©2023 Copyright by Step Wise Medical Education

All rights reserved. This book is protected by copyright. No part of this book may be reproduced in any form or by any means, including photocopying, or utilized by any information storage and retrieval system without written permission from the copyright owner.

This publication is not responsible (as a matter of product liability, negligence, or otherwise) for any injury resulting from any material contained herein. This publication contains information relating to general principles of medical care that should not be construed as specific instructions for individual patients.

Library of Congress Cataloging-in-Publication Data

DISCLAIMER

Care has been taken to confirm the accuracy of the information present and to describe generally accepted practices. However, the authors, editors, and publisher are not responsible for errors or omissions or for any consequences from application of the information in this book and make no warranty, expressed or implied, with respect to the currency, completeness, or accuracy or the contents of the publication. Application of this information in a particular situation remains the professional responsibility of the practitioner.

Visit mscmeded.com on the internet.

Dr. Mary Ruebush
StepWise Medical Education

Mary Ruebush, PhD, is one of the nation's most experienced instructors in Microbiology and Immunology for USMLE® Step 1 review. Dr. Ruebush is the author of Becker's Step 1 USMLE® lecture notes in Immunology and Microbiology, and from 2000 to 2012 was the author of the Kaplan Step 1 Review Notes. Dr. Ruebush received her PhD from the University of Georgia and has taught Infectious Disease, Immunology and Pathology at Bowman-Gray Medical School, the Uniformed Services University of the Health Sciences and Montana State University, where she received the outstanding teacher of the year award as a professor of medical science at the WWAMI Cooperative Medical School Program. Since 1990, she has taught Board Reviews for Rush Medical College (ARC Ventures), Kaplan Medical and Becker Healthcare, has helped thousands of students excel on their Step 1 USMLE® exams, and is the proud parent of two successful MDs.

Table of Contents

IMMUNOLOGY

Chapter 1. The Design of the Immune System	01
Chapter 2. The Ontogeny of Immune Cells	07
Case History. Leaky SCID, Omenn Syndrome	23
Chapter 3. Lymphocyte Trafficking	27
Chapter 4. Acute Inflammation	33
Case History. CGD	42
Case History. LAD-1	45
Chapter 5. Antigen Presentation: The Bridge Between Innate and Adaptive Immunity	49
Case Discussion. Frontiers in Cancer Immunotherapy	61
Chapter 6. Cell-Mediated Immunity: The Response to Altered/Infected Self	63
Chapter 7. Antibodies and Humoral Immunity	73
Case History. XHIGM	83
Chapter 8. The Development of Immune Memory	85
Case History. ALPS	90
Chapter 9. Active and Passive Immunotherapy	93
Chapter 10. Primary Immunodeficiency Diseases	103
Chapter 11. Acquired Immunodeficiency: HIV	111
Chapter 12. Hypersensitivity Diseases	121
Chapter 13. Transplantation	135
Chapter 14. Immunological Techniques for Diagnosis	143
IMMUNOLOGY APPENDIX	151

MICROBIOLOGY

Chapter 1. Introduction to the Microbial World	161
Chapter 2. The Genetics of Bacterial Drug Resistance	173
Chapter 3. Medically Important Bacteria	197
Chapter 4. Medically Important Viruses	259
Chapter 5. Medically Important Fungi	305
Chapter 6. Medically Important Parasites	323

Immunology
Chapter one

The Design of the Immune System

The Design of the immune System

The goal of the human immune system is to identify microbial invasion and/or cell injury and implement a sequence of steps to remove invaders and injured cells in order to repair current and prevent future tissue injury.

Although the system is designed to work as a unified whole, it is often easiest to divide into two broad categories; innate and acquired.

The innate portion of the immune system can be thought of as a series of natural barriers; chemicals, cells and structures, which are designed to prevent the penetration of the outside world into the tissues of the human host. These barriers exist with no previous stimulation, do not become stronger with exposure, and have a limited scope of injurious stimuli to which they can respond.

The acquired (adaptive) portion of the immune response becomes activated after there has been a breach of one of the innate barriers, and is designed to make a specific and concerted response against the particular injury, and prepare to prevent any subsequent attack.

The cells responsible for acquired immunity have the individual attributes of very specific recognition of a wide spectrum of foreign molecular structures, amplification of responses to prevent future repetitions of the invasion, and intricate intercellular communication to amplify and dampen the speed and intensity of the response.

	Timing	Cells	Chemicals	Proteins	Specificity /diversity	Regulatory Control	Memory
Innate	Present at all times, minutes-hours peak	Granulocytes, mast cells, innate lymphoid cells (ILCs)	pH of skin and stomach	Complement, type 1 interferons	Microbial pattern recognition, shared structures	Signaling from microbes or damage dictates length and amplitude of response	None, response is the same with each exposure
Acquired	10 days to 2 weeks development in first exposure, faster thereafter	All lymphocytes except NK cells and ILCs	Chemokines	Antibodies, type 2 interferon	Millions of unique 3-dimensional shapes	Cell to cell signaling determines speed and amplitude of response	Response gets stronger and faster with each exposure

Medical Immunology Essentials

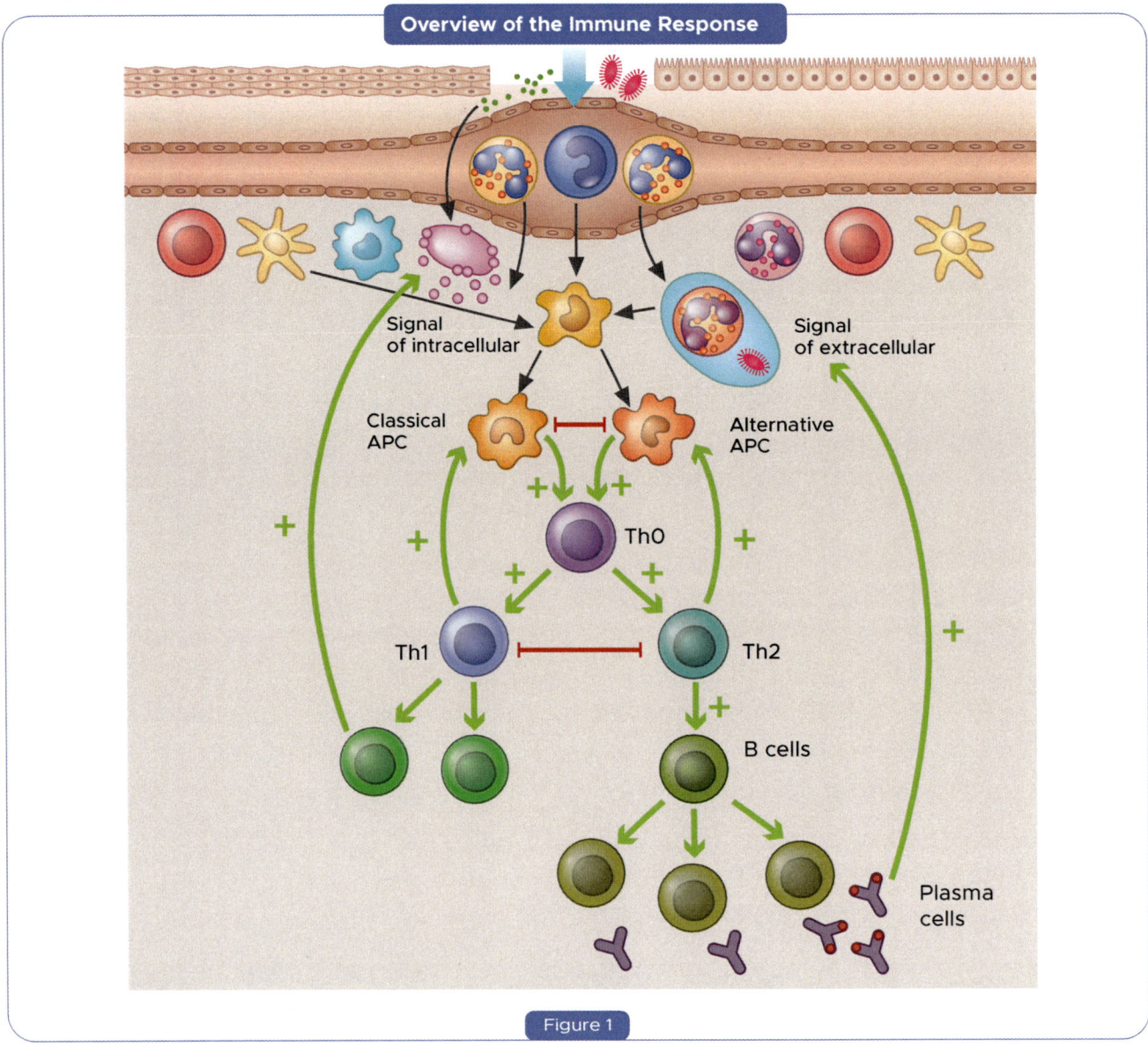

Overview of the Immune Response

Figure 1

When an injury breaks through one of the body's anatomical barriers, the acute inflammatory response brings white blood cells and proteins into the area within seconds to minutes.

If **intracellular agents** are introduced, the death of host cells results in their phagocytosis by resident antigen-presenting cells and signaling to activate TH1 cells which activate and clone the cells of **cell-mediated immunity**, which return to the infection site to kill any remaining infected cells.

If **extracellular microbes** are introduced, signals call in neutrophils and abscesses result within days. The debris of neutrophil activity is cleared by resident antigen-presenting cells which then signal activation of TH2 cells which induce B cells to produce antibodies (**humoral immunity**) against the original microbe, and in the future will increase phagocytosis if reintroduced.

Before you leave, can you...

1. Name the cellular and anatomical components of the innate and adaptive arms of the immune response.
2. Explain the general functions of innate and adaptive arms of the immune response.
3. Explain the flow of signals from acute inflammation through the development of specific adaptive immune responses.

Immunology
Chapter two

The Ontogeny of Immune Cells

The Ontogeny of Immune Cells

Hematopoiesis

The cells of the immune response originate in the bone marrow from a pluripotent stem cell, and depending on the chemical signals in the area, will differentiate down one of two pathways. In the presence of a predominance of IL-3, the myeloid pathway will be stimulated, with ultimate production of erythrocytes, platelets, granulocytes and monocytes. In the presence of a preponderance of IL-7, the lymphoid pathway will be stimulated, with the production of innate and adaptive lymphocytes.

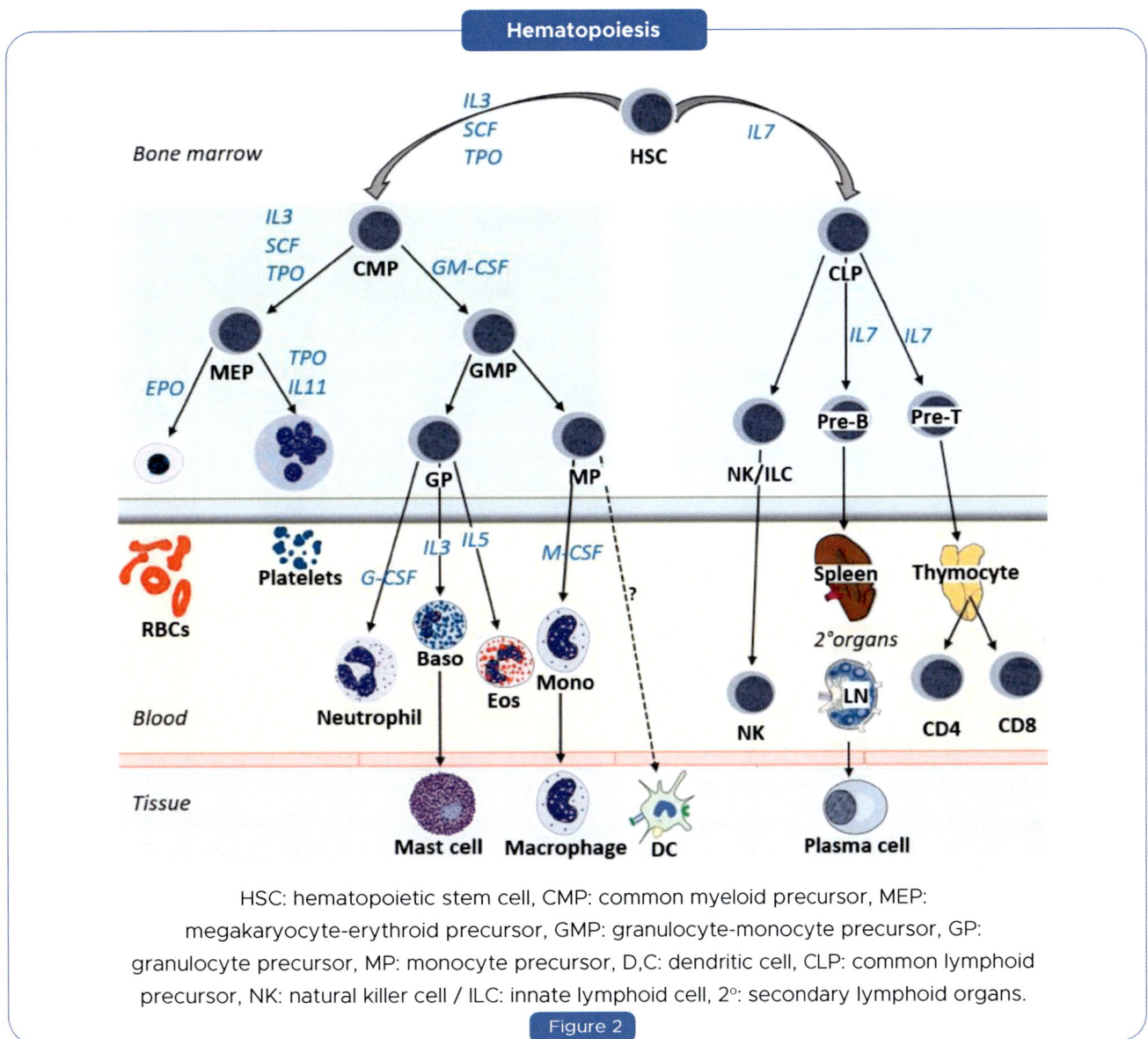

HSC: hematopoietic stem cell, CMP: common myeloid precursor, MEP: megakaryocyte-erythroid precursor, GMP: granulocyte-monocyte precursor, GP: granulocyte precursor, MP: monocyte precursor, D,C: dendritic cell, CLP: common lymphoid precursor, NK: natural killer cell / ILC: innate lymphoid cell, 2°: secondary lymphoid organs.

Figure 2

Recombinant drugs available for therapy:

For GM-CSF – Sargramostim or Molgramostim

For G-CSF – Filgrastim or Lenograstim

For IL-11 – Oprelvekin

Medical Immunology Essentials

Cells of Myeloid Origin in the Blood:

Neutrophil, PMN*	Multilobed nucleus with small pink cytoplasmic granules	1800 – 7800/μL (40-60%)	Phagocytosis and killing of extracellular organisms, abscess formation
Eosinophil	Bilobed nucleus, large pink cytoplasmic granules	0-450 μL, (1-4%) allergic and anti-helminth responses	Kill IgE-coated helminths by release of MBP*
Basophil	Bilobed nucleus, large purple cytoplasmic granules	0-200/μL (0.5-1%)	Release vasoactive chemicals during allergy and helminth infection. Corollary of mast cells in epithelium and submucosa
Monocyte	Large, half-moon shaped nucleus, non-granular cytoplasm, CD4+, CD14+, CD16+	0-900/μL (2-8%)	Phagocytosis, precursor of tissue macrophage

*PMN – Polymorphonuclear leukocyte, MBP – major basic protein
CD4 – costimulatory molecule for MHC2/TCR interaction
CD14 – endotoxin (bacterial lipopolysaccharide) receptor
CD16 – Fc receptor (tail of antibody molecule)

In the Tissues

Macrophage	Ruffled membrane, cytoplasmic vesicles, CD4+, CD14+, CD16+	Liver: Kupffer cells Kidney: mesangial cells Brain: microglia Bone: osteoclasts	Phagocytosis, antigen-presentation, secretion of cytokines. End cell of monocyte line
Dendritic cell	Long cytoplasmic arms	Epithelia and submucosa	Phagocytosis, antigen transport and presentation
Mast cell	Small nucleus, large deep purple granules	All barrier tissues	End cell of basophil line, same functions in tissue locations

CD4 – costimulatory molecule for MHC2/TCR interaction
CD14 – endotoxin (bacterial lipopolysaccharide) receptor
CD16 – Fc receptor (tail of antibody molecule)

Cells of Lymphoid Origin In the Blood

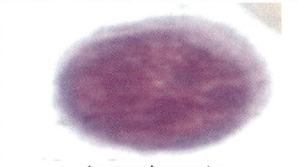 Lymphocyte	1000-4000/μL (20-40%) total	B cells (CD 19-21+) – 10%; synthesize antibody TH cells (CD4+) – 50%; produce cytokines CTLs (CD8+) – 25%; kill altered cells NK cells (CD16 & 56+) – 15%; kill altered cells

In the Tissues

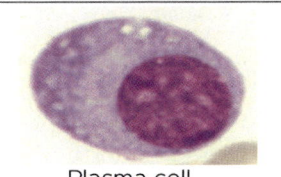 Plasma cell	Small dark, eccentric nucleus with clock-face, prominent Golgi	Lymph nodes, bone marrow, spleen, MALT*	Secretion of monoclonal antibody for two week life span

*mucosal-associated lymphoid tissue

The Development of Adaptive Lymphocyte Antigen Receptors

B and T lymphocytes have receptors on their surfaces for the 3-dimensional shape of specific foreign molecules (**antigens**). Their production is encoded in the very large "immunoglobulin superfamily of genes" which encode cell surface or soluble proteins involved in immunologic signaling, binding and adhesion. The receptors of B lymphocytes; B cell receptor (BCR) and T lymphocytes; T cell receptor (TCR) are similar in that they are "Y" shaped structures which have a cytoplasmic tail extending the COOH-terminus of the protein chains through the cell membrane to assist in signal transduction. When an appropriate shaped molecule binds to the N-terminus of the cell receptor (the idiotype or antigen binding site), a cascade of phosphorylation events will culminate in cellular cloning and activation.

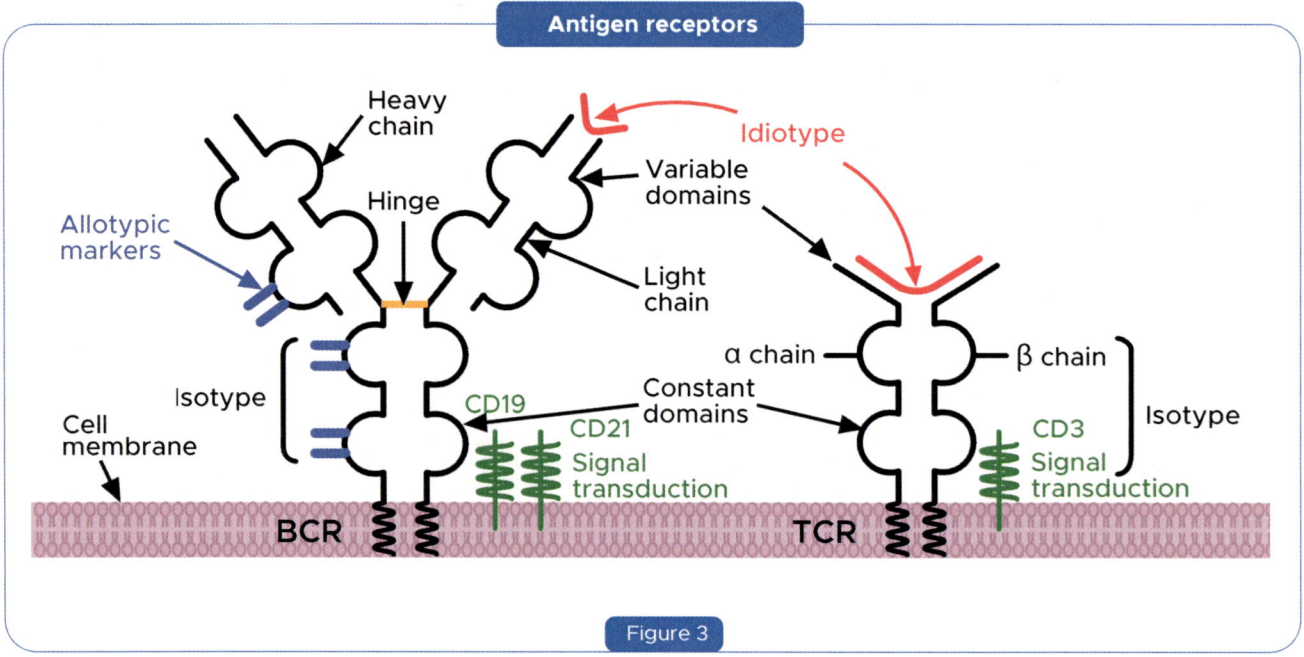

Figure 3

The heavy chains of the BCR are called:
Mu – two μ heavy chains make up IgM
Delta – two δ heavy chains make up IgD
Gamma – two γ heavy chains make up IgG (and there are 4 subisotypes of gamma chains)
Alpha – two α heavy chains make up IgA (and there are 2 subisotypes of alpha chains)
Epsilon – two ε heavy chains make up IgE

Comparison of the BCR and the TCR

	Structure	Binds to	Idiotypes /cell	Isotypes	Flexibility	Signal transduction	Secretion
BCR	Heavy and light, 2 copies each	Any chemical composition	1/cell, variable domains of H and L (2 copies, valence 2)	1 or 2/cell; heavy chains μ,δ,γ,α,ε, light chains κ, λ	Yes, hinge	CD19, 21	Yes, serum antibody
TCR	α,β, 1 copy each	Peptides presented in HLA	1/cell, variable domains of α and β (1 copy, valence 1)	1/cell; α/β or γ/δ	Rigid	CD3	Never

The Development of Lymphocyte Antigen Receptor Diversity

There is a small amount of DNA that encodes the production of the BCR and TCR...too little for it to be possible for a separate gene to exist to produce each unique receptor. Therefore, the millions of unique antigen binding molecules are created by a process of gene segment rearrangement which occurs in the primary lymphoid organs (bone marrow and thymus) in cells developing within the lymphoid lineage.

The gene segments are referred to as V (variable), D (diversity) and J (joining) and when they are randomly recombined by the action of the RAG (recombination activating) genes, they are spliced together to create the RNA coding for the N-terminal amino acids in the variable domains of the BCR or TCR.

An enzyme known as terminal deoxyribonucleotidyl transferase (Tdt) is active during this process and generates a further level of diversity by randomly inserting non-coded nucleotides (N-nucleotide addition) each time a V is joined to a D, or a D is joined to a J.

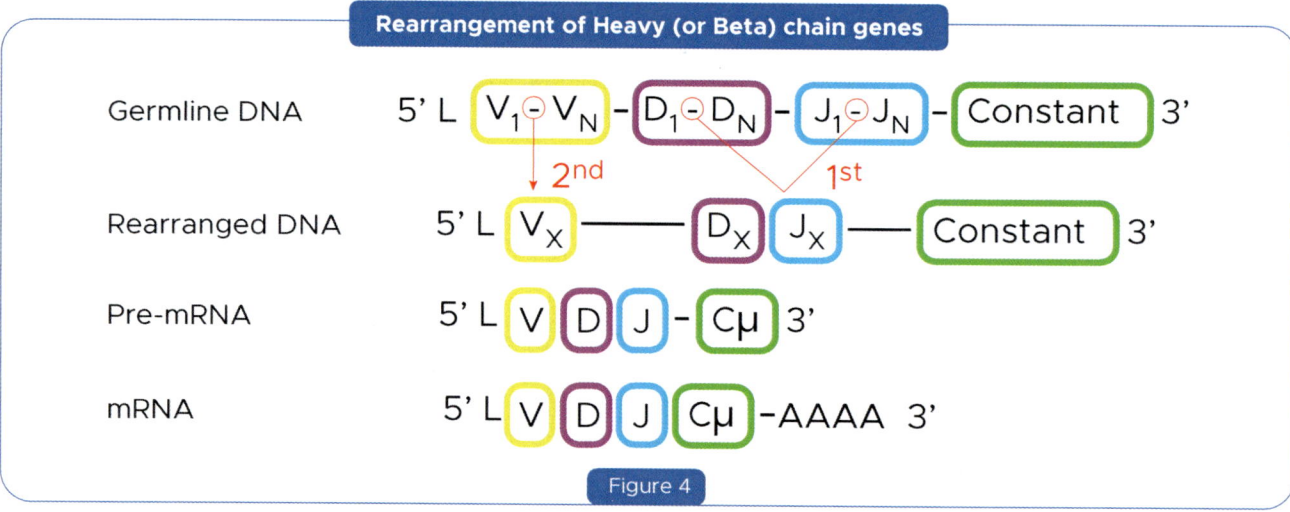

Figure 4

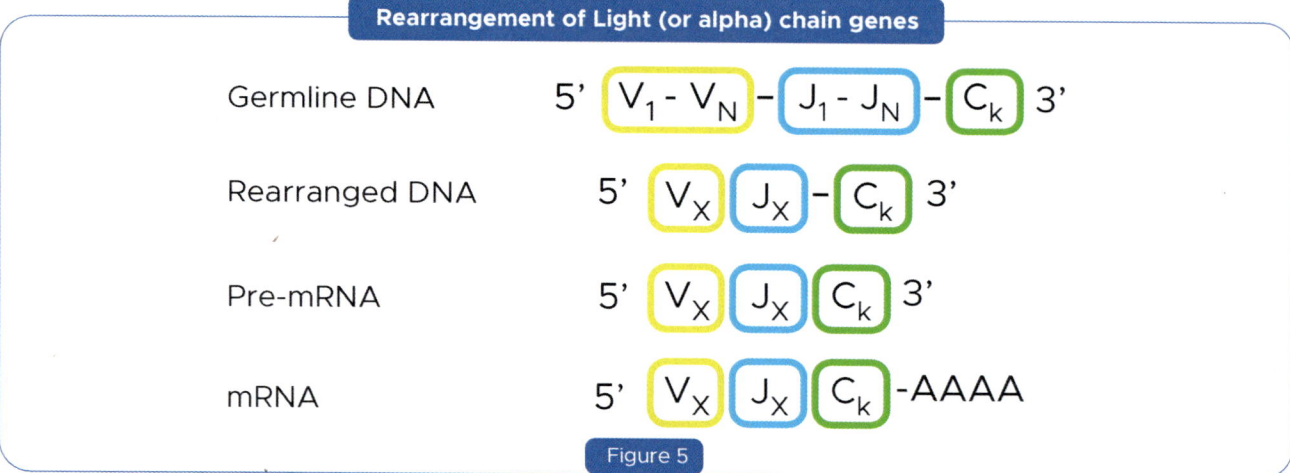

Figure 5

Allelic Exclusion

If the result of these complex, random rearrangements is an abnormal-shaped or truncated protein, the cell will be induced to undergo apoptosis. Since each diploid cell has two copies of each chromosome (one maternal and one paternal), there are two chances for each rearrangement to be successful. Whichever chromosome is randomly rearranged first, if successful in producing a functional chain, the homologous chromosome of that set will be inactivated in a process referred to as **allelic exclusion**. If unsuccessful, the failed rearranged chromosome will be inactivated, and the other one of that pair will be used to attempt a successful rearrangement. (Thus, only one allele of a given chromosome will ever be expressed at one time). Since the heavy chain genes are all on one chromosome, and the light chain genes are on two separate chromosomes, the cells have two chances to rearrange the heavy chain genes and 4 chances to rearrange the light chain genes.

Constant Domain Addition

Once VDJ rearrangement has created the coding for the N-terminal 110 amino acids (approximately), the downstream DNA contains the coding for all of the constant domain isotypes in sequence. First is the coding for addition of mu constant domains, so the first isotype of immunoglobulin produced is IgM. By alternative RNA splicing, IgD is made immediately thereafter, and mature naïve B lymphocytes are allowed to leave the bone marrow wearing those two isotypes of receptors, each with identical idiotypes.

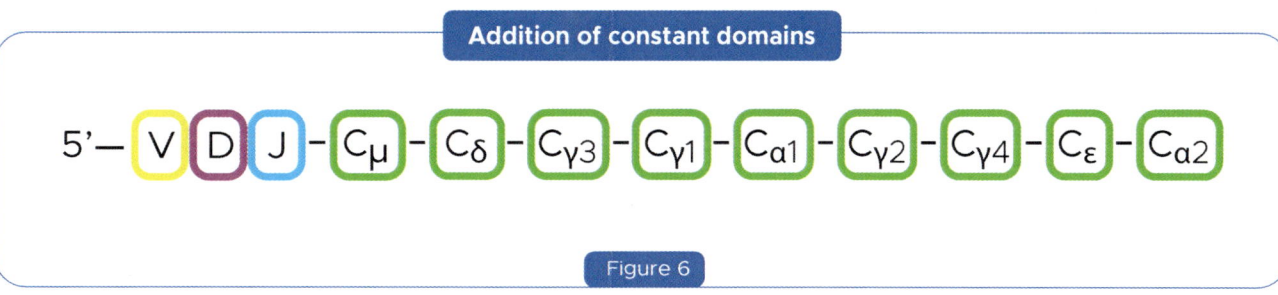

Figure 6

Selection of Receptors for Central Tolerance

Since the gene segment rearrangements we have been discussing happen in the primary lymphoid organs in the absence of any foreign antigenic stimulus, and since Tdt randomly adds bases at the junctures between V and D and J, it should stand to reason that the process is fraught with potential flaws. We have already discussed the fact that the accidental formation of aberrant or truncated peptide chains will cause cells to undergo apoptosis, but a second mechanism of cell selection is critical in the generative lymphoid organs. If a cell makes a functional receptor, but one that identifies and binds to components of self antigens, it would be dangerous to the host to allow that cell to enter the general circulation. In the B cell lineage, central tolerance is achieved by induction of apoptosis in immature B cells which bind too strongly to (have too strong affinity for) bone marrow stromal cells.

The process of induction of **central tolerance** is even more rigorous in T lymphocyte precursors. As these cells leave the bone marrow and travel to the thymus, they are allowed to continue their development only if they FAIL to respond to self antigens. Any self-reactive cell will be induced to undergo apoptosis in the thymus, and only between 1 and 5% of all T cell precursors will emerge from the process alive. The T cell receptor is designed to be complementary to molecules of the major histocompatibility complex (MHC) or the human leukocyte antigens (HLA). These membrane receptors are encoded in the immunoglobulin superfamily of genes, and bind peptides to be presented to the TCR. This is the most polymorphic genetic system in the human.

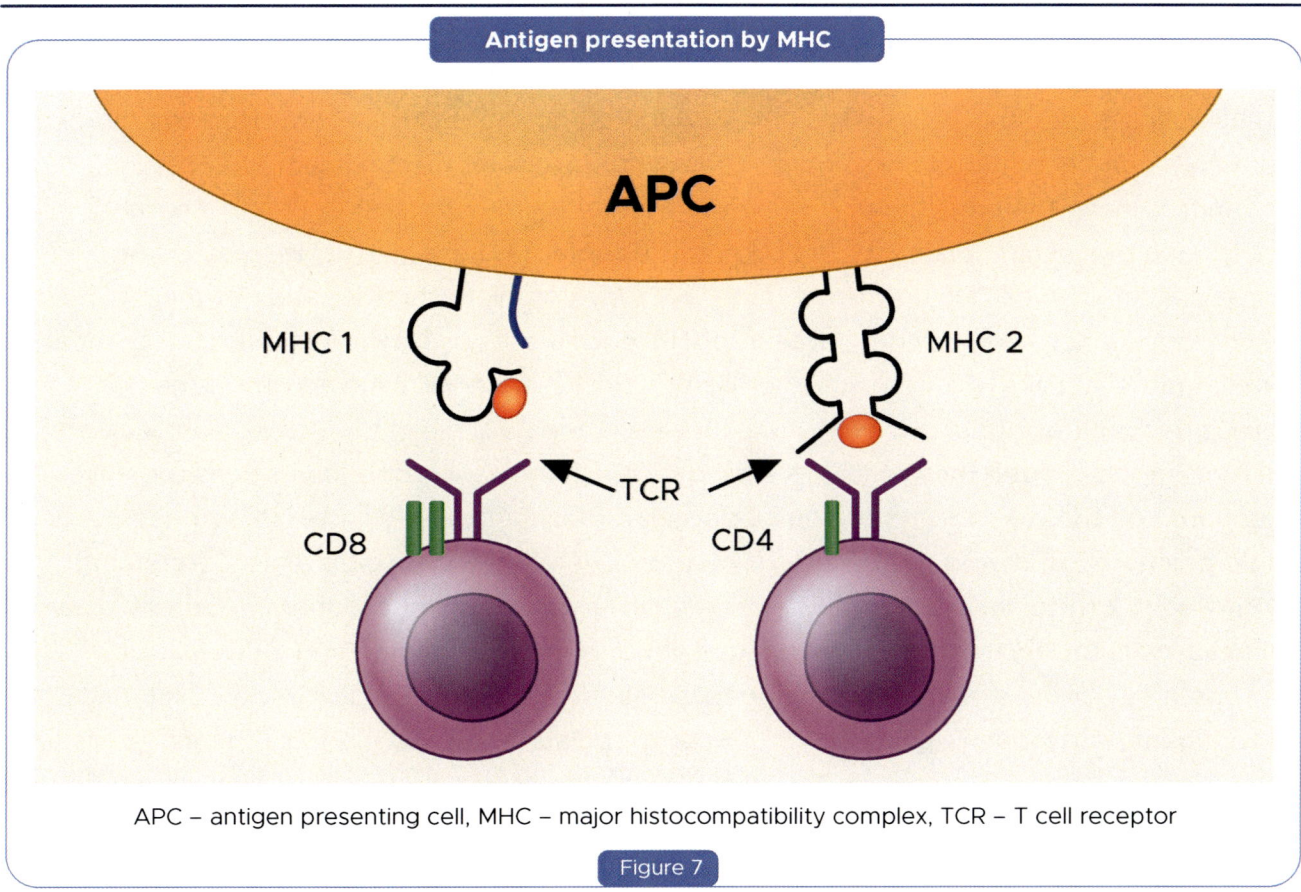

APC – antigen presenting cell, MHC – major histocompatibility complex, TCR – T cell receptor

Figure 7

Class I MHC	Class II MHC
Gene products A, B, C	Gene products DP, DQ, DR
Found on all nucleated cells	Found on antigen presenting cells
Expressed codominantly	Expressed codominantly
Long alpha chain plus β-2 microglobulin	Alpha and beta chains of similar length
Co-receptor is CD8	Co-receptor is CD4

The thymus is a bi-lobed organ in the thoracic cavity, and in the years between birth and adolescence, begins as the largest organ in the chest. It is larger than the heart and lung combined in the neonate, but by the time of adolescence, it has been converted to a fibrous scar which can be faintly seen radiographically in the superior mediastinum. As T cell progenitors leave the bone marrow, they arrive in the thymus through high endothelial venules and move immediately to the cortex as **double-negative** (DN) cells; they do not express either CD4 or CD8 on their surface. As they complete the formation of their TCR by VDJ recombination, they become **double-positive** (DP) cells which interact with the **cortical thymic epithelial cells (cTEC)** which express both MHC1 and MHC2 molecules. If the DP thymocytes are not signaled by MHC of either type, they will die in the cortex from lack of cytokine support, but if they receive a stronger signal, they will clone themselves (**positive selection**). As the cloning cells are pushed toward the inner thymic cortex, they become **single positive** (SP) thymocytes which have appropriate binding to either **MHC1 (retaining CD8)** or **MHC2 (retaining CD4)**. As these cells move to the thymic medulla, **medullary thymic epithelial cells (mTEC)** will evaluate the strength of MHC/TCR binding and deliver the appropriate cytokine signals to induce apoptosis in those cells with too strong affinity for self-antigens, and induce regulatory or effector populations of CD4 and CD8 bearing cells to leave the thymus as mature, naïve T lymphocytes. The promiscuous expression of tissue-restricted antigens in the thymic medulla is controlled by the **transcriptional regulator AIRE** and **transcription factor Fezf2**, and is necessary for the strong development of central immune tolerance.

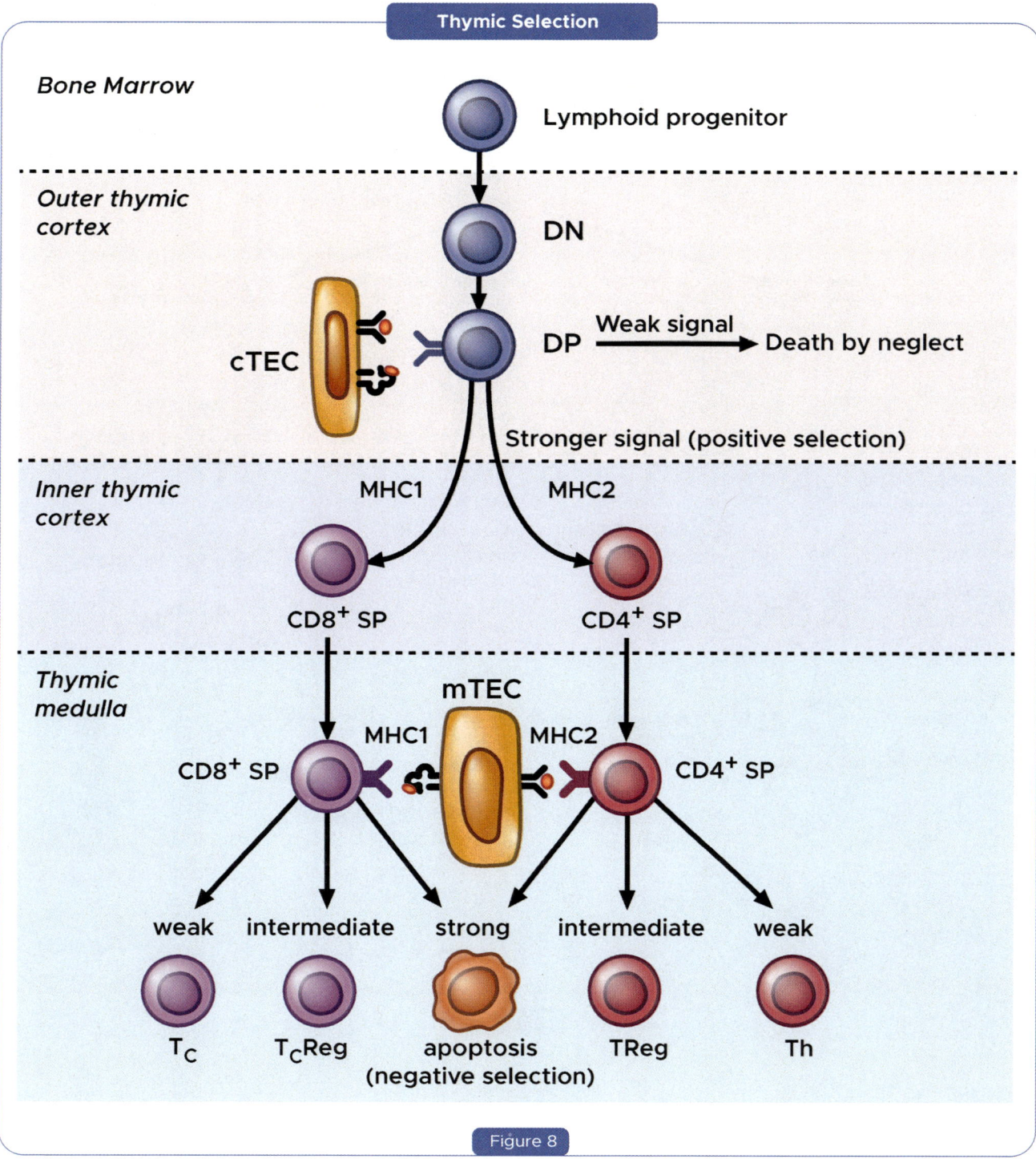
Figure 8

Summary of Adaptive Lymphocyte Development

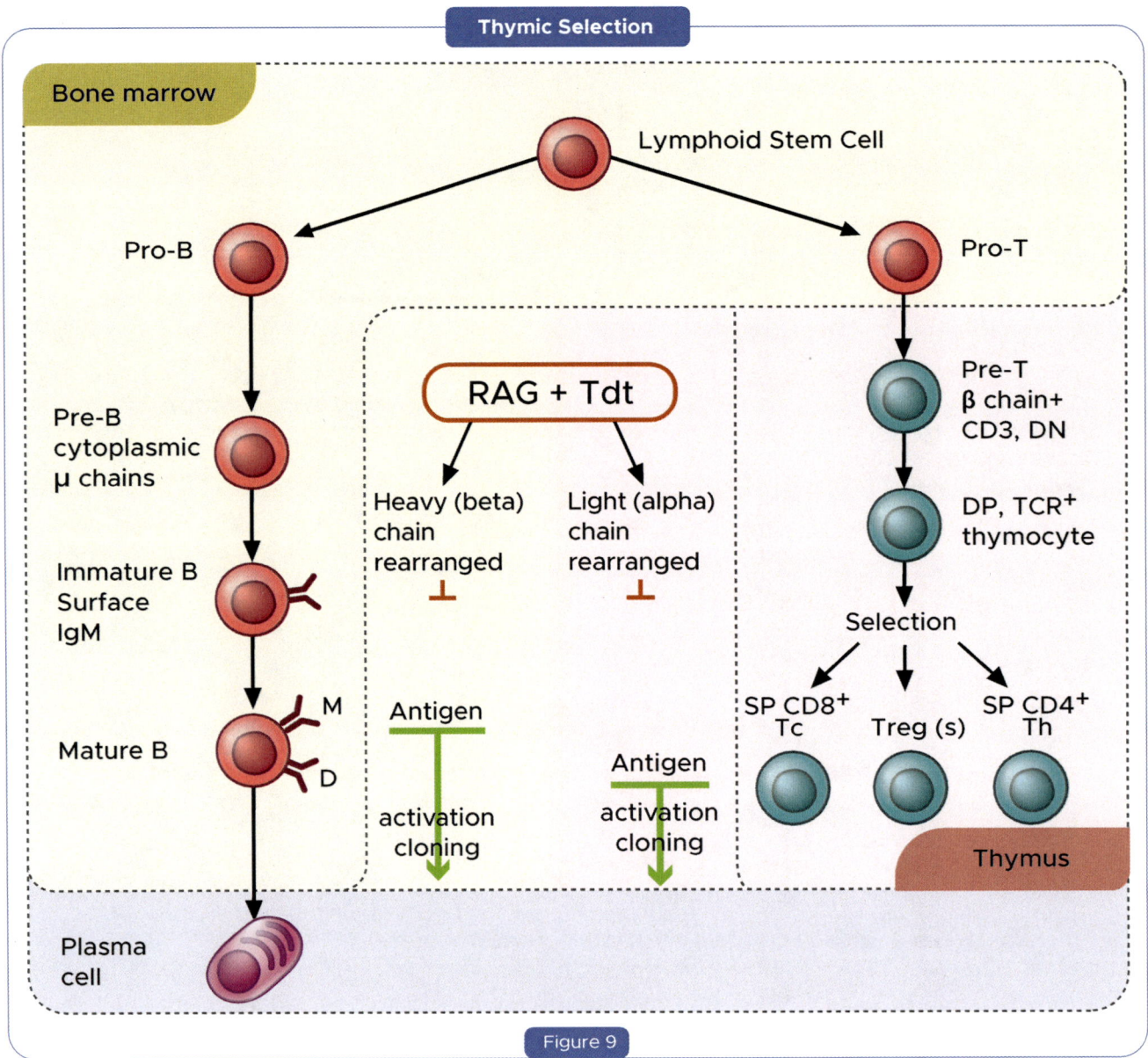

Figure 9

#MMC (Make Me Care!)

1. How do you suppose we count the different subpopulations of lymphocytes in clinical medicine?
2. Epstein-Barr virus infects cells which possess CD21 on their surface (B cells and oropharyngeal epithelial cells). What types of malignancies do you anticipate as a sequela of this infection?
3. Patients with multiple myeloma and Waldenstrom's macroglobulinemia have neoplastic cells in the B lymphocyte lineage (multiple myeloma - plasma cells; Waldenstroms - lymphoplasmacytoid cells). What do you suppose is found in excess in their urine?
4. Can you predict why the immune response to materials that contain protein is different from that produced against materials without protein?
5. Can you predict the clinical presentation of a patient with a genetic inability to produce RAG gene products?
6. A neonatal screening test for severe combined immunodeficiency (SCID) uses detection of T cell receptor excision circles (TRECs) to identify T lymphocyte development. Can you explain what process this assay is measuring and predict whether high or low numbers would associate with normal or abnormal phenotype?
7. If a patient presents with circulating lymphocytes with RAG and Tdt expression, what can you infer?
8. In cases where malignant transformation occurs in a lymphoid cell lineage, immunophenotyping is performed to determine the developmental stage of the involved cells. How would this information be useful to the clinical management team?
9. The thymus is one of 5 immunoprivileged sites in the body (brain, retina, testis, and placenta are the others). Why is a specialized barrier between the organ and the blood necessary for normal thymic function?
10. Rare genetic defects involving AIRE and Fezf2 have been described. How would you anticipate that these patients would present?
11. A key component of the amyloid which damages the tissues of patients on long-term dialysis is β-2 microglobulin. Can you explain why this is so?

Before you leave, can you...

1. Explain the origins, cytokine signals, and functions of the myeloid and lymphoid cells that originate from the bone marrow.
2. Describe the appearances or cell surface markers used to identify each of these cells in tissue or blood.
3. Describe the similarities and differences between the BCR and the TCR.
4. Explain how the diversity of antigen recognition molecules is developed in the primary lymphoid organs.
5. Explain allelic exclusion.
6. Explain central tolerance in the primary lymphoid organs.
7. Explain the roles of negative and positive selection in the thymus.
8. Understand the sequence of development of B and T lymphocytes in the primary lymphoid organs.

Case History
Leaky SCID, Omenn Syndrome

A 2-month old male infant is brought to the pediatrician for continued care of a skin condition. The child was delivered vaginally without complications, at term, weighing 6 lbs 2 oz (2.78 kg). The child has been breastfed since delivery, and has been seen previously for skin lesions that were diagnosed as pediatric atopic dermatitis. The mother is now concerned about patches of red and peeling skin appearing all over the infant's body, and the fact that his diapers continue to be soiled with loose stool. On examination, the child weighs 6 lbs (2.72 kg), and has a generalized skin rash resembling eczema. The reddened skin is thickened with irregular fissures, and there is diffuse alopecia. There is generalized lymphadenopathy and hepatosplenomegaly. Other systems appear within normal limits. The decision is made to delay the administration of the first rotavirus vaccination, and immediately refer the infant to an immunologic specialist.

Chief Complaint(s):
- Erythroderma and diarrhea

Differential Diagnoses:
- Histiocytosis
- Hyperimmunoglobulinemia E (Job) Syndrome
- Pediatric atopic dermatitis
- Pediatric Graft-vs.-Host disease (GVHD)
- Severe combined immunodeficiency (SCID)
- T cell disorders

Clinical Approach:
The cutaneous findings with diffuse alopecia and diarrhea are suggestive of a SCID (severe combined immunodeficiency). At the age of 2 months, the infant is still significantly protected by transplacentally-delivered maternal IgG (hence the normal levels of IgG detected in this infant), and a breast-fed child is also receiving passive protection of mucosal surfaces in the form of IgA contained in the breast milk and colostrum. Once those maternal protections dissipate (6-9 months after birth in the case of maternal IgG, and for as long as breast feeding occurs in the case of IgA) the presentation will progress to the finding of recurrent and potentially serious infections with all manners of microbial pathogens. Chronic diarrhea contributes to the child's failure to thrive (his weight is less at 2 months than it was at birth). The ultimate treatment for virtually all SCIDs is bone marrow transplantation or cord blood stem cell transplantation, but determination of the underlying cause can be useful in management of the patient while awaiting a suitable donor, and in genetic counseling for the parents to discuss the likelihood of sibling recurrence.

Immunologic Workup:
CBC and Differential:
- unremarkable except for elevated eosinophils
- T cell numbers normal, (CD3+CD4+ GATA3+)
- B cells undetectable (CD 19-21)
- NK cells present (CD16, CD56)

Other findings:
- Total IgA and IgM markedly low, IgG normal, total IgE elevated
- Lymphocyte stimulation with T cell mitogens profoundly reduced
- Interleukins 4 and 5 elevated
- Skin biopsy negative for Langerhans cell infiltrate
- T cells in the child are of autologous (not maternal) origin by HLA analysis

Diagnosis: Atypical or Leaky SCID; Omenn Syndrome (OS)

The virtual absence of B cells, presence of T cells with impaired function (failure to respond to T cell mitogens), and NK cells (T⁻B⁻NK⁺) with hypereosinophilia defines the immunophenotype of "leaky" or atypical SCID. Erythroderma, diarrhea and failure to thrive are common findings in all infantile SCIDs, but lymphadenopathy, hepatosplenomegaly and pachydermia distinguish OS from other variants of SCID. The condition is distinct from complete RAG1/2 deficiency in which both T and B cell counts would be undetectable. OS is genetically heterogeneous, but most cases result from hypomorphic missense mutations of RAG1/RAG2 genes, mapping to chromosome band 11p13. In such cases OS exhibits autosomal recessive inheritance and is therefore often associated with consanguineous parents. It is the prototype syndrome of immune dysregulation and other hypomorphic defects have been implicated such as IL7R, IL2R and autoimmune regulator (AIRE). The clinical appearance may mimic histiocytosis, or when engraftment of allogeneic maternal T cells causes graft-vs.-host disease (GVHD). In this case, histiocytosis and GVHD were ruled out by skin biopsy and HLA typing of infant and mother, respectively. A characteristic finding in OS is the presence of markers of activation or memory, such as HLA-DR, CD25, CD30, CD45RO and CD95, and underexpression of bcl-2 (an anti-apoptotic factor). These cells can be demonstrated to be oligoclonal, autoreactive TH2 cells by their expression of GATA3 transcription factor and their secretion of IL-4 and 5. Impaired VDJ recombination leads to the generation of a few autoreactive T cell clones which populate the skin and gut, resulting in the erythroderma and colitis. Protein loss from skin and gut contribute to a generalized edema. The eosinophilia results from IL-5 production by the TH2 cells, and IgE production results from the production of IL-4.

Management:

Isolation, hygienic care, empirical broad spectrum antibiotics and parenteral nutrition while awaiting stem cell reconstitution. Gene therapy is a hope for the future.
- Interferon-γ to reduce the Th2 cell activity
- Steroids and cyclosporin A to treat the skin reaction
- Intravenous immunoglobulin replacement

Prognosis:

Omenn syndrome is fatal in the first two to six months of life if untreated. Although life-threatening viral, bacterial and fungal infections can be observed in any SCID, patients with OS commonly develop *Staphylococcus aureus* sepsis, secondary to the generalized dermatitis. Vaccination with live viral vaccines can prove fatal. Chronic diarrhea and protein loss via skin and gut may cause malnutrition which also contributes to death. Mortality even following BMT has been reported to be between 18 and 47%. Diagnosis at birth might prevent infection and improve transplantation outcomes, but neonatal screening specific to OS is not currently available.

Immunology
Chapter three

Lymphocyte Trafficking

Lymphocyte Trafficking

The adaptive lymphocytes which have finished their development in the primary lymphoid organs (bone marrow and thymus) have not yet "seen" the foreign molecule (antigen) that will bind to their BCR or TCR and are said to be "naïve" or "virgin". The anatomical locations in which these cells can now be exposed to their cognate antigen and "trained in battle" are the **secondary lymphoid organs**; the **lymph nodes, spleen** and **mucosal associated lymphoid tissues (MALT)**. These organs have evolved to sample the fluids at key points of entry for microbial pathogens. The lymph nodes filter lymph and therefore sample entry from any cutaneous or mucosal surface. The spleen filters the blood and therefore catches pathogens that have become blood borne. The MALT (specifically the Peyer's patches) sample the intestinal contents to evaluate the difference between potentially harmful invaders and harmless commensals and useful calories.

The trafficking or recirculation of lymphocytes is controlled by chemokines and adhesion molecules. Different categories of lymphocytes have receptors for different **chemokines**, which attract them, along a chemical gradient toward specific regions of the secondary lymphoid organs. The lymph nodes and Peyer's patches contain **high endothelial venules (HEV)** which allow the **L-selectins** on the lymphocytes to bind to their complementary **addressin molecules (Sialyl Lewis-X)** on HEVs, and "home" to particular locations in those organs. The spleen does not contain HEVs, but instead lymphocytes leave the blood sinusoids which make up the red pulp and travel by a process of diapedesis (discussed with inflammation in the next chapter) to establish residence in the white pulp. All of the secondary lymphoid organs are designed to be locations where lymphocytes can be exposed to their cognate antigen and collaborate with one another to make the most effective immune response possible. The rate of recirculation of mature, naïve lymphocytes through these areas is quite dramatic: it is estimated that on average, a given lymphocyte will check in to each lymph node in the body once a day, and the spleen every other day.

The Architecture of the Lymph Node

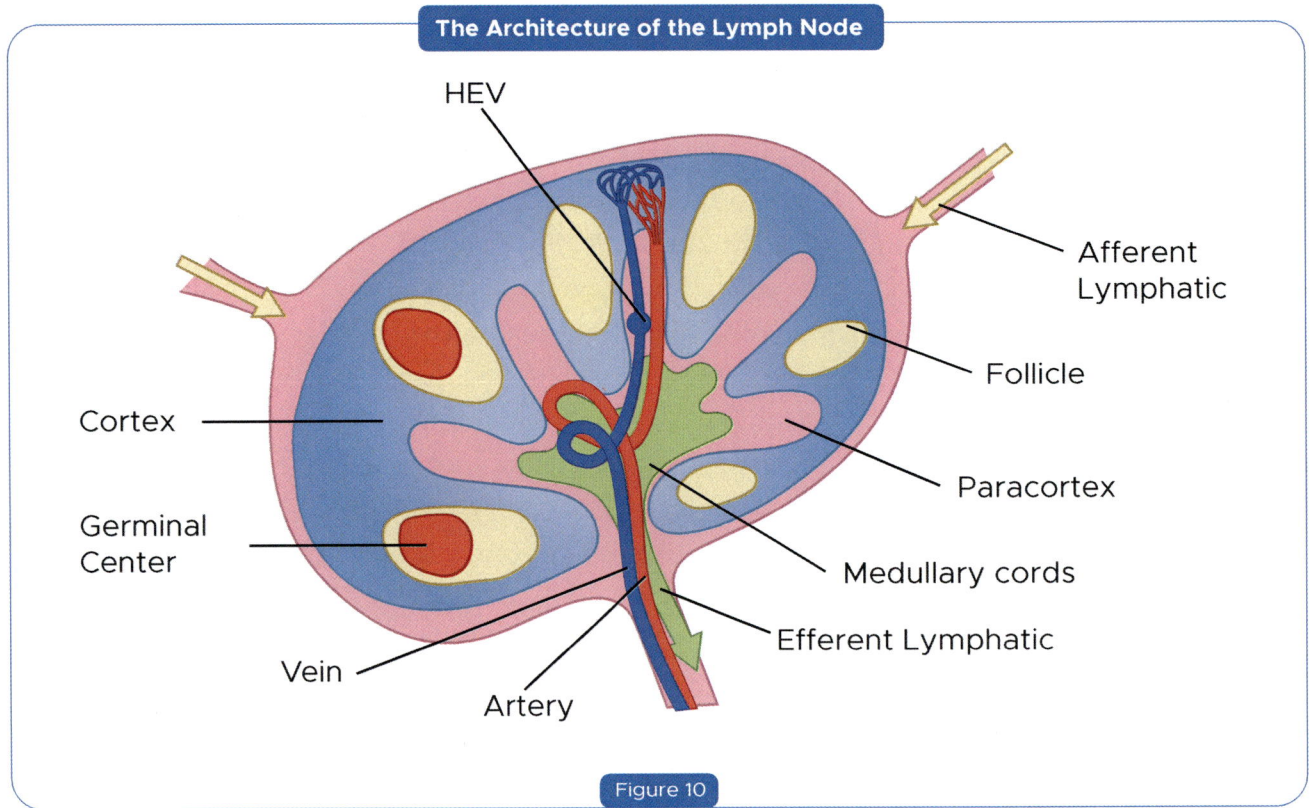

Figure 10

Lymph and foreign antigen enter the lymph node through afferent lymphatics and the subcapsular sinus. The subcapsular sinus is lined with macrophages. Lymphocytes arrive through high endothelial venules and move to their respective regions; **B lymphocytes to the cortex** where they form **follicles** and **germinal centers**, and **T lymphocytes to the paracortex.** As antigen percolates over the layers of cells, it would first have the opportunity to be captured by macrophages, then B lymphocytes and follicular dendritic cells in the cortex. If it is not bound by any of these cells, the medullary cords are also lined with macrophages for a final chance at capture. If lymphocytes are activated, they will clone themselves and the node will swell in size. Immunologic products of their activation (antibodies, effector cells, memory cells) will leave through the hilum, and circulate in lymphatic vessels until they are combined into the **thoracic duct** which drains into the systemic circulation through the **left subclavian vein.**

Medical Immunology Essentials

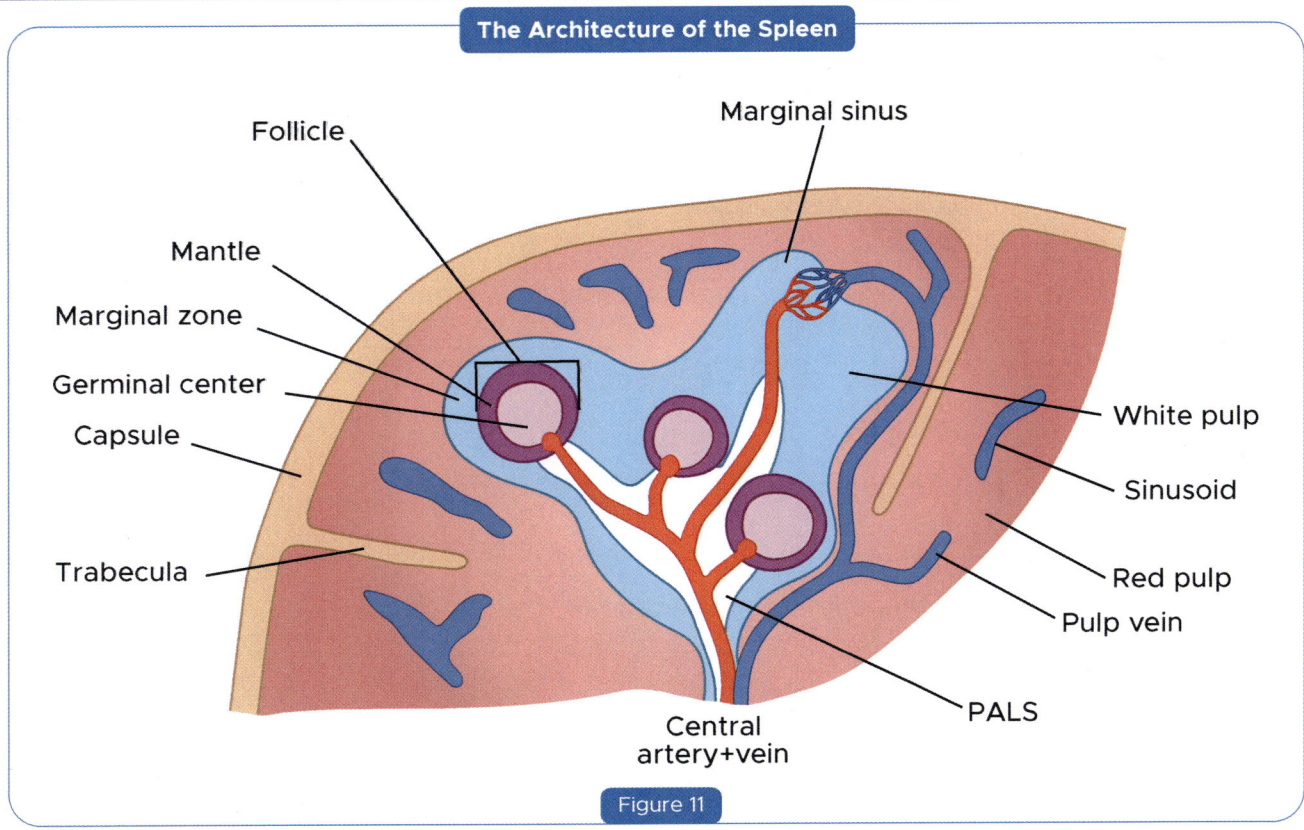

Figure 11

The spleen is the body's largest secondary lymphoid organ. The spleen red pulp serves the function of filtering the blood through sinusoids which are lined with macrophages. Aged red blood cells are removed here, and any foreign material that has gotten into the blood will also be phagocytized. The blood supply to the spleen is by the single splenic artery, and the arterioles which branch off become surrounded by **periarteriolar lymphoid sheaths** which are **T cell rich** areas. B lymphocytes create **follicles** outside of the T cell area. The lymphocyte rich areas comprise the **white pulp.**

Mucosal Associated Lymphoid Tissue

The Peyer's patches which form in the submucosa of the small intestine begin to develop before birth. They do not have incoming lymphatics, but instead sample antigen from the lumen of the small intestine through M cells to the tissues beneath. **M cells** are not covered with mucus, but instead trap antigens with ability to bind to the surface of the cell (an obvious determinant of pathogenicity).

These are endocytosed in vesicles and then released for recognition by the lymphocytes beneath. Over a lifetime, these areas become populated with memory B cells dedicated to the production of IgA and memory T cells necessary to provide help for them. The chemokine receptor and adhesion molecule patterns of naïve and memory adaptive lymphocytes are tailored to the location in which they first met their cognate antigen, so over a lifetime, this concentrates the "troops" where they are most likely to be quickly effective.

#MMC (Make Me Care!)

1. Virchow's node is a supraclavicular lymph node found near the junction of the thoracic duct and the left subclavian vein. Palpation of its enlargement is called Troisier's sign. Can you explain why this finding would be suggestive of an advanced malignancy?
2. Patients who have been surgically or naturally splenectomized (sickle cell anemia) require special vaccination protocols to protect them from encapsulated microbes which can invade the blood. Can you explain why this would be so?

Before you leave, can you....

1. Explain the structure and function of the secondary lymphoid organs.
2. Describe the locations in each of these organs where T cells, B cells and macrophages would be found.
3. Explain the role of chemokines and adhesion molecules in lymphocyte trafficking.

Immunology
Chapter four

Acute Inflammation

The immediate response to injury

Acute inflammation is the body's stereotyped response to any injury. Its cardinal signs; *rubor* (**redness**), *tumor* (**swelling**), *calor* (**heat**), *dolor* (**pain**), and *functio laesa* (**loss of function**) have been recognized since the dawn of medicine. It depends on the interplay between chemicals released during injury, activities of resident sentinel cells and hemodynamic changes, all of which are designed to stop further invasion or injury and call in the immune first responders.

Hemodynamic changes

In the first few seconds after any injury, there is a **transient neurogenic vasoconstrictive reflex**. After this, **vasodilation and leakage** result from release of chemical mediators from resident cells in the area:

Source	Mediator
Macrophages and dendritic cells	IL-1 and TNF cause mast cell histamine release
Endothelial cells	NO and PGI_2
Damaged tissue	Bradykinin
Mast cells	Histamine

Chemoattractants

A variety of small chemicals produced in the area of injury serve to attract leukocytes into the area of increased blood flow. White blood cells have receptors for these chemicals (chemokine receptors) and they move up the chemical gradient toward the source.

Source	Chemoattractant
Clotting cascade	Fibrinopeptides
Bacteria	F-met peptides
Complement cascades	C5a
Resident and entering leukocytes	Interleukin-8
Arachidonic acid cascade	Leukotriene B4

Local signals of injury and/or invasion

The signals that injury or invasion has occurred in an area are recognized by receptors on the membranes of resident and entering innate immune cells. These receptors have evolved to recognize patterns of substances which do not occur in healthy normal tissue.

DAMPs (damage-associated molecular patterns)
- Nucleotide-binding Oligomerization Domain-like receptors (NLRs) are found in the cytosol of cells and recognize uric acid, free ATP, loss of potassium and some microbial products.
- A multiprotein complex called the inflammasome signals to activate caspase-1 to cleave precursor IL-1 into the active form.

PAMPs (pathogen-associated molecular patterns)
- **Pattern recognition receptors (PRRs)** have evolved to bind the unique lipids, carbohydrates and peptides of microbial invaders. There are about a thousand of these evolutionarily conserved moieties recognized by 100 PRRs. Compare this to the millions of unique shapes which can be recognized by the receptors of lymphocytes (BCR and TCR).

1. TLRs (Toll-like Receptors)

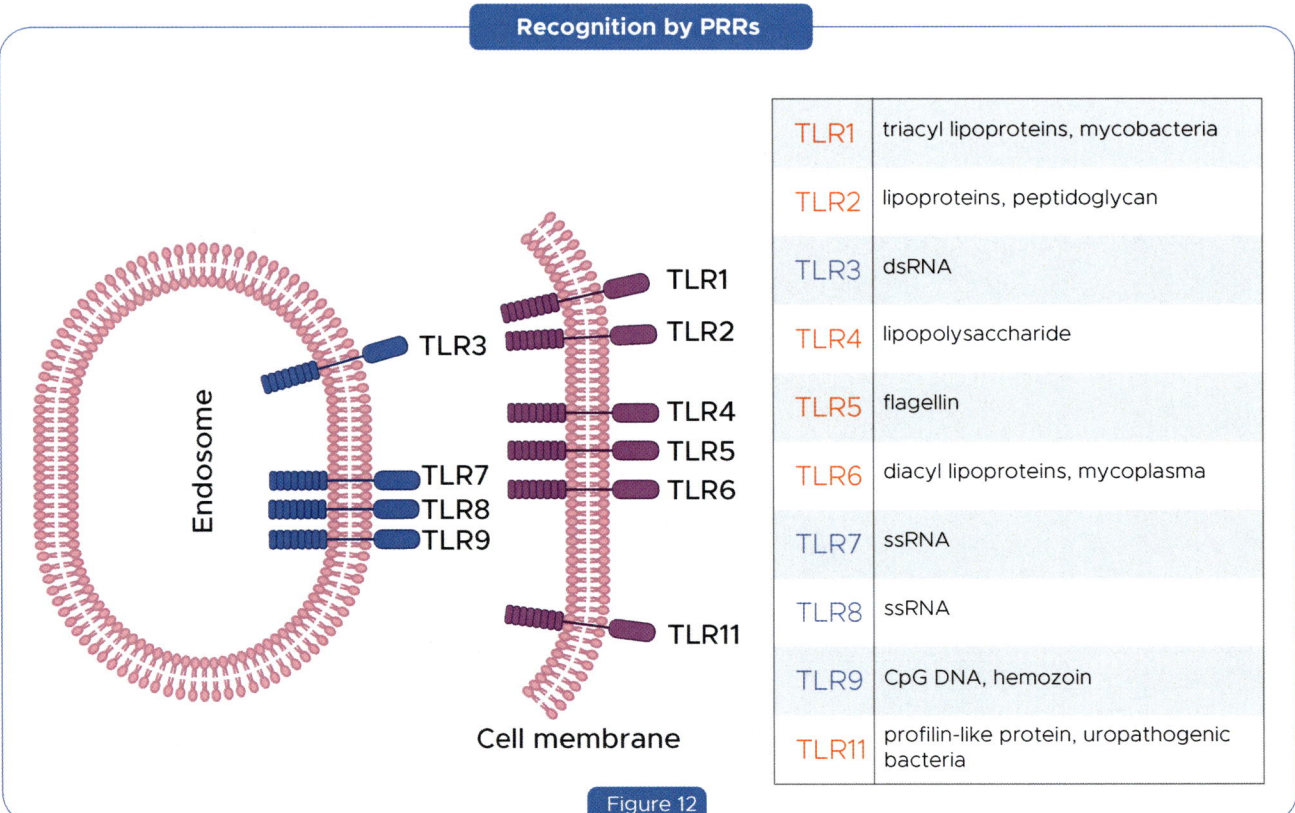

Recognition by PRRs

TLR1	triacyl lipoproteins, mycobacteria
TLR2	lipoproteins, peptidoglycan
TLR3	dsRNA
TLR4	lipopolysaccharide
TLR5	flagellin
TLR6	diacyl lipoproteins, mycoplasma
TLR7	ssRNA
TLR8	ssRNA
TLR9	CpG DNA, hemozoin
TLR11	profilin-like protein, uropathogenic bacteria

Figure 12

2. CLRs (C-type Lectin Receptors)

and Mannose receptors recognize **fungal glycans** and are found on the plasma membrane of dendritic cells and macrophages.

3. RLRs (Retinoic Acid-Inducible Gene Like Receptors)

are found in the cytosol and detect the nucleic acids of viruses that replicate in the cytoplasm.

Once these receptors are engaged, transcription factors such as NFκB or IRF7 direct the production of **proinflammatory cytokines** or **type 1 interferons**, respectively.

Diapedesis

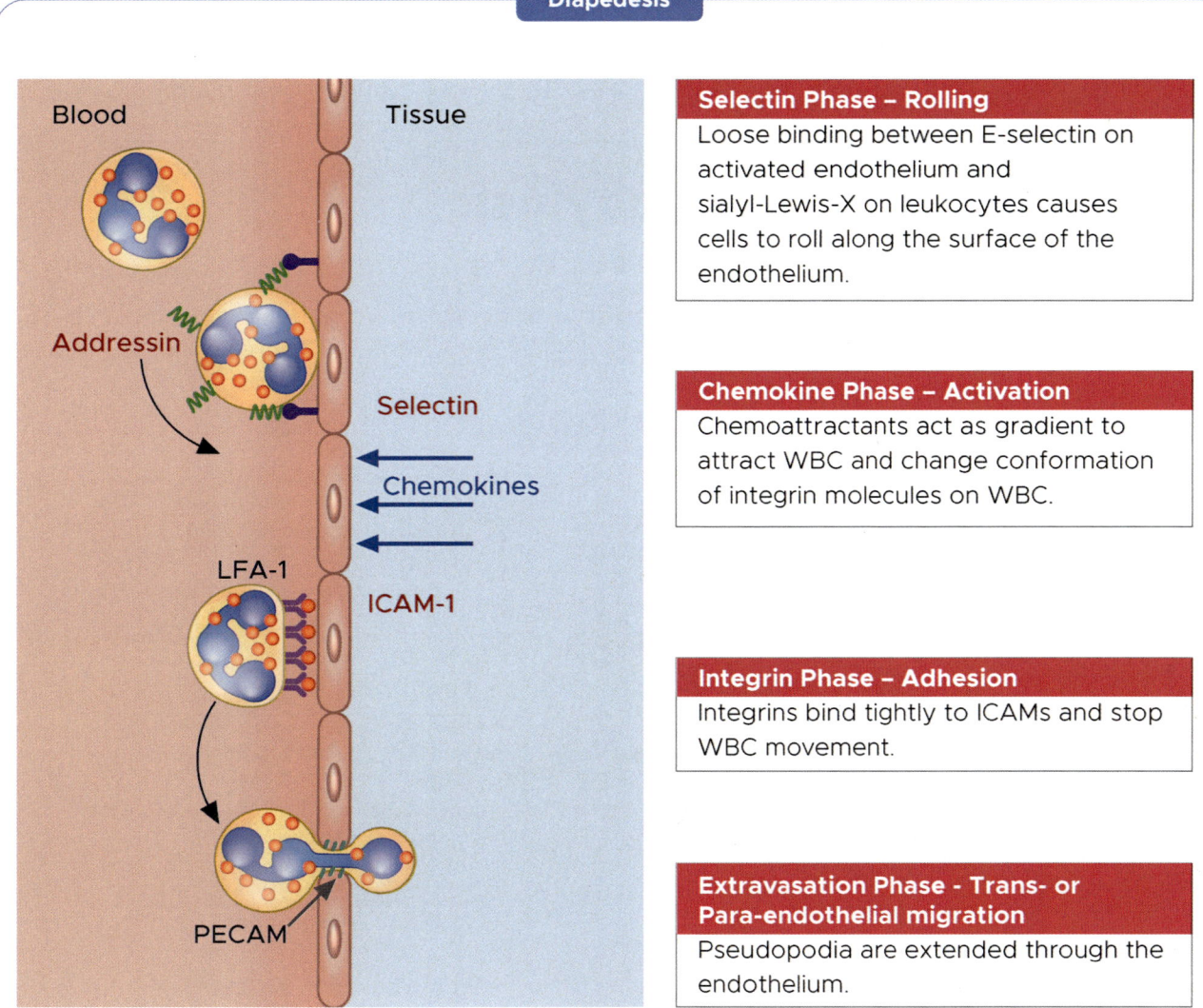

Figure 13

Summary of Adhesion molecules

Molecule		Tissue	Ligand
Selectins (loose binding to carbohydrates)	E-selectin	Activated endothelium	**Addressins** (sialyl-Lewis X)
	L-selectin	Leukocytes exiting circulation through HEVs	
	P-selectin	Platelets and activated endothelium	
Integrins (tight binding to extracellular matrix and cell adhesion molecules (CAMs)	LFA-1	Dendritic cells, macrophages, PMNs, T cells	**ICAMs** 1 and 2 on activated endothelium
	MAC-1	Dendritic cells and monocytes	
	VLA-4	Monocytes, T cells	VCAM-1

Phagocytosis

Many of the first cellular responders (either resident or newly arriving) have in common that they are phagocytic: they ingest and digest the debris of injured cells and invading microbes.

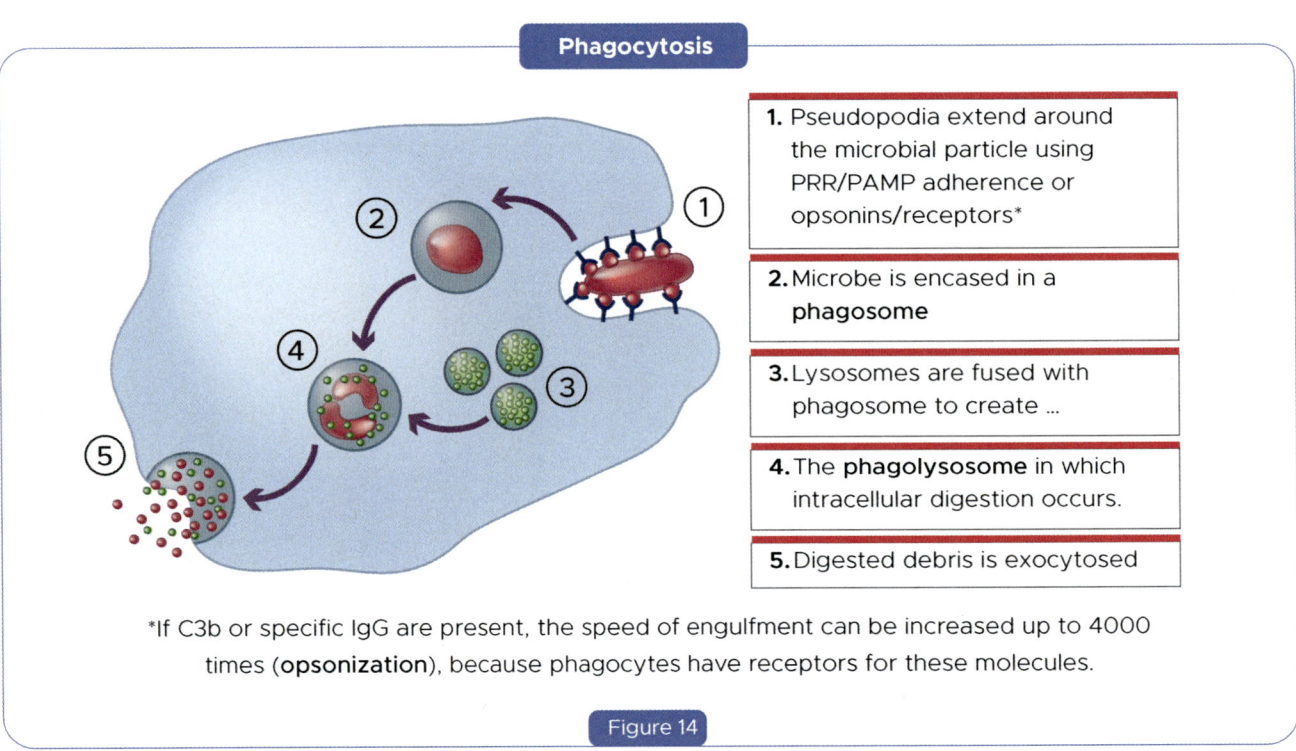

Phagocytosis

1. Pseudopodia extend around the microbial particle using PRR/PAMP adherence or opsonins/receptors*
2. Microbe is encased in a **phagosome**
3. Lysosomes are fused with phagosome to create …
4. The **phagolysosome** in which intracellular digestion occurs.
5. Digested debris is exocytosed

*If C3b or specific IgG are present, the speed of engulfment can be increased up to 4000 times (**opsonization**), because phagocytes have receptors for these molecules.

Figure 14

Mechanisms of intracellular killing

There are both oxygen-dependent and oxygen-independent mechanisms of microbial killing that are activated after phagocytic engulfment. The oxygen-dependent mechanisms are started when a "**respiratory burst**" of oxygen consumption activates a membrane-bound oxidase, **NADPH oxidase**. This causes the production of the reactive oxygen species:
- Superoxide anion
- Hydroxyl radical
- Hydrogen peroxide

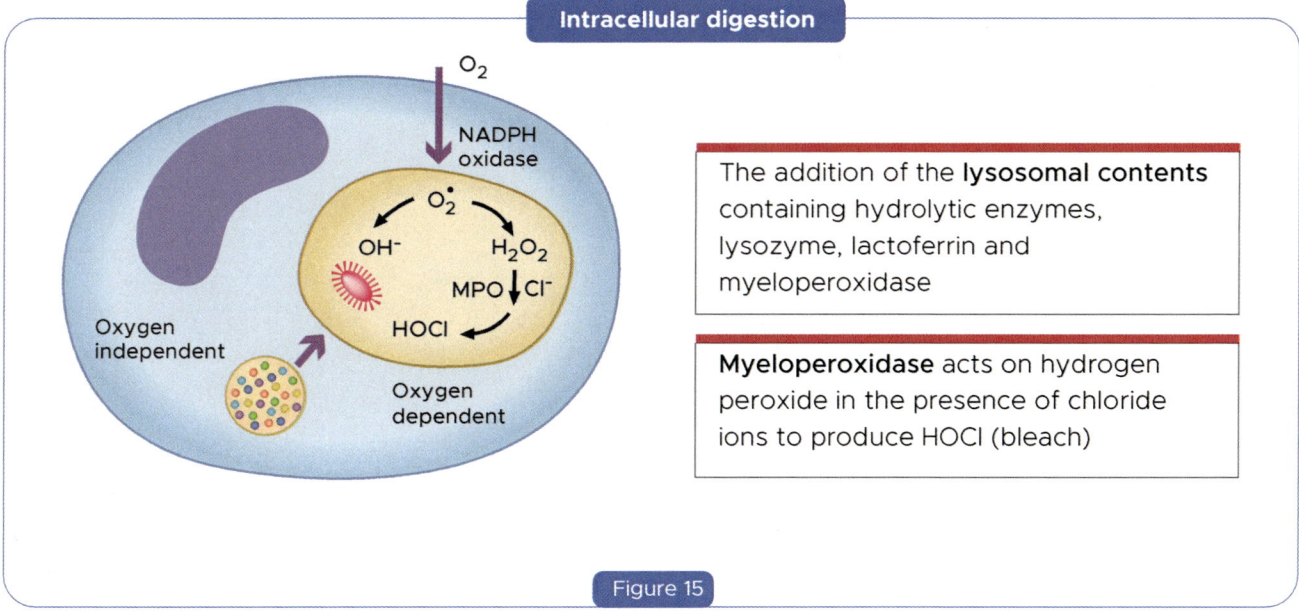

The addition of the **lysosomal contents** containing hydrolytic enzymes, lysozyme, lactoferrin and myeloperoxidase

Myeloperoxidase acts on hydrogen peroxide in the presence of chloride ions to produce HOCl (bleach)

Figure 15

Summary

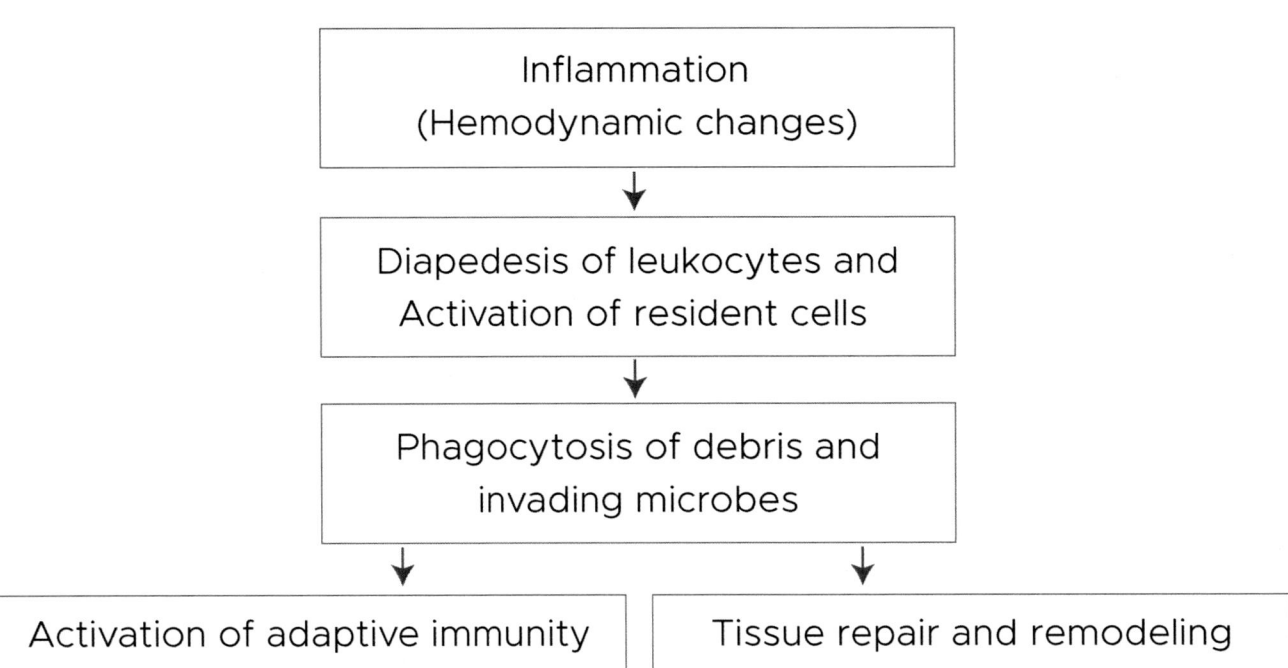

#MMC (Make Me Care!)

1. Microbial pathogens have evolved mechanisms to evade acute inflammation. Can you predict the outcomes of production of:
   - *Streptococcus pyogenes* IL-8 protease
   - *Pseudomonas aeruginosa* C3a and C5a protease
   - *Streptococcus pyogenes* C3b protease
   - *Staphylococcus aureus* protein A which binds IgG
2. Imiquimod is a biologic therapeutic which acts by stimulating Langerhans cells through TLR-7. Given what you know about this TLR, what must be true of the targeted agent and the cytokines which would result?
3. With your understanding of the signaling and cellular communication involved in the phases of the acute inflammatory process, can you predict how long it should take for the arrival/occurrence of:
   - Proteins
   - Cells
   - Tissue remodeling
4. If a patient had a genetic inability to produce integrin molecules, what would you predict would be the presentation?
5. If a patient had a genetic inability to produce NADPH oxidase in phagocytic cells, what would be the predicted outcome?

Before you leave, can you....

1. List the sequence of steps involved in acute inflammation.
2. Describe the types and sources of molecules involved in vasodilation.
3. Describe the types and sources of molecules involved in chemotaxis.
4. Explain the signals for injury and invasion and their cellular receptors.
5. Explain the mechanisms of phagocytosis and intracellular killing.
6. Identify the molecular basis and role of opsonization.

> **Case History**

CGD

A 3-month-old male child is referred to a specialist because of severe, recurrent skin infections. The child was born at term by uneventful vaginal delivery, but since the age of two weeks, has been seen 3 times by his pediatrician for recurrent skin abscesses in the diaper area and on the scalp. Cultures of the lesions grew *Staphylococcus aureus* from the scalp and gram negative enterics from the diaper region. The infections responded to antimicrobials but recurred within days of discontinuation of therapy. A pseudomonal respiratory infection one month ago was treated aggressively with antibiotics and has not recurred.

On examination, the child is alert and responsive. Height and weight determinations are at the 75th and 60th percentiles, respectively. There are numerous pustular lesions on the skin of the diaper area, the axillae and the scalp. All other systems are within normal limits.

Chief Complaint(s):
- pyoderma

Differential Diagnoses:
- Chronic granulomatous disease (CGD)
- Cystic fibrosis
- Glucose 6-phosphate dehydrogenase (G6PD) deficiency
- Glutathione synthetase (GS) deficiency
- Hyperimmunoglobulin E (Job) syndrome

Clinical Approach:
The presentation of this patient with recurrent infections in early infancy points towards a primary immunodeficiency. Because the skin and mucosal barriers are normally protected by resident and mobilizing phagocytic cells, recurrent infections in this age group and anatomical locale are suggestive of problems with innate defenses of these barrier systems. It is of note that the infectious agents in this case (*Staphylococcus aureus*, most gram negative enterics and *Pseudomonas*) have in common that they are catalase positive. The child is slightly behind on measures of height and weight, but not enough to suggest a severe combined immunodeficiency.

Immunologic Workup:
- Culture and sensitivity of exudate from multiple skin lesions grows *Staphylococcus aureus* (MSSA) and *Candida albicans*.
- CBC and Differential: Total WBC count 10,500/μL, 35% neutrophils, 51% lymphocytes, with normal proportions of B and T lymphocytes. Microcytic, hypochromic anemia.
- Erythrocyte sedimentation rate and C-reactive protein levels normal. Levels of IgM, IgG are slightly elevated, with IgA and IgE values within age reference range.
- Nitroblue tetrazolium (NBT) slide test showed failure to produce formazan inside neutrophils. Flow cytometric measurement of neutrophil respiratory burst activity using dihydrorhodamine showed a 90% decrease in intensity of fluorescence from control values.

Diagnosis: Chronic Granulomatous Disease

The diagnosis of CGD is confirmed by the NBT dye reduction test and the respiratory burst activity test. Both of these tests measure the failure of CGD neutrophils to reduce an oxidized dye. The NBT test is the standard diagnostic screening test for gene carriers and has also been used for prenatal diagnosis. Because of its increased sensitivity, the flow cytometric test can also detect the X-linked carrier state.

The phagocytes of CGD patients are able to engulf particles but are unable to generate reactive oxygen species (ROS) which are necessary for microbial killing. The microbes cultured from the cutaneous lesions and earlier respiratory infection in this case are all catalase positive. This allows microbes to incapacitate the second oxygen-dependent intracellular killing mechanism that utilizes myeloperoxidase (MPO) in the presence of chloride ions to convert hydrogen peroxide into bleach. Since aerobic organisms produce hydrogen peroxide as a biproduct of their metabolism, catalase negative organisms can be killed by their own hydrogen peroxide (with MPO). There is no oxygen-dependent mechanism for killing in a CGD patient infected with a catalase-positive organism, and the remaining lysosome-dependent mechanisms are insufficient to prevent chronic recurrent infections.

This patient's peripheral blood leukocytosis ($>8.5 \times 10^3$/μL) is an additional finding that reflects increased numbers of circulating neutrophils, and a microcytic, hypochromic anemia is consistent with chronic disease.

The finding of normal IgE levels rules out hyper IgE syndrome, and although G6PD and GS deficiencies may associate with similar phagocytic defects, they are much more commonly identified by their association with hemolytic anemia, which is absent here.

CGD is a genetically heterogeneous primary immunodeficiency disorder which can result from defects in any of the 5 subunits of NADPH oxidase in phagocytic cells. The NADPH oxidase complex is responsible for the respiratory burst which generates ROS to kill ingested microbes. Because of the locus heterogeneity of the causal gene defects, the patterns of presentation differ from patient to patient within the syndrome. Commonly lung, skin, liver and bone are the affected sites. Patients with CGD are at increased risk of life-threatening infections with catalase-positive bacteria and fungi and inflammatory complications such as CGD colitis.

The most common form of CGD inheritance is X-linked recessive. 80% of all cases involve males with hemizygous mutations of the gene coding for gp91phox which has been mapped to the p21.1 region of the X chromosome. Subtypes of the disease which are autosomal recessive in inheritance are generally associated with milder disease. The degree of superoxide anion production is determined by the involved mutation, so molecular diagnosis may be useful for deciding prognosis and therapy.

Management:

Early diagnosis and treatment with antibiotics to manage infections and prednisone to manage inflammatory and autoimmune complications are the mainstays of CGD therapy. Aggressive anti-infection prophylaxis using trimethoprim-sulfamethoxazole and antimycotics such as itraconazole are combined with interferon-gamma therapy to increase the production of superoxides in cases where the genetic variant is one of reduced but not totally absent ROS production.

Prognosis:

With prompt and aggressive antimicrobial and immunomodulatory therapy, the average life span for patients with CGD is now 40 years. It tends to be somewhat longer for females (autosomal recessive inheritance) than for males (X-linked recessive inheritance). Early gene therapy trials have not shown prolonged benefit, and stem cell transplant remains the only curative therapy.

Case History

LAD-1

A 2-month old female infant with perirectal cellulitis of one-week duration is referred for immunological workup. The infant was born uneventfully at term to a single mother who has declined to identify the biological father. There was no obvious dysmorphism nor neonatal complications. Her umbilical cord detached late, one month after birth and she has been returned to her pediatrician three times since then to treat *Staphylococcus aureus* omphalitis. In each case, the infections resolved with oxacillin, but returned within days. At the present time, the umbilical area is still edematous, oozes a serosanguineous fluid and is and surrounded by faint bluish scars.

On presentation the infant ranks within the 70th percentile for height and weight. Temperature is 38.4 C (101.1 F), respirations 36/min, heart rate 80 beats/min. Other physical exam parameters are within normal limits.

Chief Complaint(s):
- cellulitis, omphalitis

Differential Diagnoses:
- Chronic granulomatous disease (CGD)
- Hyper IgE syndrome (formerly Job Syndrome)
- Interleukin 1 receptor-associated kinase-4 (IRAK-4) deficiency
- Leukocyte adhesion deficiency (LAD)
- Myeloperoxidase (MPO) deficiency
- Sepsis

Clinical Approach:
In an infant with mild growth delay and recurrent cutaneous infections, the possibility of primary immunodeficiency disease must be considered. Since the primary protection of the skin is via myeloid-origin phagocytic cells, a complete work-up should include evaluation of defects in number, mobilization and phagocytic function. Because one of the earliest roles of neutrophils and wound healing is in the management of the umbilical stump, delays in this process are extremely suggestive of problems in the ability of neutrophils to perform diapedesis into areas of injury. Healthy infants with delayed umbilical cord loss are not uncommon, but such findings in the setting of extreme leukocytosis would not be expected. Epinephrine and corticosteroids are known for their ability to demarginate leukocytes and impede adherence but there is no indication of their use in this patient.

Immunologic Workup:
- CBC and differential: Leukocytosis ($1.4 \times 10^5/\mu L$) with neutrophil predominance (70%)
- Elevated C-reactive protein.
- Serological tests for CMV, *Toxoplasma* and HIV negative.
- Flow cytometry: normal populations of CD3, CD4, CD8, CD19 and CD56 lymphocytes, CD18 absent from populations of monocytes and neutrophils.
- Neutrophil oxidative index normal. Karyotype normal but genetic analysis suggestive of consanguinity.

Diagnosis:
LAD-1 is a rare genetic condition which presents clinically with localized bacterial infections in the setting of extreme leukocytosis. The infections tend to be those of gram positive normal flora and gram negative coliforms, as would be anticipated in patients with neutropenia. The condition results from failure to express CD18 which is the common β2 subunit of LFA1 family integrins (β2 integrins). The gene defect maps to chromosome 21q22.3 and may involve point mutations (50%) or missense, nonsense and splice mutations (all others). It is inherited in an autosomal recessive fashion and is therefore often associated with cases of parental consanguinity. Cases occur worldwide, displaying a lack of ethnic predisposition.

The LFA1 family integrins play important roles in lymphocyte trafficking, antigen presentation, cytotoxic killing and leukocyte adhesion to endothelial cells in acute inflammation. The ligands for the β2 integrins are IgCAMs (molecules in the immunoglobulin superfamily of genes) which are important in the tight binding of leukocytes to the extracellular matrix or activated endothelium to perform diapedesis or wound healing. Integrin/IgCAM interactions are also essential for the efficient opsonization and phagocytosis by neutrophils, monocytes and macrophages.

LAD-1 is distinguished from hyperimmunoglobulin E syndrome or CGD/MPO deficiency by its extreme neutrophilia. Patients with CGD or MPO deficiency would have changes in the neutrophil oxidative index. It is distinguished from IRAK-4 deficiency because those patients cannot develop fever. The neutrophils are mature, containing vacuoles and granules in the presence of infection, in distinction to the cells of myeloid leukemias.

LAD-2 is an extremely rare, autosomal recessive defect described in infants of Middle Eastern or Brazilian descent. It results in the lack of fucosylation of the ligands for selectin molecules, and causes complete failure of expression of sialyl-Lewis X necessary for the first, reversible step of leukocyte diapedesis. It is associated with severe growth and mental retardation. These patients manifest the Bombay type blood group phenotype since they are also unable to fucosylate the H blood group polysaccharide. They also cannot fucosylate IgM and IgG, but have normal levels of these antibodies detected in the blood.

Management:
Control of bacterial infections with antibiotics until an appropriate donor for stem cell transplantation can be achieved. Transplantation has unusually high success even if a non haplo-identical donor is used, presumably because integrins are important in lymphocyte costimulation to produce rejection. Prophylactic antibiotics, interferon-gamma therapy or leukocyte transfusions have not shown significant benefit. Gene therapy to insert the CD18 subunit is currently under investigation.

Prognosis:
LAD-1 is typically fatal within the first two years of life unless stem cell transplantation can be performed. LAD-2 is less likely to be a fatal condition, but patients display mental retardation and neurologic impairment.

Immunology
Chapter five

Antigen Presentation: The Bridge Between Innate and Adaptive Immunity

Antigen Presentation

Introduction:

If acute inflammation is sufficient to stop the invasion of microbes and isolate the injured area, the debris will need to be cleaned up, and the tissue returned to its normal function as much as possible. This process is under the control of the resident phagocytes, and their evaluation of the cause of the damage will cause signaling to the cells of adaptive immunity, so that if the same injury were to be repeated again, there would be memory of the previous assault, and a more rapid and specific response to it in the future.

The neutrophils which drove acute inflammation are phagocytic cells which ingest, kill with reactive oxygen species and die, with the production of pus and abscess formation. Antigen presenting cells (APCs) such as macrophages and dendritic cells are extremely long-lived cells which similarly phagocytize and kill intracellularly with reactive oxygen species, but afterwards take the peptide-containing debris of their meal and display it on their cell membrane. The molecules which anchor these foreign peptides into the membrane of the APC belong to the immunoglobulin superfamily of genes and are called the major histocompatibility complex (MHC) as a general term, or the human leukocyte antigens (HLA) in the human.

Role of the Major Histocompatibility Complex

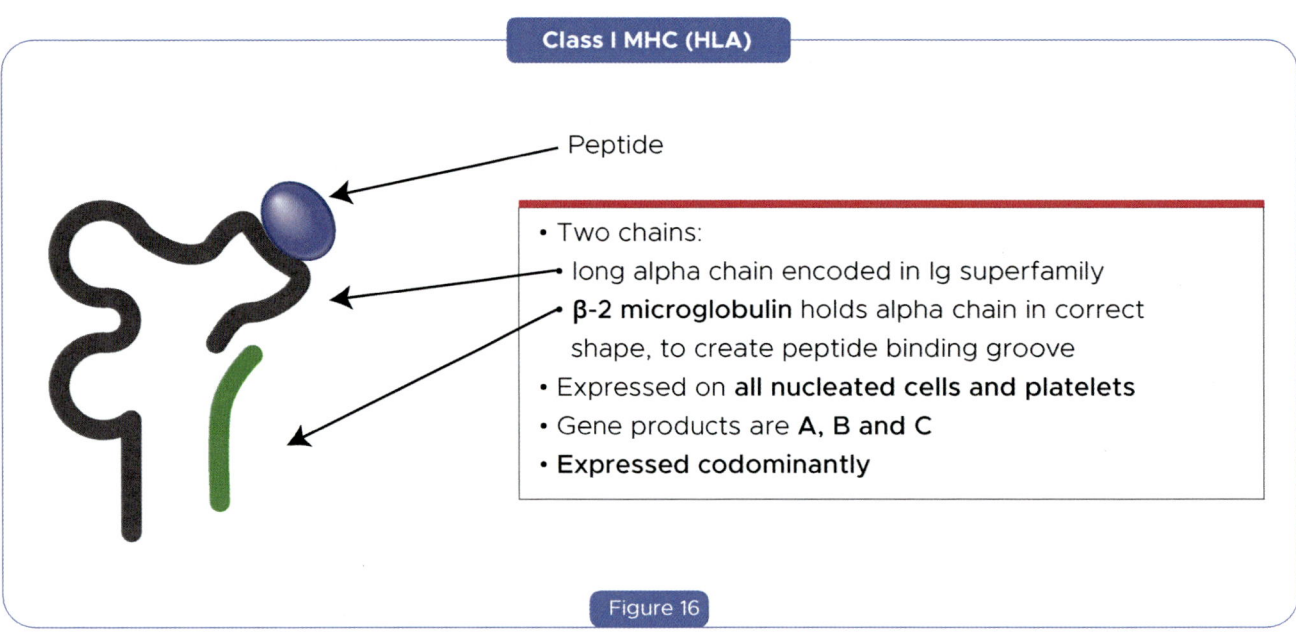

Class I MHC (HLA)

- Two chains:
  - long alpha chain encoded in Ig superfamily
  - **β-2 microglobulin** holds alpha chain in correct shape, to create peptide binding groove
- Expressed on **all nucleated cells and platelets**
- Gene products are **A, B and C**
- **Expressed codominantly**

Figure 16

Where do the peptides come from?

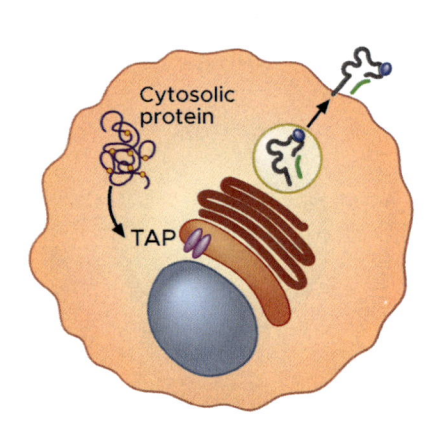

Class I MHC Loading

- MHC Class I molecules are loaded with peptides via the **endogenous pathway.**
- Peptides produced in the cytosol of the cell are degraded in proteasomes and transported by a TAP transporter complex to the site of production of the class I molecule in the ER.
- The combination of MHC 1 and internally produced peptide is then transported to the cell surface.
- Normal cells wearing normal peptides will be ignored because of central tolerance induced in the thymus.
- Cells producing abnormal or microbial peptides will be targeted for killing with **CD8⁺ T cells (CTLs).**

Figure 17

Class II MHC (HLA)

- Alpha and beta chains of similar length, both encoded in same genetic region.
- **Expressed codominantly** on **antigen-presenting cells** (macrophages, dendritic cells, B cells, activated T cells and endothelial cells)
- Gene products are DP, DQ, DR.

Figure 18

MHC 2 Loading

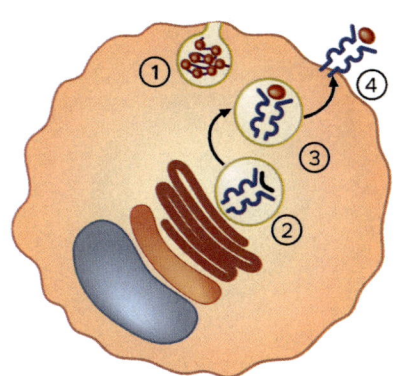

1. Peptides loaded into class II MHC molecules originate in acidic vesicles after phagocytosis/endocytosis by the presenting cell (**exogenous pathway**).
2. MHC molecule is produced in the endoplasmic reticulum and has an **invariant chain** blocking the peptide binding groove.
3. Release of the MHC molecule into the acidic vesicle causes digestion of the invariant chain, and the ingested peptides bind in the now vacant groove.
4. The combination of MHC II/peptide is transported to the cell membrane where it is available for recognition by **CD4+ TH cells**.

Figure 19

Summary of MHC/HLA Molecules

Class I molecules (A, B, C)	Function	Identification of **altered self** cells (neoplasms or intracellular microbes)
	What cells have these?	**All nucleated cells, platelets**
	Where did the peptides come from?	Produced endogenously in infected, altered cells
	Who recognizes this signal?	**CD8$^+$ CTLs**
Class II molecules (DP, DQ, DR)	Function	**Stimulate TH** to "help"
	What cells have these?	**Antigen-presenting** cells (DC, macrophages, B lymphocytes, activated T cells and endothelial cells)
	Where did the peptides come from?	**Phagocytized and/or processed** in acidic vesicles
	Who recognizes this signal?	**CD4$^+$ TH cells**

Transportation of the Signal to the Secondary Lymphoid Organs

Within hours of the ingestion and digestion of debris by resident, phagocytic antigen-presenting cells, they will begin to move toward the secondary lymphoid organs carrying their cargo of MHC II/peptide signals. As you recall, our mature but naïve T lymphocytes have been recirculating through these organs, and now, the interaction of these antigen-specific lymphocytes with the MHC II/peptide complex complementary to their TCR will begin their stimulation. B lymphocytes residing in the follicles and germinal centers of these secondary lymphoid organs can bind free antigen of any chemical composition to their membrane Ig receptors, and can themselves serve as antigen presenting cells for TH cells.

Differentiation of APC Signaling

In the microenvironment of the inflammatory focus where the APCs are cleaning up debris, there are multiple chemical signals which encourage the APCs to differentiate down one of two pathways. Mast cells, NK cells and other innate lymphoid cells, and microbial pathogens themselves (PAMPs) are the origin of these signals, and they deliver important insights about the nature of the invader to the APCs so that this can be additionally communicated downstream.

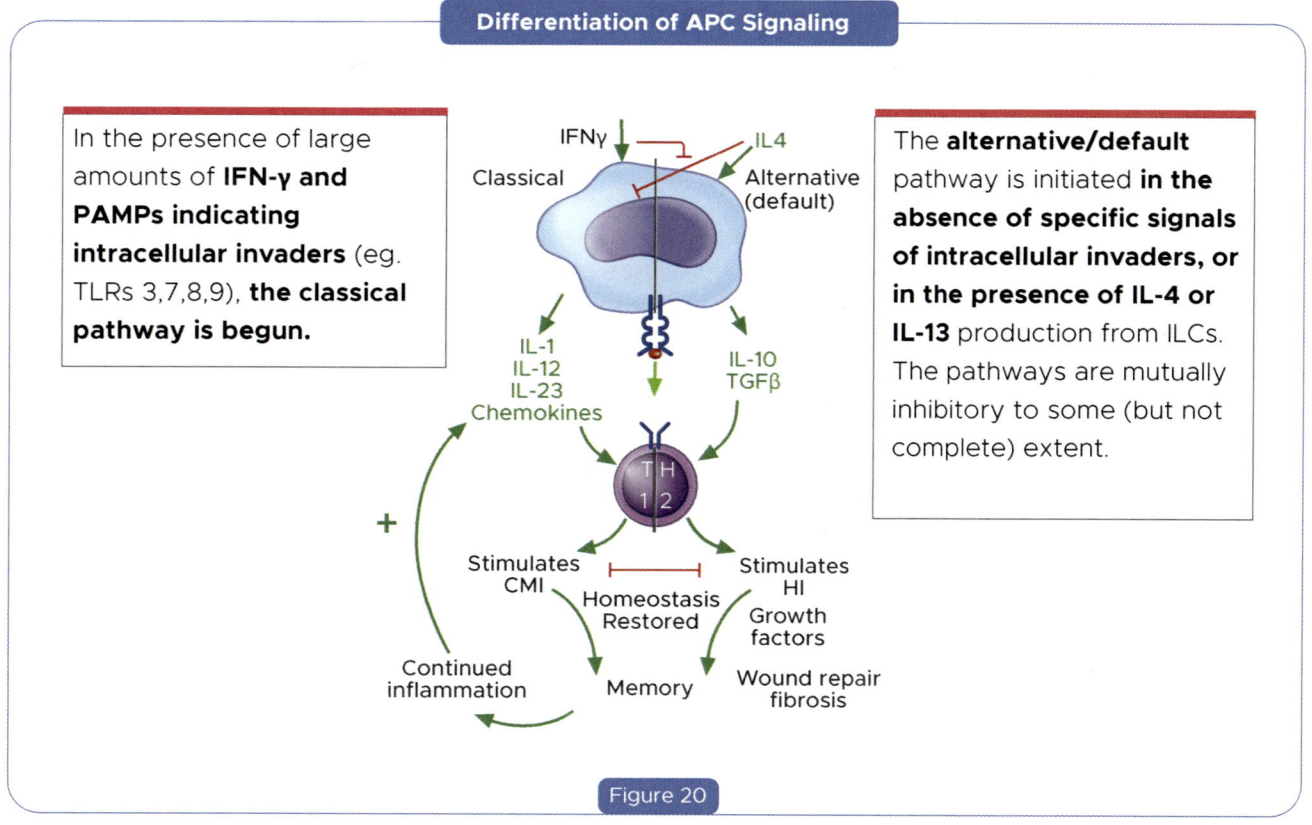

Figure 20

The cytokine signals from the classically activated APCs, along with the signal from the MHC class II/peptide binding to the TCR, induce the mature, naïve TH cell to differentiate down the pathway to become the TH cell controlling the cell-mediated immune response (CMI; TH1). This is because **CMI is the most efficient pathway for identification of altered/infected self cells to target them for elimination.**

The cytokine signals from the alternatively activated APCs (again along with MHC II/peptide signaling) induce the mature naïve TH cell to differentiate down the pathway to become a **TH2 cell which will control the development of antibodies from B lymphocytes (the humoral immune (HI) response).** This pathway is adapted for the removal of extracellular microbes via enhancement of phagocytosis (**opsonization**) or complement activation).

Communication between APC and TH cells

The communication between APC and TH cells is the critical engineering checkpoint for the activation vs. inhibition of the adaptive immune response. It involves a 3-signal cascade:

Signal 1
Binding of the TH TCR to the MHC II/peptide complex presented by the APC. This is the only antigen-specific signal of the cascade. CD4 leaflets stabilize this interaction, CD3 acts as the signal transduction molecule.

Signal 2
Binding of costimulatory molecules (from left to right in diagram).
- CD80/B7 on APC binds to CD28 on TH cell. The binding of CD80/B7 to CTLA-4 delivers an inhibitory signal.
- Adhesion molecules (LFA-3 on APC binds to CD2 on TH cell)
- CD40 on APC binds to CD40L on TH cell.

Signal 3
Cytokine secretion
- APC makes IL-1 (fever), IL-6 (acute phase reaction), TNF (fever, cachexia, apoptotic cell death), IL-12 induces switch to TH1.
- TH makes IL-2 (autocrine proliferation signal binds to CD25), TH1 makes IFN-γ (stimulates APC activity).

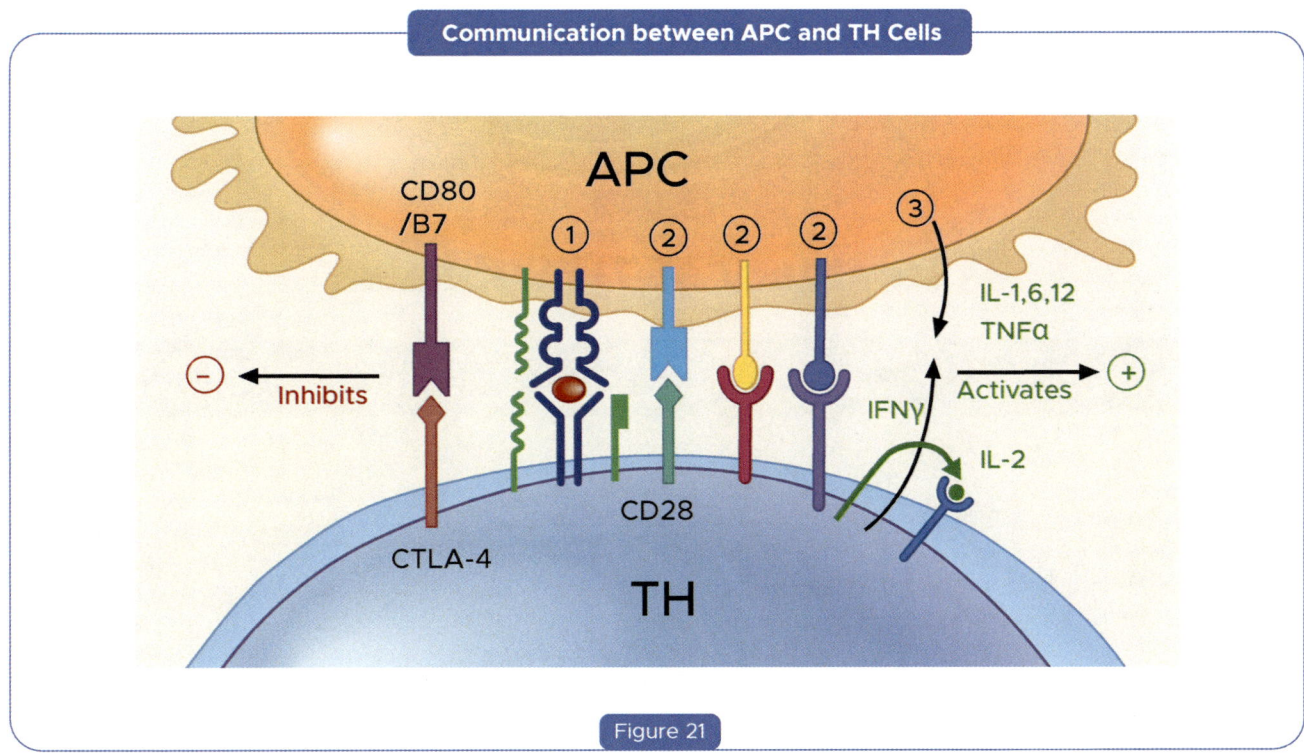

Figure 21

Differentiation of TH cell subsets

All TH cells possess the same cell surface markers with which they are identified. CD3 is the signal transduction molecule on all T cells. CD4 is the marker specific to TH cells. The two major types of TH cells are the TH1 (controls CMI) and the TH2 (controls humoral immunity), but discovery of new categories of TH cells is accelerating with the study of their specific chemokine receptors, signal transducers and activators of transcription.

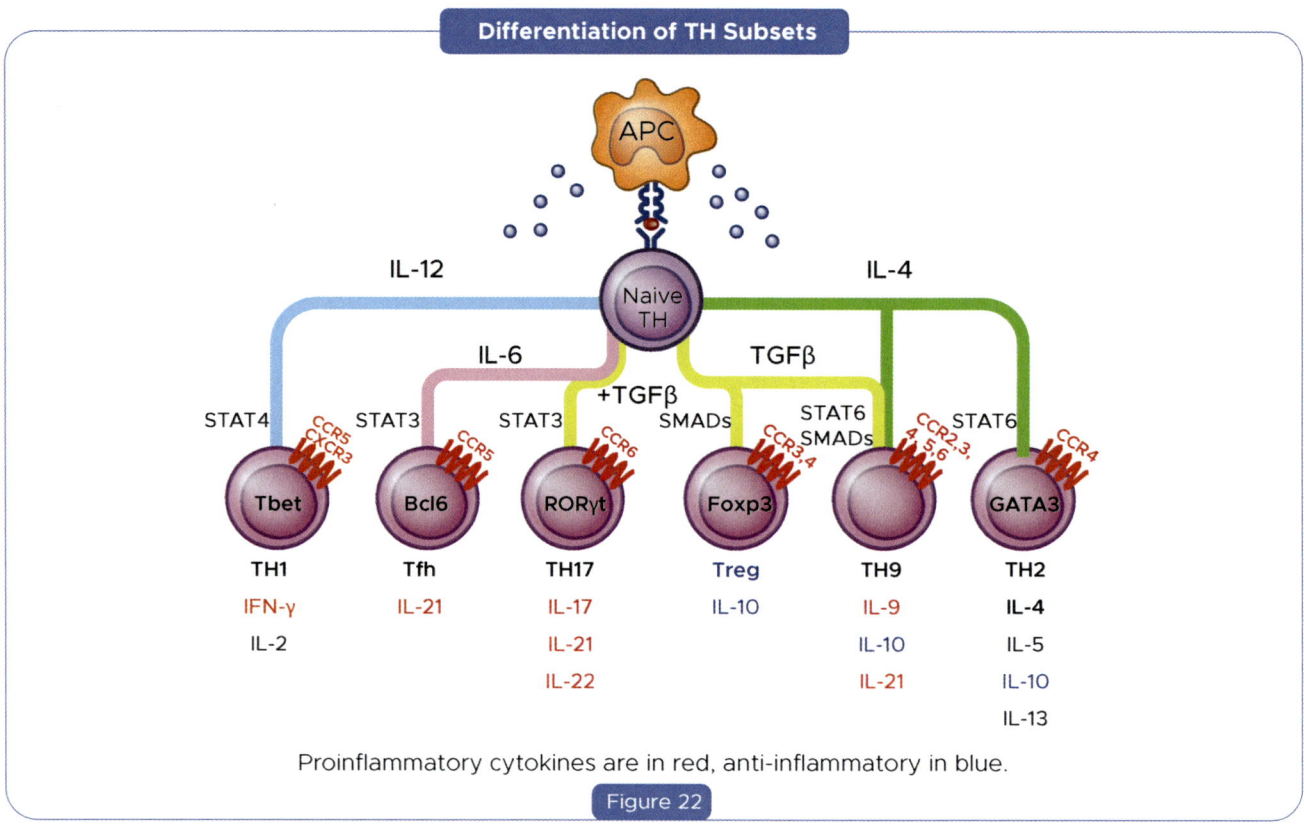

Proinflammatory cytokines are in red, anti-inflammatory in blue.

Figure 22

Summary of TH Subsets

Cell	Stimulus	Chemokine Receptors	Signal receptor	Transcription Factor	Product	Function
TH1	IL-12	CCR3,5	STAT4	Tbet	IL-2, IFN-γ	Defense vs. intracellulars
Tfh	IL-6	CCR5	STAT3	Bcl6	IL-21	Defense vs. autoimmunity
TH17	IL-6 + TGFβ	CCR6	STAT3	RORγt	IL-17,21,22	Defense vs. extracellulars
Treg	TGFβ	CCR4,8	SMADs	Foxp3	IL-10	Immune regulation & prevents autoimmunity
TH9	IL4 + TGFβ	CCR2,3,4,5,6	STAT3, SMADs	?	IL-9,10,21	Anti-tumor & prevents autoimmunity
TH2	IL-4	CCR4	STAT6	Gata3	IL-4,5,10,13	Defense vs allergy & asthma

Summary

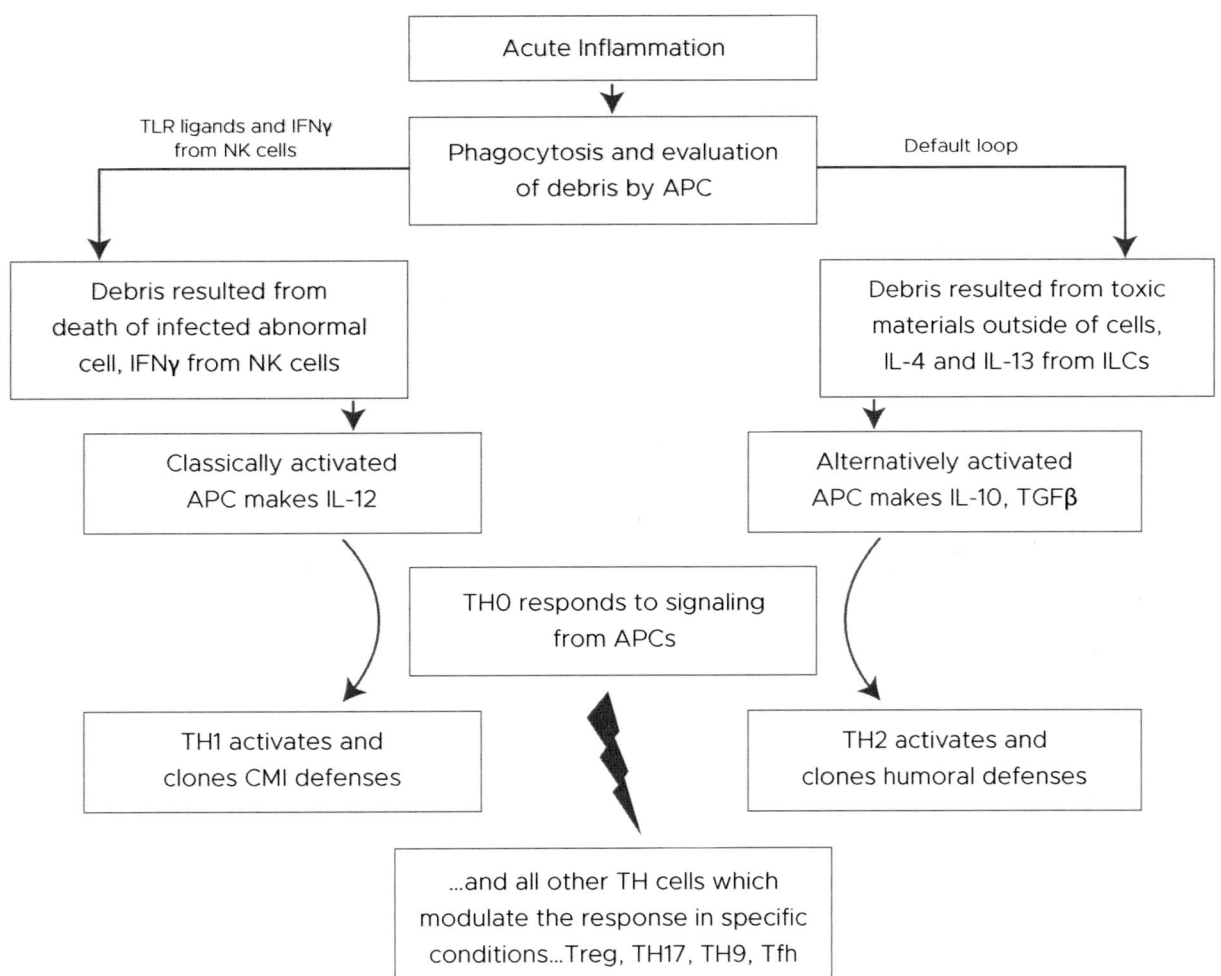

#MMC (Make Me Care!)

1. In the engineering design of the immune system, acute inflammation can be thought of as a nearly instantaneous first response to prevent the attack of something that can kill you right now. The adaptive response then ensues as a more focused subsequent response which is tailored to be maximally effective against the injury, and minimally damaging to host tissues. What two attributes of TH cells make them a critical target for medical therapies which either increase or decrease immune activation?
2. Abscesses and granulomas can be considered the two end pathologic lesions of acute vs. adaptive immune responses. If abscesses are made of neutrophils and granulomas are made of TH1 cells and macrophages, what does this tell you about the different stimuli which caused their development?
3. Ipilimumab is a new monoclonal antibody which blocks CTLA-4. Based on this information, can you project the clinical situations in which this therapy would be beneficial, and those when it would be immunologically contraindicated?
4. If you were going to design a therapy to increase or decrease adaptive immunity in the most efficient way possible, would you design it to be functional at the APC, the TH or the effector cell level, and why?
5. Many cancer cells exhibit complex abilities to evade immune recognition and destruction. Can you explain why a cytokine profile including decreased IL-2 and IFN-γ and increased TGF-β and IL-10 would be "tumor permissive"?

Before you leave, can you....

1. Explain the distinction between a phagocyte and an antigen presenting cell and give examples of each.
2. Enumerate the complex signals between the innate immune response and the bridge to adaptive immune response.
3. Describe the structure, loading, and function of the Class I and II HLA molecules.
4. Explain the complex signaling from the initial injury/infection site which results in the activation of the classical and alternative pathways of APC activation.
5. Explain the signals delivered downstream from APCs which cause the stimulation of the main TH populations (TH1 and TH2) and lesser TH cells (Treg, TH17, TH9, Tfh).
6. Explain the outcome of the stimulation of different TH populations on the outcome of immune stimulation at the organismal level.

Medical Immunology Essentials

Case Discussion
Frontiers in Cancer Immunotherapy

As this diagram of the signaling between APC and TH cells illustrates, the critical engineering "choke" point for the immune engine has the capacity to turn up (activate) or turn down (inhibit) responses downstream. One of the challenges in management of neoplasia is that neoplastic cells have evolved complex mechanisms to skew the response in the direction that they prefer...the dampening down of any potentially threatening immune response. Each of these of neoplastic techniques of immune evasion has become a focus of intense interest in the immunotherapy of cancer.

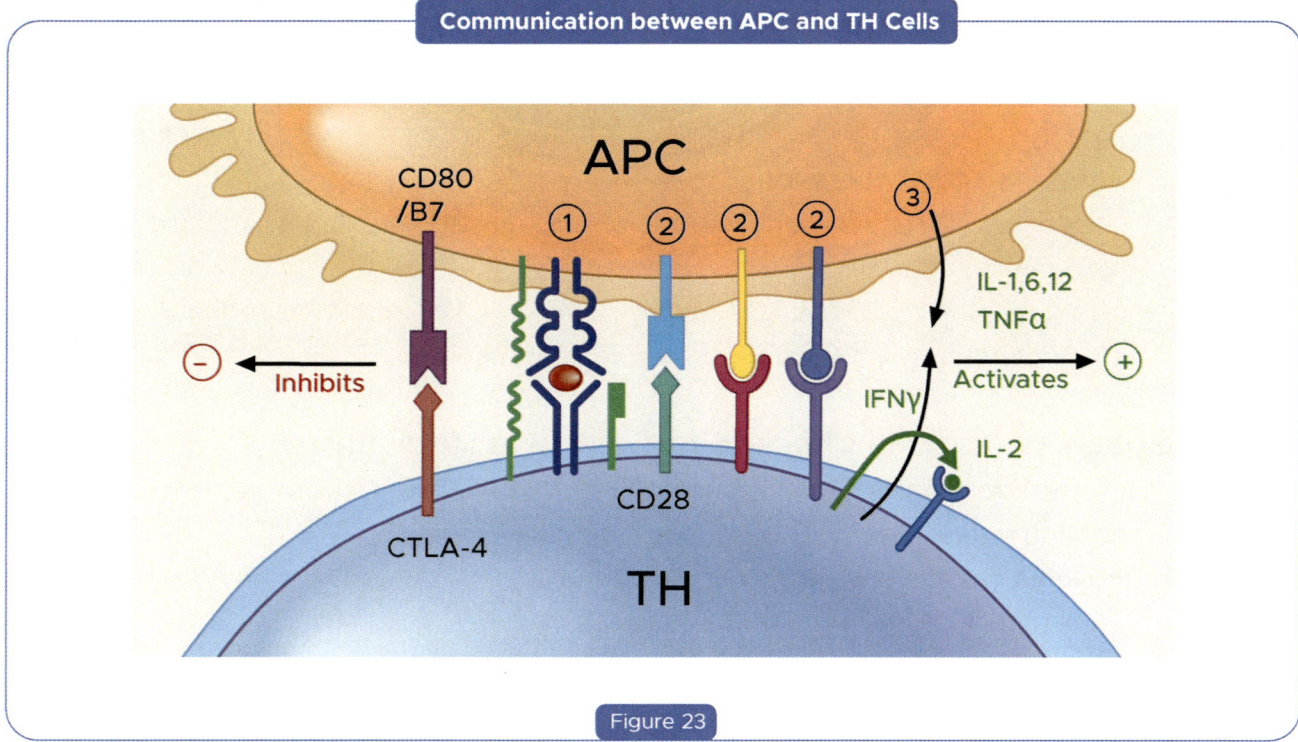

Figure 23

Cancer Avoidance Techniques vs. Immunotherapies
Signal 1: MHC and TCR recognition
- Many neoplastic cells will down-regulate expression of both MHC II and I molecules. This will stop the production of "help" from TH cells...the major source of amplification of immune signals, and inhibit the ability of effector cells of CMI (CTLs) to recognize the neoplastic cells.
- **Type 1 interferons (IFN-α and IFN-β)** are anti-viral interferons which increase the expression of MHC I and II molecules. They have also been shown to decrease cellular protein synthesis through inhibition of eIF2 (inhibiting tumor growth), increase apoptosis through stimulation of p53, and decrease angiogenesis and proliferation of endothelial cells which is required for tumor mass growth.

Signal 2: Costimulatory vs Coinhibitory Molecule Signaling
- The CD28/CTLA-4 family of receptors on T cells binds to the B7/CD80 family of molecules on APC. Binding of CD80 to CD28 gives an activating signal to the TH cell, and binding to CTLA-4 is inhibitory.
- **Inhibitors of CTLA-4 like ipilimumab** and tremelimumab act to inhibit the immune suppressive activity of tumors.
- PD-1 (programmed cell death protein-1) is a member of the CD28/CTLA-4 family. Expression of its ligands (PDL-1 and PDL-2) on tumor cells is believed to cause the T-cell exhaustion found in many cancers and chronic infections.
- **Inhibitors of PD-1 – pembrolizumab** and nivolumab
- **Inhibitors of PDL-1 – durvalumab**, atezolizumab

Signal 3: Production of a cytokine environment which favors tumorigenesis
- The cytokines produced in the microenvironment of the APC/TH interaction can favor immune suppression.
- Tregs and alternatively activated APC favor an environment of immune escape and neovascularization.
- Therapies which favor the TH1/classical APC axis of immunity and inhibit the TH2/alternative APC axis are under development.

Other Aspects of Immune Checkpoint Control In Medicine
Natural immunosuppression: pregnancy, self-tolerance, tolerance to microbiome.
Natural immunoactivation: control of infectious agents.
Pathologic activation: hypersensitivity and autoimmunity.

Immunology
Chapter six

Cell-Mediated Immunity: The Response to Altered/Infected Self

Cell-mediated Immunity

Introduction:
As we have discussed before, acute inflammation is designed to combat microbes with rapid reproductive rates that must be stopped quickly before they enter critical tissue spaces. The cell-mediated immune response, on the other hand, is designed to manage much more insidious invaders...those that invade host cells and hide inside them, hijacking the cell's own synthetic machinery and spreading from cell to cell to cause the disease as a result of loss of normal cell or tissue function. The eradication of invaders hiding intracellularly requires precise mechanisms of identification of the difference between normal and altered host cells. The evolutionary struggle between the microbes that carry out their lifecycles inside our cells, and the immune effector cells that must control them, has caused the development of a variety of mechanisms to control a variety of pathogens.

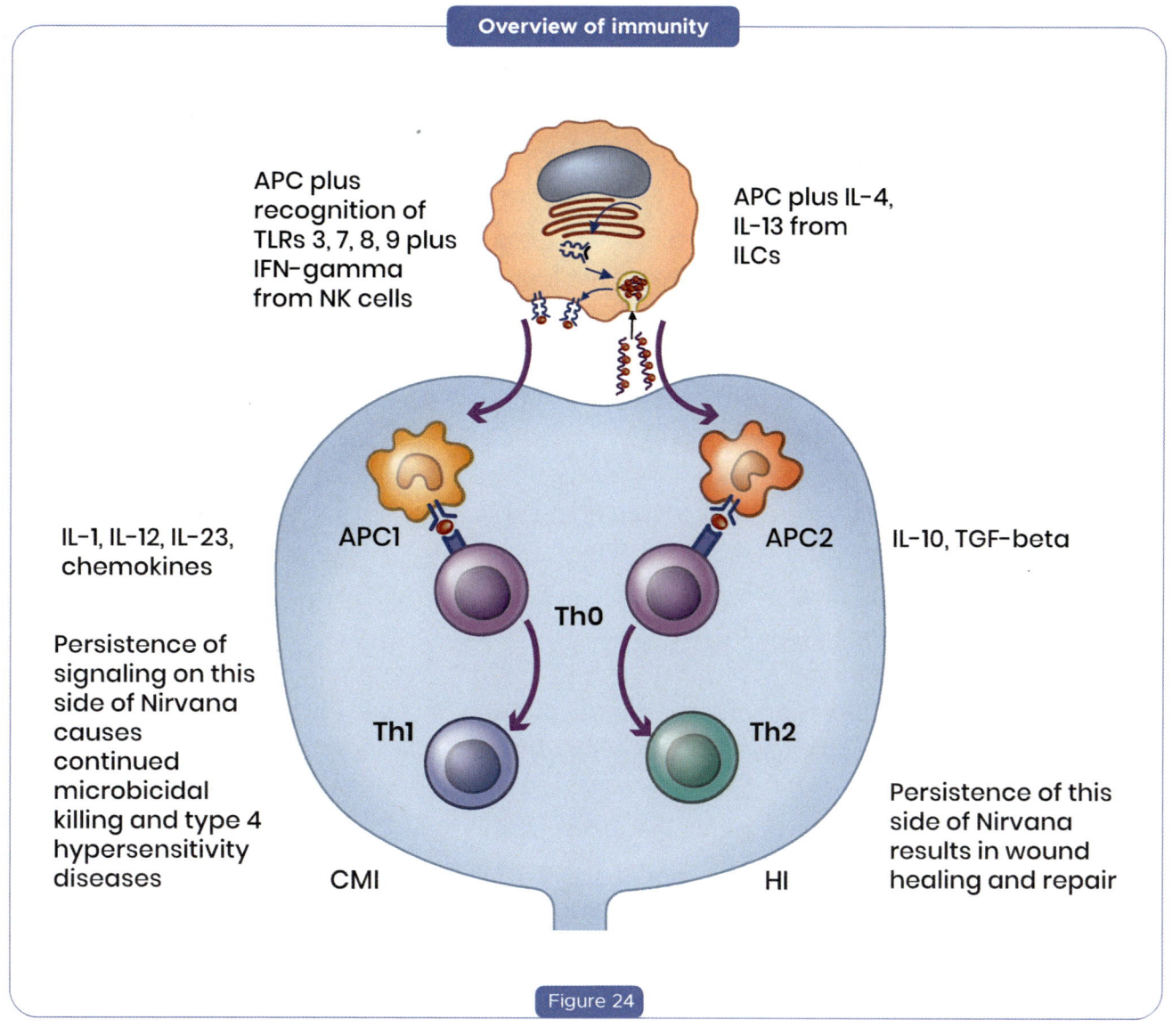

Figure 24

Early Signaling for CMI

Microbes which invade host cells as soon as they are transmitted to man do not set off the complex signals which we associate with acute inflammation. However, innate lymphoid cells exist in virtually all barrier tissues (skin and mucosa) and these cells recognize signals indicating cellular injury and altered function (DAMPs) and synthesize cytokines which induce APCs to differentiate down the classical pathway of activation. In the presence of IFN-γ (from resident NK cells) and TLR ligands which indicate unusual intracellular processes (double-stranded RNA, CpG DNA etc.), macrophages and dendritic cells will phagocytize cellular debris and process and present it to mature naïve TH cells in the context of MHC class II. This, along with the cytokine signal of IL-12, will induce the activation and differentiation of TH1 cells which will control all of the effector mechanisms downstream.

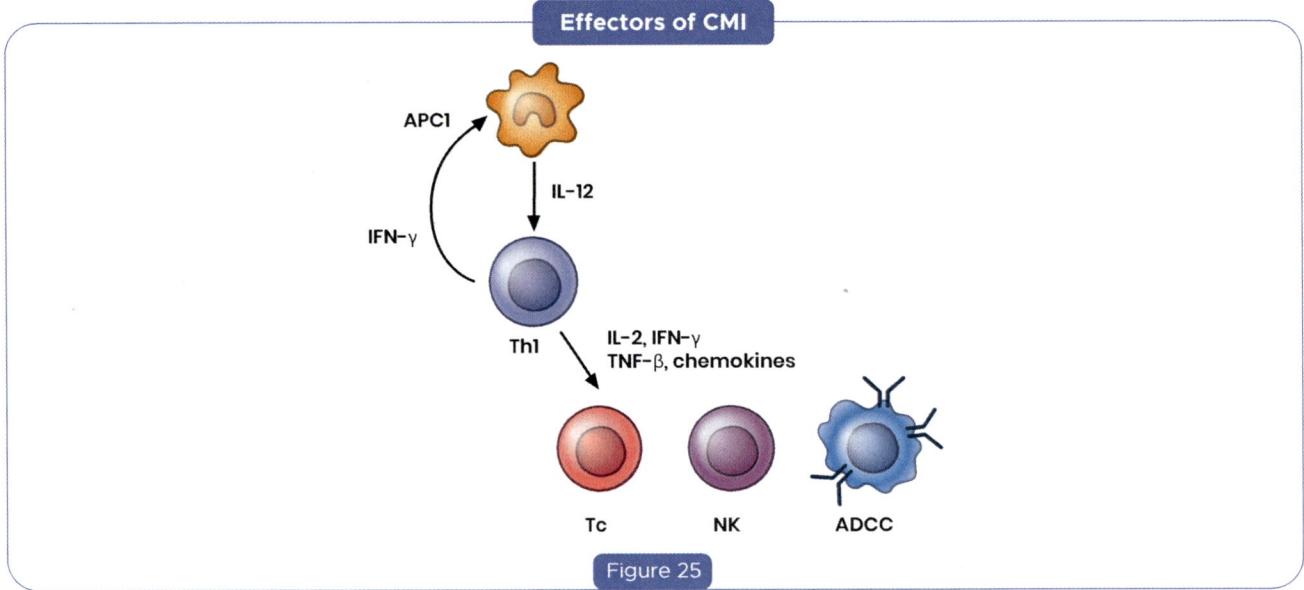

Figure 25

Effectors of Cell-Mediated Immunity

1. Macrophages

In the special case where the infected host cell is actually an APC in the mononuclear phagocytic system, the TH1 delivers IFN-γ to cause the increased efficacy of intracellular killing mechanisms.

- The best membrane marker to identify macrophages is CD14 (the endotoxin receptor).
- This is the preferred mechanism of control of facultative intracellular microbes such as mycobacteria, *Listeria, Francisella, Brucella, Legionella, Yersinia pestis, Salmonella typhi, Nocardia* and *Histoplasma capsulatum*.
- This is the one case within the CMI system where the APC and the effector cell are the same cell.
- The end pathologic lesion of all such infections is the granuloma: a spherical accumulation of TH1 cells and activated, highly secretory macrophages (epithelioid cells).

2. Cytotoxic T Lymphocytes (CTLs)

The CTL is the most efficient effector cell for most **obligate intracellular** microbes (viruses, *Chlamydia*, *Rickettsia*, sporozoan protozoa and *Leishmania*). They are also a critical defense against neoplastic change.

CTLs are attracted to the location of infection or malignant transformation by TH1 production of IFN-γ and chemokines. IL-2 produced by TH1 cells induces their proliferation.

Remember that all nucleated cells make MHC 1 molecules and load them with peptides made inside the cell. If the cell has neoplastic change or if there is an intracellular pathogen infecting it, then the abnormal peptides can serve as a signal to the CTL that the cell needs to be removed.

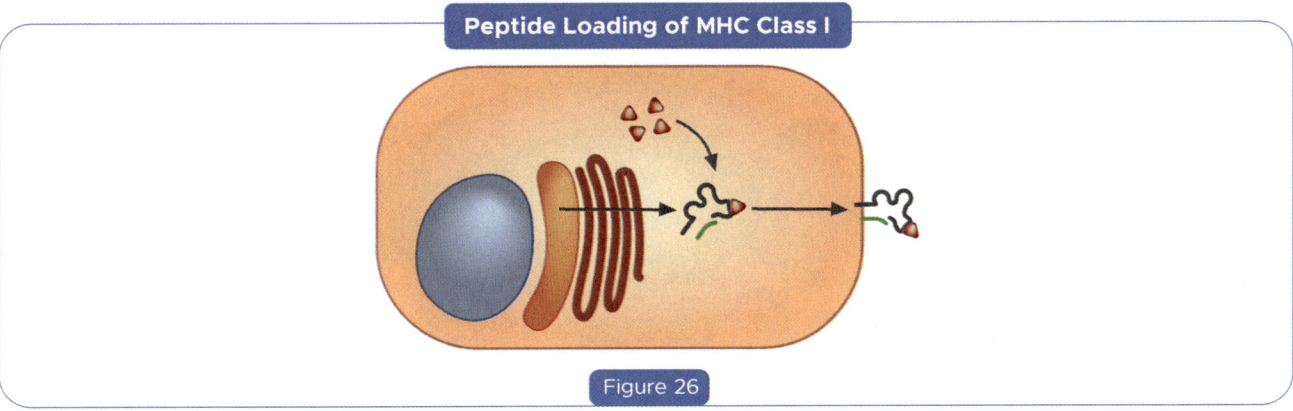

Figure 26

CTLs kill extracellularly if their TCR binds to an altered cell wearing abnormal peptides in the groove of an **MHC 1 molecule.**
- Cytoskeletal rearrangement leads to exocytosis of granules against the target cell.
- **Perforin and granzymes** activate the **extrinsic cascade of apoptosis** through caspase 8.

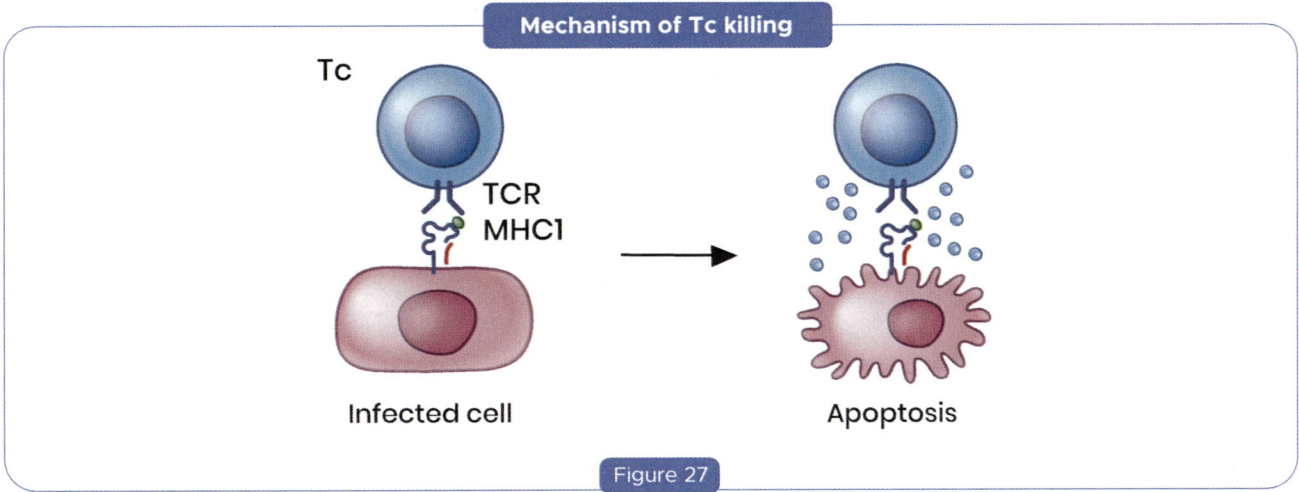

Figure 27

3. Natural Killer (NK) Cells

NK cells are a category of **innate lymphoid cell** that targets cells that do NOT express MHC 1. This is important because many viruses (**herpesviruses** and **HIV**) as well as cancers have "learned" to avoid CTL killing by downregulating expression of MHC. Although they are never as effective as a CTL in removal of infected or malignant cells because they exhibit no memory, they are important when other mechanisms do not work.

- NK cells are identified by their CD markers – **CD16 (the Fc receptor)** and **CD56 (unknown function)**
- Target cell identification is with a 2-signal system of killer Ig-like receptors (KIRs).
    - An activating signal is received from binding to a DAMP.
    - An inhibitory signal is received from binding to MHC 1.
- Killing is extracellular through **perforin and granzymes.**

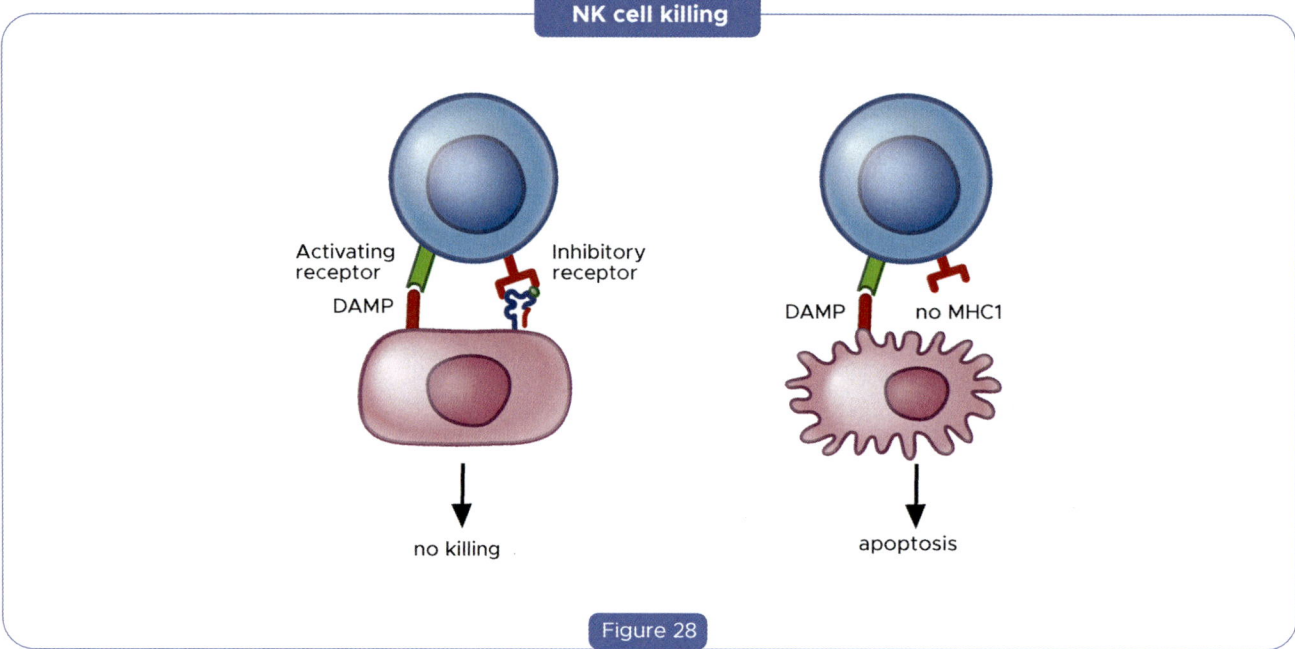

Figure 28

4. Antibody-dependent Cell-Mediated Cytotoxicity (ADCC)

The final effector mechanism controlled by the TH1 cell is ADCC.

- This mechanism of target cell killing can be exercised by any cell with an Fc receptor **(CD16; monocytes, macrophages, NK cells, neutrophils and even eosinophils).**
- The targeting is done by the binding of specific antibody, and once identified, the target cell is induced to undergo apoptosis in response to the release of perforin, lytic enzymes and tumor necrosis factor (TNF) from the ADCC cell.
- The antibody is **IgG** with exception of that used by **eosinophils** to target helminth parasites; in that case it is **IgE.**

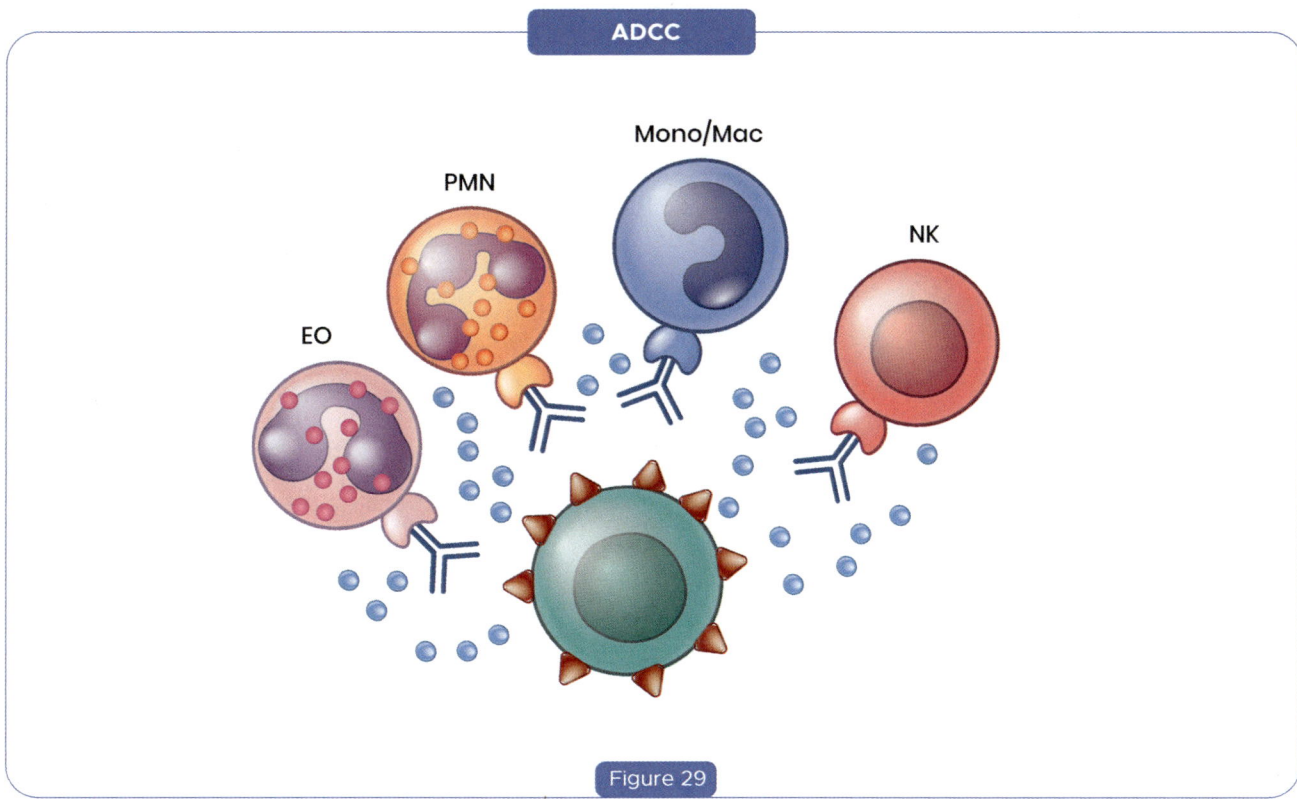

Figure 29

#MMC (Make Me Care!)

1. Cytomegalovirus (CMV) is a herpesvirus that causes the cells that it infects to produce a fake MHC 1 molecule. What would you predict about the pathway for infected cell killing by the immune response?
2. Infliximab is an inhibitor of TNF-α which is used in the therapy of rheumatoid arthritis, Crohn disease and other chronic inflammatory conditions. Can you predict what category of infectious agents would be a risk in patients treated with this monoclonal antibody, and explain why?

Before you leave, can you....

1. Explain the molecular signaling necessary to stimulate the APC1-TH1 pathway and name the infectious or pathological situations in which it would be important.
2. Name the 4 effector mechanisms within CMI and give examples of when each would be important.
3. List the identifying markers for each of the effector cells and describe the mechanisms by which they kill.

Immunology
Chapter seven

Antibodies and Humoral Immunity

Antibodies and Humoral Immunity

Introduction:

Macromolecules such as antibodies, complement proteins and antimicrobial peptides which circulate in the blood and lymph constitute the **humoral immune response.** In any case where an antigen has enough size and complexity to be recognized as being foreign (an **immunogen**), the immune response can respond by creating an antibody which binds to it. Thus, the humoral immune response is the response to the introduction of any immunogen, regardless of whether it originated as an intracellular or extracellular invader.

As the result of successful CMI, in our previous chapter, the products of apoptosis will be processed by APC to generate antibodies. The debris from a successful innate inflammatory response will generate antibodies as well. Antibodies, as the secreted product of the B lymphocyte lineage, can be thought of as "tags" to identify foreign invaders in any subsequent invasion, but their efficacy in destruction of the material depends on their activation of the processes of phagocytosis or complement system activation. Antibodies can only function outside of cells, so their role in the management of intracellular microbes is only during the stages when the microbe moves from host cell to host cell.

Direct B Cell Activation

When we left B lymphocytes last, they were emerging from the bone marrow as mature, but naïve cells, and they recirculated to the secondary lymphoid organs to create germinal centers. When a foreign epitope complementary to the idiotype of the BCR arrives in the lymph node through afferent lymphatics draining the site of inflammation, or via the blood in the case of the spleen, the antigen-stimulated centroblasts undergo a burst of proliferation (**blastogenesis**). Mutational changes can occur in the idiotype-encoding regions, and this creates variations in populations with slightly different shapes to their BCR (**somatic hypermutation**). This can be seen in the **dark zone of the germinal center** where proliferation is at its peak. The cells with receptors which have the best strength of binding (**affinity**) will then be selected by natural selection because their receptors will be occupied more than those with weak affinity. In the competition for binding to the antigen, the cells with the best fit will receive continued stimulation to multiply (**affinity maturation**). Some of these cells will differentiate into plasma cells which will migrate to the medullary cords where they will secrete antibody of IgM or IgD isotype, at the rate of thousands of molecules per second, for a period of about **two weeks**, and then they will die.

If there are no TH cells encountered by a proliferating B lymphocyte during this process, **only IgM and IgD can be produced,** and there is **no memory** of the response, thus the advances in receptor shape which occur during somatic hypermutation are lost with the short lifespan of the mature B lymphocyte. This type of **T cell independent B cell activation** occurs when the antigen contains **no peptides**. Fortunately, this type of response is not the norm, since proteins are a necessary building block of living cells. It is only when individual constituents of living cells are the antigen that the T cell independent response is observed (individual lipids, polysaccharides, nucleic acids).

Remember that mature, naïve B cells leaving the bone marrow are wearing membrane receptors in equal numbers of molecules of IgM and IgD monomers. The secreted form of **IgM is a pentamer**, held together by a **joining** or **J chain.**

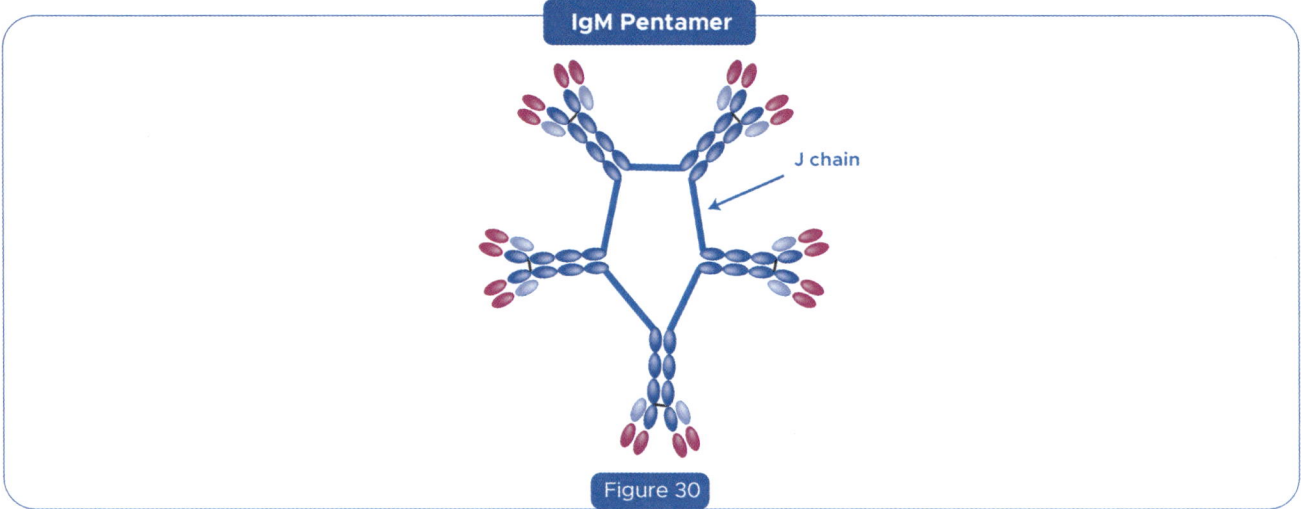

Figure 30

The function of IgD is not known and it has a very short half-life free in the serum, but IgM is uniquely suited to enhance the **innate inflammatory response.** Indeed, since there is no IgM memory, it can be argued to be a component of innate immunity.

- IgM (the macroglobulin) is too large to escape from the vasculature, so its major effects occur **intravascularly.**
- It has more identical idiotypes **(a valence of 10)** than any other molecule of immunoglobulin. It therefore has the **highest avidity** of any Ig; a measure of the number of combining sites that can be engaged at one time. Think of it acting in an early response as a sort of immunological sponge, soaking up available antigen and holding it so that other cells can respond.
- It is the strongest **activator of complement** of any immunoglobulin, and the complement cascade attracts neutrophils and enhances inflammation. The binding site for the C1q component of complement is immediately behind the hinge region of each monomer, so the pentamer effectively has 5 times the complement activating activity of any monomer.
- Since it has no free tail (Fc) outside of its sterically hindered center, it **cannot act as an opsonin,** since opsonization requires the availability of an Fc tail to fit into the Fc receptor (CD16).

The acquisition of T cell help

As the proliferating B cells are pushed outwards from the center of the clone of dividing cells, they must receive signals from follicular dendritic cells and TH cells in the paracortex to survive. As with the interaction between TH0 and APCs, there is a 3-signal system for the activation of B cells and the differentiation of TH0 to TH2 cells. In the humoral immune response, it is most common for the B lymphocyte to serve as the APC, after processing antigen bound to its BCR in acidic vesicles, and presentation in the context of MHC class II molecules.

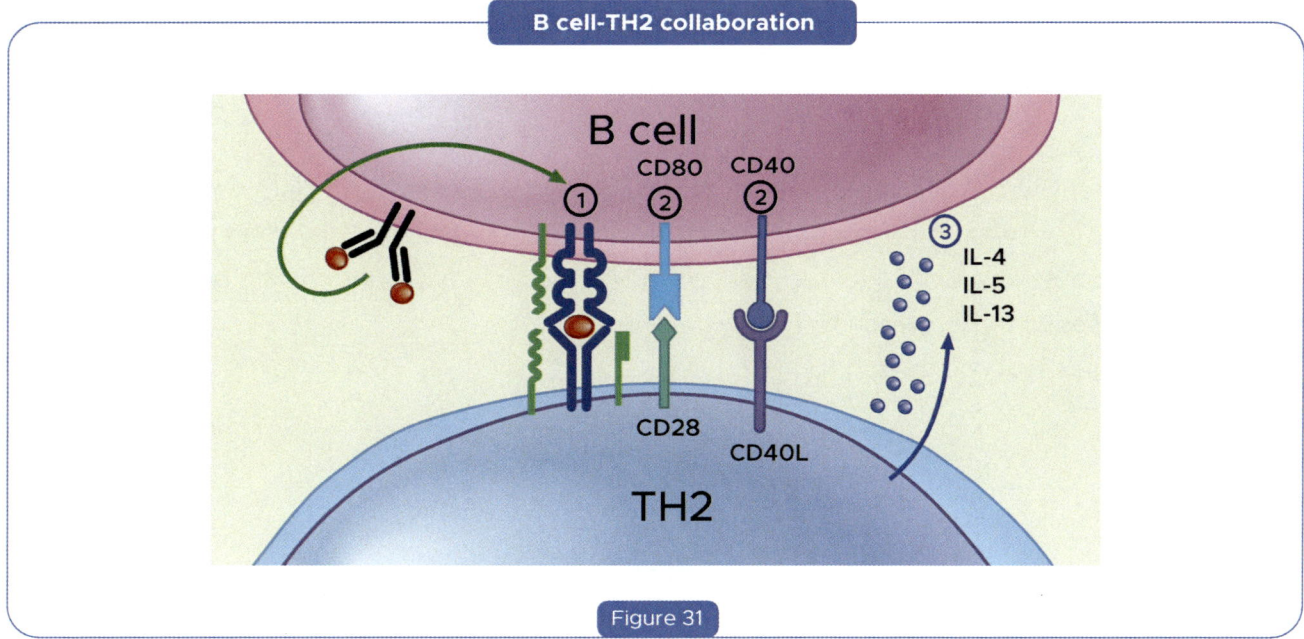

Figure 31

Signal 1:
B cell binds epitope of antigen to its BCR, endocytoses, processes in acidic vesicle, and **presents peptide component in the groove of MHC class II molecule**. This binds to the TCR of an appropriate TH cell and serves as the only antigen-specific signal between the two cells.

Signal 2:
Binding of costimulatory molecules. CD28 binds to CD80 and CD40L binds to CD40. The engagement of CD40 and CD40L have been shown to be necessary for cytokine secretion and isotype switching.

Signal 3:
Cytokines produced by TH2 cell bind to cytokine receptors on B cell and induce cloning, isotype switching, differentiation to plasma cells and B cell memory.

Isotype Switching

When CD40L and CD40 are bound on the surface of TH2 cell and B cell respectively, the expression of activation-induced cytosine deaminase is induced. This enzyme is essential to allow the modification of the germ-line B cell DNA so that isotype switching can occur. Depending on the cytokine signal from the TH2 cell, which is in turn dependent on the signaling of tissue location and category of antigen (chemical nature, bacterial, viral, parasitic or fungal origin), the switch region for a new set of constant domains is activated, and the idiotype coding is spliced to a new isotype. Because the function of the antibody molecule resides in the characteristics of the constant domains, the specificity of the resulting molecule is left the same (or improved by affinity maturation) but the functional capacity of the molecule is changed.

Since the excised DNA is destroyed and run through nucleotide salvage pathways, the cell cannot return to synthesizing a constant domain that was upstream. The cytokines involved in switching are complex, pleiotropic and situational, so the only two that can be easily tested are:
- **IL-5 causes isotype switch to IgA** in the mucosa
- **IL-4 causes isotype switch to IgE**

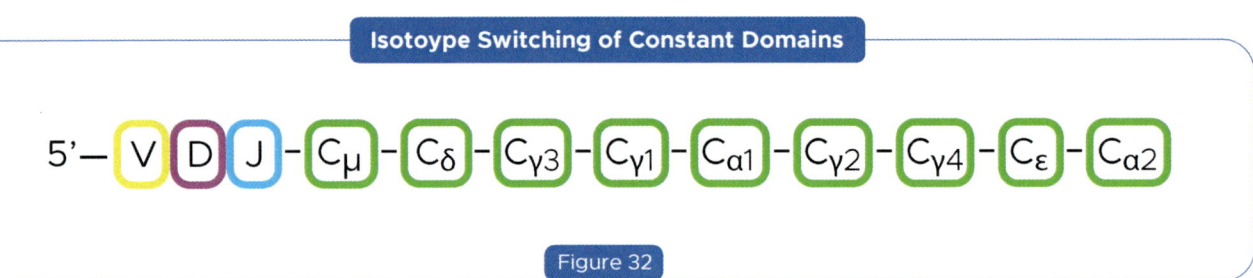

Figure 32

IgG

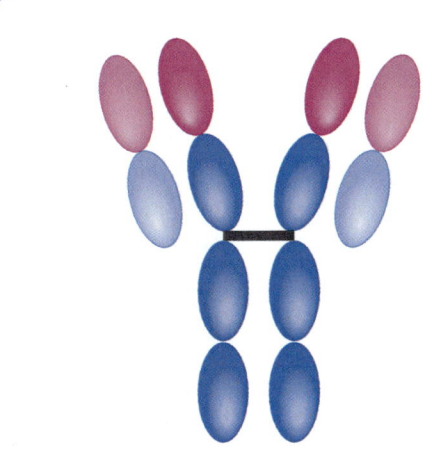

- **Gamma heavy chains**
- **4 subisotypes** with slightly different functions
- **Most common isotype** made after IgM
- Largest number of effector functions
- **Complement activation**
- **Opsonization**
- **ADCC**
- **Active transport across the placenta**
- Distributes inside and outside of vasculature

Figure 33

IgA

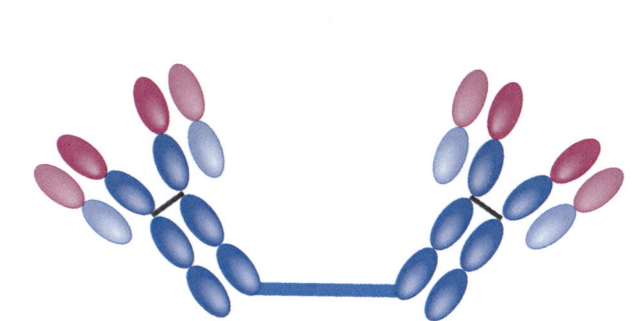

- **Alpha heavy chains**
- **Two subisotypes**
- **Dimeric** in secretions
- Major immunological component of **breast milk and colostrum**
- Prevents binding of microbes to mucosal surfaces
- Does not activate complement or opsonize

Figure 34

The majority of IgA is produced in the submucosa and is transported into the lumen of the organ by binding to a poly-IgA receptor on the internal surface. After transport, the receptor is retained as **secretory component**, protecting the molecule against the possibility of proteolytic cleavage in the intestine, urogenital and respiratory systems.

IgE

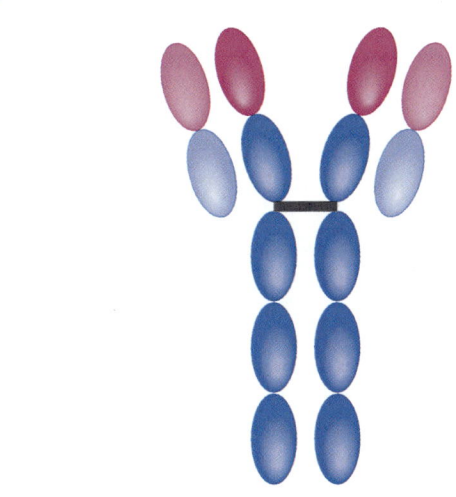

- Epsilon heavy chains
- There is only one switch region associated with IgE synthesis and it is located at the end of the germ-line DNA
- It is secreted as a monomer
- It has affinity for **Fcε receptors on mast cells and basophils**
- It is the protective antibody against **helminth parasites**
- When misdirected it causes **type 1 hypersensitivities**

Figure 35

Medical Immunology Essentials

The Complement Cascades

Complement proteins are produced in the liver and can be considered acute phase reactants. They are a set of zymogenic enzymes which cleave one another in a sequential pattern and liberate split products which have roles in increasing acute inflammation.

The two more evolutionarily primitive cascades are the lectin cascade and the alternative cascade. The **lectin cascade** is begun by recognition of **mannose binding lectin** on the surface of various microbial pathogens, and the **alternative cascade** is believed to recognize surface charge differences between microbial cells and host cells. The only cascade which requires antibodies to activate it is the **classical cascade** and it can be begun by a single pentamer of IgM or two monomers of IgG.

The sequence of the cascade follows the order **1,4,2,3,5-9**, and the cascades start at different points:
- The classical cascade begins with **C1**
- The lectin cascade begins with **C4**
- The alternative cascade begins with **C3**

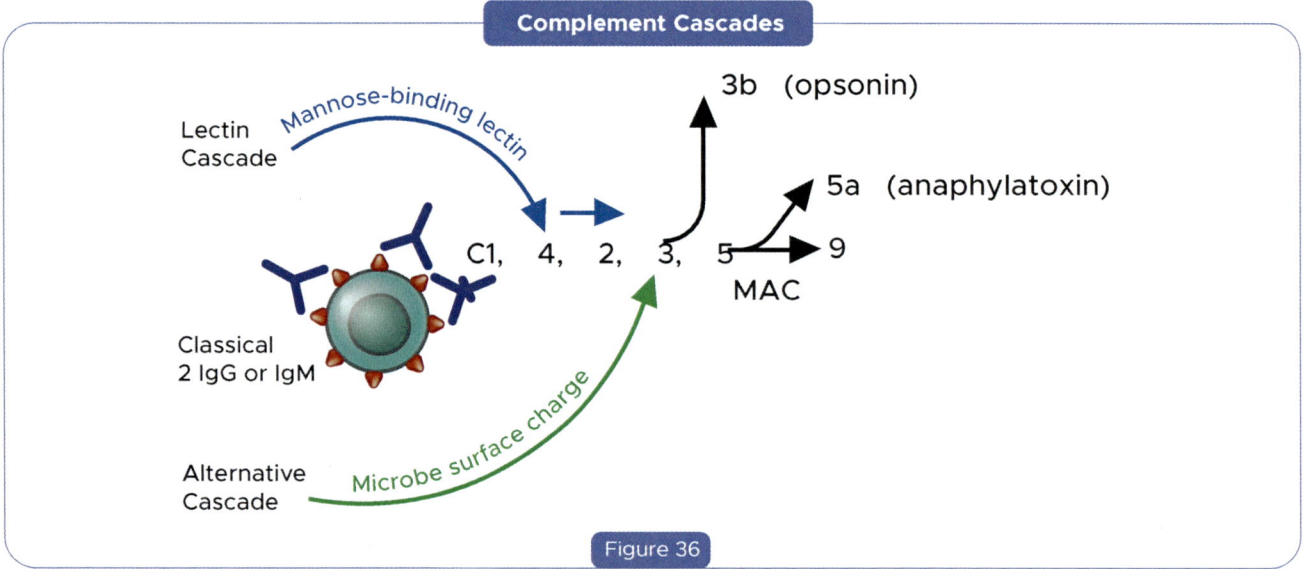

Figure 36

Biological functions of Complement Split Products
- C3a, C4a, C5a – the **anaphylatoxins**. Attract cells into the area.
- C3b – the **opsonin**, enhances phagocytosis.
- C5-9 – the **membrane attack complex**, causes lysis of cell membranes.

Regulation of Complement

"Brakes" on the complement cascade exist at the C1, C3 and C5 levels.
- C1 inhibitor
- C3 inhibitor (**DAF**, decay-accelerating factor, **CD55**)
- C5 inhibitor (**MIRL**, membrane inhibitor of reactive lysis, **CD59**)

Summary of the Humoral Immune Response

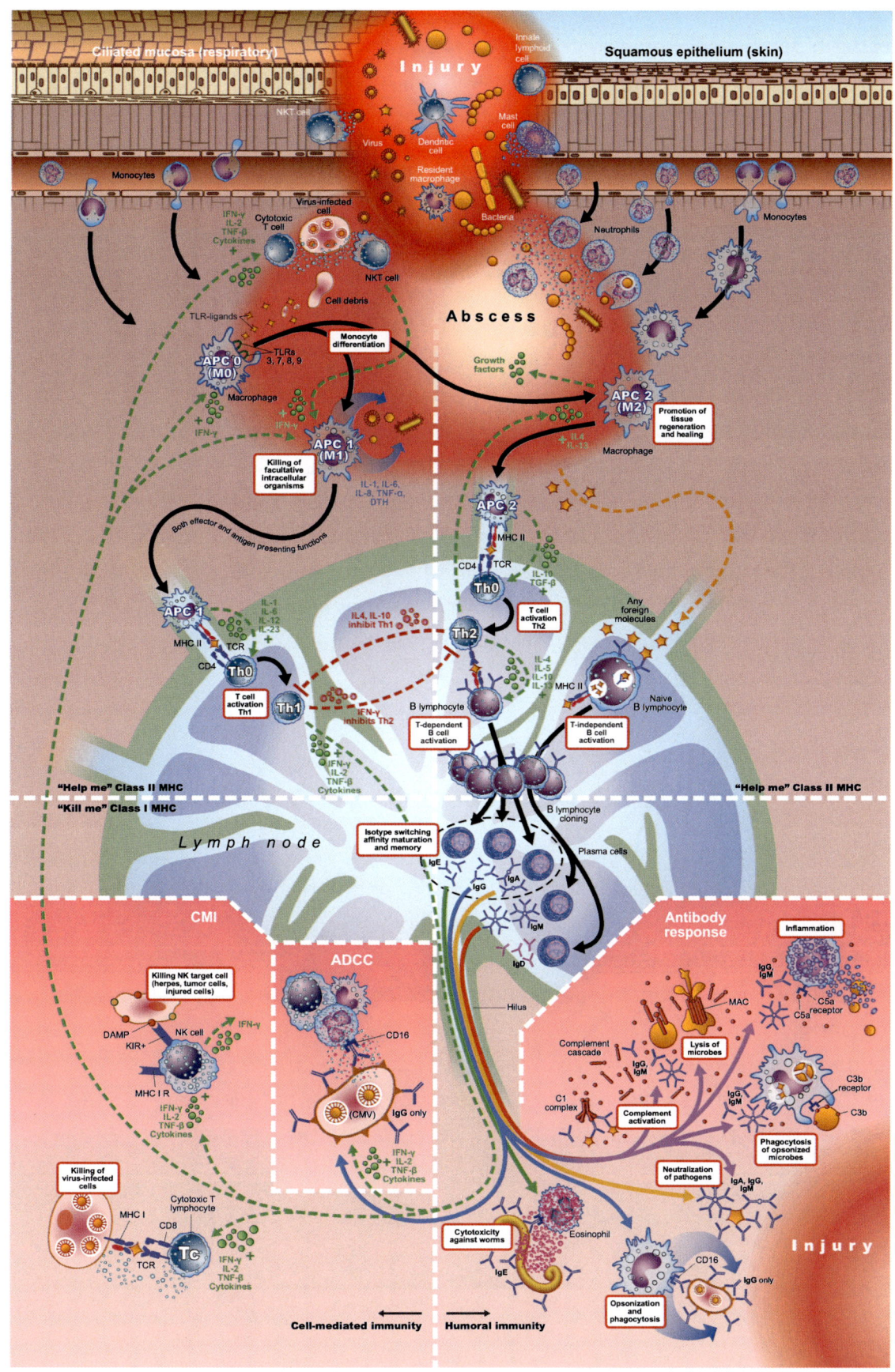

#MMC (Make Me Care!)

1. It has been established that the presence of protein in a vaccine improves its efficacy and the duration of its protective response. Can you explain this based on what you know of the development of the humoral immune response?
2. The genetic absence of CD40L on the surface of TH2 cells is a condition which generally proves lethal by the age of 25. How would you expect a patient with such a deficiency to present?
3. Opsonization of antigen-antibody immune complexes with C3b is a critical step in their removal from the blood by the spleen. Can you explain:
   - Why patients with genetic deficiencies of C3b develop immune complex disease?
   - Why patients with immune complex disease develop small-to-medium sized blood vessel vasculitis and have depressed complement levels in the blood?
4. Glycosylphosphatidylinositol (GPI) is a common membrane anchor on the surface of erythrocytes for DAF (CD55) and MIRL (CD59). Can you anticipate the result of a genetic absence of this molecule?
5. *Mycobacterium leprae* is an obligate intracellular organism (cannot be grown outside of eukaryotic cells) that lives inside human cells of the mononuclear phagocytic system. There are two polar forms of the disease, with the more serious, lepromatous form resulting when the alternative APC/TH2 axis of the immune response is activated. Can you explain why this is so?

Before you leave, can you....

1. Explain the difference between T cell-dependent and -independent humoral responses.
2. Explain the signaling that causes B cell activation, isotype switching and TH2 differentiation.
3. Explain somatic hypermutation and affinity maturation.
4. Describe the structure, function, and anatomical location of the 5 major isotypes of immunoglobulin.
5. Describe the 3 pathways by which complement can be activated.
6. Name the biological functions of the split products of the complement cascade.
7. Name the points at which the complement cascade can be arrested.

Case History

XHIGM

A 2-year-old male is referred for immunological workup because of failure to thrive and recurrent infections including otitis media, diarrhea, sinusitis and pneumonia. The recurrent infections began at about 6 months of age, and have included *Staphylococcus aureus*, *Pneumocystis jirovecii* and *Cryptosporidium parvum*. He is up to date on all recommended vaccinations.

On presentation, the child ranks in the 65th percentile for height and weight. His temperature is 38.4 C (101.1 F), respirations 30/min, heart rate 80 beats/min. There is mild anterior cervical and auricular lymphadenopathy. Several ulcerations are found on the oral mucosa, but the remaining physical findings are within normal limits.

Chief Complaint(s):
- Recurrent infections and failure to thrive

Differential Diagnoses:
- Agammaglobulinemia
- Bruton agammaglobulinemia
- Common variable immunodeficiency
- Severe combined immunodeficiency
- Transient hypogammaglobulinemia of infancy

Clinical Approach:
The finding of growth delay and recurrent/chronic infections with opportunists in this age group is suggestive of the possibility of primary immunodeficiency. The presence of recurrent infections of mucosal surfaces with normal flora and opportunistic pathogens suggests that there may be a problem with mucosal immunity such as IgA synthesis.

Immunological Workup:
- CBC and differential: neutropenia
- Immunoglobulin levels normal for IgM, low for IgG, IgA and IgE
- Elevated C-reactive protein
- Serology for CMV, HIV and *Toxoplasma gondii* negative
- Specific IgG antibodies against tetanus and hepatitis B surface antigen negative
- Isohemagglutinins against allo-ABO blood groups normal
- Normal numbers of CD3, CD4, CD8, CD19 and CD56 lymphocytes by flow cytometry, CD40L missing from TH cells
- Stool examination for *Cryptosporidium* oocysts positive
- Molecular genetic testing

Diagnosis: X-linked Hyper IgM Syndrome (XHIGM)

Hyper IgM syndrome is a group of rare primary immunodeficiencies which impede the ability of the B lymphocytes to undergo isotype switching. Affected individuals may have normal to high levels of IgM, but are unable to make IgG, IgA or IgE, and are thus susceptible to a broad range of pyogenic and opportunistic infections. The most common form (70%) of hyper IgM syndrome is inherited in an X-linked recessive fashion because the CD40LG gene is located on the long arm of the X chromosome (Xq26). Production of an abnormal variant of CD40L or an inability to produce enough of the molecule, causes the inability to start the cytokine activation required for isotype switching. X-linked hyper IgM syndrome is believed to occur in about 2 in a million births of male children.

Other forms of hyper IgM syndrome are inherited in an autosomal recessive fashion and reflect problems with activation-induced cytidine deaminase (AID) deficiency, uracil nucleoside glycosylase (UNG) deficiency, or CD40 deficiency. AID and UNG are enzymes important in somatic hypermutation, so in some cases of hyper IgM syndrome, this process is also affected.

Some patients with XHIGM have neutropenia with maturation arrest of the myeloid lineage at the promyelocyte-myelocyte stage. They may also display autoimmune disorders, neurologic complications from central nervous system infections, liver disease, and gastrointestinal tumors and increased risk of lymphoma.

Management:

Patients with all forms of HIGM are treated with immunoglobulin replacement therapy to prevent infection and reduce the likelihood of development of lymphoid hyperplasia. Anti-microbial therapy should be prompt and pathogen-specific (not empirical). Prophylactic therapy to prevent infection with *Pneumocystis* (trimethoprim-sulfamethoxazole) and *Cryptosporidium* (nitazoxanide and azithromycin) should be used. Treatment with granulocyte colony stimulating factor (G-CSF) may be of benefit in patients with neutropenia.

Stable patients should be monitored every 2-3 months. Water that is boiled or treated by reverse osmosis to avoid *Cryptosporidium* infection is advised. Daycare environments, farm animals, puppies and kittens should be avoided. Liver function tests should be performed yearly because subclinical hepatitis is not uncommon, and antigen testing for viral hepatitis is necessary since patients are unable to produce antibodies.

Prognosis:

The overall prognosis for patients with XHIGM is guarded, with 20% survival to 25 years postdiagnosis. The severity of disease varies widely, but without treatment, the condition can result in death during childhood or adolescence. Stem cell transplantation has been used to successfully cure XHIGM, and gene therapy is being studied as another approach. Recombinant CD40L has been shown to restore missing TH1 cytokines but has shown no effect on differentiation of B cells and isotype switching.

Immunology
Chapter eight

The Development of Immune Memory

The Development of Immune Memory

Introduction:
If you notice, we have now traveled through all the steps of both the innate and adaptive immune responses, so in our last section of immune theory, we need to discuss how the adaptive immune response "remembers" what it has done and improves on it with each exposure. The steps we have already discussed have required about 10 days to 2 weeks to be complete.

After an immune response has been successful at removing an invader or healing an injury, it is important to return the system toward a baseline homeostatic level. This avoids wasting biological energy fighting an invader that has been vanquished and allows the system to "reset" to pay attention to new challenges.

Humoral Immune Memory
On the humoral side of the immune response, the very short lifespan of the plasma cell effector (2 weeks) causes antibody production to return toward normal when the cells die. Unless the antigen persists in the system, there is no additional stimulation of the dividing B lymphocyte pool to cause them to make more plasma cells. Since the system is totally antigen driven, if there is no antigen to occupy the idiotype of the BCR, the cell receives no stimulation to clone, and becomes quiescent. The B lymphocytes which remain in lymphoid follicles after the primary immune response are **memory cells** with about a **10-year life span.** Because they have undergone a round of activation, somatic hypermutation and isotype switching, they have improved affinity for the antigen, and their BCR is made of molecules with a new isotype.

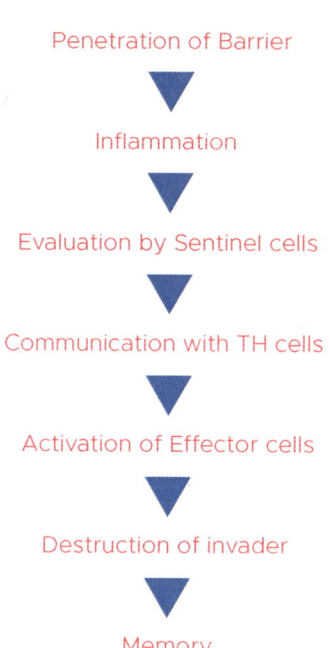

Cell-Mediated Immune Memory
T lymphocytes exert most of their activity through the production of cytokines, and once activated in a primary immune response are said to be memory cells with the ability to "last a lifetime". That may have been true when the lifetime of the average homo sapiens was about 40 years, but now, with increased life expectancy, memory T cells of both TH and CTL categories need to be refreshed with new stimulation as we age. Because continued cytokine production after the removal of an infectious process would be energy intensive and potentially harmful, some proportion of T cells that have become activated are induced to undergo a process of **activation-induced cell death (AICD).**

This is accomplished through the trimerization of **Fas and FasL molecules** which are coexpressed on the surface of activated T cells after they have been stimulated with IL-2. This triggers the activation of the extrinsic cascade of apoptosis and returns the number of memory T cells toward, but always above, the original baseline. Memory TH cells and CTLs are quiescent, generally non-dividing, and will recirculate through the body to areas of inflammation.

Medical Immunology Essentials

Tissue Signals in Dissemination

Although the primary immune response occurred either at the location of the injury/infection or at the site of a draining secondary lymphoid organ, during the memory induction phase of the response, the cells tend to generalize the protection throughout the body. Tissue specific expression of adhesion molecules and chemokines attract memory cells to the anatomical areas similar to the site of the primary response. This serves to focus the cellular memory in the locations where the battle occurred before, so that the "troops" are waiting there for a further invasion.

Anamnestic (Memory) Responses

As a generality, each administration of an antigen increases the speed, precision and amplitude of an adaptive immune response of any kind. Remember that each response depends on specific clones of lymphocytes whose receptors are complementary to the shape of a foreign antigen, so each response is independent of all others. This is because each administration of the immunogen causes cloning of specific responding cells, and therefore the pool of responding cells rises with each exposure. This is a way of building your immunological "muscles" and although it may seem counterintuitive in the field of medicine, the best way to develop a strong immune response is to allow it to "experience" its environment completely!

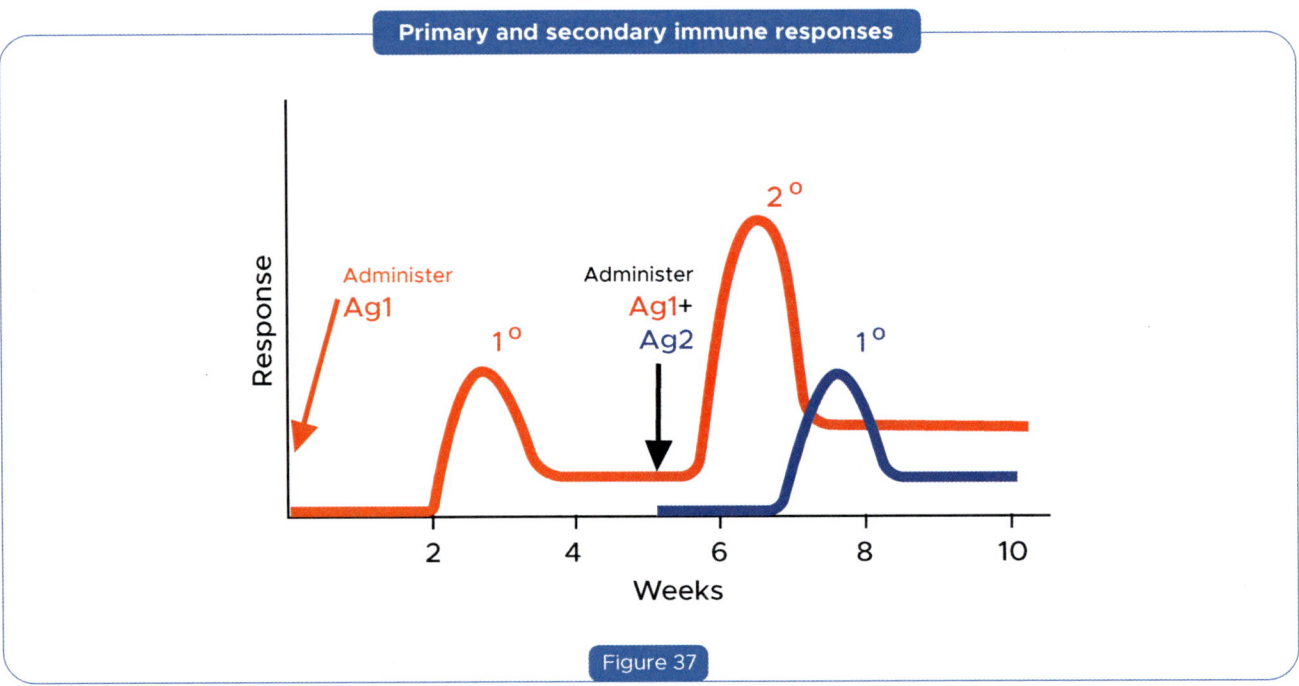

Figure 37

#MMC (Make Me Care!)

1. An extremely rare genetic mutation in the FAS gene has been shown to cause Canale-Smith Syndrome. Can you anticipate the clinical picture of a patient with such a deficiency?
2. Given what you know about the lifespans of memory B and T lymphocytes, can you predict the intervals at which booster vaccinations will need to be administered for protective immunity if the necessary response is:
    a. Humoral
    b. Cell-mediated
3. Can you explain why the route of vaccine administration (oral, intramuscular, etc.) would have a role in its efficacy?
4. Can you explain to a recalcitrant anti-vaxxer parent why the administration of 3 immunogens in one vaccine (like the MMR) does not overwhelm the child's immune response?

Before you leave, can you....

1. Explain what induces activated lymphocytes to become memory cells.
2. Predict the lifespan of memory B, TH and CTLs.
3. Explain the mechanism and purpose of AICD.
4. Explain the purpose of tissue specialization of the immune response.
5. Explain how primary, secondary and subsequent immune responses differ from one another.

Case History

ALPS

A 10-year-old male is referred for immunologic workup because his parents are concerned about enlarging, disfiguring lumps on his neck. His history is remarkable for a surgical splenectomy performed three years ago, following a minor playground accident that resulted in splenic rupture. Since that time, the child has been hospitalized for episodes of pneumococcal sepsis, vasculitis and bleeding disorders. The parents deny family history of relatives with immunodeficiency, thrombocytopenia or lymphoid malignancy. On examination, the child is afebrile and within low/normal standards for height and weight. The cervical, axillary, femoral and inguinal lymph nodes are dramatically enlarged. There is conjunctival and mucosal pallor, and bruising is evident on the trunk and extremities.

Chief Complaint(s):
- Chronic lymphadenopathy

Differential Diagnoses:
- Hyper IgM (HIGM) syndrome
- Interleukin (IL)–2 receptor alpha-chain deficiency
- Lymphoma (Hodgkin and non-Hodgkin)
- Mycobacterial disease
- X-linked lymphoproliferative syndrome (XLP)

Clinical Approach:
The age of the patient and persistent lymphadenopathy, apparent cytopenias and infections are suggestive of a genetic defect in the immune system. Lymph node biopsy should be ordered to rule out infectious (EBV) and neoplastic (lymphoma) causes of lymphadenopathy.

Immunological Workup:
- CBC and differential - Neutropenia, reticulocytosis, anemia, thrombocytopenia and lymphocytosis.
- Hypergammaglobulinemia with IgG and IgA, low levels of IgM.
- Flow cytometry - elevation of double-negative T lymphocytes.
- Monospot and EBV VCA IgM negative.
- Positive direct Coombs test and antiplatelet antibodies.
- Elevated plasma level of soluble Fas ligand (FasL).
- Molecular genetic testing for TNFRSF6 (FAS receptor gene), TNFSF6 (FasL gene) or CASP-10 (caspase 10 gene) – TNFRSF6 negative.

Diagnosis: Autoimmune Lymphoproliferative Syndrome (Canale-Smith Syndrome)

Autoimmune lymphoproliferative syndrome (ALPS) is a rare genetic disorder of programmed cell death and lymphocyte homeostasis. In 75% of cases, it results from mutations in the FAS gene, which is responsible for the ability of the adaptive immune response to return towards a homeostatic baseline after stimulation. It results in chronic (more than 6 months duration) uncontrolled, but non-malignant proliferation of lymphocytes and can be associated with the development of autoimmunity and lymphomas. The discovery of an autosomal dominant mutation in the FAS gene in 1995 was followed by the discovery of other associated genetic defects in the apoptotic pathway, which cause ALPS-like syndromes. Patients may present with familial history of lymphoproliferative disorder, but as in many autosomal dominant defects, ALPS may arise from new mutation.

Management:

Patients with ALPS are treated with immunoglobulins and immunosuppressive drugs such as mycophenolate mofetil. Preservation of the spleen is paramount whenever possible since splenomegaly in the treatment of severe cytopenias increases risk of sepsis, is often ineffective and rarely leads to permanent remission. Stem cell transplantation remains the only curative treatment but is considered only in severe cases without response to immunosuppressive medications.

Prognosis:

With proper surveillance and education, the prognosis for patients with ALPS is good. Most are expected to live a normal lifespan, although significant interventions such as hospitalization, immunosuppression, splenectomy and antibiotic therapy may be required. Childhood onset cytopenias are often chronic and refractory. There is wide variability in the mortality and morbidity of ALPS, depending on the severity of autoimmune disease, as well as development of sepsis, hypersplenism and lymphoma. The lymphoproliferative aspects of the disease tend to wax and wane randomly before resolution after the age of 20.

Immunology
Chapter nine

Active and Passive Immunotherapy

Active and Passive Immunotherapy

Introduction:
One of the most important interfaces between immunological theory and medical practice has been the development of vaccination and immunotherapy. Other than improvements in sanitation, vaccination can be asserted to be the single greatest advancement in human health and wellbeing in the 19th and 20th centuries.

Immunization can be either active or passive, natural or artificial, and we use each of these in medicine today:
- **Active, natural** – recovery from disease confers memory and resistance to subsequent infection.
- **Active, artificial** – vaccination. Introduction of an altered immunogen to create memory and resistance in the absence of disease and recovery.
- **Passive, natural** – in utero and during breast feeding, the child receives immune products passively from the mother.
- **Passive, artificial** – in cases where post-exposure prophylaxis is needed, individuals are given pre-formed immune products from other individuals.

Vaccination
The Centers for Disease Control and Prevention (CDC) publish the national standards for vaccine protocols yearly (below). These standards consider:
- The **immunological capacity** of the age group to be treated.
- The **epidemiology of exposure** to a given pathogen.
- The **mechanism of pathogenesis** of a particular microbe and the best immune response to prevent it.

Remember that the development of an active immune response requires 10 days to 2 weeks to reach protective levels. Therefore, vaccination must be begun at least two weeks in advance of the potential exposure.

Childhood vaccination recommendations:

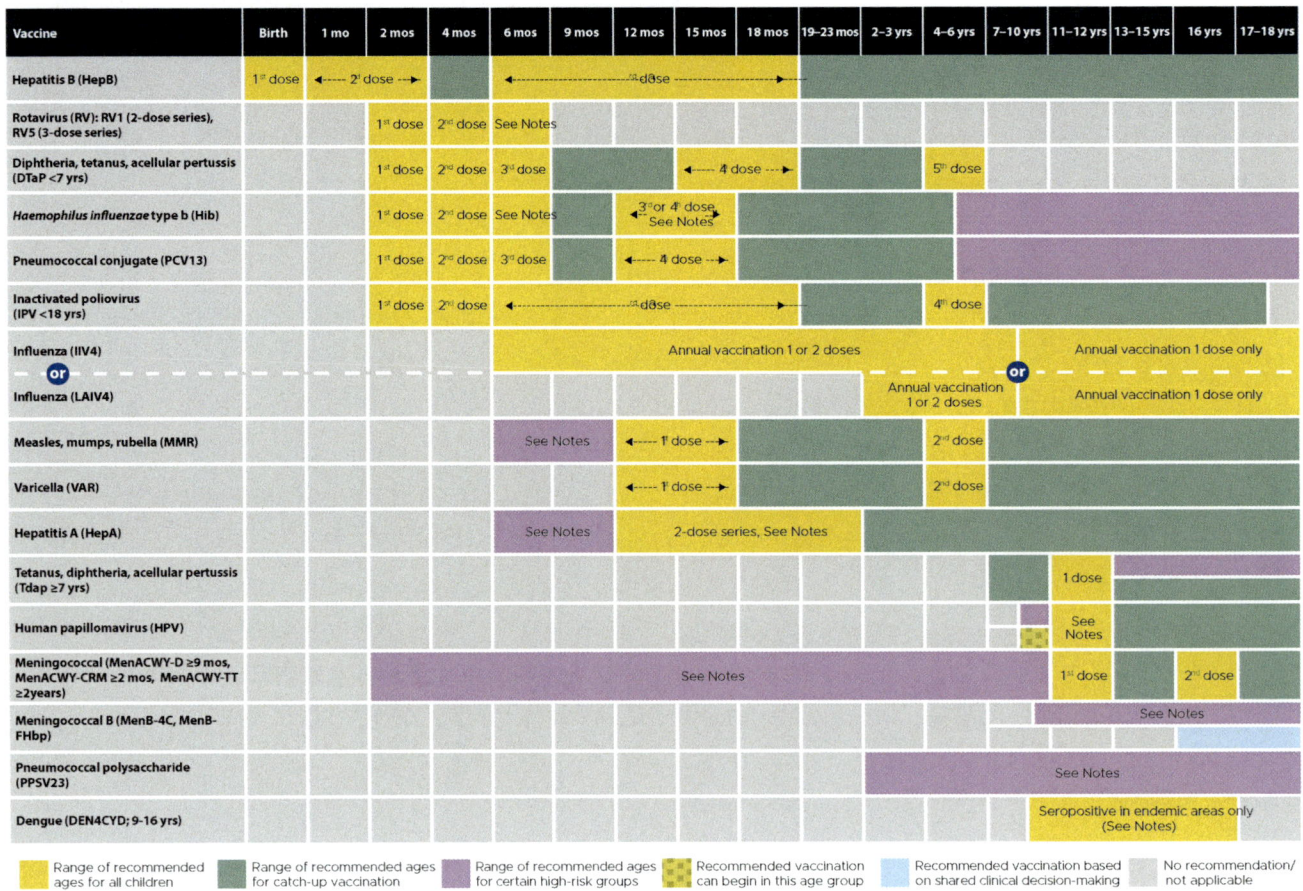

cdc.gov/vaccines/schedules 2022

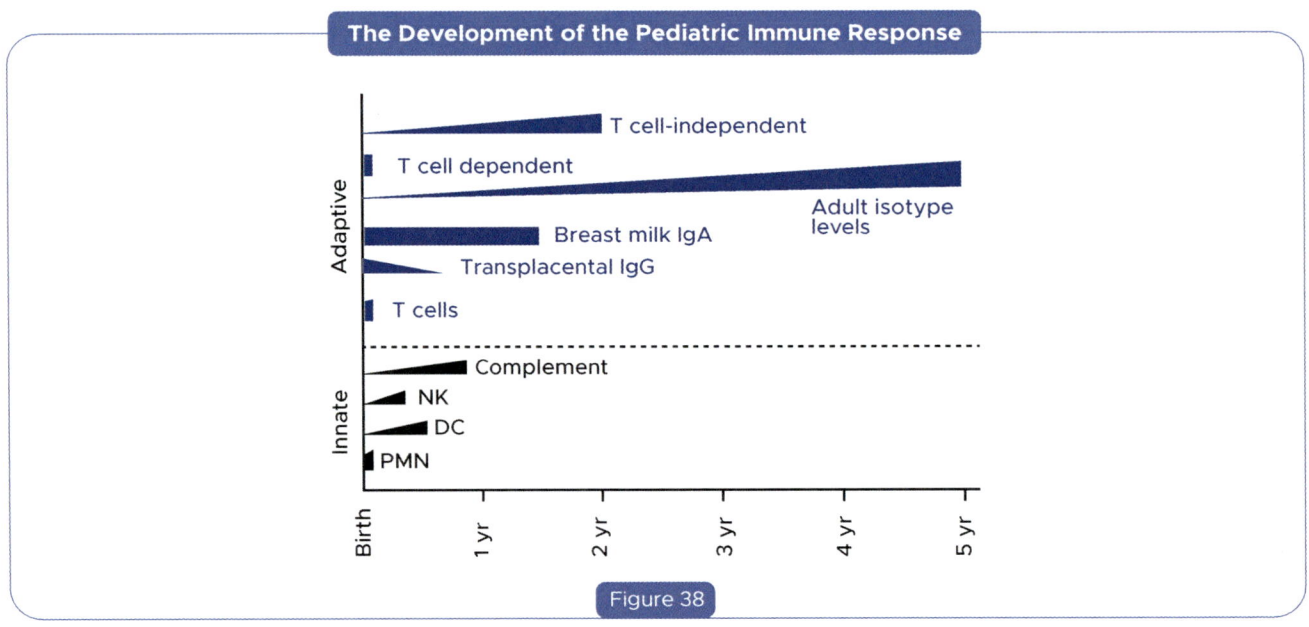

Figure 38

- In utero and in early months, the child's immune response is tilted toward tolerance.
- Innate immune responses are at adult levels by 1 year.
- T cells are fully functional, but naïve at birth.
- T cell-independent antibody responses require 2 years for development
- Adult levels of all antibody isotypes are not present until 5 years.
- Transfer of **transplacental IgG begins at 28 weeks** and peaks before birth.
- Transplacental IgG protects the child for the first 6 months after birth but is undetectable by 1 year.
- IgA in colostrum and breast milk passively protects oral mucosa, upper respiratory and gastrointestinal tracts and inner openings of eustachian tubes.

Pediatric Bacterial Vaccines

Epidemiology	Vaccine	Contents*	Response
Respiratory or traumatic	DTaP	Toxoid of *C. diphtheriae*	Antitoxin, IgG
		Toxoid of *C. tetani*	Antitoxin, IgG
		Toxoid plus filamentous hemagglutinin of *B. pertussis*	Antitoxin, IgG
Respiratory	HiB	Capsule type B (polysaccharide) of *H. influenzae* conjugated to diphtheria toxoid (protein)	Anti-capsular antibodies, IgG
Respiratory	PCV	13 capsular serotypes of *S. pneumoniae* conjugated to diphtheria toxoid	Anti-capsular antibodies, IgG
Respiratory	MCV4	4 capsular serotypes of *N. meningitidis* (YWCA) conjugated to diphtheria toxoid	Anti-capsular antibodies, IgG
Respiratory	MenB (ages 19-23)	4 outer membrane Proteins of Serogroup B	Anti-Serogroup B membrane proteins, IgG

*All pediatric vaccines must be T-cell dependent antigens (contain protein) or isotype switching will not happen. The protein acts as the **carrier** (recognized in the MHC groove by the TCR) and the capsular polysaccharide acts as the **hapten** (bound to the BCR).

Pediatric Viral Vaccines

Live, attenuated – best immunogenicity but potential for danger in immunocompromised. Measles, mumps, rubella, rotavirus, varicella zoster, Sabin Polio, intranasal influenza.

Killed – safe in all patients, elicits only humoral response. Salk polio, rabies, injectable influenza, hepatitis A. Mnemonic: **R**est **I**n **P**eace **A**lways

Recombinant DNA – safe in all patients, elicits only humoral response. Hepatitis B, human papilloma virus

Epidemiology	Vaccine	Route	Contents*	Response
Respiratory	MMR	Injection	Live, atten	CMI and HI
	Varicella			
	Influenza		killed	HI
	Influenza	Intranasal	Live, atten	CMI and HI
				mucosal
GI	Polio Salk	Injection	killed	HI
	Polio Sabin	oral	Live, atten	CMI and HI
				mucosal
	Rotavirus	oral	Live, atten	CMI and HI
				mucosal
	Hepatitis A	Injection	killed	HI
	Hepatitis B	Injection	Recombinant	HI
Sexual	HPV	Injection	Recombinant	HI

*Adjuvants are added to vaccines to increase the speed and amplitude of the immune response. They do not change the nature of the response but are believed to increase non-specific inflammation. The only adjuvants cleared for use in the US are the mineral salts alum and calcium phosphate. Adjuvants cannot be used in live, attenuated vaccines because they would inactivate the virus.

Vaccines in Special Patient Populations

VACCINE	Pregnancy	Immunocompromised status (excluding HIV infection)	HIV infection CD4+ count[1] <15% or total CD4 cell count of <200/mm³	HIV infection CD4+ count[1] ≥15% and total CD4 cell count of ≥200/mm³	Kidney failure, end-stage renal disease, or on hemodialysis	Heart disease or chronic lung disease	CSF leak or cochlear implant	Asplenia or persistent complement component deficiencies	Chronic liver disease	Diabetes
Hepatitis B										
Rotavirus		SCID[2]								
Diphtheria, tetanus, and acellular pertussis (DTaP)										
Haemophilus influenzae type b										
Pneumococcal conjugate										
Inactivated poliovirus										
Influenza (IIV4)										
Influenza (LAIV4)						Asthma, wheezing: 2–4yrs[3]				
Measles, mumps, rubella	*									
Varicella	*									
Hepatitis A										
Tetanus, diphtheria, and acellular pertussis (Tdap)										
Human papillomavirus	*									
Meningococcal ACWY										
Meningococcal B										
Pneumococcal polysaccharide										
Dengue										

Legend:
- Vaccination according to the routine schedule recommended
- Recommended for persons with an additional risk factor for which the vaccine would be indicated
- Vaccination is recommended, and additional doses may be necessary based on medical condition or vaccine. See Notes.
- Precaution—vaccine might be indicated if benefit of protection outweighs risk of adverse reaction
- Contraindicated or not recommended—vaccine should not be administered
- No recommendation/not applicable
- *Vaccinate after pregnancy

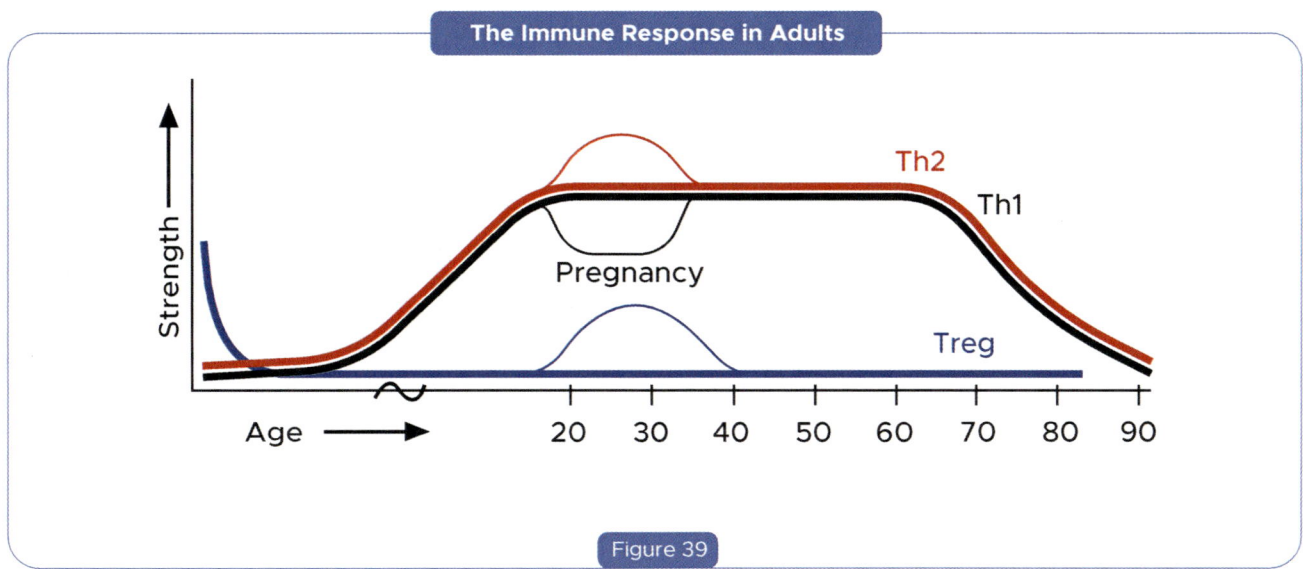

The Immune Response in Adults

Figure 39

Vaccines for the Elderly
1. Varicella zoster – live attenuated (1 dose) or recombinant DNA (2 doses) to prevent shingles, 60 years of age.
2. Pneumococcal – one dose of PCV13 followed by one dose of PPSV23 (no protein conjugation) starting at 65
3. Influenza – intramuscular, killed, yearly
4. Tetanus/diphtheria (Td) – 10 year boosters

Passive Immunotherapy
When there is insufficient time for a protective response to be made after exposure to a pathogen, or when the patient is incapable of making a response because of immunodeficiency, preformed antibodies can be administered. It is important to remember that administration of immunoglobulins from other humans is always more dangerous than vaccination, because the antibodies themselves can be regarded as foreign proteins. Minor differences in amino acid sequences within the constant domains of heavy and light chains (**allotypes**) are inherited from one's parents and may be recognized as foreign by others. When the result of such immune recognition is the production of an antibody against the therapy, immune complex disease can result (**type III hypersensitivities**), and when the antibody made is of IgE isotype, fatal anaphylaxis can result (**type 1 hypersensitivity**).

#MMC (Make Me Care!)

1. Patients with selective IgA deficiency are at high risk for development of anaphylactic responses against minute amounts of IgA contained in matched whole blood transfusions. Can you imagine why this is so?
2. Why are live viral vaccines not given before 6 months of age?
3. A child is born with positive specific serology, IgG isotype, against HIV. Is this diagnostic? Explain.
4. Can you predict when children will first present with primary immunodeficiencies involving antibody synthesis? Why?
5. Premature infants delivered before 28 weeks gestation are at high risk for respiratory and systemic pathogens. Based on what you understand about the development of the gestational and pediatric immune response, should the vaccination schedule for preemies be age-adjusted? In other words, should vaccines be delayed to correct for the gestational age of the early delivery?
6. The adenovirus vaccine developed by the military uses live virulent respiratory strains of the virus administered orally in enteric coated capsules. Can you explain the strategy?

Before you leave, can you....

1. Describe the types of immunotherapies which are used in medicine.
2. Explain how the development of the pediatric immune response affects our strategies for vaccination.
3. Know the contents of the bacterial and viral vaccines, and the strategies for their use.
4. Describe the pros and cons of the 3 categories of viral vaccines as pertains to their safety and immunogenicity.
5. Be able to list the common pediatric vaccines and explain how they work at the molecular level.
6. Explain the role of the hapten/carrier effect in the HiB, PCV and MCV4 vaccines.
7. Know the contraindications for the major vaccines.
8. Predict the vaccination protocol for special risk and elderly patients and explain why they are used.

Immunology
Chapter ten

Primary Immunodeficiency Diseases

Primary Immunodeficiency Diseases

Mutations that result in the malfunctioning of the immune response are referred to as primary **immunodeficiencies**. Depending on their severity, they normally manifest early in life, in the period after maternal passive protection has waned.

1. Defects of Phagocytic and Antigen Presenting Cells

Child with repeated infections with extracellular microbes

| Chronic Granulomatous Disease (deficiency of NADPH oxidase) Catalase positive organisms, Nitroblue tetrazolium dye reduction test negative, Neutrophil oxidative index < 73, Rx IFN-γ **G6PD deficiency** affects the same pathway upstream, but will present with anemic crisis | Leukocyte Adhesion Deficiency (absence of **CD18** from **β2 integrins**) Failure of diapedesis, no abscesses or pus, defects of wound healing, omphalitis | Chediak-Higashi Syndrome (defect in **LYST** or **CHS1** gene, affects synthesis and storage of granules in phagocytes and NK cells) Chemotactic and degranulation defects, **partial oculocutaneous albinism**, absent NK activity | Hyper IgE Syndrome (defect in **STAT3**, affects production of IL-17, 21, 22) Eosinophilia, eczema, increased IgE, cold abscesses, retained primary teeth, recurrent skin and pulmonary infections |

*Myeloperoxidase deficiency – usually clinically silent. Catalase positive organisms: **S**taph **N** **E**nterobacteriaceae **A**re **L**isted **C**atalase **P**ositive (*Staphylococcus, Nocardia,* Enterobacteriaceae, *Aspergillus, Listeria, Candida, Pseudomonas*)

2. Defects of the Humoral Immune System
a. Antidody defects

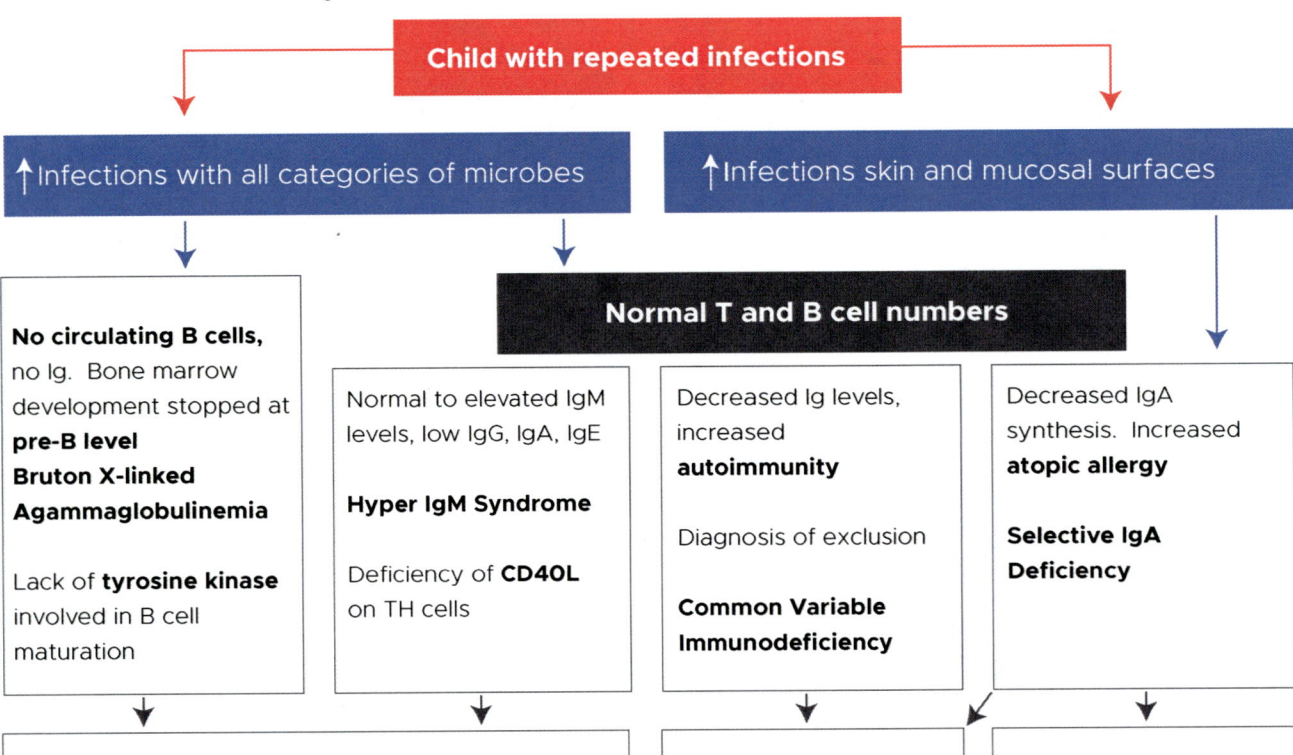

b. Complement Deficiencies

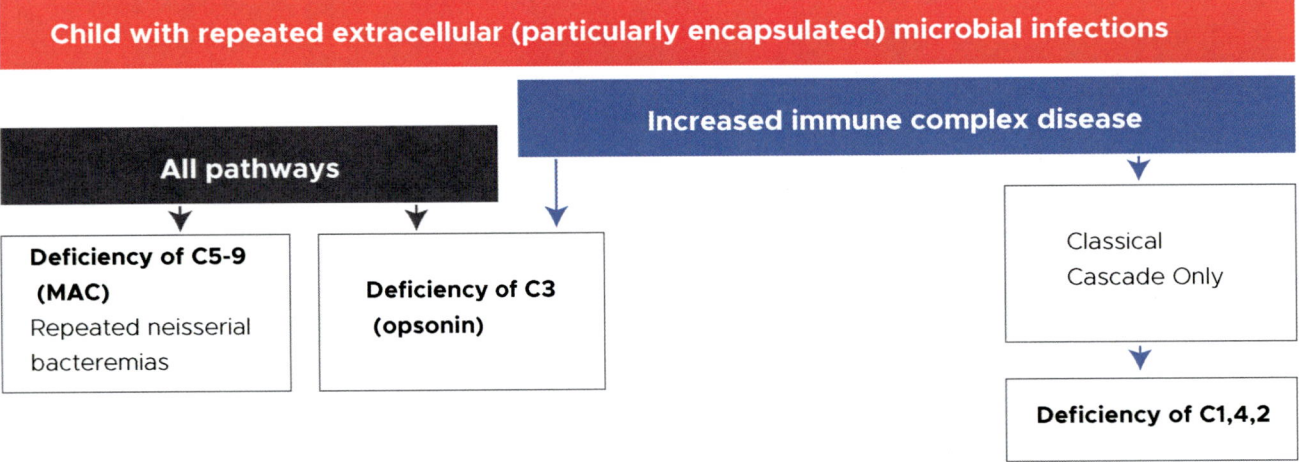

c. Deficiencies of Complement Regulation

All pathways	Classical Cascade Only
Pt with morning hemoglobinuria, thrombocytopenia, leukocytopenia. **Paroxysmal Nocturnal Hemoglobinuria** **Absence of CD55 (DAF) and CD59 (MIRL)** (inhibitors of C3 and C5 convertases) on myeloid stem cells due to absence of glycosylphosphatidylinositol (GPI) Rx: stem cell transplant, Eculizumab (blocks MAC)	Pt with overt, noninflammatory swelling of skin and mucous membranes. **Hereditary Angioedema** **Absence of C1-Inh** Rx: ecallantide, lanadelumab to decrease plasma kallikrein. Ruconest – recombinant C1Inh

3. Combined Partial Lymphocyte Defects

- Male child (X-linked) in first year.
- Microthrombocytopenia, eczema and recurrent infections.
- Profound bleeding after circumcision.
- IgM low, IgG normal, IgA and IgE elevated.

Wiskott-Aldrich Syndrome.
Genetic defect of WASp involved in cytoskeletal signaling of non-erythroid hematopoietic cells.

Rx – stem cell transplantation

- Ataxia with onset in infancy.
- Telangiectasias of the conjunctiva (3-6 years).
- Thymic aplasia, sinopulmonary infections.
- Dysgammaglobulinemia (IgA).
- Low T cell counts and mitogenesis.

Ataxia Telangiectasia.
Genetic defect of ATM protein kinase (key regulator of repair of ds breaks in DNA). Chromosome 11, autosomal recessive.

Rx - antibiotics

4. Defects of T lymphocytes

Decreased T cell numbers, all categories
↓
- Conotruncal cardiac abnormalities
- Neonatal hypocalcemia
- Cleft palate
- Thymic aplasia
- 22q11.2DS (DiGeorge Syndrome)

Failure of formation of **3rd and 4th pharyngeal pouches**

Dx - Low TREC detected by PCR

Rx – thymic transplant, calcium supplementation

Decreased CD8 T cell numbers, increased NK and γδT cells
↓
- Child < 6 years old
- Recurrent bacterial infections of URT
- Necrotizing granulomatous skin lesions
- Severe viral infections absent
- TAP deficiency

Bare Lymphocyte Syndrome Type 1

Dx – FACS for HLA class I

Rx – antibiotics and chest physiotherapy

5. Severe Combined Immunodeficiencies (SCIDs)

6 month and beyond infant onset, chronic, recurrent infections of all microbial origins including opportunists and normal flora, lymphocytopenia.

Failures of the Ruebush Rule of 2's (MHC II → IL-2 (or 4) → divide in 2)
- Bare Lymphocyte Syndrome type 2, ↓TH cells, no GVH, ↓T-dependent Abs
- IL-2R deficiency – common γ chain of IL-2, 4, 7, 9 and 15. Inability of cell proliferation

Failure of BCR/TCR rearrangement
- RAG1 or RAG2 gene nonsense mutations

Toxicity of purine product in bone marrow
- Adenosine deaminase deficiency

Medical Immunology Essentials

Summary of the Origins of Immunodeficiency

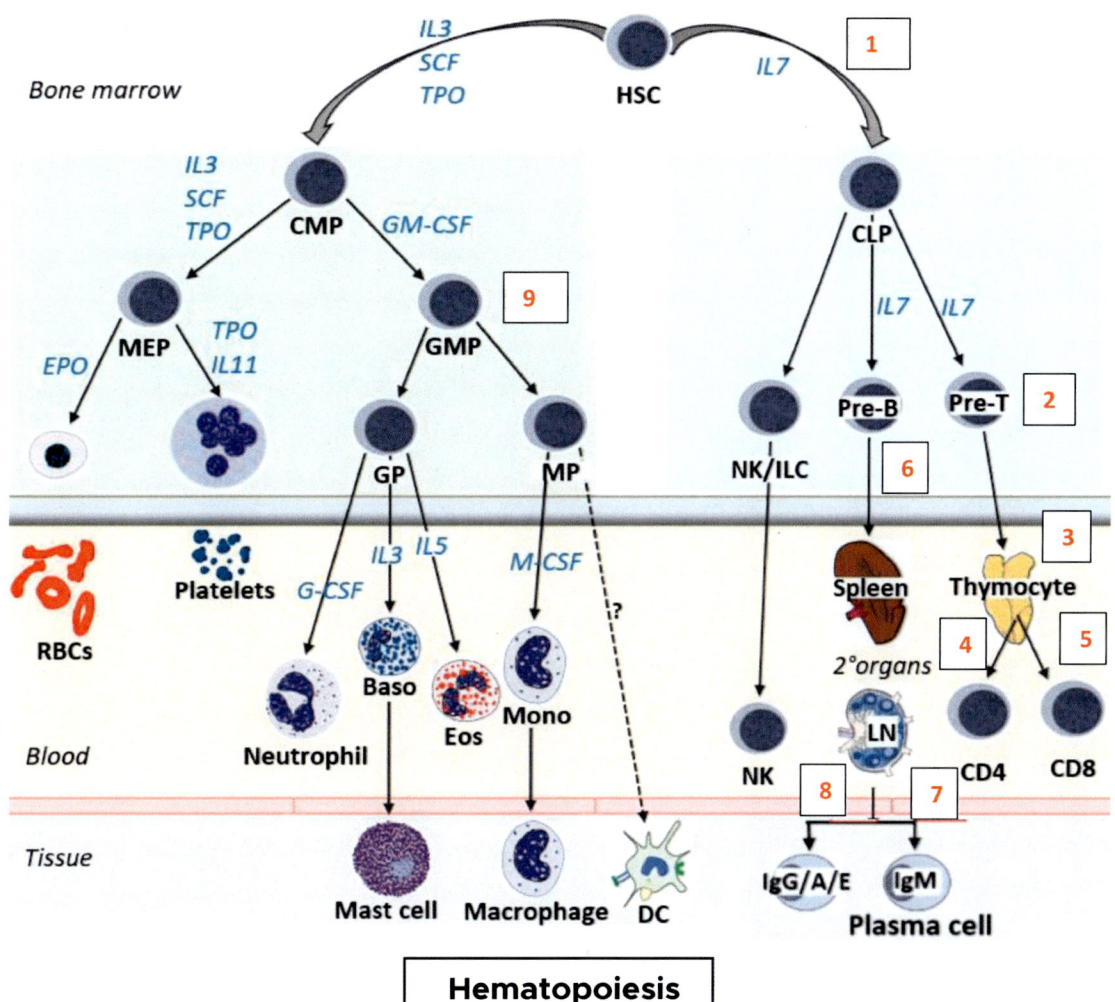

Hematopoiesis

HSC: hematopoietic stem cell, CMP: common myeloid precursor, MEP: megakaryocyte-erythroid precursor, GMP: granulocyte-monocyte precursor, GP: granulocyte precursor, MP: monocyte precursor, DC: dendritic cell, CLP: common lymphoid precursor, NK: natural killer cell / ILC: innate lymphoid cell, 2°: secondary lymphoid system

	Disease	Pathophysiology
1	SCID1, ADA2, deficiency	Key macrophage purine metabolism enzyme
2	SCID, IL-2R deficiency	IL-2 receptor dysfunction
3	22q11 DS3 (DiGeorge syndrome)	Thymus hypoplasia
4	MHC II deficiency	Deficiency of CD4 TH lymphocytes with Ig4
5	MHC I deficiency	Failure of TAP proteins in ER5
6	Bruton agammaglobulinemia	Defect in tyrosine kinase in B lymphocytes
7	Hyper IgM syndrome	Defective isotype switching (esp. CD40 ligand)
8	Seletive IgA deficiency	Unknown cause, mild effects; important in transfusion
9	Chronic granulomatous disease	Deficiency in NADPH oxidase
	Chediak-Higashi diseasea	Defective protein trafficking

1. Severe combined immunodeficiency disease, 2. Adenosine deaminase, 3. Deleteion syndrome, 4. Immunoglobulin, 5. Endoplasmic reticulum.

Before you leave, can you...

Diagnose the primary immunodeficiencies of phagocytes, B and T lymphocytes, complement and severe combined immunodeficiencies and explain their patient presentation and therapy down to the molecular basis.

Immunology
Chapter eleven

Acquired Immunodeficiency: HIV

Acquired Immunodeficiency: HIV

The virus

Human Immunodeficiency Virus (HIV) is a positive sense RNA virus in the **retrovirus** family. It carries two copies of its genome (it is diploid) and encoded reverse transcriptase, integrase and protease enzymes. It is said to be a lymphotropic virus because it infects lymphocytes by binding to the **CD4 molecule**. It uses chemokine coreceptors to target macrophages early (**CCR5 chemokine receptor**; M-tropic) and switches over to targeting T cells later (**CXCR4 chemokine receptor**; T-tropic).

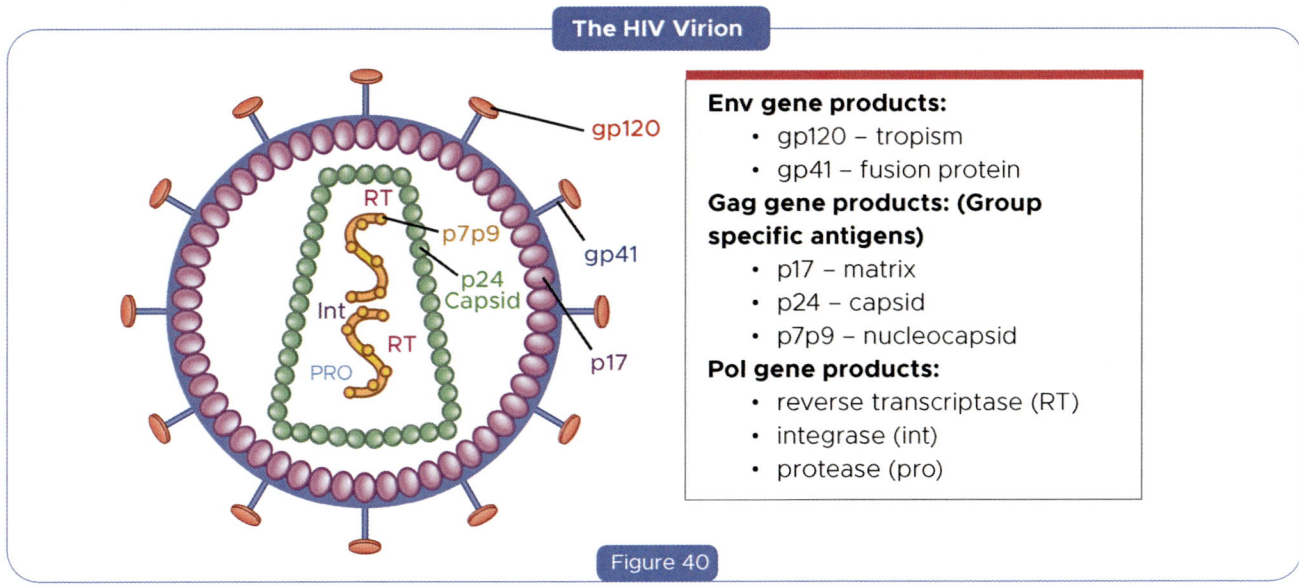

Figure 40

Epidemiology
- Sexual, blood and products, intrapartum, perinatal, breast milk
- Current US epidemiology - most new cases in **females or i.v. drug users**

The Lifecycle (there is a nice animation on YouTube @HIV Replikation)
- Binding to **CD4 and chemokine receptor** using **gp120** (establishes **tropism** of the virus, frequent mutations cause **genetic drift**)
- **Fusion protein (gp41)** causes fusion of viral envelope with cell membrane (**enfuvirtide** counteracts)
- Virus enters cell, and viral genome is reverse transcribed to create double-stranded DNA (**NRTIs and NNRTIs** work here). RT is extremely error prone, responsible for **genetic drift**. Vif gene product inactivates APOBEC3G and stops proteasomal degradation pathway.
- **Integrase** enzyme clips off long terminal repeats and transports the DNA genome (**provirus**) into the nucleus, integrating it into the chromosomes (**Raltegravir** inhibits this stage). Vpr gene product facilitates nuclear entry and arrests cell division.
- Proviral DNA is transcribed into messenger RNA using cellular transcriptases. *Tat* gene product activates this step.

- Unspliced viral mRNA molecules are transported to the cytoplasm. Controlled by viral *rev* gene product.
- Spliced viral mRNAs are translated on cellular ribosomes and cleaved by viral protease enzyme. Unspliced mRNAs are destined to be genomic copies during assembly.
- Virions are assembled (under control of viral vpu gene product) and released by budding off the cellular membrane.

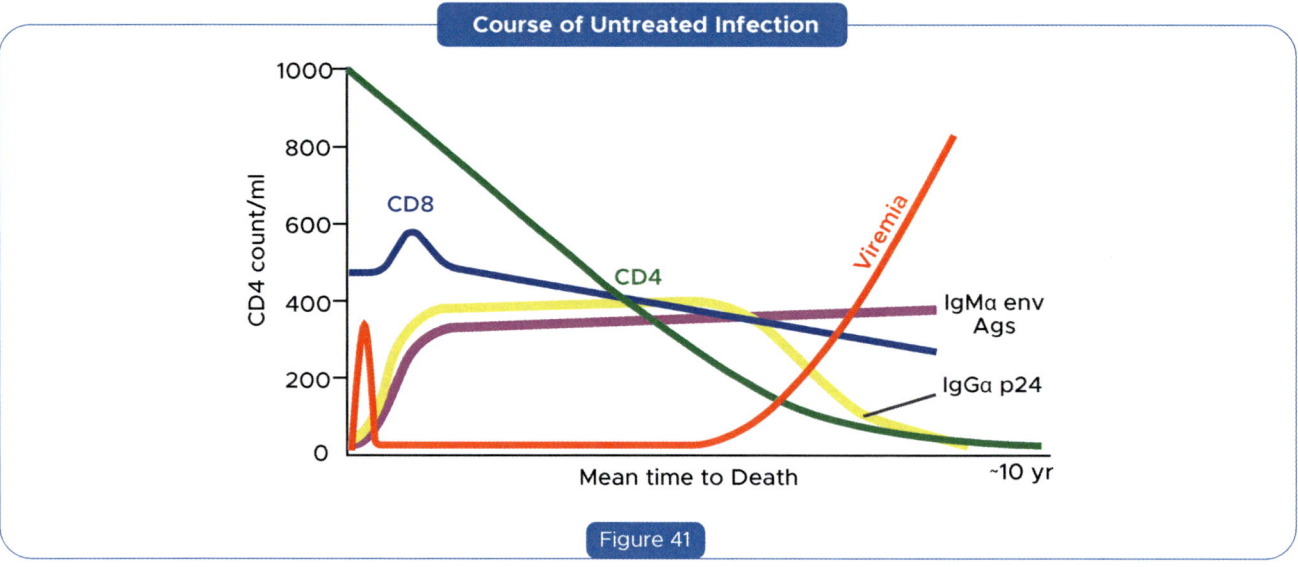

Figure 41

Acute infection (first 2 to 6 weeks)
- Asymptomatic to mono-like symptoms
- CD4 count normal (800 to 1200/μL)
- Reservoir established in macrophages, and virus spread throughout the body
- Strong CMI and HI response against the virus keeps viremia low.

Clinical latency (time variable)
- Lasts until CD4 count falls below 600/μL
- Antibodies against p24 capsid and envelope glycoproteins keep viremia low.

Early Symptomatic
- Shift of viral chemokine co-receptor preference toward CXCR4 (found primarily on TH cells) increases infection rate of TH cells.
- Signs of immunological dysfunction as TH cells are killed by viral lysis, syncytia formation, CTL killing, complement-mediated lysis and apoptosis.
- TH1 cells are lost in a skewed fashion, leading to immunological deviation toward the TH2 response.
- Constitutional symptoms begin (fever, diarrhea, fatigue and weight loss)
- As CD4 count falls to 400/μL, isotype switching becomes impossible. P24 antibodies (IgG isotype) fall, viremia begins to rise.
- Mild opportunistic diseases increase in incidence (oral and vaginal candidiasis, bacillary angiomatosis, listeriosis)

Acquired Immunodeficiency Syndrome (AIDS)

- At a count of 200 CD4 cells/µL, the immune response collapses
- AIDS-defining conditions (candidiasis of bronchi, trachea, lungs, esophagus, invasive cervical cancer, HSV chronic ulcers, Burkitt lymphoma, *Pneumocystis* pneumonia, Kaposi sarcoma, etc.)

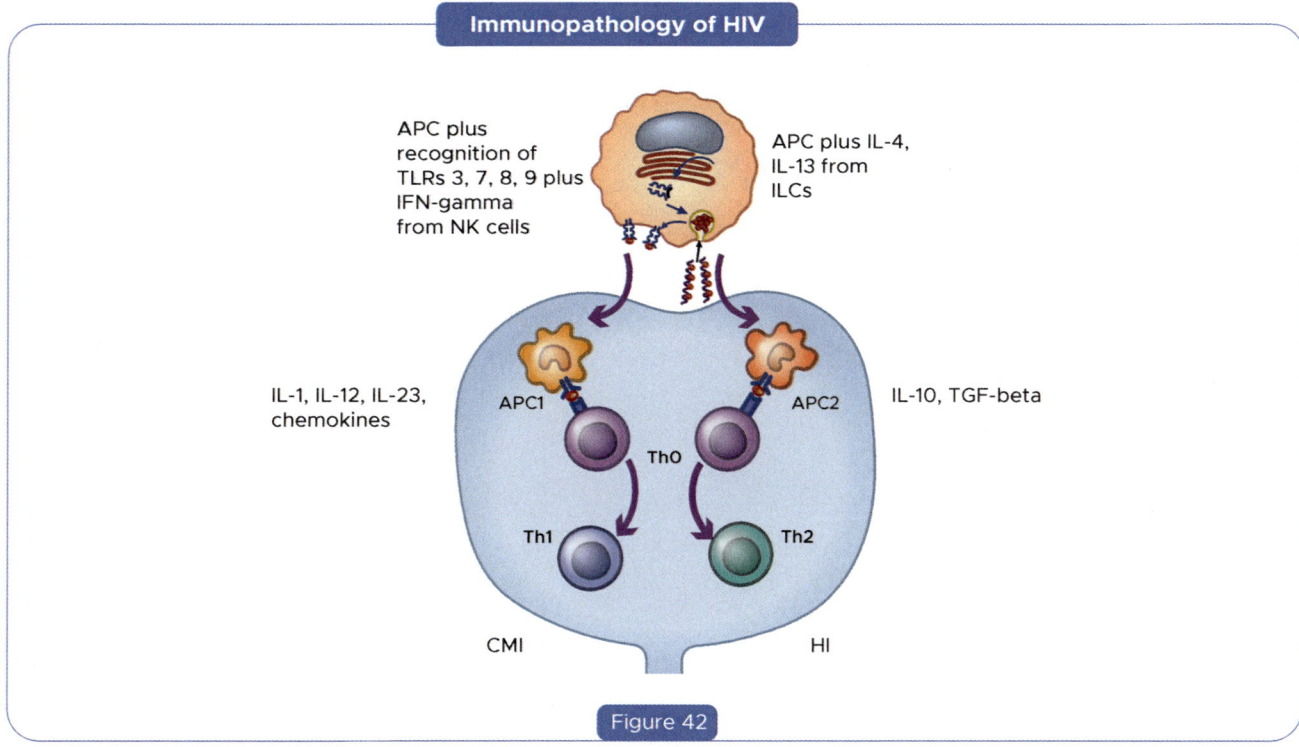

Figure 42

Direct Mechanisms	Indirect Mechanisms
Virus budding causes loss of membrane integrity	Abnormal intracellular signaling
Accumulation of unintegrated viral DNA	Innocent bystander killing of cells coated with virus
Impaired cellular RNA processing	Apoptosis
Syncytia formation	Inhibition of lymphopoiesis
Cell activation increases viral load	AICD
	Immune responses eliminate infected Th cells
	Nef gene product downregulates cellular expression of CD4 and MHC 1 (essential for progression to AIDS)

So what does the advent of opportunists tell us about the immune system status?

CD4*	Opportunistic Disease	Comment
200	Herpes simplex virus	Failed TH1 and CMI
175	Herpes zoster	
100	Cryptosporidiosis	
100	Kaposi sarcoma	
75	*Candida* esophagitis	Failure of barriers
75	*Pneumocystis* pneumonia	
50	Cryptococcal meningitis	CNS
50	Non-Hodgkin lymphoma	
50	AIDS dementia complex	
40	Progressive multifocal leukoencephalopathy	
35	Wasting syndrome	TNF
30	*Toxoplasma* encephalitis**	Systemic collapse
30	Cytomegalovirus	
30	Secondary *Pneumocystis* pneumonia	
25	*Mycobacterium avium* complex	

*(cells/µL^3) ***Toxoplasma* encephalitis is the number one diagnosis at autopsy in AIDS

Diagnosis

Purpose	Test
Initial screening	HIV-1/2 Ag/Ab immunoassay
Confirmation	HIV 1 + 2 Ab differentiation immunoassay and NAAT*
Detect virus in blood (viral load)	RT-PCR
Detect infection in newborn (provirus)	PCR
Early marker of infection	p24 antigen
Progression of disease	CD4:CD8 ratio

*nucleic acid amplification test

Management
- Monitor CD4+ cell count (directly or as a percentage determined by flow cytometry of the total lymphocyte count)
- Serum level of HIV RNA determined by RT-PCR or branched DNA (bDNA) should be monitored every 3-6 months. Extremely sensitive, but false positives.
- Anti-retroviral therapy for life (2 NRTIs or NNRTIs plus one protease inhibitor). Change "cocktail" if viral load begins to rise.

Mechanism of Action of Anti-Retrovirals
- Macrophage co-receptor antagonist – maraviroc (CCR5 antagonist)
- Anti-fusion protein - enfuvirtide
- Anti-integrase enzyme - raltegravir
- "anivir/enavir/inivir/onivir"drugs – protease inhibitors
- Nucleoside reverse transcriptase inhibitors (NRTIs)
    ◇ Abacavir (ABC)
    ◇ Didanosine (ddI)
    ◇ Emtricitabine (FTC)
    ◇ Lamivudine (3TC)
    ◇ Stavudine (d4T)
    ◇ Tenofovir (nucleotide prophylactic)
    ◇ Zalcitabine (ddC)
- Non-nucleoside reverse transcriptase inhibitors (NNRTIs)
    ◇ Delaviridine
    ◇ Efavirenz
    ◇ Nevirapine

Recommendations for Prophylaxis against Opportunists in AIDS

Disease Agent	Begin Prophylaxis	Therapy
Pneumocystis jirovecii	< 200 CD4	Trimethoprim-sulfamethoxazole
Histoplasma capsulatum	<100 CD4 (endemic area)	Itraconazole
Toxoplasma gondii	<100 CD4	Trimethoprim-sulfamethoxazole
Cytomegalovirus	<50 CD4	Gancyclovir, valgancyclovir
Mycobacterium a-i	<50 CD4	Azithromycin, clarithromycin
Cryptococcus	<50 CD4	Fluconazole
Cryptosporidium	<50 CD4	Nitazoxanide, hygiene

Prevention

- Pre-exposure prophylaxis (PrEP) cuts down infection 99% in sexually-transmitted cases, and 74% in iv drug users
    - Truvada[R] contains tenofovir (inhibits the activity of HIV-1 reverse transcriptase by competing with substrate, deoxyadenosine 5'-triphosphate) and emtricitabine (cytidine analog)
- Blood and organ donor screening
- Safe sex

Before you leave, can you...

1. Relate the progression of disease during HIV infection to CD4 count.
2. Explain the lifecycle of the virus and its effects on the immune system.
3. Explain the goals of the categories of anti-retroviral drugs.
4. Explain the standard protocols for anti-microbial prophylaxis depending on CD4 count and relate them to the decline in the immune response.

Immunology
Chapter twelve

Hypersensitivity Diseases

Hypersensitivity Diseases

Introduction:

Just as we have seen previously that immunodeficiency diseases occur when there is insufficient immune response to protect the host, too much immune response can also be damaging. Taken together, the diseases of hypersensitivity discussed in this chapter can be manifested against foreign or self antigens. In cases where the injurious stimulus causing hypersensitivity is a foreign immunogen, protection of the host from exposure can stop the tissue damage. Failures of self-tolerance are called autoimmune diseases. In cases where the excessive immune response is directed against one's own tissues or cells, the only thing that will stop the activation and damage is the suppression of the immune response.

The hypersensitivity diseases are classified into 4 types, based on the mechanism of immune response on which they depend. In each case, they require an initial "sensitizing" exposure which is usually asymptomatic, and symptoms ensue with re-exposures.

- **Type I hypersensitivity** is also known as immediate hypersensitivity or atopic allergy. It depends on **IgE antibodies** and the degranulation of **mast cells and basophils.** This is the physiologic response to helminth parasites, so when this response is misplaced, against things that are not helminthic, the damage to host tissues ensues.

- **Type II hypersensitivity** is mediated by **IgM or IgG autoantibodies** against one's own **cells** or **tissues**, and the subsequent complement activation, opsonization, phagocytosis, immune lysis and inflammation against those cells and tissues in a **localized** fashion.

- **Type III hypersensitivity** is caused by **immune complexes** of antibody and protein antigen **(not whole cells)**. When the production of these circulating complexes overwhelms the ability of the spleen to remove them (using C3b opsonization), then complement-mediated opsonization, phagocytosis and inflammation occurs throughout the small-to-medium sized vasculature of the body. Thus, the damage is systemic, and not tissue- or organ-specific.
  **Notice that type II and III hypersensitivities have a common mechanism of damage through complement-mediated inflammation. The difference between them is the nature of the eliciting antigen.

- **Type IV hypersensitivity** is also known as **delayed-type** hypersensitivity. It is a manifestation of the over activation of the **TH1 arm** of the immune response, and the activation of the **effector cells of CMI**. It requires **48-72 hours** to observe peak activity because of the complex cell-to-cell communication required for CMI. The effectors of damage can be either macrophages or CTLs and their cytokines.

Many **type IV hypersensitivities** culminate in becoming **"mixed"** meaning that autoantibodies are eventually made once tissue damage begins, and those autoantibodies can exacerbate the damage via immune complex mechanisms. Nevertheless, hypersensitivities are defined by their initial inciting response, so hopefully it is not surprising to you at this point that once a TH1 response begins, antibodies can also be produced.

Type I Hypersensitivity

Examples: allergic rhinitis (hay fever), systemic anaphylaxis to drugs, insect stings, asthma

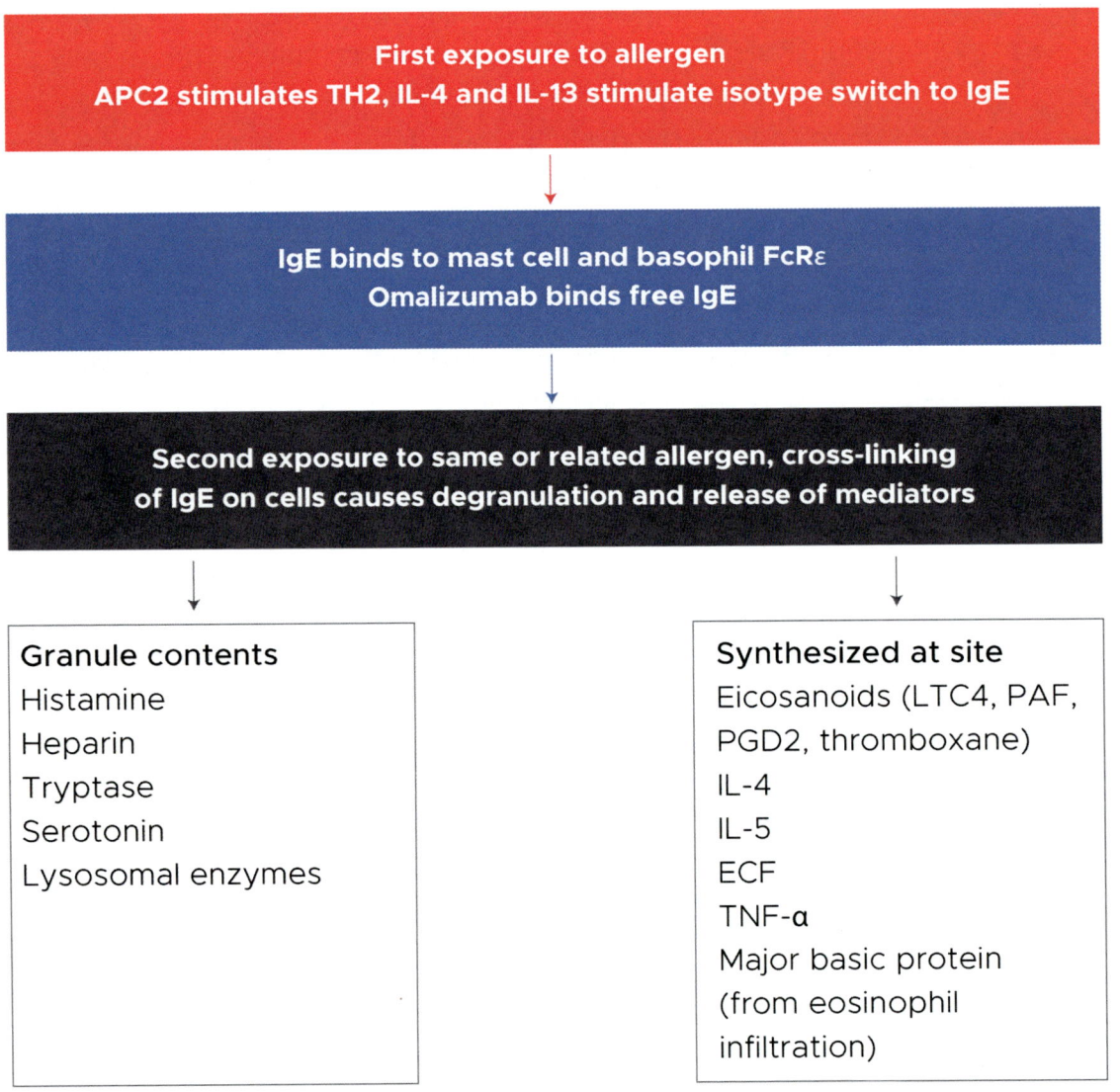

Mediator	Action	Therapy
Histamine	Vasodilation, intestinal hypermotility	Release inhibitors: Cromolyn, Nedocromil
Tryptase	Tissue damage, complement activation	
PGD2	Bronchoconstriction	β2 agonists: salmeterol, formoterol, albuterol binds M3 muscarinic receptors (antagonizes acetylcholine)
		Tiotropium methylxanthine – theophylline (relaxes smooth muscle)
LTC4	Mucus secretion, increased endothelial cell adhesion	Lipoxygenase inhibitor: Zileuton
		CysLT1 receptor antagonists: zafirlukast, montelukast
		Corticosteroids inhibit: fluticasone, budesonide, mometasone, beclomethasone
PAF, ECF	Leukocyte migration	Steroids
IL-4	Isotype switch to IgE, lymphocyte activation	Steroids
IL-5	IL-5 recruits eosinophils and causes switch to IgA in submucosa	Steroids Benralizumab (anti IL-5R)
TNF-α	↑ vascular permeability	Steroids
Major basic protein (eosinophils)	Lysis helminth cuticle	Corticosteroids can cause eosinopenia and reduce MBP toxicity

Type II Hypersensitivity

Type II hypersensitivities are all caused by **autoantibodies directed against cells or tissues.** Some autoantibodies (**cytotoxic**) cause cell death by complement activation, opsonization and inflammation, some (**non-cytotoxic**) cause alteration of the function of cells by binding to cells without causing lysis. In some cases, the antibodies can be visualized, **binding linearly** to tissues, via immunofluorescence or electron microscopy.

Cytotoxic Type II Hypersensitivities:

HDNB*	RF	Goodpasture Syndrome	Transfusion Rxn**	ITP
IgG antibodies Rh negative mother against Rh positive fetus	Antibodies against *Strep pyogenes* cell wall antigen – x-react with myocardium	Ab against type IV collagen in basement membranes	IgM antibodies against ABO glycoproteins	Abs against platelet membrane proteins
Hemolysis, anemia, hydrops fetalis	Myocarditis, arthritis	Pneumonitis, nephritis	Hemolysis	Bleeding into epithelia, mucosa
Dx: IgG anti-Rh	Dx: ASO titer > 200	Dx: anti-BM	IgM isohemagglutinins	Dx: anti-platelet membrane
Rx: RhoGAM	Anti-inflammatories	Cyclophosphamide, corticosteroids	Stop transfusion	Steroids

*Hemolytic disease of the newborn, rheumatic fever, immune thrombocytopenia
**Because of cross-reactive glycolipids on the surface of GI normal flora, all humans are sensitized against ABO glycoproteins unlike their own. Therefore, transfusion reactions can occur without evidence of previous mismatched transfusions.

Non-cytotoxic Type II Hypersensitivities

Graves Disease	Myasthenia gravis	Type II Diabetes
Ab against TSH receptor stimulates secretion of T3, T4	Ab against acetylcholine receptor, blocks release of acetylcholine	Ab against insulin receptor blocks binding of insulin
Dx: anti-TSH receptor	Dx: anti-AchR, edrophonium test Image: exclude thymoma	Dx: glycated hemoglobin (A1C) test above 6.5%
Rx: radioiodine therapy, methimazole	Rx: pyridostigmine (acetylcholinesterase inhibitor), chronic immunosuppression, plasma exchange plus IVIG and thymectomy	Rx: behavior modification, metformin, meglitinides and sulfonylureas, DPP-4 inhibitors, thiazolidinediones, α-glucosidase inhibitors, SGLT2 inhibitors, bile acid sequestrants and dopamine receptor agonists.

Type III Hypersensitivities

Type III hypersensitivities are caused by the circulation of **antigen-antibody complexes**. These are normally removed by the spleen after opsonization with C3b, but when the ability of the spleen is overcome (if there are complement deficiencies or simply too many) the binding of the complexes in small-to-medium sized blood vessels can activate complement and cause inflammation in those sites. The antibodies involved can be autoantibodies or antibodies against foreign antigens, but notice, by definition, the type III hypersensitivities **are not mounted against intact cells** (but perhaps components of those cells). Because the inflammation can occur in any blood vessel of the appropriate size, the type III hypersensitivities are **system-wide vasculitides** associated with fibrinoid necrosis.

SLE*	PSGN*	Arthus Rxn	Serum Sickness	HBV-PAN*
Nephritis, arthritis, vasculitis, malar rash	Nephritis, granular deposits on IF or EM, 10 days after GAS pharyngitis or 3 weeks after GAS impetigo	**Local** pain and edema 4-12 hours after vaccination	Arthritis, vasculitis, nephritis 12 hrs to 3 wks after administration of foreign protein or serum	Fever, malaise, fatigue, anorexia, myalgia, arthralgia (large joints)
Abs against dsDNA, Sm, other nucleoproteins	Abs against streptococcal cell wall Ags	Abs against any injected protein	Abs against various proteins	Abs against HBV or HCV, other cases idiopathic
Dx: ANA titer > 1:40, 4 ACR* criteria	Dx: Hematuria, proteinuria, positive streptozyme	History	History	Dx: immune complexes to HBV or HCV, low CH50
Rx: hydroxychloroquine, NSAIDs, corticosteroids	Rx: Symptomatic depending on severity	Rx: Symptomatic	Rx: Withdrawal of offending stimulus	Rx: Treat underlying infection

*Systemic lupus erythematosus, poststreptococcal glomerulonephritis, polyarteritis nodosa, American College of Rheumatology

Type IV Hypersensitivities

Type IV hypersensitivities are cell-mediated responses involving TH1 cells and/or TH17 cells directing killing by macrophages, CTLs or neutrophils. Because of the level of cell-to-cell communication involved, these responses require 48-72 hours to reach their peak. Once the tissue damage and destruction begin, antibodies can also be produced which may be used in diagnosis (eg rheumatoid arthritis and pernicious anemia) and may also contribute to type III hypersensitivity symptoms. In such cases, the response is said to be mixed, but still categorized by the mechanism of its origination.

TB test*	Contact dermatitis	RA*	Hashimoto Thyroiditis
Ag – tuberculin and mycolic acid	Hapten/carrier response to Ni, plant catechols No Ab	Ag in synovium	Ag in thyroid
No Ab	Itching vesicular lesions	IgM Abs against IgG Fc, anti-CCP	Abs against microsomes, thyroglobulin
"Granuloma" at injection site		Destruction articular cartilage and bone	CTL killing in thyroid leads to hypothyroidism
Dx: Size of induration	Dx: determine exposure	Dx: ↑ESR, CRP, anti-CCP	Dx: ↑ thyroid hormone, ↓TSH, Abs against TPO (thyroid peroxidase)
	Remove stimulus, topical corticosteroids for symptomatic relief	Rx: NSAIDs, steroids, disease-modifying anti-rheumatic drugs (DMARDs), Biologic agents	Rx: levothyroxine sodium for life

*tuberculin, rheumatoid arthritis
*pernicious anemia, multiple sclerosis

...continued

PA*	MS*	Type 1 Diabetes
Ag – parietal cells	Ag – myelin basic protein	Ag – islet cells
Abs against intrinsic factor	Abs against myelin	Abs against insulin, glutamic acid decarboxylase
Decreased vitamin B12 absorption, megaloblastic anemia	Progressive demyelination, paralysis	Polydipsia, polyphagia, polyuria.
Dx: indirect bilirubin, LDH, serum cobalamin, folic acid, methylmalonic acid and homocysteine assays	Dx: MRI of brain and spinal cord, CSF exam. Duration of deficit days to weeks	Dx: Random, non-fasting plasma glucose of 200 mg/dL or fasting level of 126 mg/dL
Rx: hydroxycobalamin	Rx: mitoxantrone, teriflunomide, immunomodulatory therapy	Rx: injected insulin

Other type IV hypersensitivities include:

- Guillain-Barré syndrome – response to peripheral nerve gangliosides or myelin. Ascending paralysis.
- Crohn disease – unknown antigen. Chronic intestinal inflammation.
- Celiac disease – gliadin, CTLs against MHC class 1-like molecule. Anti-gliadin, transglutaminase and endomysial antibodies. Gluten-sensitive enteropathy.

Why does Autoimmunity Happen?

The short answer is that we don't know. At its root, it is a failure of self tolerance. There are triggers that are hormonal, environmental, genetic and infectious. Many microbes make molecules similar to those of humans, and **molecular mimicry** can start a patient responding against the microbe, and then generalizing to attack his or her own tissues.

HLA molecules have a strong association with autoimmune disease, perhaps because the shape of individual molecules predispose to presentation of antigens for recognition:
- HLA B27 – a constellation of diseases such as ankylosing spondylitis, inflammatory bowel disease, reactive arthritis, juvenile idiopathic arthritis and anterior uveitis. The identification of this haplotype is important in diagnosis.
- HLA DR 2 – Multiple sclerosis, Goodpasture syndrome, narcolepsy.
- HLA DR 3 – celiac disease, Graves disease, systemic lupus erythematosus and type 1 diabetes.
- HLA DR 4 – rheumatoid arthritis.

Therapies of Hypersensitivities and Autoimmune Disease

Most therapies target the modification of T cell function:
- Proliferation inhibition – cyclosporine
- Cytokine synthesis inhibition – corticosteroids
- T cell killing – cyclophosphamide

New monoclonals have revolutionized the therapy of chronic autoimmune diseases and are now altered to minimize the possibility that the patient will make an immune response to the therapy over time. The standardized nomenclature will help you anticipate the reaction:
- If the name contains "o" it is made in mice (high immunogenicity)
- If the name contains "u" it is a human antibody (less immunogenicity)
- If the name contains "xi" it is **chimeric**: the variable domains are the only part of non-human origin
- If the name contains "zu" it is **humanized**: only the hypervariable regions are of non-human origin
- If the name contains "xizu" it is **chimeric and humanized**

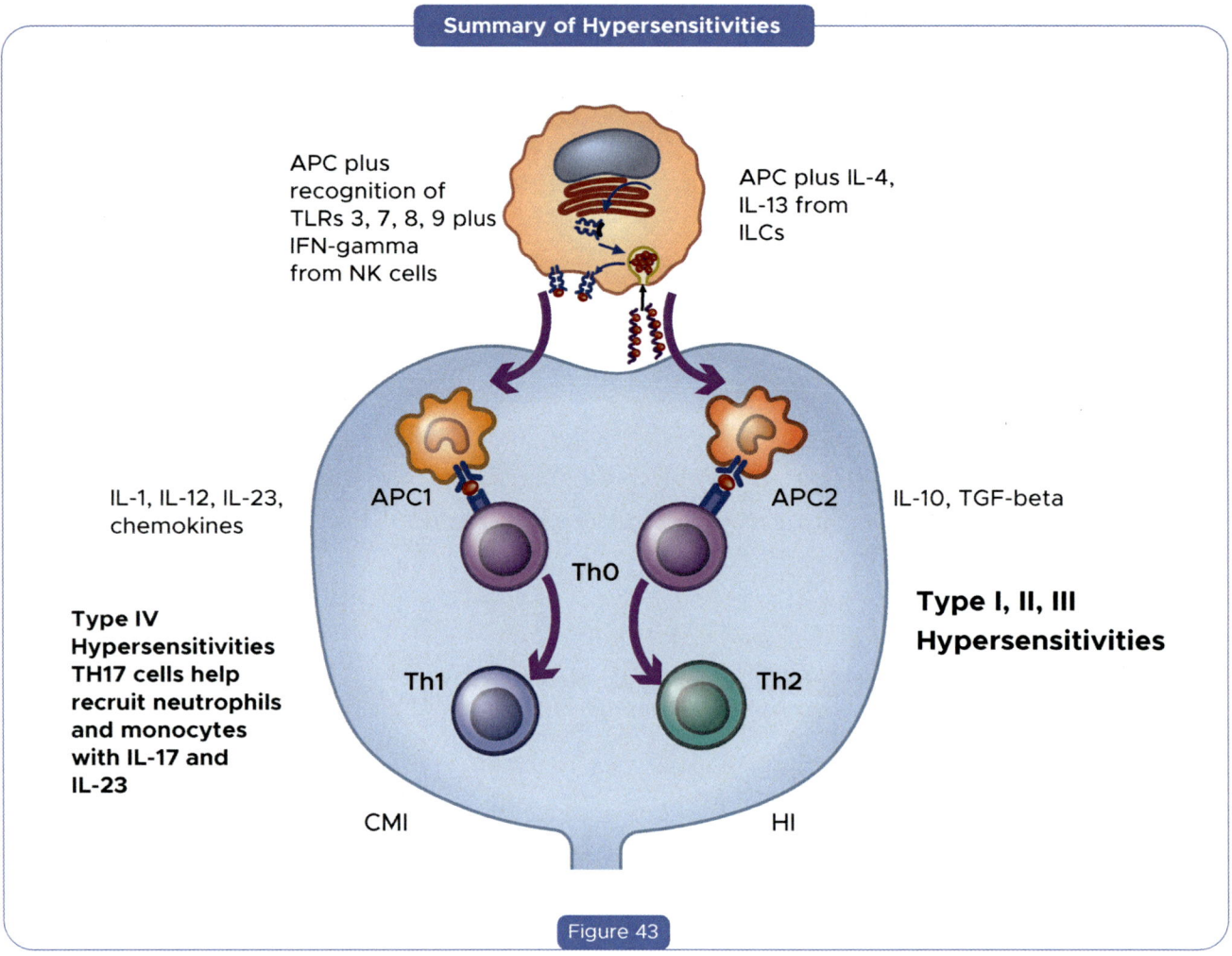

Figure 43

Before you leave, can you...

1. Explain the molecular basis of pathogenesis of the 4 types of hypersensitivity diseases.
2. Identify the cell, tissue or molecule targeted by the major autoimmune diseases.
3. Understand the broad strategies for diagnosis and management of each of these diseases.

Immunology
Chapter thirteen

Transplantation

Transplantation

Introduction:
The difficulty of surgically moving tissues/organs from one human to another is that the entire immune response is designed to identify self vs. non-self. This is the very foundation of protection from invading microbes and malignantly transformed cells, and the immune system has no mechanism to recognize the "good intentions" of the goal. The HLA is the most polymorphic genetic system in our species so by definition even transplants between closely related individuals will eventually be recognized and destroyed.

Definitions:
1. **Transfusion**
   Transplantation of blood cells. Because erythrocytes have no HLA on their cell membranes, there is no danger of immune rejection, although pre-formed alloantibodies against ABO glycoproteins can cause hemolytic destruction.
2. **Autograft**
   A transplant from one location to another on the same patient. This is used for skin grafting following burns, and coronary artery bypass surgery. Since it is the patient's own tissue, there is no danger of rejection. The immune system recognizes foreignness, not location.
3. **Isograft**
   A transplant between monozygotic twins. Since mutational changes can occur during gestation and development, even monozygotic twins are not genetically identical, and therefore isografts will also require immunosuppression for success.
4. **Allograft**
   A transplant between non-identical humans.
5. **Xenograft**
   A transplant from an animal to human. Pig heart valves can be used in humans because it is an avascularized tissue which does not perfuse with destructive immune cells.

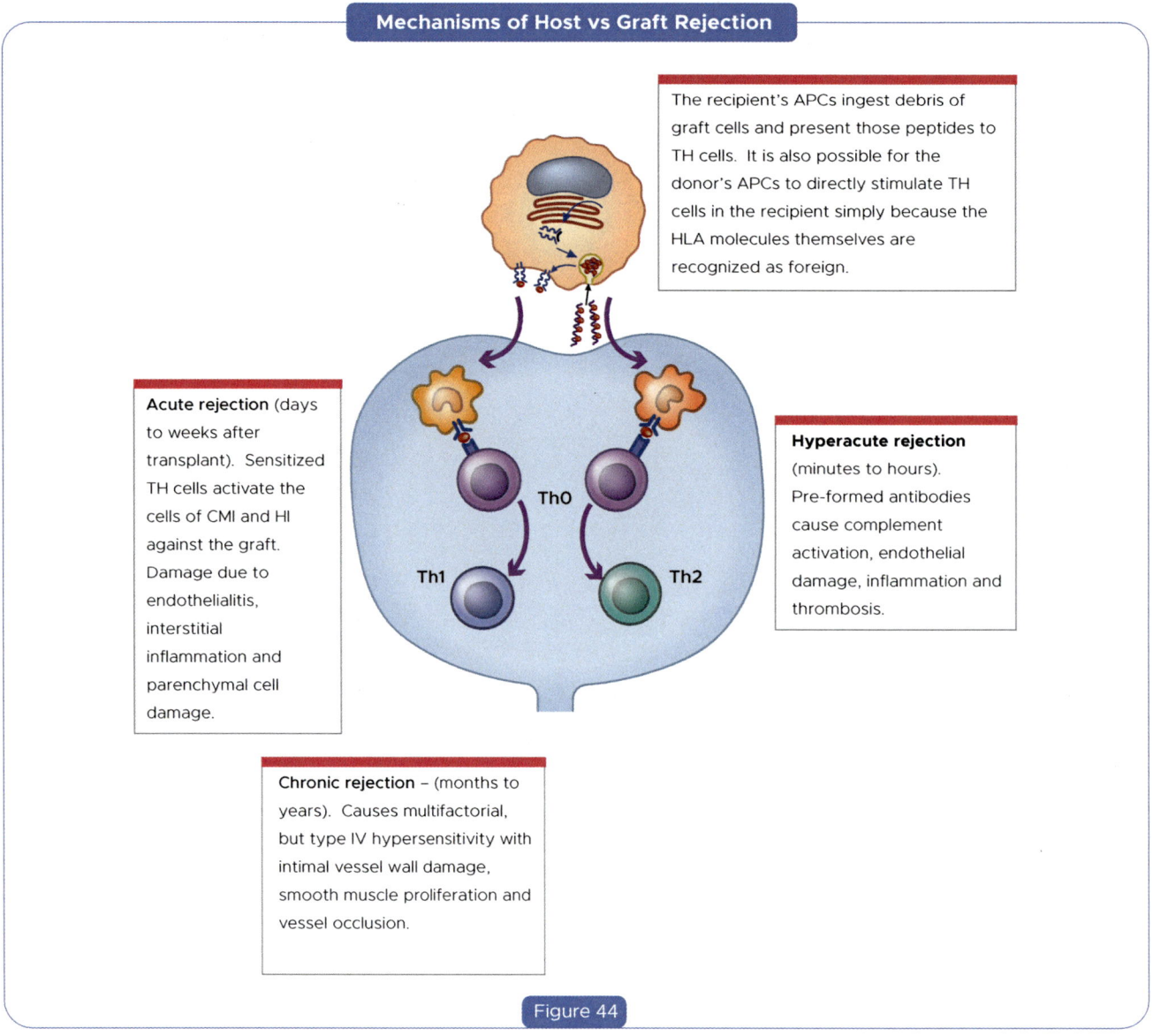

Figure 44

Graft vs Host Disease

In the special case where the tissue transplanted is bone marrow (or to a lesser extent liver), it is possible for immunocompetent cells in the transplant to react against the recipient who has received them. This is the reverse of the direction of recognition of foreignness in most transplants, with the graft cells recognizing the recipient as foreign. It depends on the ability of the TH cells to proliferate to a level at which they can become life-threatening to the recipient. Any rapidly proliferating cell population is at risk of cytotoxic killing, and the result is rash, jaundice, diarrhea and gastrointestinal hemorrhage.

Matching Donor and Recipient

In cases where a patient is critically ill and there is insufficient time to do tissue compatibility testing, surgery will proceed with only the requirement of **ABO blood grouping** and cross-matching. This is essential because all humans have preformed antibodies blood group antigens other than their own. Matching the donor and recipient for ABO blood group avoids the possibility of hyperacute graft rejection from these preformed antibodies.

Cross-matching involves mixing the cells of the donor with serum from the recipient. If there are any, as yet unidentified pre-formed antibodies which react with the donor cells, this too would cause hyperacute rejection.

ABO blood testing is done by mixing erythrocytes with known sera. Agglutination (clumping) of the red blood cells indicates that antibodies have recognized their antigen and caused the erythrocytes to clump. Lack of agglutination indicates a failure of the antibody to recognize its antigen. Humans are sensitized to cross-reactive glycolipids found on the surfaces of their intestinal normal flora. Self-tolerance protects them from making antibodies against their own blood group antigens, but they will produce IgM isohemagglutinins against the blood groups that are different from their own.

• Persons with type O blood have neither A nor B antigens, and therefore produce anti-A and anti-B isohemagglutinins. These persons are therefore considered the "**universal donor**" for blood transfusions.
- Persons with A blood have A antigens and make anti-B antibodies.
- Persons with B blood have B antigens and make anti-A antibodies.
- Persons with AB blood have A and B antigens and make no isohemagglutinins. These patients are safe to receive any blood type and are called "**universal recipients**" for blood transfusions.

HLA Matching of Donor and Recipient

In cases of potential living donor transplantation (kidney, partial liver, partial lung, bone marrow), efforts are made to match the donor and recipient at as many loci as possible. Remembering that this is the most polymorphic gene system in the human, and that allele products are codominantly expressed, a "perfect" match would mean 12 identical alleles (6 class 1 and 6 class II), and this is rarely possible. For practicality, the alleles tested are **A, B and DR** since these have been shown empirically to have the most value in matching. Because all of the signaling for proliferation is delivered at the MHC class II level (TH cells receiving stimulation from APCs), it is best to try to **match the class II alleles first.** This may seem counterintuitive, since the signal for killing is delivered at the class I recognition level, but remember that a lone CTL is not likely to cause much damage unless it is stimulated to activate and proliferate by the cytokines of a TH1 cell.

The Mixed Lymphocyte Reaction (Class II testing)

The **Ruebush Rule of Two's** states that MHC II stimulation leads to the production of **IL-2**, which causes cells to divide in **two**, so this assay measures cell proliferation in mixed cultures.

- Cells from donor are irradiated so that they cannot proliferate.
- Cells from recipient are added in culture.
- Culture is provided with a source of radiolabeled nucleotide precursor so that any newly formed DNA will cause radioactivity of culture to rise.
- The "best" result would be NO increase in radioactivity over background: this would signify that the recipient did not recognize the donor class II antigens as foreign.

Class I testing (Microcytotoxicity or Flow cytometry)

The discussion of flow cytometry will follow in our final chapter, but the microcytotoxicity assay for class I antigens will be discussed here.

- Sequentially treat the cells of donor and recipient with antisera against the known class I antigens. This requires a very large stockpile of specific antisera since there are so many alleles, but some focus can be achieved by understanding the most common haplotypes in particular ethnic groups.
- Add complement to each of the cultures. If the antibody added bound to the cells, it will activate complement and cause the cell membrane to become leaky.
- Add a colored dye so that cells with leaky membranes (those identified by specific antisera) will take up color and be visualized.
- Repeat this process until you have identified 2 A and 2 B alleles on the cells of donor and recipient.

Anti-Rejection Drug Strategies

With the advent of strong and effective immunosuppressive therapies the quality and length of life after transplantation has been dramatically improved. Remember that all grafts except autografts will need to be followed by life-long immunosuppression. There are usually 4 categories of immunosuppressant maintenance drugs:

- **Calcineurin inhibitors** – cyclosporine and tacrolimus
- **Anti-proliferative drugs** – mycophenolate mofetil and azathioprine
- **mTOR inhibitor** – sirolimus
- **Steroids** – prednisone

Additionally, two monoclonal antibody therapies are now in use for the prevention of acute rejection. **Basiliximab** and **dacliximab** bind the **alpha chain of CD25**, the high affinity receptor for IL-2 on the surface of activated T cells.

Before you leave, can you...

1. Define the types of transplantation practiced in the United States today.
2. Explain the immunological mechanisms of graft rejection at the molecular level and predict the timing under which they will be observed.
3. Explain how tissue compatibility testing is done.
4. Describe the pharmacotherapy of rejection avoidance.

Immunology
Chapter fourteen

Immunological Techniques for Diagnosis

Immunological Techniques for Diagnosis

Introduction:
More than a decade ago, the USMLE announced that they would no longer test on techniques of laboratory procedure. The purpose of this chapter, therefore, is not to focus on how these tests are done, but on their uses in clinical diagnosis and how a physician should interpret their results.

Principles of Agglutination and Precipitation
The immunological interactions that we have been discussing up until this point have been happening at the molecular level, invisible to the naked eye. Early immunologists discovered that when antibodies were combined with their complementary antigen, they would make visible deposits that would settle out of a liquid. This is the basis of tests which visualize the results of agglutination and precipitation. The only difference between these two things is that **agglutination involves the settling out of particles from a suspension** (RBC, latex beads) and **precipitation involves the settling out of proteins** from a solution when bound to their specific antibodies. In each case, the complex of antigen and antibody has too much density to remain in suspension or solution, and a visible deposit forms in the bottom of a test tube or microtiter well. In each case, it is the valence of the antibody and its ability to cross-link between molecules of antigen that gives the complex its size and density. Therefore, if antibodies are partially digested to separate their antigen-bearing arms, precipitation and agglutination will no longer occur.

- Digesting antibodies with **pepsin** cuts them behind the hinge, so the combining arms are still connected.
- Digesting antibodies with **papain** cuts them in front of the hinge, so individual binding arms are separated and these will not cause either agglutination or precipitation.
- A single idiotype-bearing arm is called an **FAb** (fragment, antigen-binding). This will bind antigen but cannot agglutinate or precipitate it.
- Two held together (after pepsin cleavage) are called an **F(Ab)'2**. These can agglutinate or precipitate specific antigen.
- The tail (left after papain cleavage) is called the **Fc**. Cells with Fc receptors bind to this tail and can remove immune complexes from the circulation.

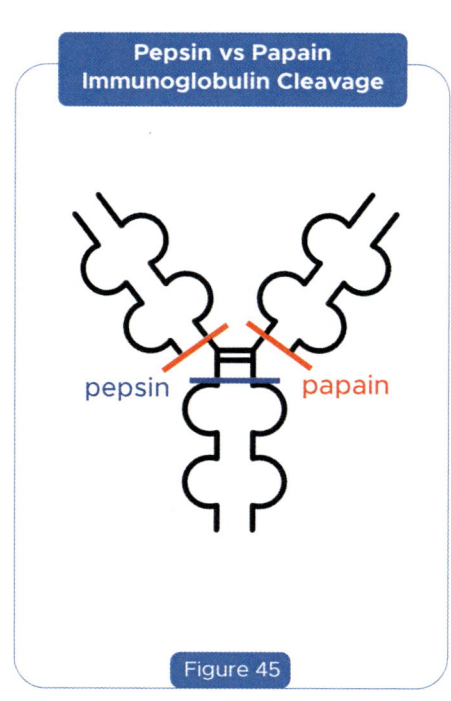

Figure 45

Medical Immunology Essentials

Development of Immune Complexes during Infection

As a patient is first exposed to a pathogen and that microbe carries out its lifecycle, rapid proliferation of the microbe will precede the body's ability to make antibodies. After a lag of 10 days to 2 weeks, specific antibodies will rise and will bind to the microbial antigens. These complexes will be removed from the blood by the spleen, and the complexes will be of maximal size during the **equivalence zone** when every idiotype of every antibody molecule is binding to every epitope of antigen. This is also the period of maximum precipitation or agglutination in a laboratory assay. In the patient, the equivalence zone is normally identified when the free antigen (which has previously been in excess) disappears from the serum. As the immune response stops the lifecycle of the microbe, the patient enters a period when the amount of antibody being produced exceeds the amount of antigen, so a rising titer of antibody is measured during convalescence.

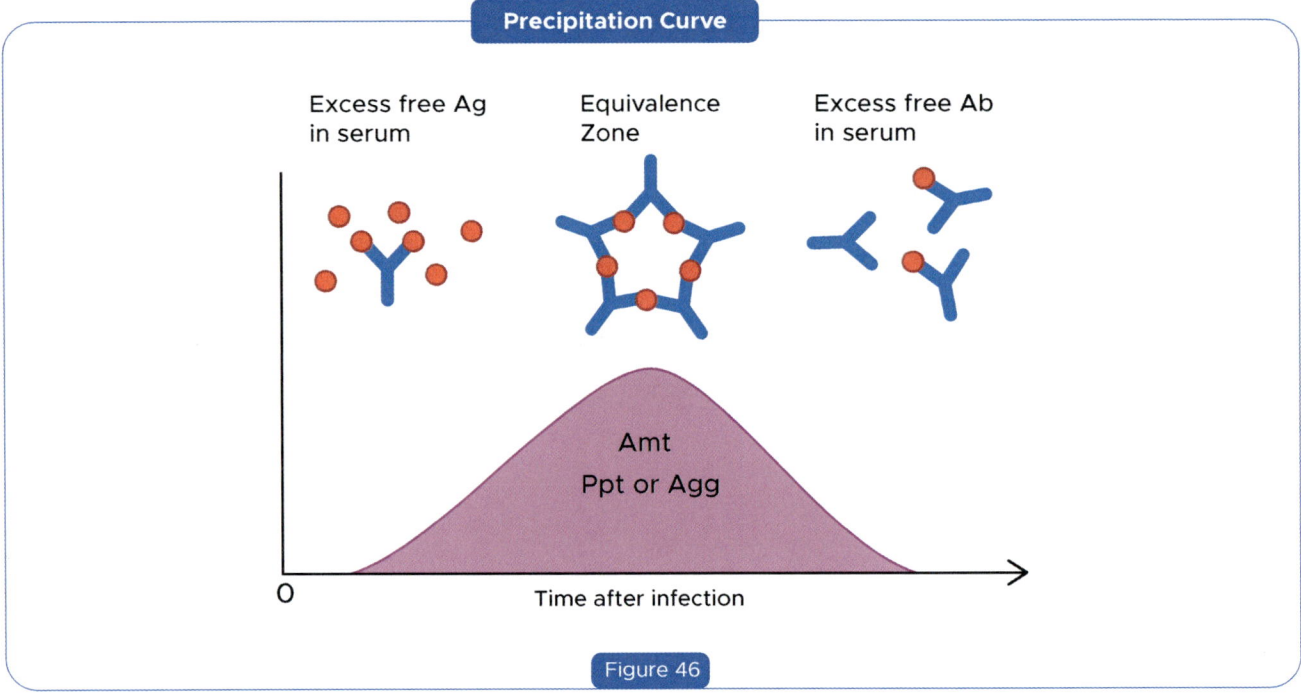

Figure 46

Antiglobulin (Coombs) test

The antiglobulin, or Coombs test is an agglutination test used to detect IgG antibodies against red blood cells. Because IgG is not large enough to bridge between erythrocytes, once it binds to red blood cells in an autoimmune condition (autoimmune hemolytic anemia or hemolytic disease of the newborn, HDNB) the cells will not agglutinate until a developing serum (Coomb's serum; anti-human IgG) is added. The assay comes in two forms, direct and indirect.

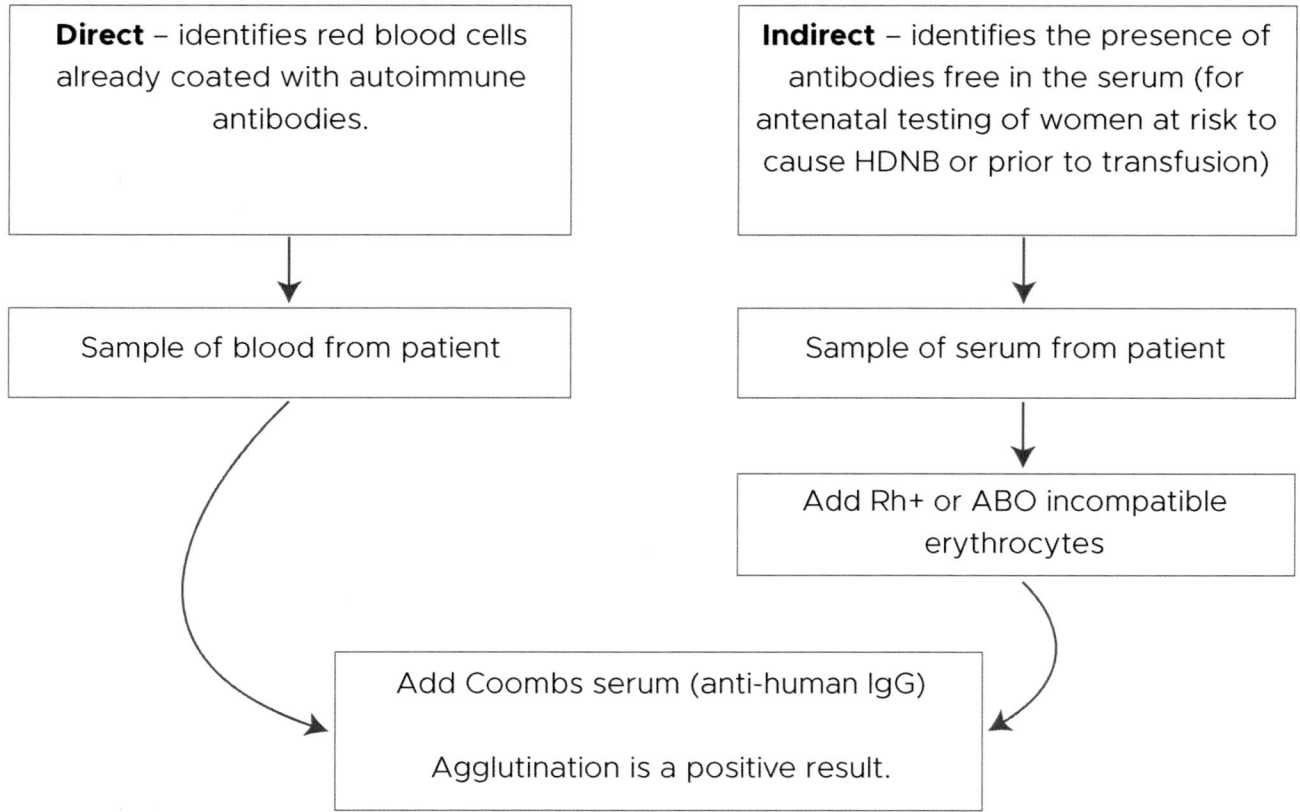

Enzyme Immunoassay

The **enzyme-linked immunoassay (EIA or ELISA)** and the **radioimmunoassay (RIA)** are extremely common diagnostic techniques which differ only in the means of visualizing the result. With EIA, a change in color caused by enzymatic cleavage of a substrate is observed, and in RIA, increased radioactivity is used as the measure of binding. Both assays are extremely sensitive, capable of detecting 10^{-9} g of material, but as such, they can produce **false positive** results. These tests can be used to detect antigen or antibody. The radioallergosorbent test (RAST) is an RIA to detect IgE antibodies in atopic patients.

If we consider the process of initial HIV testing with EIA:
- The first step is to coat the wells of a microtiter plate with a viral antigen, usually the p24 capsid.
- Next a sample of serum from the patients to be tested is placed in column 1 of each row, A – H being the different patients that can be simultaneously tested.
- A serial dilution is made from column 1 to column 10, and columns 11 and 12 are retained as positive and negative controls (known positive serum in column 11 and no serum in column 12).
- After washing with saline, an enzyme-linked anti-human gamma globulin is now added to each well.
- After washing again with saline, the substrate for the enzyme is added, and change in color in the wells is noted.
- The titer is determined as the reciprocal of the dilution in the last positive well.

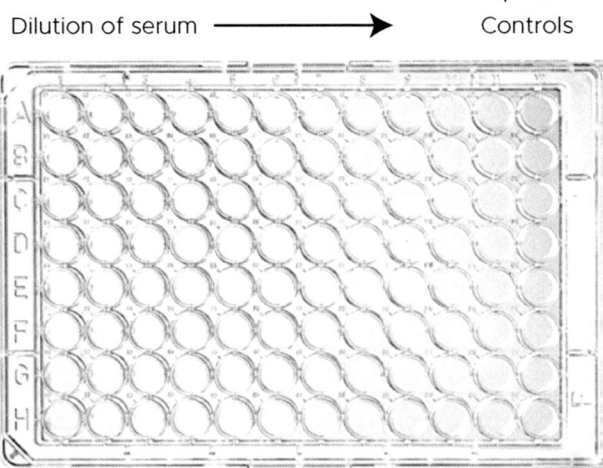

Immunofluorescent Assays
Immunofluorescent antibody tests use fluorescence microscopy to identify the binding of labeled antibodies to antigens. There are direct and indirect versions.

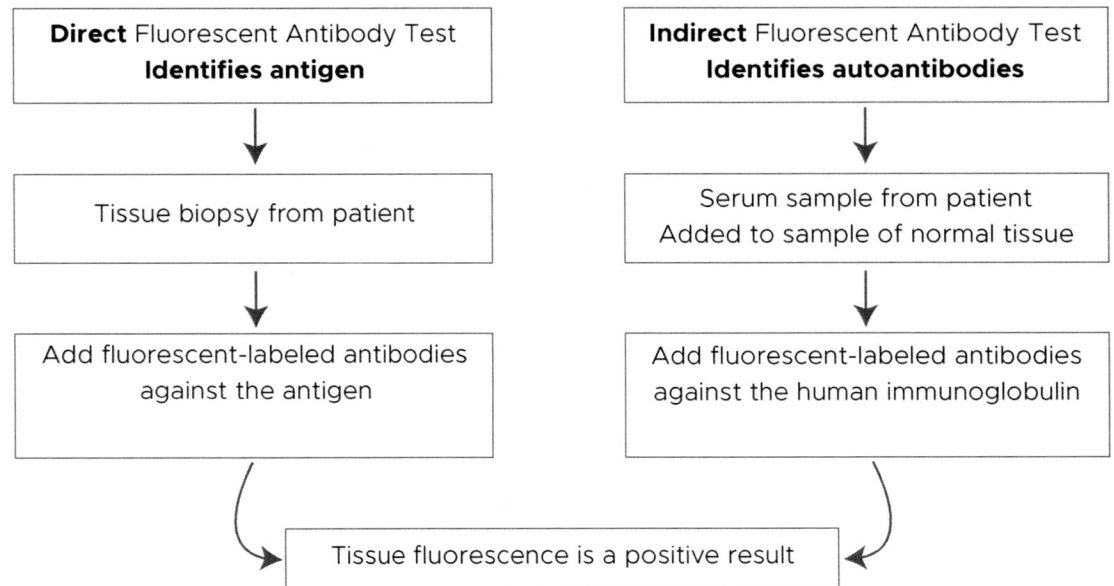

Fluorescence-Activated Cell Sorter

The fluorescence-activated cell sorter (FACS) is a computerized apparatus designed to separate cells out of a complex mixture, based on fluorescent dyes with which they have been labeled. The working of the FACS is beyond the scope here, but the interpretation of the data produced is highly testable.

Starting with a population of peripheral blood cells, if the physician wanted to determine the proportion of T cells and B cells, the cells would first be mixed with fluorescence-labeled antibodies against important cell surface markers and then run through the sorter. For example, one might use a blue-labeled antibody against CD3 and a yellow-labeled antibody against CD19. The apparatus will run the cells in the sample through an electromagnetic aperture in single file and evaluate the color and intensity of fluorescence for each. What is generated is a graphic showing color and intensity for the populations, plotted against one another.

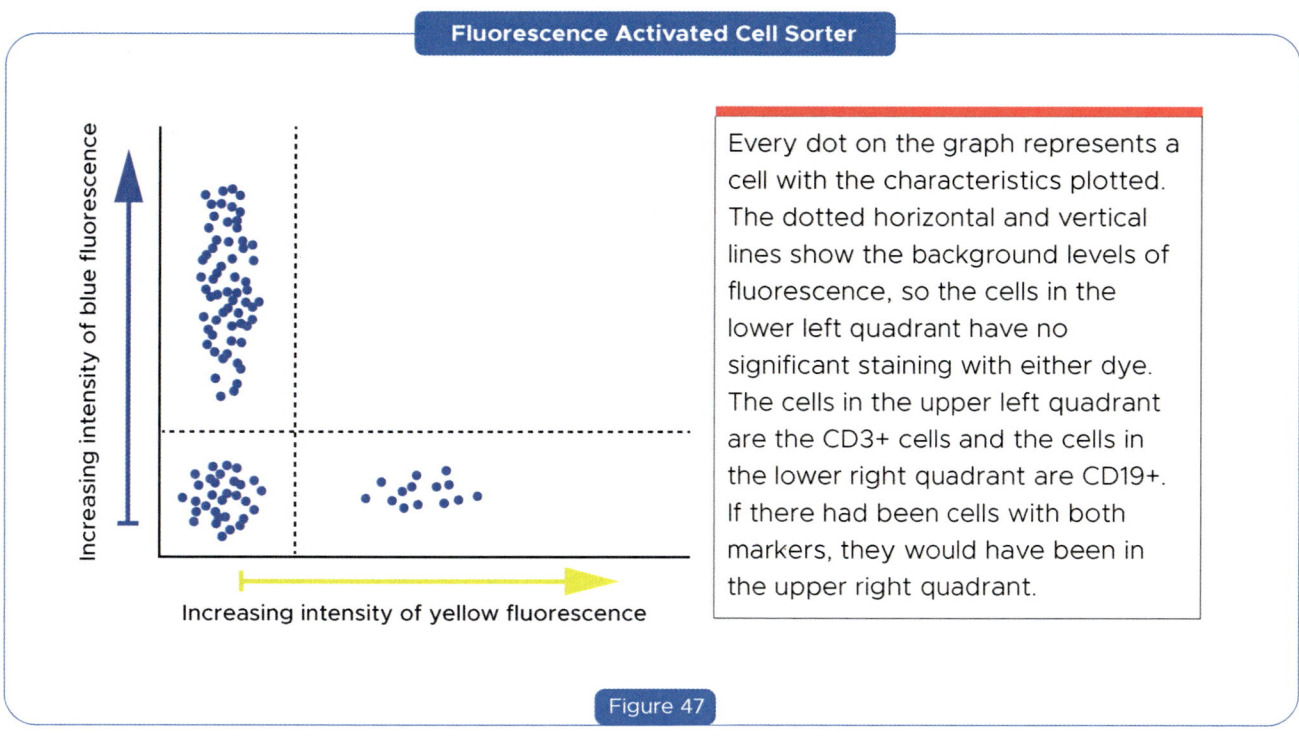

Every dot on the graph represents a cell with the characteristics plotted. The dotted horizontal and vertical lines show the background levels of fluorescence, so the cells in the lower left quadrant have no significant staining with either dye. The cells in the upper left quadrant are the CD3+ cells and the cells in the lower right quadrant are CD19+. If there had been cells with both markers, they would have been in the upper right quadrant.

Figure 47

#MMC (Make Me Care!)

Hepatitis B virus has three major antigens C (main core), E (second core) and S (surface). Patients make antibodies against all three antigens at some point in their infection (unless they develop a chronic case of infection). A prognostic indicator of recovery is the disappearance of the S antigen before 6 months post-infection. Can you explain why this would be so in the context of what you know about the development of immune complexes?

Before you leave, can you....

1. Understand the general procedures and uses for the most common immunological diagnostic tests.
2. Be able to interpret data provided from a laboratory to diagnose disease.

Immunology

APPENDIX

Key Cytokines and their Actions

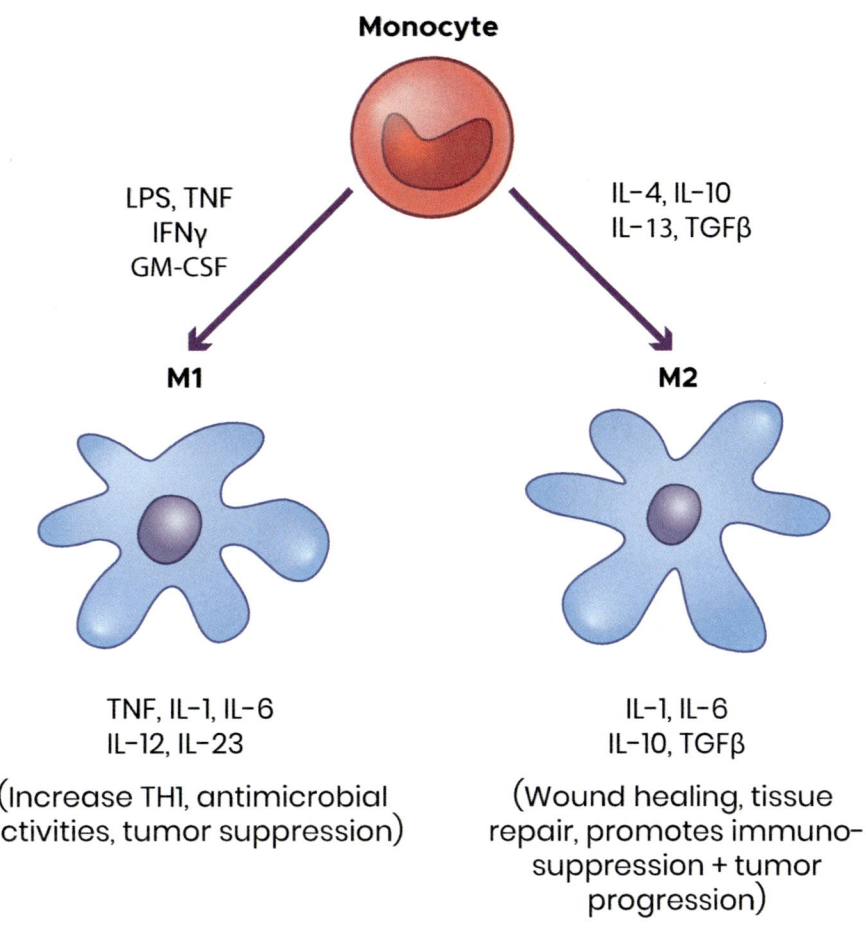

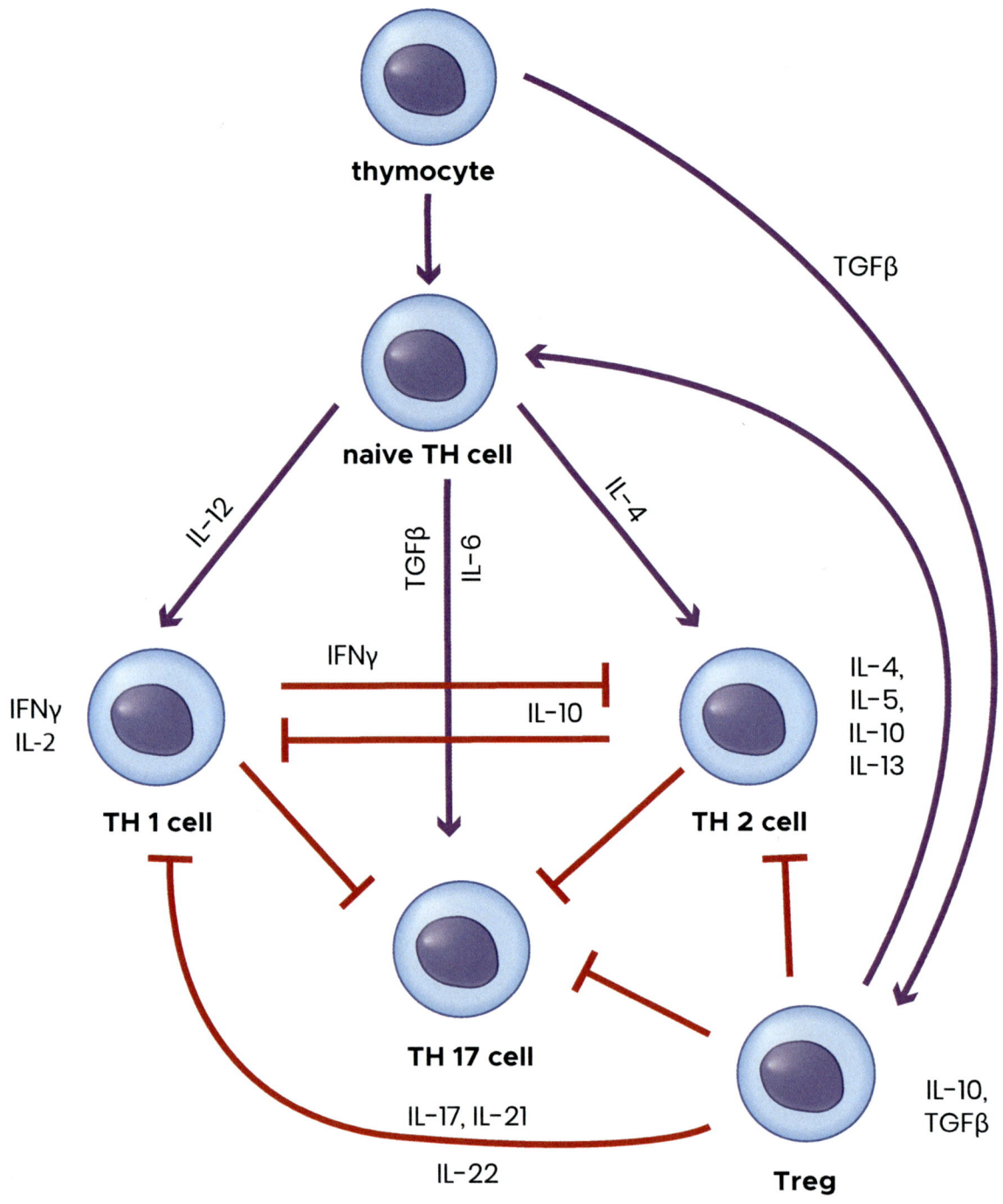

Medical Immunology Essentials

Family	Cell of Origin	Target tissue	Action
Interleukins			
IL-1	Mononuclear phagocytes, B cells, endothelial cells	Hypothalamus	↑ fever
	Inflammasome (any cell)	Leukocytes Liver	Pro-inflammatory, acute phase response
IL-2 (aldesleukin*)	T cells, NK cells	T and B lymphocytes	Cloning
		Mononuclear phagocytes	Activation
IL-3	T cells	Bone marrow progenitors	Stimulates myeloid cell growth and differentiation
IL-4	T cells	TH0	Differentiation and cloning into TH2
		B cells	Activation, cloning, isotype switch to IgE
IL-5	T cells and mast cells	B cells	Isotype switch to IgA
		Bone marrow	Production of eosinophils
IL-6	T cells, fibroblasts, macrophages	T and B cells	Costimulatory
		Mature B cells	Cloning
		Liver	Acute phase response
IL-7	Stromal cells of bone marrow and thymus	Lymphoid stem cells	Cloning and differentiation
IL-8	Endothelial cells, macrophages, platelets	Neutrophils	Activation and chemotaxis
IL-10	TH2 and Treg cells	Macrophages	↓ activation
		T lymphocytes	Inhibits TH1 activation
IL-11 (oprelvekin*)	Bone marrow stroma	Myeloid precursors	↑ megakaryocyte differentiation
IL-12	M1 macrophages, NK cells	TH0 cells	Differentiation into TH1 cells

IL-13	TH2 and mast cells	B cells	Isotype switch to IgE, IgG1
		Epithelium	Mucus secretion
IL-17	TH17 and γδT cells	Fibroblasts, endothelial cells, macrophages	Proinflammatory, attracts PMNs
IL-21	TH17 cells	NK, CTLs	cloning
IL-22	TH17 cells	Epithelial and stromal cells	Wound healing
IL-23	Macrophages, dendritic cells	TH0	Differentiation to TH1
		TH17	↑ IL-17
		Macrophages	Produce IL-1, IL-6 and TNF
IL-35	Treg cells	TH1, TH2, TH17	Anti-inflammatory, stimulates Treg cells

Family	Cell of Origin	Target tissue	Action
Colony Stimulating Factors			
G-CSF (filgrastim*)	Macrophages and TH cells	Bone marrow	↑ granulocyte precursors
GM-CSF (sargramostim*)	Macrophages and TH cells	Bone marrow	↑ granulocyte-monocyte precursors
Interferons (Type 1)			
Interferon-α (Infergen, intron A, roferon A*)	Virus-infected cells	Uninfected cells in the vicinity	↓ viral replication, ↑ MHC 1 and 2 expression
Interferon-β (avonex, betaseron*)	Fibroblasts, macrophages	Lymphocytes, endothelial cells	Anti-inflammatory, pro-immunoregulatory cytokines, Rx for MS
Interferons (Type 2)			
Interferon-γ (Actimmune, imukin*)	TH1, CTLs, NK cells	Macrophages	↑ activity, Rx for CGD
		B cells	Blocks class switch to IgG1 and IgE
		TH2 cells	↓ proliferation
TNF Family			
TNF-α	Macrophages and NK cells	Tumor cells	Cytotoxic effect
		Inflammatory cells	Cancer cachexia, ↑ inflammatory cytokines
TNF-β	TH1 and CTLs	Tumor cells	Cytotoxic effect
		Phagocytic cells	↑ phagocytosis
		Endothelial and stromal cells	↑ tertiary lymphoid accumulations in chronic inflammation and graft rejection
TGF Family			
TGF-β	M2 macrophages, platelets, lymphocytes, mast cells	Proliferating B cells	Isotype switch to IgA
		Fibroblasts	Wound healing, scar formation, fibrosis

CGD; chronic granulomatous disease, MS; multiple sclerosis, TNF; tumor necrosis factor, TGF; transforming growth factor
* recombinant + DNA therapeutics

Key CD Markers and their Functions

T cell Markers		
CD Number	**Found on....**	**Function/Ligand**
CD2 (LFA-2)	Thymocytes, T and NK cells	Adhesion molecule, binds CD58
CD3	Thymocytes and T cells	Signal transduction molecule
CD4	Thymocytes, T cells, macrophages, monocytes	Coreceptor for TCR/MHC2, receptor for HIV
CD8	Thymocytes, CTLs	Coreceptor for TCR/MHC1
CD25	Activated TH and Treg	High affinity IL-2 R
CD28	T cells	Receptor for CD80/B7 costimulation
CD152	Activated T cells	Receptor for CD80/B7 co-inhibition

B cell markers		
CD Number	**Found on....**	**Function/Ligand**
CD10 (CALLA)	Lymphoid progenitors and immature B cells	B cell development
CD19	B cells	Activation, signal transduction
CD20	B cells	unknown
CD21	Mature B cells	Coreceptor complex with CD19, Receptor for C3d, EBV receptor
CD40	B cells, dendritic cells, endothelial cells, macrophages	Activates when bound to CD40L
CD80 (B7.1)	Activated B cells, dendritic cells, macrophages	Binds CD28 (activates) or CTLA-4 (inhibits)
CD86 (B7.2)	Activated B cells, dendritic cells, macrophages	Binds CD28 (activates) or CTLA-4 (inhibits)

Other markers

CD Number	Found on....	Function/Ligand
CD14	Dendritic cells, macrophages, monocytes	Endotoxin receptor
CD16	Macrophages, granulocytes, NK cells	Fc receptor for ADCC, opsonization
CD18	Leukocytes, absent in LAD	Adhesion molecule, β chain of β2 integrins
CD34	Precursors of endothelial and hematopoietic cells	Loose binding, L-selectin
CD45 (LCA)	Hematopoetic cells	TCR and BCR receptor-mediated signaling
CD54 (ICAM-1)	B and T cells, endothelial cells, monocytes	β2 integrins, receptor for rhinovirus
CD55 (DAF)	Ubiquitous	C3b, C4b; inhibits complement activation
CD56	NK cells	unknown
CD58 (LFA-3)	Ubiquitous	CD2; adhesion
CD59 (MIRL)	Ubiquitous	C8, C9; inhibits MAC

LFA; leukocyte function antigen, HIV; human immunodeficiency virus, TCR; Tcell antigen receptor, BCR; B cell antigen receptor, CALLA; common acute lymphoblastic leukemia antigen, EBV; Epstein-Barr virus, ADCC; antibody-dependent cell-mediated cytotoxicity, LAD; leukocyte adhesion deficiency, LCA; Leukocyte common antigen, DAF; decay activating factor, MIRL; membrane inhibitor of reactive lysis, MAC; membrane attack complex.

Microbiology
Chapter one

Introduction to the Microbial World

Introduction to the Microbial World

Introduction:

Human beings have coexisted on the planet with billions of microbes since the beginning of time, and fortunately only a relatively small fraction of those successfully managed to invade, persist and cause disease. It is useful to organize these microbes into 3 categories: true pathogens, organisms of the microbiome which have overcome host homeostasis, and microbes which only cause disease in patients with specific immunodeficiencies.

- **True pathogens** infect a normal host and produce **virulence factors** which cause disease. Recovery of the host is followed by immunologic memory.
- **Organisms of the microbiome** can persist and cause disease in patients with mechanical failures of innate barrier systems such as cilia, mucus, epithelia or disruption of the protective effects of normal flora by antibiotics. These infections are often mixed, with multiple different microbes involved.
- **The microbes of immunodeficiency disease** are generally single microbes that are specific to a particular immune defect (neutrophils, antibody production or T cell killing).

This classification is useful to the physician to predict the patient population and underlying physiology of that patient.

A second classification of infectious disease agents is by their taxonomic grouping. This is useful to anticipate the pathogenesis and the pharmacotherapy necessary to interrupt the lifecycle. There are 5 categories of infectious agents which can be defined using these criteria: prions, viruses, bacteria, fungi and parasites.

Medical Microbiology Essentials

Categories of Infectious Agents

Agent	Size	Cells	Replication	Rx
Prion	Infectious protein	Acellular	Deposits extracellularly	
Virus	Electron microscope	Acellular	DNA or RNA, obligate intracellular	Anti-fusion, anti-nucleic acid, anti-release
Prokaryote	Light microscope	• Cells with no internal membrane-bound organelles • Replicate continuously, binary fission, asexual • Mono and polycistronic mRNA • No introns • **70S ribosomes** • Cell membrane without sterols* • Cell wall - **peptidoglycan**	DNA and RNA	• Anti-cell wall-penicillin, cephalosporins, vancomycin • Anti- 70S ribosomes – tetracycline, macrolides, lincosomides
Eukaryote • **Fungus** (ergosterol major membrane sterol, complex carbohydrate cell wall) • **Parasite** (cholesterol in membrane, no cell wall)	Light microscope to naked eye	• Cells with mitochondria, nuclei and all other membrane bound organelles • Cell cycle, mitosis and meiosis • Monocistronic mRNA • Introns and exons • 80S ribosomes	DNA and RNA	• Anti-ergosterol – nystatin, imidazoles, terbinafine • Anti-chitin – nikkomycin • Anti-glucan-echinocandins Most anti-parasitic drugs have some toxicity for human

*_Mycoplasma_ has no cell wall, and a membrane with cholesterol

The Epidemiology of Infectious Disease

The physician's understanding of where a microbe comes from is important to understand the tissue that will be affected and how the infection might spread.

1. Normal flora are extremely important to the health of the human, because they compete for space with more harmful organisms, and because they assist digestion and produce vitamin K for clotting blood. When they are not confined to their normal locations by the host immune response because there has been injury or decline in natural immunity, they tend to spread contiguously from their preferred niches:

- **Skin** – *Staphylococcus epidermidis*, *S. aureus*, diphtheroids, streptococci, yeasts, anaerobes (acne).
- **Nose** – *Staphylococcus aureus*, *S. epidermidis*, diphtheroids, streptococci.
- **Oropharynx** – viridans streptococci (plaque and dental caries), other streptococci, non-pathogenic *Neisseria* and *Haemophilus*, yeasts.
- **Gingival crevices** (anerobic niches) – *Bacteroides*, *Fusobacterium*, *Actinomyces*, streptococci.
- **Colon** - *Escherichia coli*, *Bacteroides fragilis*, *Bifidobacterium*, *Clostridium*, *Eubacterium*, *Fusobacterium*, *Lactobacillus*, various streptococci (*S. bovis* and *S. faecalis*).
- **Vagina** (during menarche) – *Lactobacillus*, *Streptococcus agalactiae*, *Bacillus fragilis*, diphtheroids, *Candida*, non-pathogenic streptococci and gram-negative diplococci. Pre-menarchal and post-menopausal females may have *Staphylococcus aureus* predominate.

Notice that in the oropharynx and vagina there are normal flora that can confuse the diagnosis of true pathogens:

> In the oropharynx - all streptococci are gram positive cocci in chains, so diagnosis of *Streptococcus pyogenes* (GAS) in this site is not possible by gram stain alone. Similarly, non-pathogenic (non-encapsulated) *Haemophilus influenzae* organisms cannot be distinguished from the pathogenic type b by gram stain alone.

> In the vagina - normal flora gram negative diplococci confuse the diagnosis of the pathogen *Neisseria gonorrhoeae*.

2. Means of infection

Includes inhalation, fecal-oral, direct contact, sexual, transplacental, parenteral (i.v. drug), vector-borne or traumatic implantation.

3. Geography

Always important when mentioned in a vignette. Particularly with vector-borne and fecal-oral spread, parasites and fungi.

Microbial Mechanisms of Pathogenesis

1. Adherence

a. Viruses

attach to specific cell membrane receptors. This causes the "tropism" of the virus and results in cell death and symptoms/signs as a result.

- **Hemagglutinin** – most RNA viruses
- **CD4 and chemokine receptors** – HIV (via gp120)
- **CD21** – Epstein-Barr virus
- **Acetylcholine receptor** – rabies virus
- **ICAM-1** – rhinovirus

b. Bacteria

- Extracellular organisms that use surface molecules
    - Gram positives – **lipoteichoic acids** bind to fibronectin
    - *Streptococcus pyogenes* **M protein** binds to fibrinogen
    - *Mycoplasma* **protein P1** binds to sialic acid
    - Gram negatives and positives – **pili** (fimbriae) bind to sugar receptors
    - *Bordetella pertussis* – **filamentous hemagglutinin** binds to integrin (?)
- Biofilm producers
    - *Pseudomonas aeruginosa*
    - *Staphylococcus aureus* and *S. epidermidis*
    - Viridans streptococci

c. Parasites

- *Plasmodium falciparum* binds to ICAM-1 and glycophorins on erythrocytes
- *Plasmodium vivax* binds to Duffy antigen

2. Evasion of Innate Immune Responses

a. Inhibition of chemotaxis and complement anaphylatoxins

- *Streptococcus pyogenes*
    - Chemokine protease degrades IL-8
    - C5a peptidase inactivates C5a
- *Pseudomonas aeruginosa*
    - Inactivates C3a, C5a anaphylatoxins

b. Inhibition of phagocytic engulfment

- **Capsules** (slime layer, glycocalyx) – slippery secretions of many organisms (mnemonic – Some Killers Have Pretty Nice Slimy Capsules:
    - *Streptococcus pneumoniae*
    - *Klebsiella pneumoniae*
    - *Haemophilus influenzae* type B

◇ *Pseudomonas aeruginosa*
◇ *Neisseria meningitidis*
◇ *Salmonella spp.*
◇ *Cryptococcus neoformans*

c. Inhibition of opsonization
- *Streptococcus pyogenes* M protein destroys C3 convertase
- *Staphylococcus aureus* protein A binds the Fc of IgG

d. Pili of Neisseria gonorrhoeae are antiphagocytic

3. Evasion of Acquired Immune Responses
a. Antigenic Variation
- Viruses
    - ◇ **Antigenic drift** – mutations cause genetic change
    - ◇ **Antigenic shift** – reassortment of segmented genomes causes dramatic change
        - › **ROBA:** **R**eovirus, **O**rthomyxovirus, **B**unyavirus, **A**renavirus
- *Neisseria gonorrhoeae* – pili and outer membrane proteins
- Enterobacteriaceae – capsular and flagellar antigens
- African trypanosomes – variant specific glycoprotein

b. Intracellular Survival – avoid humoral immunity
- **Facultative intracellular** – survive in mononuclear phagocytes
    - ◇ *Mycobacterium tuberculosis* – inhibit hagosome-lysosome fusion with sulfatides (sulfolipids which hydrolyze to H_2SO_4)
    - ◇ *Listeria monocytogenes* – 'jets" out of phagosome before lysosomal fusion
    - ◇ **Invasins** – surface proteins which promote binding of non-phagocytic cells (*Yersinia pseudotuberculosis*)
- **Obligate intracellular** – invade non-phagocytic cells and cannot live outside of cells
    - ◇ **Syncytial viruses** (Herpesviruses, HIV, paramyxoviruses) evade humoral immunity by using fusion protein to make multi-nucleated giant cells.
    - ◇ **Downregulation of MHC 1** expression – herpesviruses, adenoviruses, rubeola (avoid CTL recognition)

c. Avoidance of Mucosal Immunity – IgA proteases
- *Haemophilus influenzae*
- *Neisseria gonorrhoeae*
- *Neisseria meningitidis*
- *Streptococcus pneumoniae*

Nutrition, Penetration and Spread

- **Siderophores** – the competition for bioavailable forms of iron has been a problem since the dawn of time. Many bacteria make siderophores to chelate iron for their own cells, and the **acute phase reactant hepcidin** is the body's attempt to thwart that theft.
- **Destruction of extracellular matrix**
    - Collagenase – *Clostridium perfringens*
    - Hyaluronidase – *Clostridium perfringens* and *Streptococcus pyogenes*
    - Lecithinase - *C. perfringens*
    - Streptokinase – *S. pyogenes* (dissolves fibrin)
    - Streptodornase – *S. pyogenes* DNAse
- **Spread via the bloodstream**
    - **Bacteremia,** viremia, fungemia, parasitemia – presence of microbes in the blood
    - **Septicemia** – multiplication of microbes in the blood with symptoms

Injury Mediated by the Immune Response

1. Acute Inflammation
    - **Formyl-methionyl peptides** and **peptidoglycan-teichoic acid fragments** are chemotactic for neutrophils, and make bacteria "pyogenic"
2. Chronic Inflammation
    - **Type 1 Hypersensitivity** – misplaced antihelminthic response, allergy
    - **Type 2 Hypersensitivity** – Rheumatic fever; antibodies against *Streptococcus pyogenes* crossreact with perivascular connective tissue
    - **Type 3 hypersensitivity** – post-streptococcal glomerulonephritis – immune complexes against *S. pyogenes* serotypes M12 and M14
    - **Type 4 hypersensitivity** – tuberculosis, leprosy, chlamydial PID – CMI causes cytotoxicity and granuloma formation

Toxins – poisonous substances produced by living cells.

1. Anatomical Toxins (PAMPs)

a. Endotoxin (Lipopolysaccharide)
- Part of the **outer membrane** of a **gram negative bacterium**
- Active component – **lipid A**, released when cell dies, except in *Neisseria* which constitutively overproduces outer membrane blebs at all times.
- Mechanism of action – Binds to **CD14 and TLR4** on macrophages, dendritic cells, monocytes, stimulates overproduction of cytokines
- Cannot be inactivated in autoclave (heat stable)
- Not highly immunogenic

b. Peptidoglycan -Teichoic Acid Fragments
- Released on death of a **gram positive bacterium**

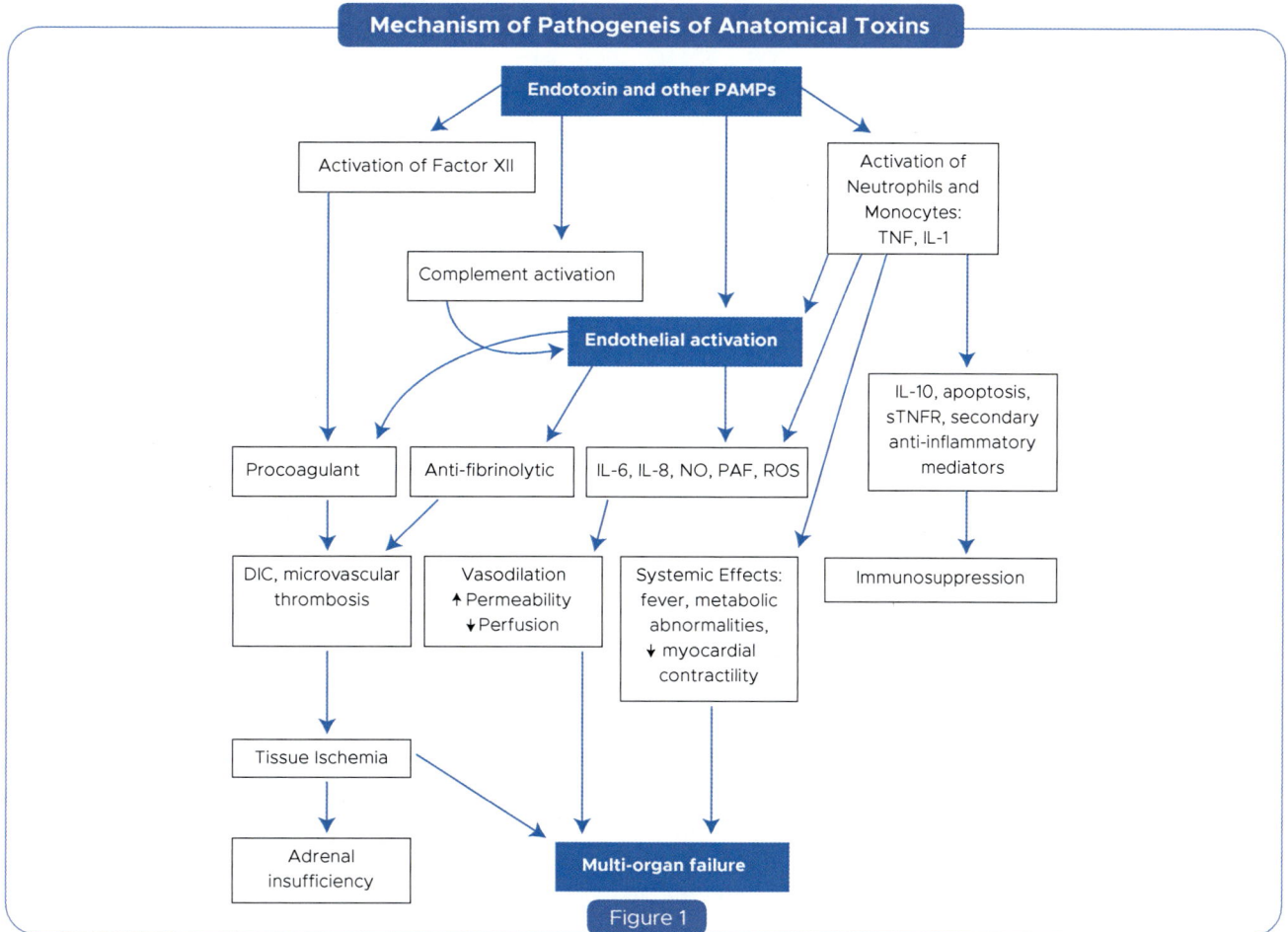

Figure 1

2. Exotoxins

Protein secretions of living cells

- Some are delivered by **type III secretion systems**
- Some have 2 components; **A = active, B = binding**
- Classified by site of action: **cytotoxins, enterotoxins, neurotoxins**
- Inactivated to make **toxoid vaccines**

Mechanism of Action of Key Exotoxins

	cAMP Inducers	Inhibitors of Protein Synthesis	Neurotoxins	Cytolysins	Superantigens
Organism	ETEC, V. cholerae, B. anthracis	C. diphtheriae, P. aeruginosa	C. tetani	C. perfringens	Staph aureus and Strep pyogenes
Toxin	Heat labile toxin, cholera toxin, edema factor	Diphtheria toxin, exotoxin A	Tetanus toxin	Alpha toxin	TSST-1 and Exotoxins A, C
Mechanism of action	ADP ribosylates GTP bp (adenylate cyclase)	ADP ribosylates eEF2 (targets heart, nerve, epithelium or liver)	Blocks release of glycine and GABA (inhibitory transmitters)	lecithinase	Cytokine storm involving APC/TH stimulation
Organism	B. pertussis	S. dysenteriae, EHEC	C. botulinum	Staph aureus	
Toxin	Pertussis toxin	Shiga toxin, verotoxin	Botulinum toxin	Alpha toxin	
Mechanism of action	ADP ribosylates G_i	Interferes with 60S ribosomal subunit	Blocks release of acetylcholine	Pore-forming	

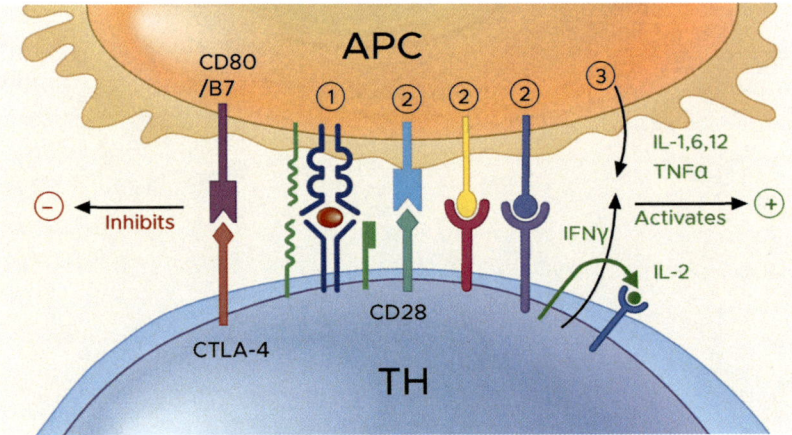

If you remember this diagram of the antigen presentation step between an APC and a TH cell, you hopefully remember that the crucial first step is the recognition of a specific peptide/MHC class II pair by the TCR. Superantigens cross-link the outside of the MHC to the TCR in the absence of any antigenic specificity and cause a cytokine storm: IFN-γ and IL-2 from the TH cell, and IL-1, 6 and TNF-α from the APC.

Figure 2

#MMC (Make Me Care!)

In this chapter we discussed the mechanisms of pathogenesis of endotoxin and superantigens. How would you expect the two patient presentations to differ?

Before you leave, can you....

1. Explain the lifecycles and physiology of the viruses, prokaryotes and eukaryotes.
2. Explain how the anatomy and physiology of microbes affects the choice of pharmacotherapy.
3. Understand the routes of entry of the major microbes of man.
4. Explain the pathogenic strategies of adherence, evasion of innate and adaptive immunity and toxin production employed by viruses, prokaryotes and eukaryotes.
5. List the molecular mechanisms of the major bacterial toxins.

Microbiology
Chapter two

The Genetics of Bacterial Drug Resistance

The Genetics of Bacterial Drug Resistance

Introduction
It is now a point of common agreement that we have entered the "post-antibiotic era" of medicine...a time when we will have more and more cases of multi-drug resistant microbes for which we have few therapeutic answers in our arsenal. This is because we have been unwise about our choices of how and when to treat, and more and more, this is becoming a topic stressed in USMLE questions. Concern that vancomycin-resistant *Staphylococcus aureus* (VRSA) and carbapenem-resistant *Klebsiella pneumoniae* (CRKP) might spread globally is well-founded, and if we want to prevent the problem from spreading, we need to understand how it began.

Forms of Drug Resistance
Since the discovery of the first antibiotic in 1928 it has been established that there are three general categories of drug resistance:

- **Intrinsic**
  If a microbe lacks the target molecule for a given drug, it is said to be intrinsically resistant. For example, *Mycoplasma* lacks a cell wall, the target for the penicillin-style drugs. Therefore, *Mycoplasma* is **intrinsically resistant** to penicillin.

- **Chromosomal**
  This means that the genes encoding resistance are found on the chromosome of the microbe. The most important example of such a trait in medicine is **methicillin-resistant *Staphylococcus aureus* (MRSA)**, which arose shortly after the introduction of methicillin in 1959. The mutation produced an altered **penicillin-binding protein (PBP)** which had diminished affinity for the drug. In the six decades since its first appearance, it has now become the predominant isolate found in hospitals worldwide. Most chromosomal genes encode structural proteins.

- **Plasmid-mediated**
  This means that the resistance genes are carried on plasmids which are extrachromosomal circles of DNA within the bacterial cell. Most plasmid resistances encode enzymes. The drug resistances encoded on plasmids include:
    - **β lactamases** which inactivate penicillin and cephalosporins
    - **Efflux pumps** for tetracycline and sulfonamides
    - **Phosphorylases**, acetylases and adenosylases which modify aminoglycosides and chloramphenicol
    - Ribosomal **methylases** for macrolides, lincosamides
    - Enzymes which **inactivate ribosomal binding** sites for tetracycline
    - **Ligase** which creates cell wall pentapeptides that end in D-Ala-D-Lac which will not bind vancomycin

The problem, of course, is that microbes would simply like to remain alive. It is actually not in their best interests to kill their hosts, but often medicine has taken a "scorched earth" approach to kill all of them rather than foster a more healthy and realistic discussion of management of well-being in the presence of a diverse microbiome.

The mutations which gave us the first drug resistances arose in chromosomes spontaneously, and those microbes which possessed the resistance genes had selective advantage in the presence of our drugs. Over many decades, the resistant populations became the predominant clones, and so we have been forced over time to develop more and more antimicrobics.

The DNA of Bacteria

Bacteria have 3 types of DNA molecules which can be transcribed and translated to create the proteins they need.

1. Chromosome
- The largest molecule of DNA in the cell which contains all genes essential for life. It is a large, closed circle.
- Most chromosomal genes encode **structural proteins**.
- Because the chromosome encodes all essential genes, mutations in chromosomal genes have a high chance of damaging the bacterium.

2. Plasmid
- Circular genetic elements outside of the chromosome which encode non-essential (but potentially useful) genes.
- About 1/10th the size of the chromosome.
- Most plasmid genes encode enzymes.
- Today, the most common newly arising drug resistances are encoded on plasmids, and as you will see in our discussion, bacteria have developed accelerated techniques for trading plasmids with one another to assist their survival.

3. Bacteriophage genome
- The viruses of bacteria (bacteriophages or phages) may integrate their DNA into the chromosome of the cell they infect.
- This is an attribute of the lifecycle of the "temperate" or "lysogenic" phage, and for as long as the viral DNA is stably integrated into the bacterial chromosome, its genes are transcribed and translated just as if they belonged to the bacterium.

- This type of symbiosis is referred to as lysogenic conversion, and is the source of many important pathogenic traits in bacteria:
    - **L**abile toxin of ETEC
    - **O** antigen of *Salmonella*
    - **V**erotoxin of EHEC
    - **E**rythrogenic exotoxins of *Streptococcus pyogenes*
    - **D**iphtheria toxin
    - **C**holera toxin
    - **B**otulinum toxin
    - **S**higa toxin

We will go through the mechanism by which this occurs in detail, but for now, the mnemonic **LOVED CBS** can help you remember these important traits. (If you are **loved**, that Can Bring Sequelae…like pregnancy, since the bacteria in each of these cases, are "pregnant" with phage.)

Recombination

Since prokaryotes do not have a nuclear membrane (or any internal membranes), they do not have a mechanism to protect their DNA from enzymatic processes happening in the cytosol. If DNA were donated from one bacterial cell to another, therefore, the newly received DNA would not survive long. The process of **recombination** is designed to solve this problem by packaging DNA into circles which cannot be cleaved open, because their restriction endonuclease sites are protected by methylation. There are two forms of recombination which depend on the shape of the newly arrived, donated DNA molecule:

- **Homologous recombination** (for **short linear pieces**)
- **Site-specific recombination** (for **circular pieces** with restriction endonuclease sites in common with the chromosome or plasmid).

Remember that recombination must happen AFTER any DNA has been donated from one cell to another, or the donated DNA will be lost. It is simply easiest to explain it first, since every form of genetic exchange except one will require some sort of recombination at the end.

1. Homologous Recombination

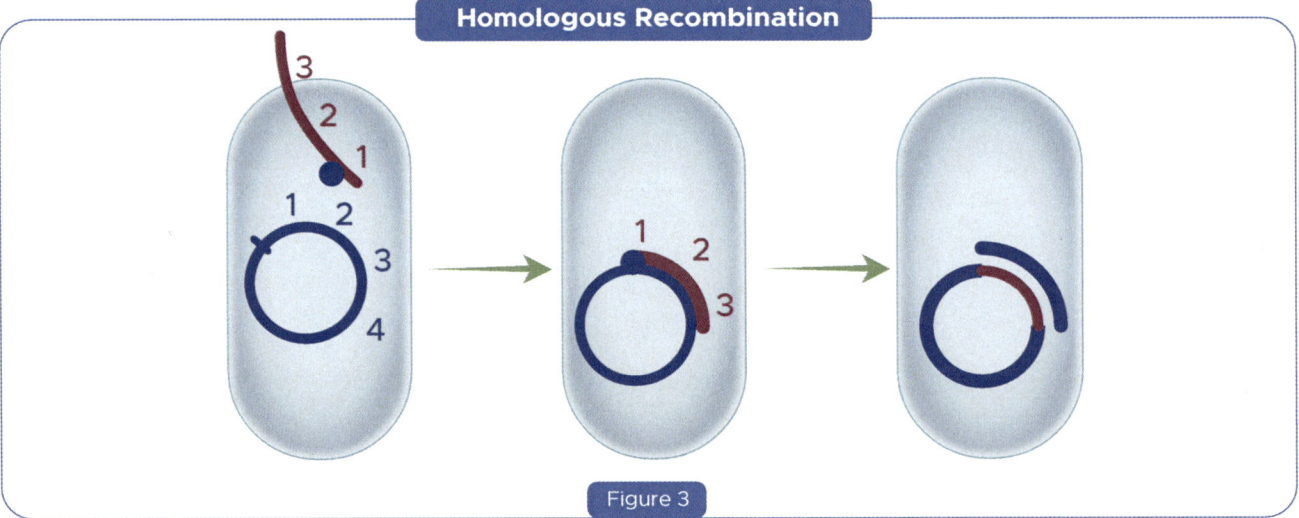

Figure 3

- The **exogenote** DNA (entering from outside) must be a linear piece with some sequence homology with the chromosome.
- The recipient cell must have **recombinase A**, which lines up the homologous sequences and does the cutting and pasting that removes the chromosomal piece and replaces it with the exogenote DNA.
- There is a **one-to-one exchange** of incoming DNA for what was previously in the chromosome.
- The newly excised DNA is destroyed by exonucleases.

2. Site-specific recombination

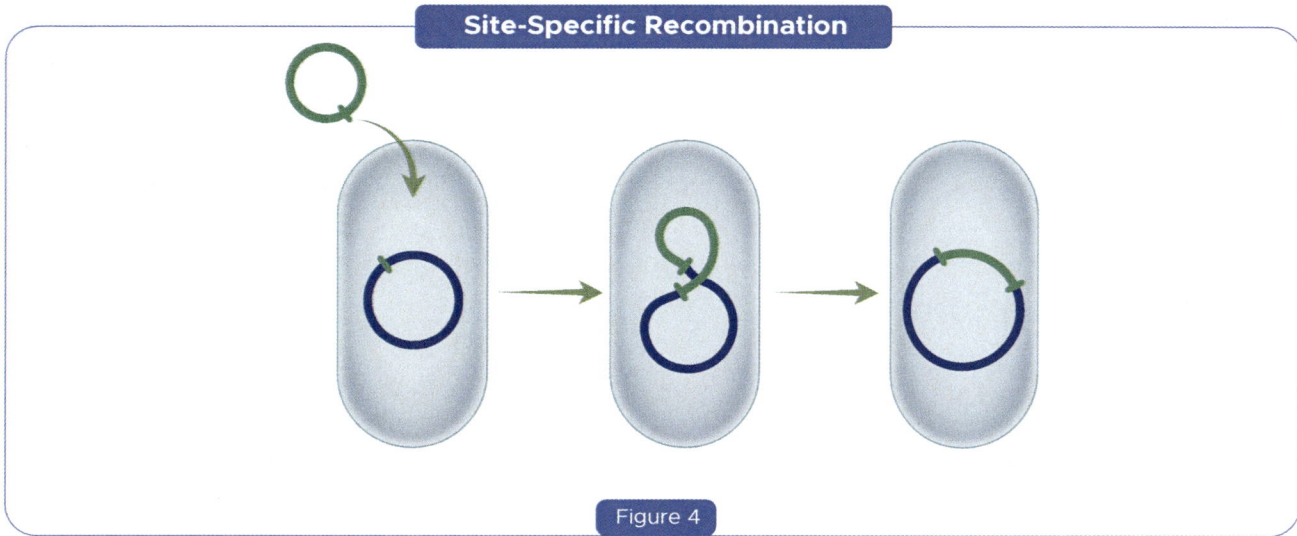

Figure 4

Site-specific recombination is a mechanism by which small circles of DNA (**plasmids, temperate phage** or **transposons**) can be incorporated into the chromosome.
- The incoming circle must have a **restriction endonuclease site** in common with the chromosome.
- When a cut is made in both circles of DNA at the restriction endonuclease sites, the sticky ends can re-anneal making the two circles into a figure eight.
- This effectively incorporates all of the small circle into the large circle, and **no DNA is lost** in the process.

Horizontal Gene Transfer

Since bacteria reproduce by binary fission, in the absence of mutation, there is no built-in mechanism for genetic exchange. Early experiments by Griffith, Lederberg and Tatum showed that bacteria were able to exchange DNA when grown together in culture.

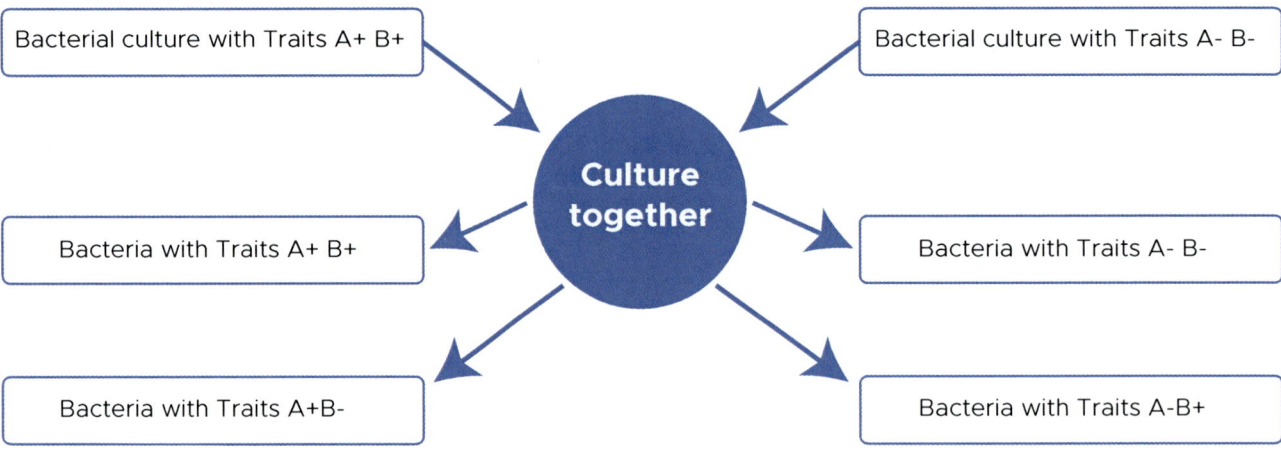

Although it would take decades to elucidate the mechanisms behind these results, we now know that horizontal genetic exchange in bacteria can occur via 3 mechanisms:
- Transformation
- Conjugation
- Transduction

If one of these mechanisms creates a new variant with improved survival ability, then natural selection will cause that variant to become a larger proportion of the population. Unfortunately, we provide the selection pressure to cause bacteria to continuously adapt to the pharmacologic agents that we use.

Mechanisms of Genetic Exchange
1. TransFormation (Free DNA)

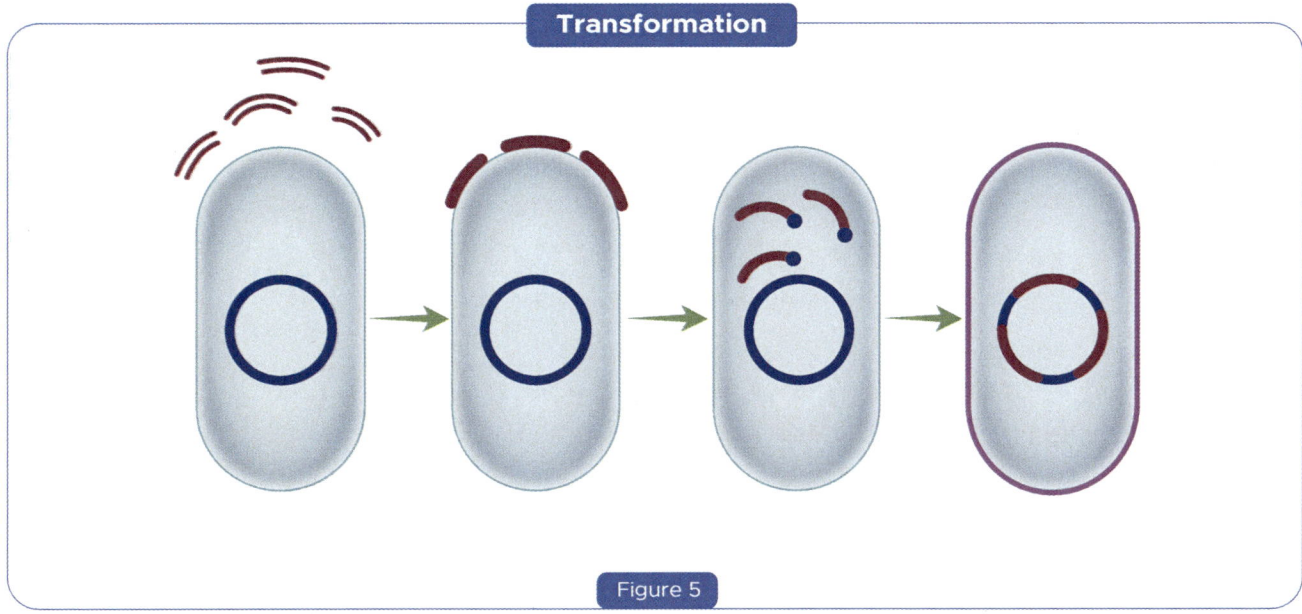

Figure 5

- Uptake and incorporation of **free DNA** from the environment by competent cells, followed by incorporation using **homologous recombination**.
- In order to do this, cells must become **"competent"** or able to bind free DNA to their membrane and import it. Some bacteria are **naturally competent (natural transformers)**:
    - **S**treptococcus pneumoniae
    - **B**acillus spp.
    - **H**aemophilus influenzae
    - **N**eisseria spp.

    (mnemonic: **S**ome **B**acteria **H**ave **N**atural competence)
- Once the DNA is inside the cell, the remainder of the process is **homologous recombination**, requiring recombinase A, and a one-to-one exchange of exogenote DNA for what was previously in the chromosome.
- If the acquisition of the new DNA allows the bacterium to have selective advantage (e.g. become encapsulated), then it has acquired a virulence trait by this method.

2. Conjugation

Conjugation is transfer of DNA using **cell-to-cell contact**. It is the analogy to sexual exchange in eukaryotes, and as such, requires a donor (male) and recipient (female). The gender role of the bacterium is determined by the presence or absence of a **fertility factor**, which is a plasmid with the genetic coding for the process.

- **Tra (transfer) operon** – a group of genes which control the production of sex pili, the conjugal bridge and the enzymes for DNA metabolism
- **oriV** – the origin of vegetative replication. The site where a replication fork will form when the plasmid replicates.
- **IS** – insertion site, a restriction endonuclease site that can allow the plasmid to integrate into the chromosome.
- **oriT** – the origin of transfer. The site of a break in one strand of the DNA duplex that will lead the strand across the conjugal bridge and into the recipient.

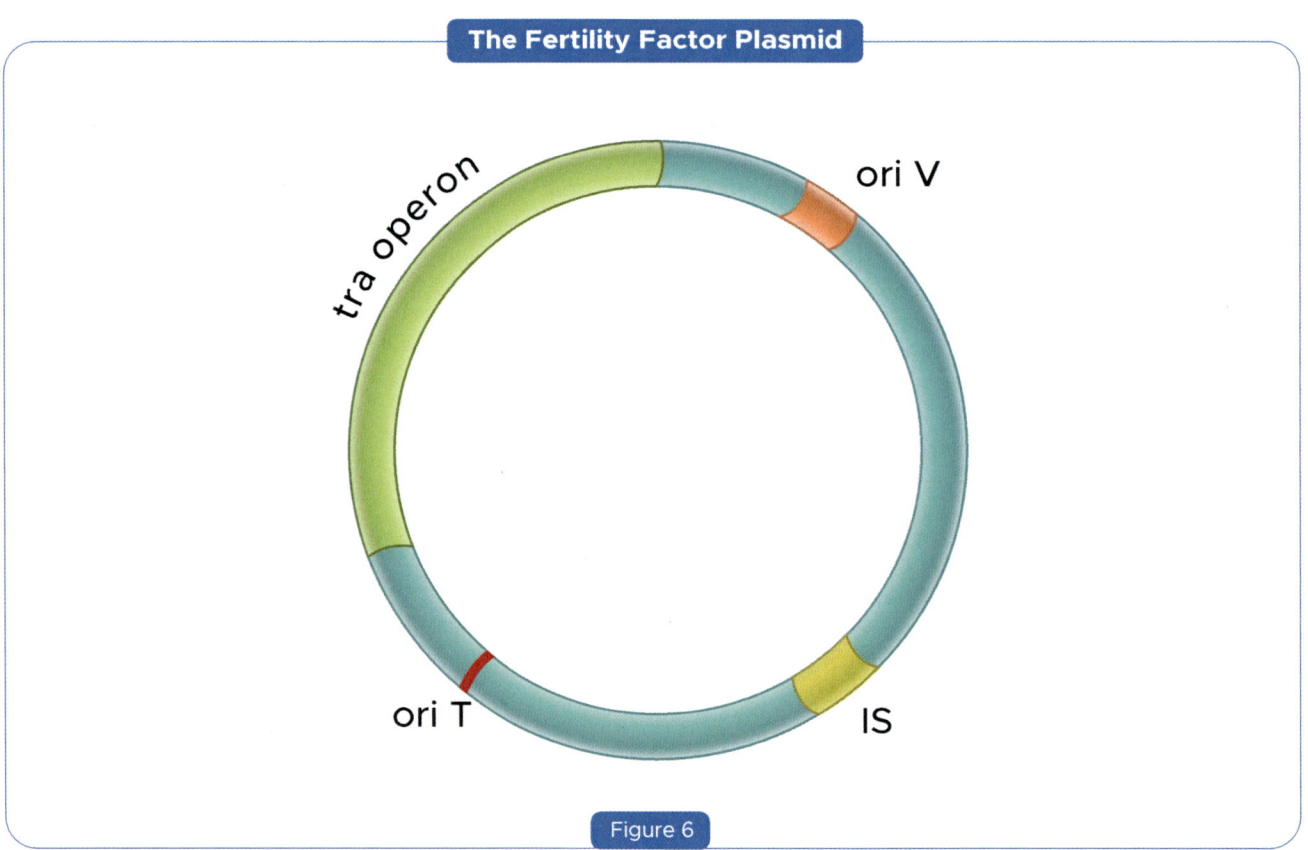

The Fertility Factor Plasmid

Figure 6

Mating Types of Bacteria

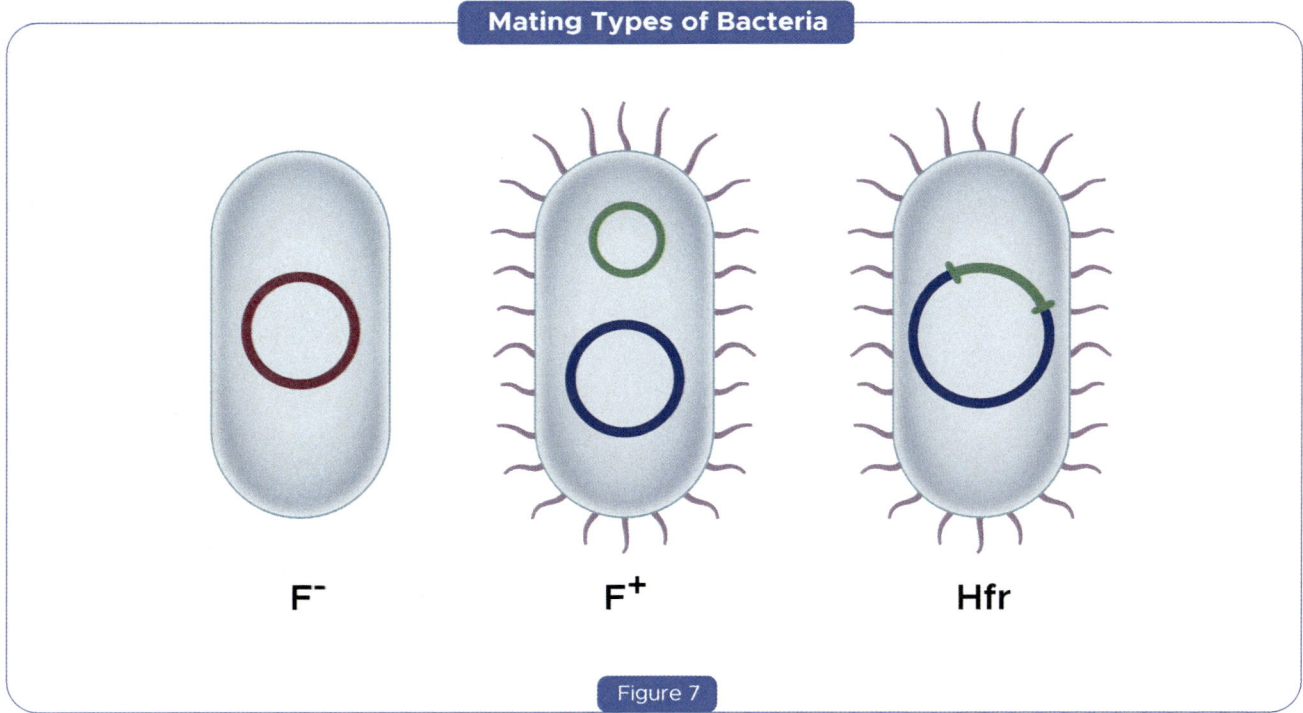

Figure 7

- There are 3 **mating types** of bacteria.
    - The **F⁻** cell is the **recipient** in any cross. It has chromosomal DNA but does not have a fertility factor.
    - The **F⁺** cell is a **donor** and has both chromosomal and fertility factor DNA in plasmid form.
    - The **Hfr (high frequency recombinant)** cell is a donor and has its fertility factor integrated into the chromosome as an **episome.**
- There are two possible conjugal crosses. Each requires a donor and a recipient, so they are **F⁺ to F⁻** and **Hfr to F⁻**.

The F⁺ by F⁻ Conjugal Cross

The F⁺ by F⁻ Conjugal Cross

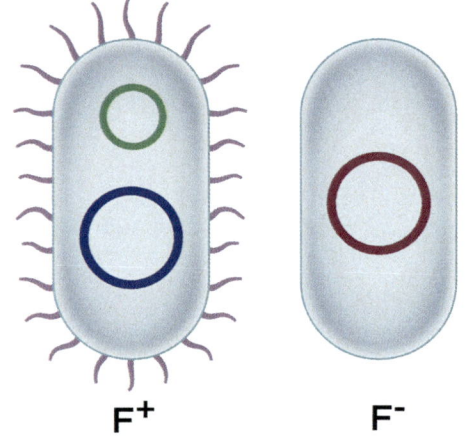

- The F⁺ cell modifies one of its sex pili to create a bridge to the cytoplasm of the F⁻ cell.

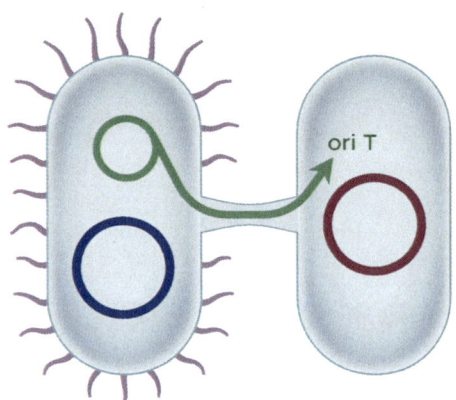

- A break in plasmid DNA is made at oriT and a single strand is transferred to the recipient.

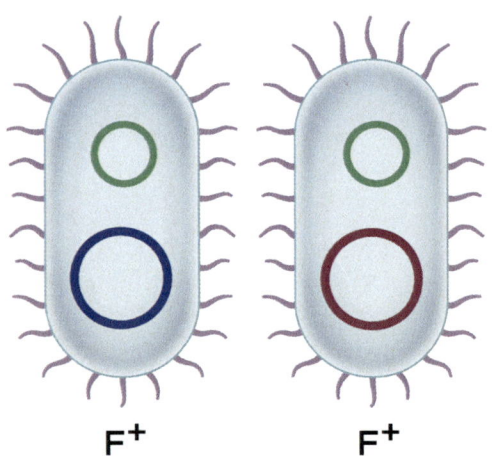

- Both cells duplicate the second strand of plasmid DNA.
- Each cell at the end has a fertility factor, so the recipient has become a donor in the process.

Figure 8

The Hfr x F⁻ Conjugal Cross
The Hfr Chromosome

Remember that in the Hfr chromosome, the fertility factor plasmid incorporated into the chromosome by the process of **site-specific recombination**. The two ends of the original restriction endonuclease site serve as the flanking sequences separating the two types of DNA. The process is still begun with a break at oriT, but now, because the **episome** is included within the chromosome, chromosomal alleles will follow oriT across the conjugal bridge. Which chromosomal genes will be successfully transferred depends on their **genetic proximity to oriT**, since it is a race to get across the conjugal bridge before it breaks.

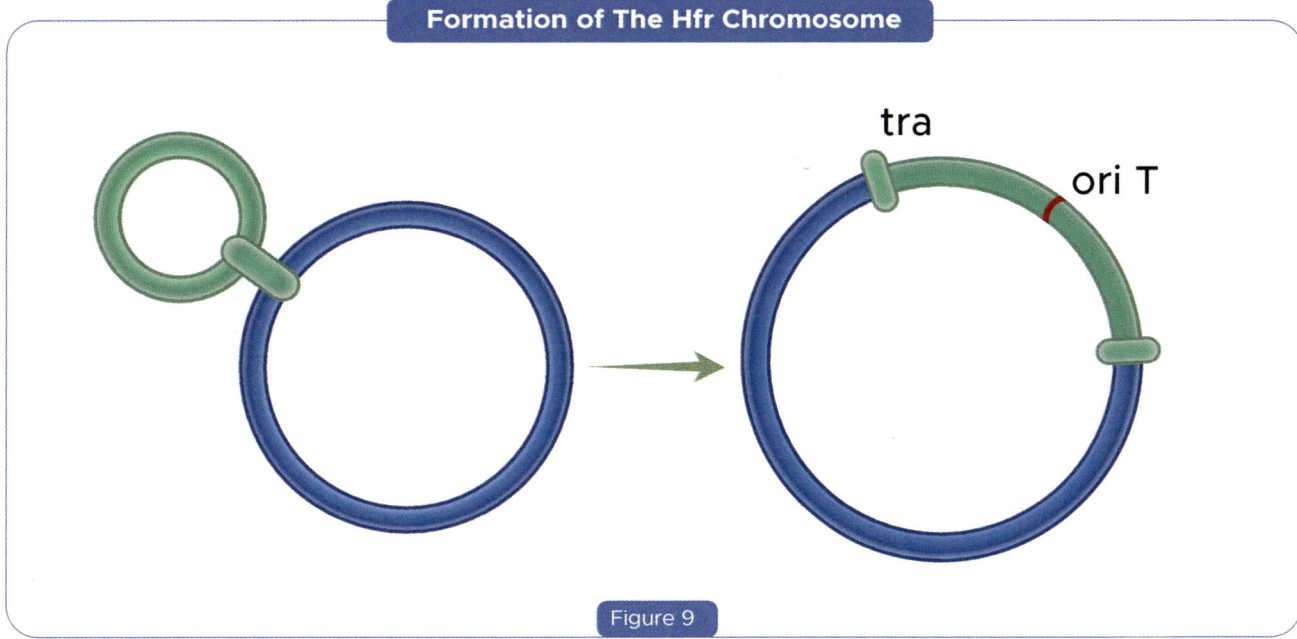

Figure 9

The Hfr x F⁻ Conjugal Cross

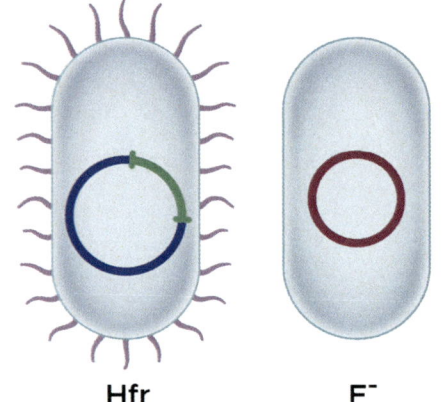

Hfr   **F⁻**

- The Hfr cell creates a conjugal bridge to the cytoplasm of the F⁻ cell by modifying one of its sex pili.

- A break is made in a single strand of the episome at oriT and leads across the bridge.

- The first few genes behind oriT are from the original fertility factor, but thereafter, chromosomal genes are pulled in order.

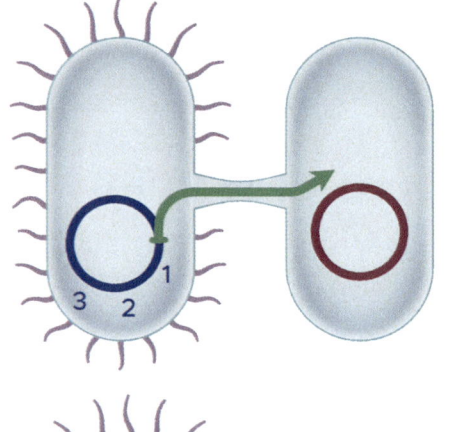

- Because of the fragility of the conjugal bridge, and the size of the entire Hfr chromosome, it is not possible for the entire molecule to cross over.

- The bridge breaks, and the DNA that has made it into the F⁻ cell must be homologously recombined in order to be saved.

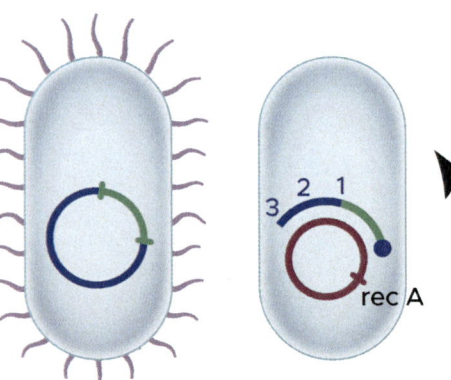

rec A

- The only possible homology in the chromosome of the F⁻ recipient is that of the **chromosome-origin DNA** (not episomal).

- Because there are 2 time-dependent variables (speed of getting across the bridge and speed of recombination), it becomes true that the **genes closest to oriT** are those that are most likely to be successfully transferred.

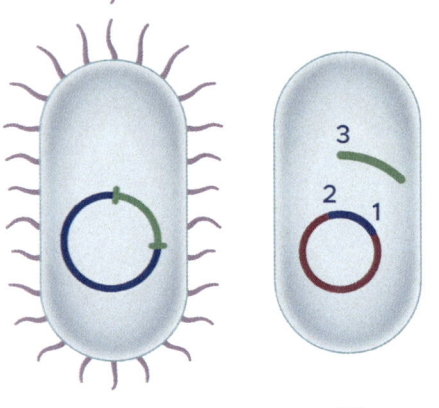

Hfr   **F⁻**

- Because the tra operon is not transferred, the **F⁻ cell remains a recipient with new chromosomal genes.**

Figure 10

3. Transduction

Transduction is the **delivery** of DNA from one bacterium to another using a phage as a vector. Because phages have two types of lifecycles, there are two types of transduction, both of which are accidents of the viral lifecycle.

a. Generalized transduction (an error of the lytic phage lifecycle)

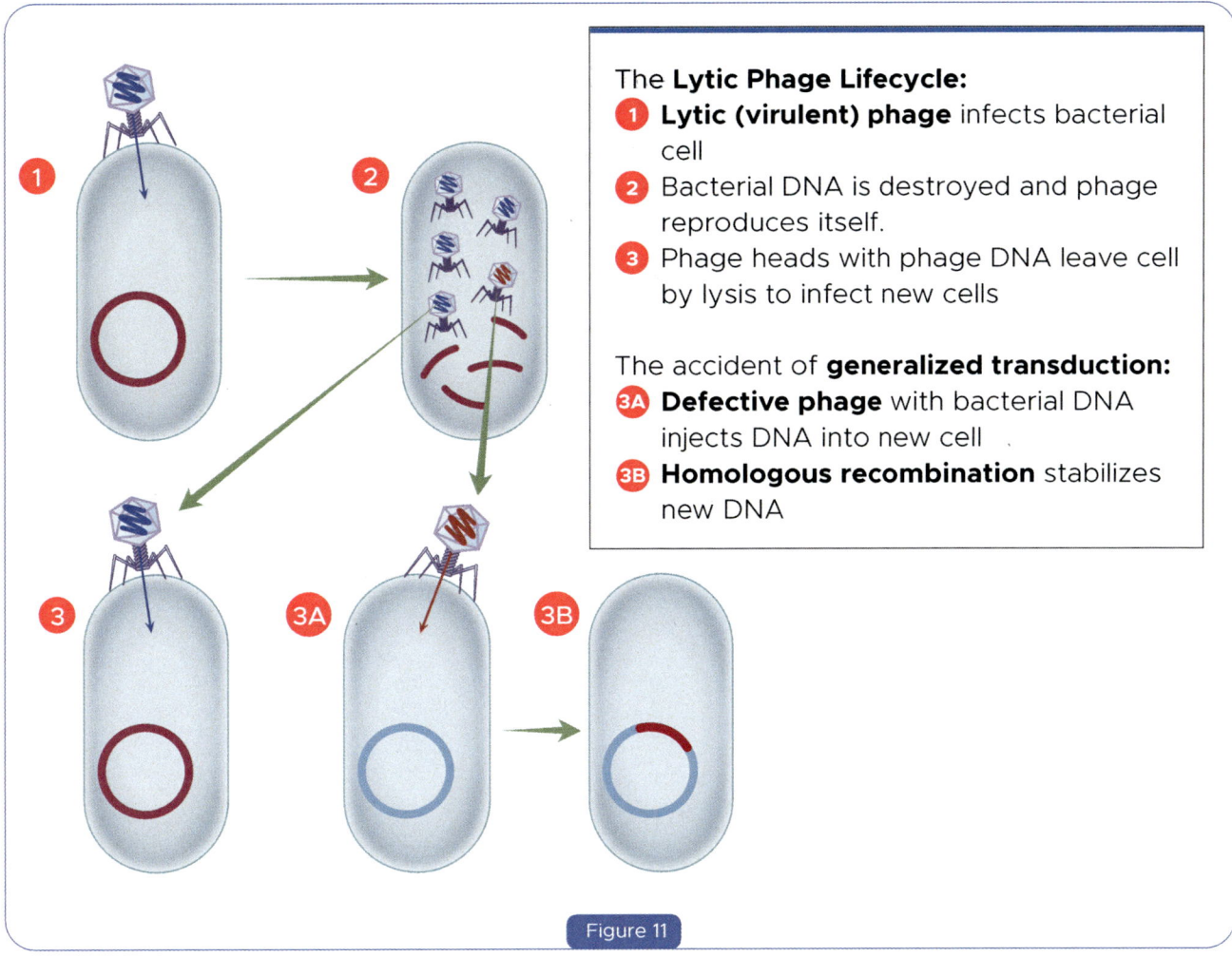

The **Lytic Phage Lifecycle:**
1. **Lytic (virulent) phage** infects bacterial cell
2. Bacterial DNA is destroyed and phage reproduces itself.
3. Phage heads with phage DNA leave cell by lysis to infect new cells

The accident of **generalized transduction:**
3A. **Defective phage** with bacterial DNA injects DNA into new cell
3B. **Homologous recombination** stabilizes new DNA

Figure 11

b. Specialized Transduction

Bacteriophages that undergo a stage of stable association of their genome within the bacterial cell are referred to as **temperate** or **lysogenic** phages. The association remains stable as long as a **repressor gene** in the viral genome prevents disassociation of the two, and the phage genome is replicated with each binary fission of the host bacterial cell. If the repressor gene is inactivated, the phage enters **induction**, removing its genome from the chromosome and beginning a phase of rapid lytic replication.

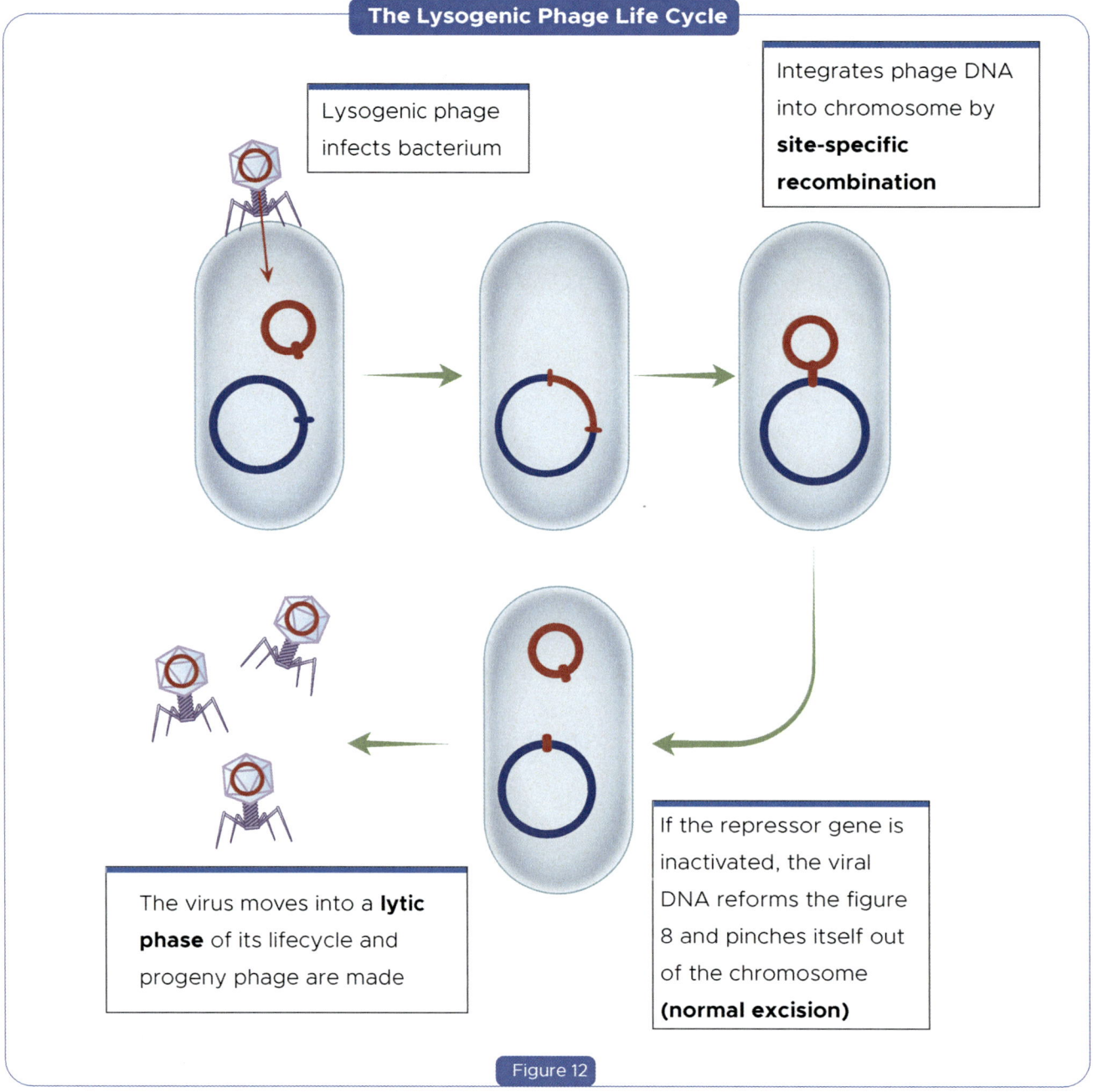

Figure 12

If an **error of the excision process** fails to excise all the viral DNA and instead takes bacterial DNA along, then this defective DNA is capable of causing **specialized transduction**.

Specialized Transduction

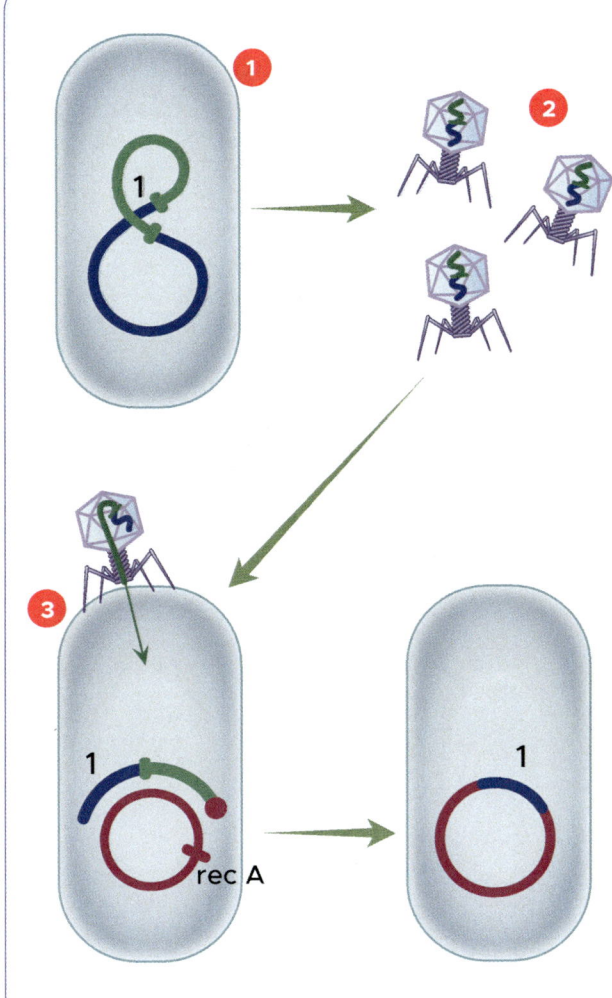

1 If during excision, the two restriction endonuclease sites fail to realign, the two molecules of DNA are pinched apart from one another in an erroneous fashion. This leaves a portion of the viral genome in the chromosome and puts a portion of the chromosome within the viral shells that are formed. Neither microbe can live without the DNA it needs.

2 A generation of defective tranducing phages are created, which are capable of injecting the defective DNA, but are not able to complete the lysogenic life cycle.

3 If rec A is available in the next infected cell, however, the genes captured from the chromosome of the first bacterial cell can be transferred to the other via **homologous recombination.**

Figure 13

Summary of Genetic Exchange Mechanisms

	Transformation	Conjugation		Transduction	
		F⁺ x F⁻	Hfr x F⁻	Generalized	Specialized
Mechanism	Free DNA from environment	Cell-to-cell transfer through sex pilus		Error of packaging	Error of excision
DNA transferred	Any	Fertility factor plasmid	Chrom. genes closest to oriT of episome	Any	Chrom. next to integration site of phage
Recombination	Homologous	No	Homologous		
Comments	Requires competency, sensitive to extracellular DNAses	Sex change in F⁻	No sex change	Error of lytic virus LC	Error of temperate phage LC
Important Examples	*Streptococcus pneumoniae* PBP mutations	Most gram negatives (all resistances), VRSA*		MRSA	

Neisseria gonorrhoeae is a special case of transfer via conjugation: it takes two plasmids to accomplish the job of one, because the plasmid with the DR genes has lost its tra operon. As long as there is another fertility factor in the cell that can build the conjugal bridge, the DR plasmid can sneak across in a process known as **mobilization.** So, if you ever see mention of "**conjugation using non-conjugative plasmids**" this is what they are referring to.

Transposition and the Development of Multi-Drug Resistance Plasmids

Barbara McClintock was awarded the Nobel Prize in 1983 for her pioneering work on "**mobile genetic elements**" in a plant related to corn. Since then, we have learned that it is similar elements capable of moving themselves from place to place **inside a bacterial cell** that have been the origin of an explosion of multiple drug resistance plasmids.

Transposition can be **replicative** (make multiple copies of a section of DNA), or **conservative** in which case it simply moves the single copy from one place to another. This may sound trivial since it is, by definition, happening INSIDE a single cell, but remember that not all molecules of DNA within a bacterium are equally easily transmitted, so if the movement causes insertion into a fertility factor, the mechanism of transfer to other cells is assured.

Transposable elements come in multiple sizes (**cassettes, integrons, insertion sequences, transposons**) depending on the amount of genetic material contained within. **Insertion sequences** are often considered the smallest mobile element, encoding simply the genes which cause transposition. **Transposons** by definition have additional genes, so our interest is in those that encode drug resistances.

Transposable elements are identified by the **indirect repeats** that flank the mobile segment. An indirect repeat reads identically right to left on the bottom strand and left to right on the top strand. This allows protection as a circle when it moves.

The transposase enzyme carried with the transposon makes a staggered cut in a new location of DNA inside the cell and pastes the transposon into that location. This creates gaps on either side of the location where the transposon landed, and those gaps are repaired to create **direct repeats** (directly superimposable nucleotide sequences) on either side of the mobile element. When transpositional events collect multiple resistance genes in a fertility factor plasmid, the result is a **resistance transfer factor**, of which the plasmid of vancomycin-resistant *Enterococcus* is an example.

Screening for Antibiotic Susceptibility
1. Kirby-Bauer Agar Disc Diffusion
The Kirby-Bauer is a rapid screening assay to test the isolate from a patient against a variety of antibiotics at a variety of concentrations.
- A confluent lawn of bacteria from the patient is created on an appropriate agar dish.
- Filter paper discs soaked in different antibiotics are dropped onto the surface of the dish. The antibiotics diffuse out from the disc, creating a concentration gradient that will either inhibit the microbe or not.
- The dish is incubated and examined for zones of inhibited growth in the proximity to the filter paper with antibiotics.
- This yields a quick, qualitative result that the isolate is resistant, intermediate or sensitive to the drug.

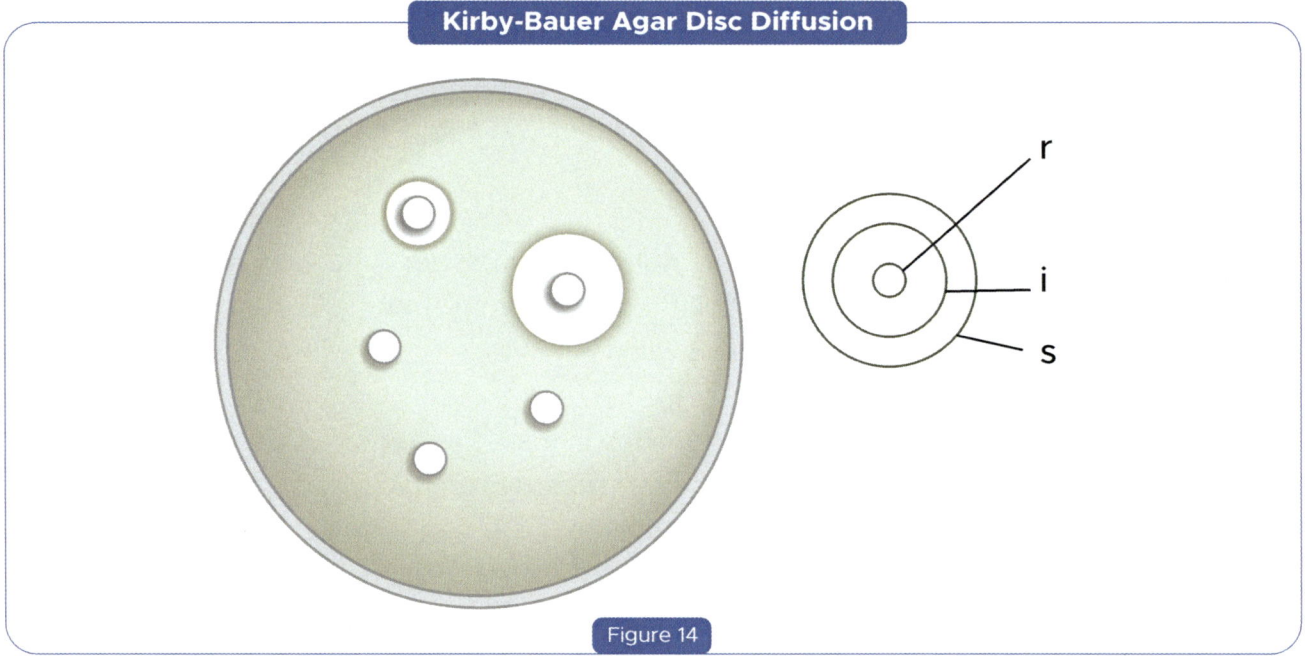

Kirby-Bauer Agar Disc Diffusion

Figure 14

2. Minimal Inhibitory Concentration (MIC)

The follow up to the Kirby-Bauer screening is to test for the minimum concentration of the drug which will inhibit growth of the isolate (**MIC**).

- Make a serial dilution of the drug in buffer and include a no drug control.
- Put a known number of bacteria from the patient's isolate into each tube, incubate and examine for turbidity as a measure of increased cell count.
- The MIC is the concentration of drug in the last tube in the dilution series with no visible growth. In this case 2 µg/mL.

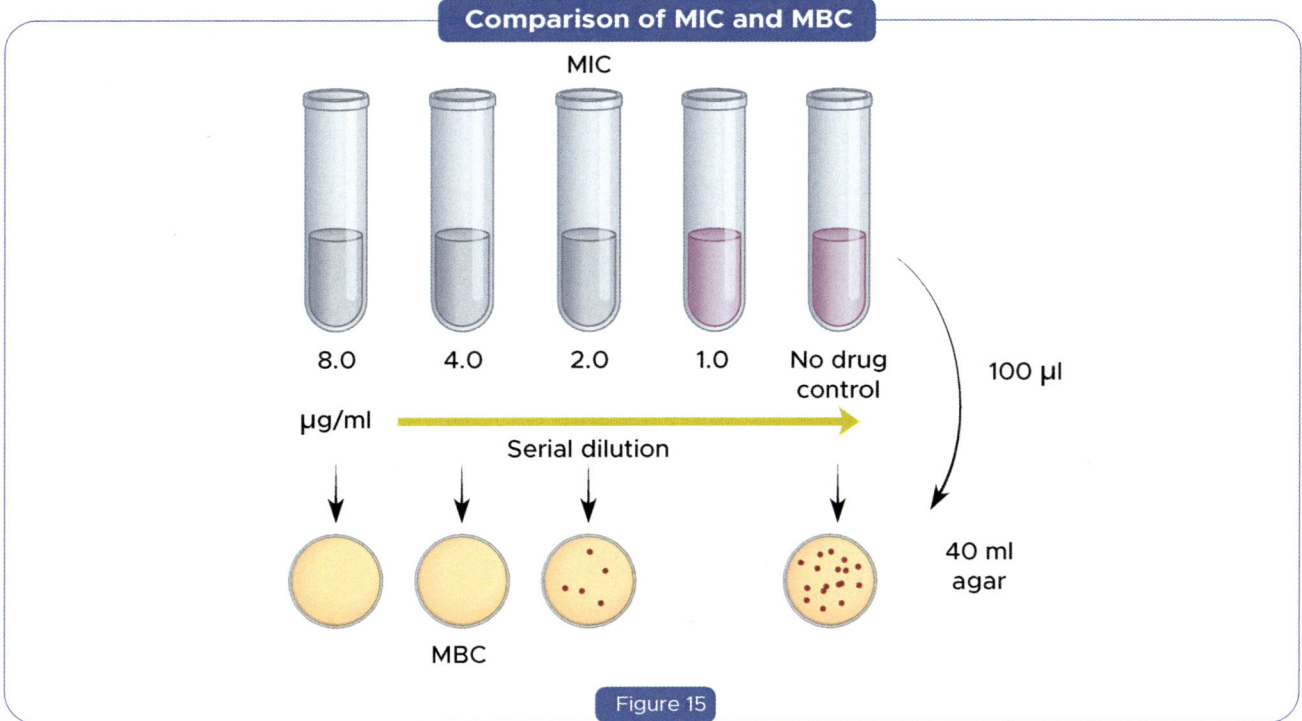

Figure 15

3. Minimal Bactericidal Concentration (MBC)

The MBC is a sub-plating step following the MIC and is not done routinely in all hospital labs.

- Take a small amount of culture fluid from the tubes of MIC series that have no visible growth (usually 100 µL) and plate it on 40 mL of agar.
- This dilution effectively removes the drug from the presence of the bacteria.
- If colonies grow after culture, the organisms were not dead. Thus, the MBC shown here is 4 µg/mL, one concentration above the value of the MIC.

Techniques of Infection Control

Definitions:
- **Sterilization**
  complete removal or killing of any viable agent.
- **Disinfection**
  removal of pathogens from an area.
- **Antiseptics**
  disinfectants for the skin.
- **Pasteurization**
  rapid heating and cooling of a liquid to remove pathogens.

Techniques of Physical Control:
- **Heat**
  autoclaves (steam under pressure) operate at 121°C, for 15-20 min. Dry heat requires 180°C for 2 hours to sterilize.
- **Radiation**
  creates thymine dimers in DNA
- **Filtration**
  removal based on size. Most bacteria will be removed with a 0.45μ filter, but smaller forms like *Mycoplasma* and spores require a 0.22 μ filter.

Techniques of Chemical Control:
- **Membrane-targeting agents**
  alcohol, phenol, detergents. **Enveloped viruses** can be inactivated with these agents.
- **Protein denaturing agents**
  chlorine, ethylene oxide, formaldehyde, glutaraldehyde, heavy metals, hydrogen peroxide, iodine. **Naked viruses** can be inactivated with these chemicals.

Before you leave, can you...

1. Define the roles of bacterial genes found in the chromosome, plasmid and bacteriophage genome.
2. Explain the means by which genetic material can be transferred horizontally between bacteria (conjugation, transformation, transduction).
3. Explain the role of lysogenic conversion and the bacterial pathogenicity factors which result from it.
4. Explain the mechanisms by which donated DNA can be stabilized in the genome of a recipient cell.
5. Explain how transposons move and have contributed to the rise of multi-drug resistant plasmids.
6. Identify the means by which the major bacterial pathogens acquire and trade resistance genes.
7. Explain how drug resistance is quantified in the laboratory and how hospitals disinfect and sterilize to prevent disease transmission.

Microbiology
Chapter three

Medically Important Bacteria

Medically Important Bacteria

1. Anatomy

The bacteria are divided into 3 major groups depending on their response to the Gram stain, which identifies the thickness and permeability of the cell wall.

- Gram positive
- Gram negative
- Non-Gram staining (some are too small to see, some lack a cell wall, some are intracellular, some are totally impermeable to stain)

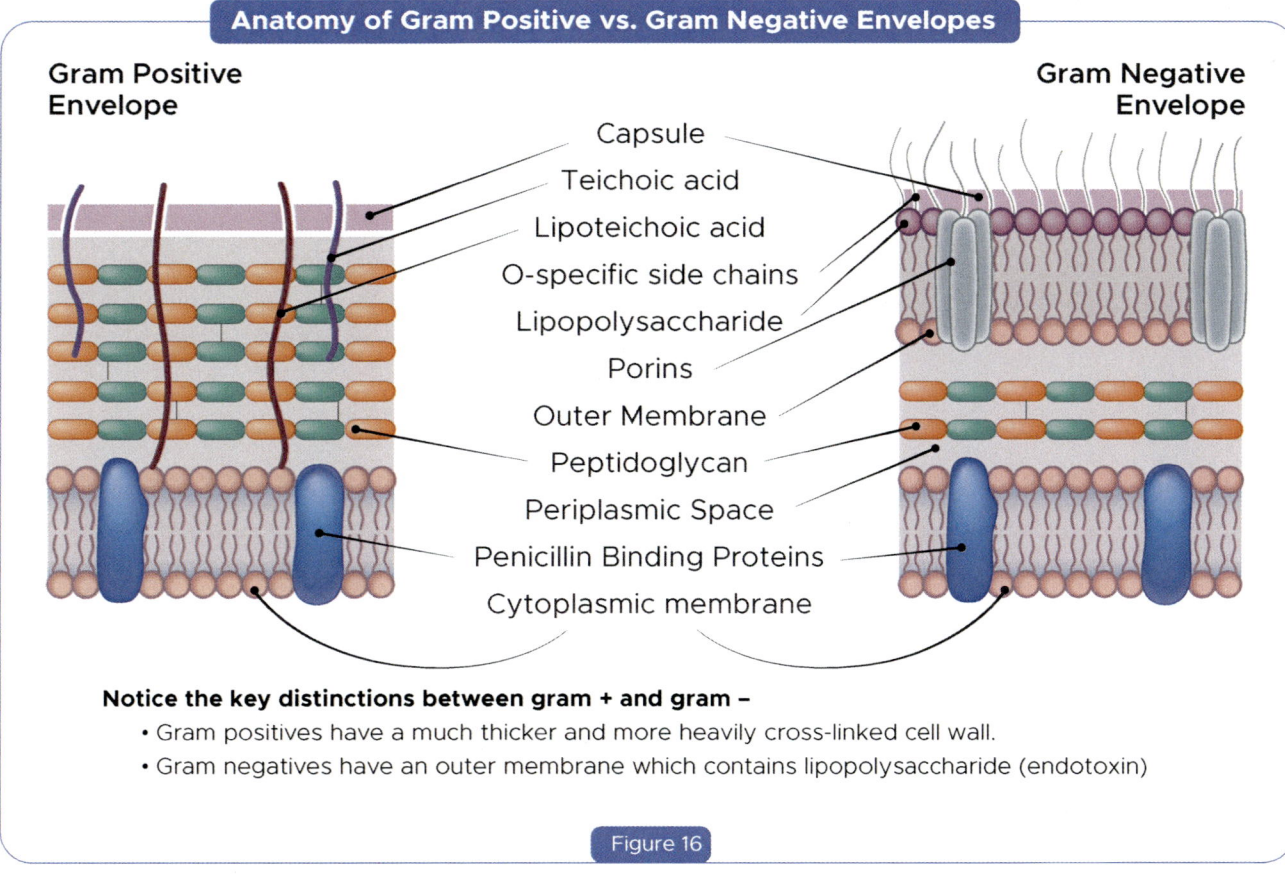

Anatomy of Gram Positive vs. Gram Negative Envelopes

Labels: Capsule, Teichoic acid, Lipoteichoic acid, O-specific side chains, Lipopolysaccharide, Porins, Outer Membrane, Peptidoglycan, Periplasmic Space, Penicillin Binding Proteins, Cytoplasmic membrane

Notice the key distinctions between gram + and gram −
- Gram positives have a much thicker and more heavily cross-linked cell wall.
- Gram negatives have an outer membrane which contains lipopolysaccharide (endotoxin)

Figure 16

Structure and Function of the Layers of the Bacterial Envelope

Layer	Gram positive	Gram negative
Capsule (slime layer, glycocalyx)	• **Polysaccharide gel*** which protects from phagocytosis. • Immunogenic except for *Neisseria meningitidis* type B (sialic acid) and *Streptococcus pyogenes* (hyaluronic acid)	
Outer membrane	none	• Lipopolysaccharide = endotoxin. Lipid A toxic component • Outer membrane proteins – antigenic variation, adherence • Porins – passive transport
Cell wall	Thick and highly cross-linked	Thin
	• **Peptidoglycan** – mesh of N-acetylglucosamine and N-acetylmuramic acid. • Rigidity, shape and protection from osmotic pressure • Gives Gram stain results • Target molecule for largest number of antibiotics	
Periplasmic space	none	• Space where molecules accumulate as they diffuse in and out of cell • Regulates osmotic pressure
Cytoplasmic (inner, plasma) membrane	• **Penicillin-binding proteins** (carboxypeptidases and transpeptidases) which create the cross-linkages in the cell wall. • Penicillin-style drugs bind here and inactivate.	

*Bacillus anthracis has a polypeptide capsule of poly-D-glutamate

2. Bacterial Replication

Bacteria reproduce by the process of binary fission. When placed in a new culture medium, there are 4 phases of growth:

- In the lag phase, the bacteria turn on the enzymes and coenzymes they need for the new culture medium. Note that there is no increase in cell number in the culture during this time.
- In the **logarithmic (exponential) growth phase**, the bacteria are dividing in two as quickly as they can, and each binary fission is said to be a **generation time**. Different bacteria require different times for doubling, but this phase will continue until something becomes rate limiting.
- In the **plateau phase**, the bacteria have either run out of nutrients or there has been a build up of toxic metabolites so that the number of cells dividing is roughly equivalent to the number dying.
- In the **decline phase**, for the same reasons, there are now more bacteria dying than dividing.

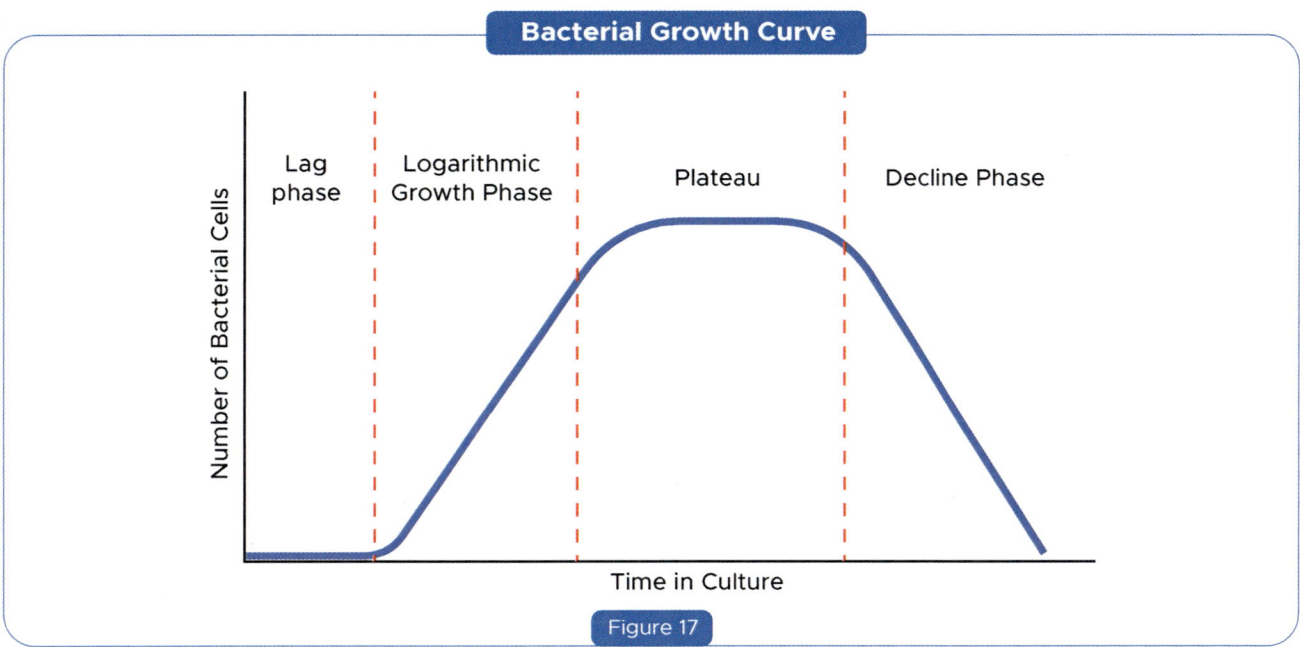

Figure 17

3. Spore Formation

There are two genera of bacteria that will produce spores when environmental conditions are not favorable for normal metabolism and replication: *Bacillus* and *Clostridium.*

This process occurs for survival purposes, to resist changes in temperature or pH, and is accompanied by the formation of a thick resistant coat of **keratin** and **peptidoglycan**, and the formation of enzymes which assist in the resistance to dessication and toxic materials.

Calcium dipicolinate and **dipicolinic acid synthetase** serve this function and are unique to bacterial spores.

Notice that **bacterial spores do not serve the purpose of reproduction**, although fungal spores are both protective and reproductive.

4. Bacterial Metabolism and Physiology

Although the USMLE has phased out questions regarding the details of laboratory procedures, some bacteria have special nutritional requirements which can be mentioned in stems as clues toward a diagnosis:

- *Mycoplasma*
  requires purines, pyrimidines and cholesterol
- *Francisella, Brucella, Legionella and Pasteurella*
  require cysteine (the 4 sisters "Ella" worship in the cysteine chapel)
- *Haemophilus*
  requires factors X and V (protoporphyrin and NAD) which can be obtained from lysed red blood cells (chocolate agar).

a. Oxygen Utilization

Most bacteria that infect humans use oxygen as their terminal electron acceptor for as long as it is available. When oxygen is not available they will ferment: they are **facultative anaerobes.** In order to capture oxygen from their environment, they use **superoxide dismutase,** (SOD) which combines oxygen with hydrogen to produce H_2O_2 (hydrogen peroxide). Most aerobes will then take the additional step of using **catalase** to convert their toxic, metabolic H_2O_2 back into water and singlet oxygen.

The outliers in this process that will require growth in special incubators are:

Bacterial oxygen Requirements

Obligate aerobes	Microaerophiles	Obligate anaerobes
• Require oxygen • Cannot ferment • Have SOD • **M**ycobacterium, **N**ocardia, **P**seudomonas, **C**orynebacterium, **B**acillus (**M**y **N**asal **P**assages **C**an **B**reathe)	• Require less than normal atmospheric pressure of oxygen • *Campylobacter, Helicobacter*	• Killed by oxygen • Lack SOD and usually catalase* • Are fermenters • Cannot use oxygen as their terminal electron acceptor • *Clostridium, Bacteroides, Actinomyces* (**C**an't **B**reathe **A**ir) *aerotolerant anaerobes can produce catalase to increase their survival in mixed cultures.

Figure 18

5. Pharmacotherapy

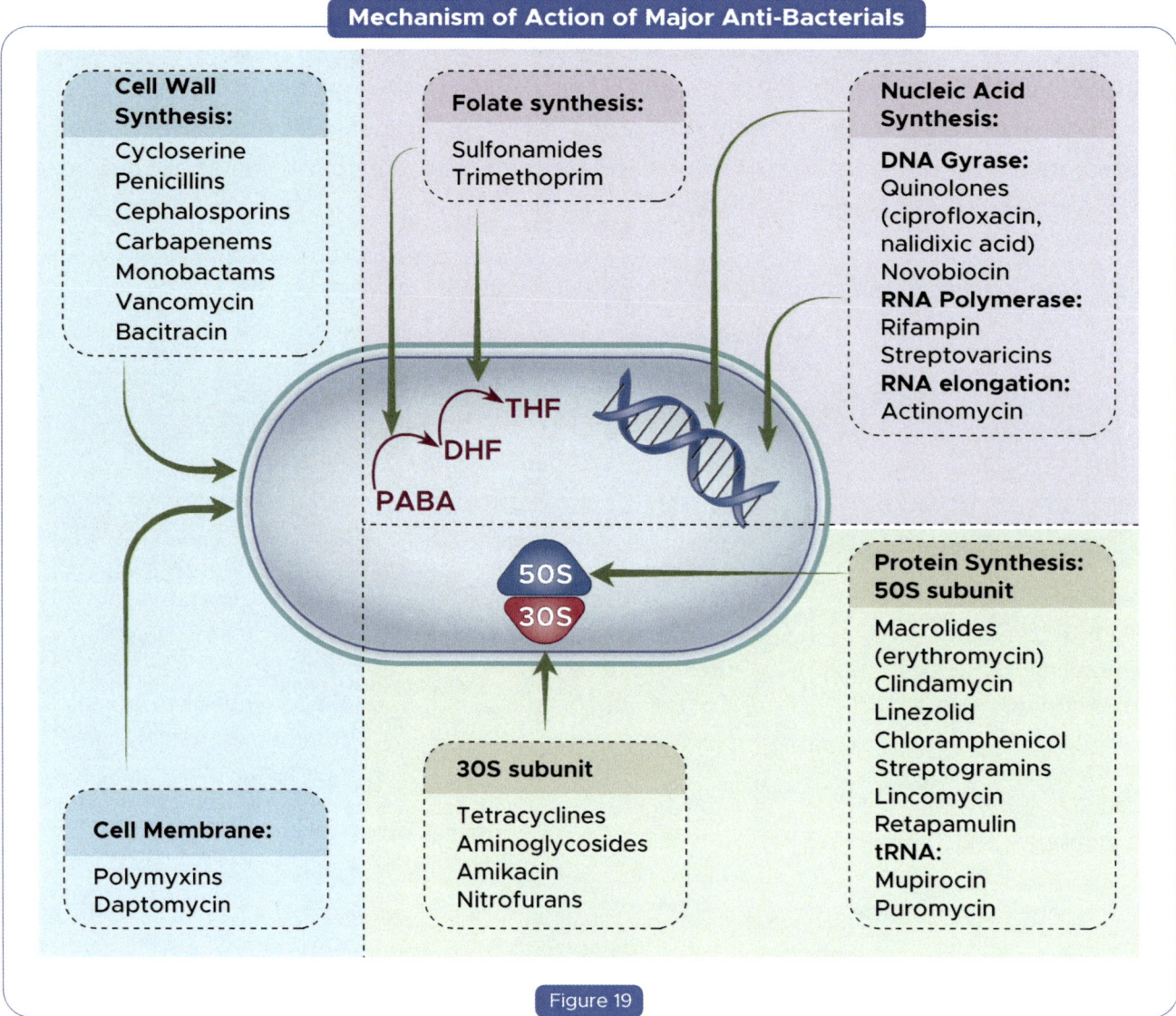

Figure 19

6. Laboratory Techniques
a. Principles of Culture
- **Obligate intracellular** organisms must be grown in tissue or cell culture.
- **Extracellular** or **facultative intracellular** organisms can be grown on agar or in broth.
    - **Selective media** add special nutrients to encourage a particular organism or inhibit others with antimicrobics.
    - **Differential media** allow multiple organisms to grow but allow for their differentiation on the basis of colony shape or color.

b. A Few Media for Name Recognition:
- Respiratory
  - *Corynebacterium* – Loeffler's or Tellurite (differential) gray/black colonies
  - *Mycobacterium* – Lowenstein-Jensen (selective)
  - *Legionella* – charcoal-yeast extract agar (contains cysteine and iron, selective)
- Gastrointestinal
  - Enteric bacteria – Eosin Methylene Blue or MacConkeys, differential to identify lactose fermenters vs. non-fermenters
  - *Vibrio cholerae* – thiosulfate citrate bile salts sucrose (TCBS) for high pH preference
- Genitourinary
  - *Neisseria* from sites with normal flora – Thayer-Martin (selective)
- CNS
  - *Neisseria* – chocolate agar

c. Microbiological Stains
1) Gram Stain
- All cocci are gram positive except *Neisseria*, *Moraxella* and *Veillonella*
- Both spore-formers are gram positive
- Human tissues will stain pink (no cell wall)

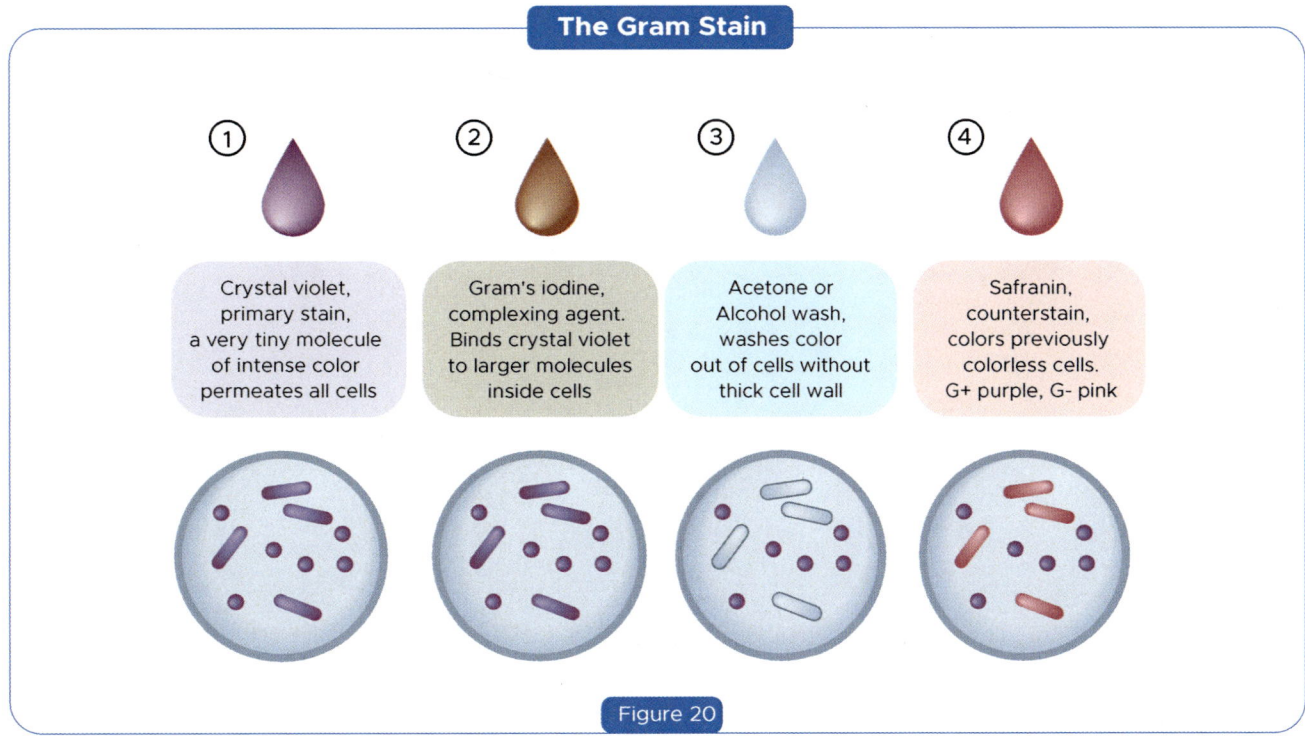

Figure 20

2) Acid-fast Stain (Ziehl-Neelsen or Kinyoun)

The acid-fast stain is used for cells that have a cell envelope rich in mycolic acids (long chain, waxy, fatty acids). The primary stain must be forced into the cells with heat or a shocking pH change. Once the stain is inside, the rest of the stain is conducted at room temperature, so once in, the primary stain cannot be washed out.

- *Mycobacterium* is acid-fast.
- *Nocardia* is partially acid-fast
- Human tissues will stain blue (no mycolic acids)

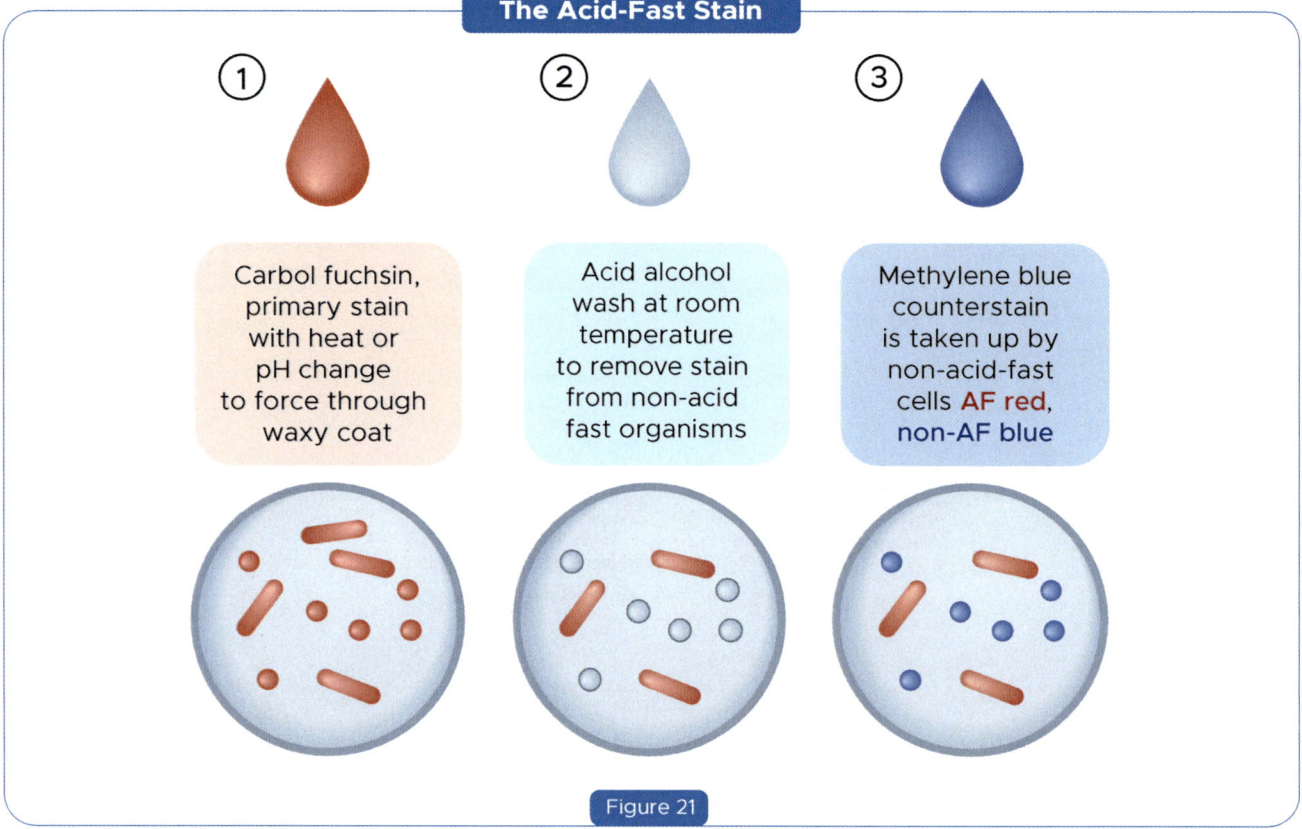

Figure 21

Medical Microbiology Essentials

Taxonomy of the Medically Important Bacteria

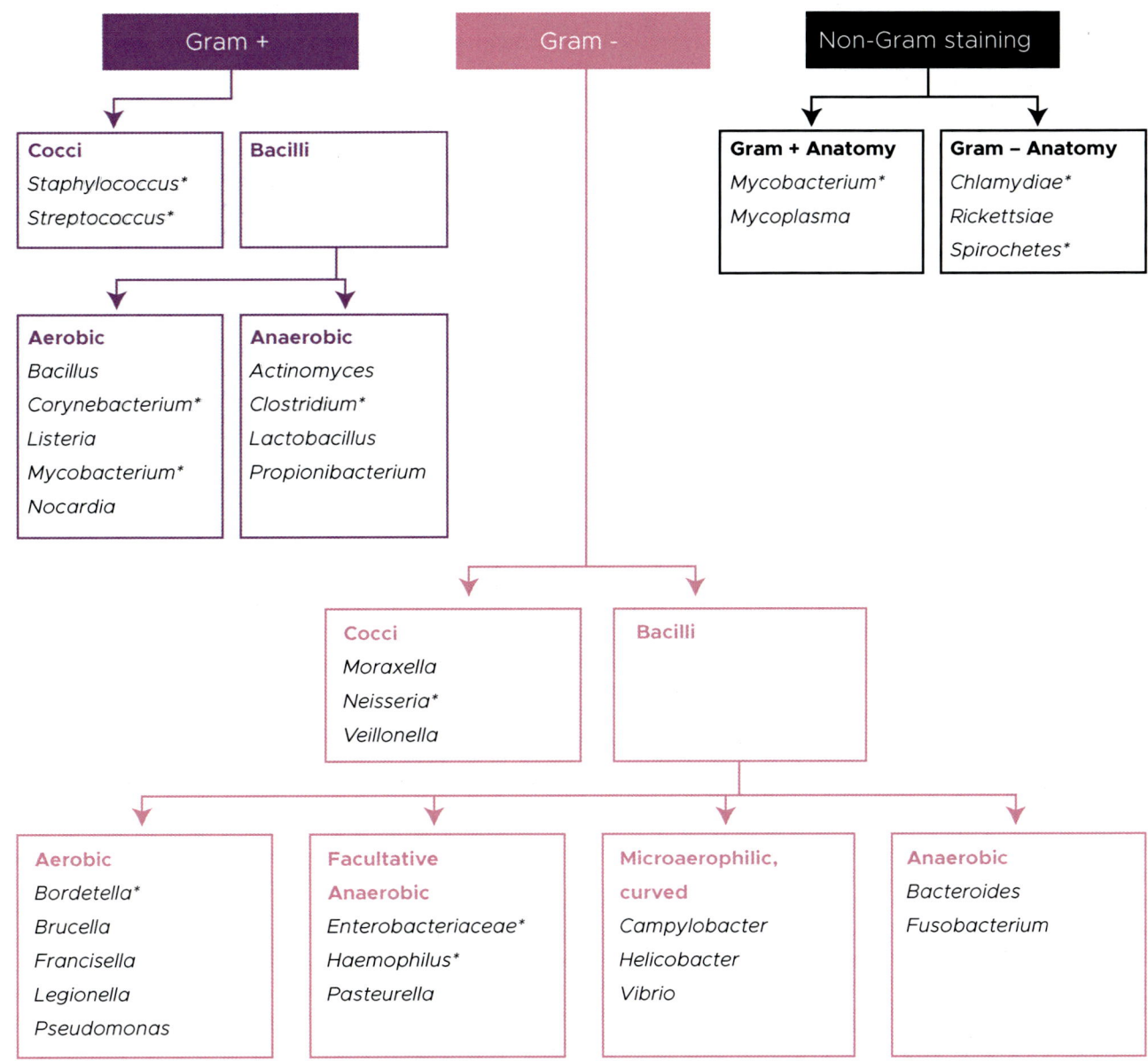

*Denotes microbes that are likely to generate more than one question

Gram-positive Cocci

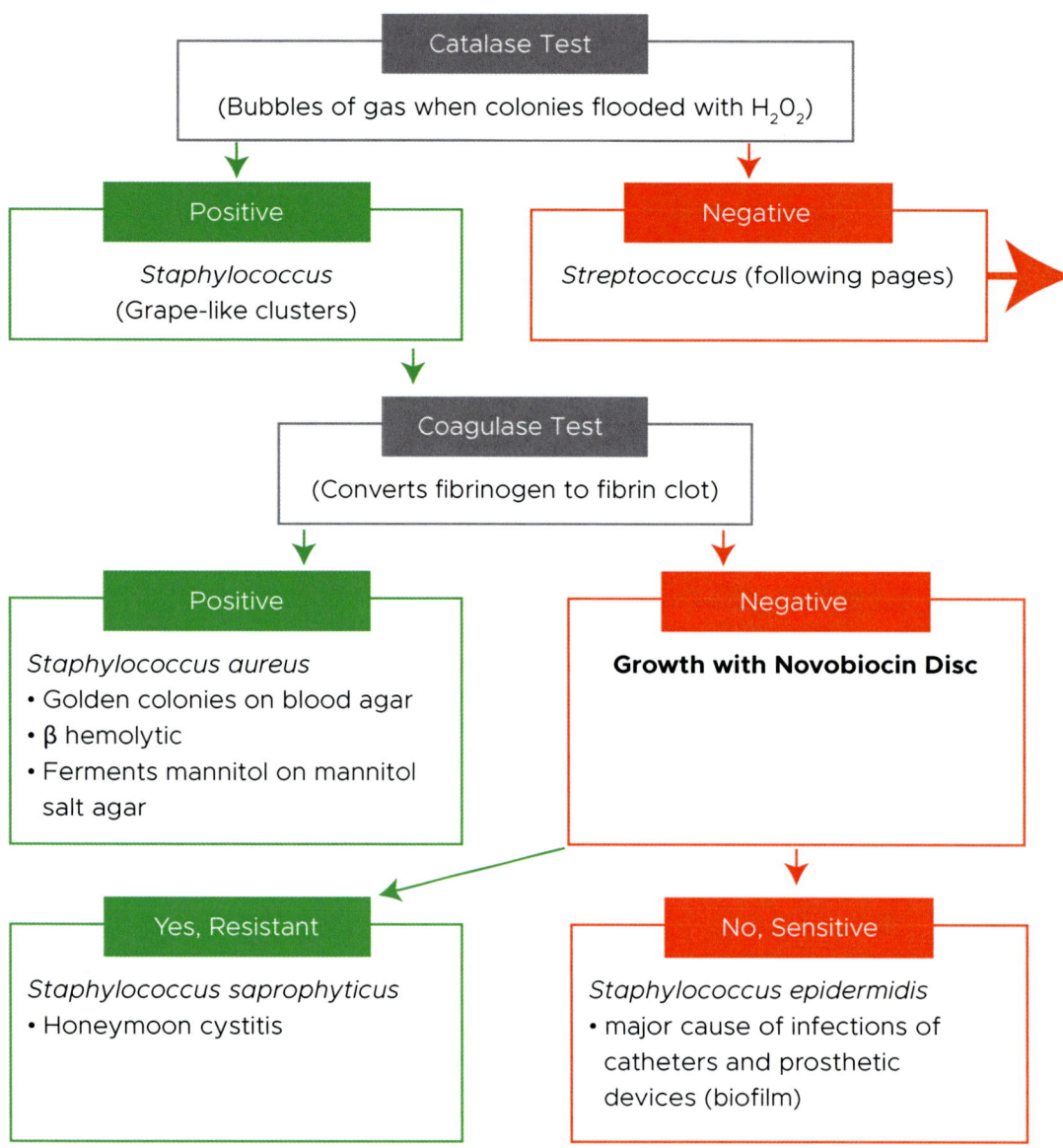

Gram positive, Catalase positive Cocci

a. Staphylococcus aureus
1) Epidemiology:
- normal flora of nose and skin (**halophilic**)
- 95% of all hospital isolates worldwide, **#1 cause of osteomyelitis**
- Transmission
    - sneezing
    - surgical wounds
    - contaminated food
- Predisposing conditions
    - Breaks in barrier system, foreign body, iv drug use
    - Failures of innate immunity against extracellular microbe
        - Neutropenia
        - CGD
    - Cystic fibrosis (neutrophil overload, chloride imbalances)

Medical Microbiology Essentials

2) Patients, Pathogenesis and Pharmacotherapy:

Chief Complaint	Vignette Clues	Pathogenesis	Rx
(Food Poisoning) Vomiting and diarrhea	**3-6 hrs** after meal, **Salty or creamy** foods, picnic	Preformed enterotoxins (A-E) heat stable in food	Supportive
(Endocarditis) Fever, fatigue, malaise, **acute onset**	**Acute** onset and clinical course, heart murmur	• Coagulase (inhibits phagocytosis) • alpha toxin (cytolytic)	MSSA – nafcillin, gentamicin MRSA - Vancomycin VRSA- quinupristin, dalfopristin, linezolid
(Pneumonia) Cough, fever	**Typical pneumonia**, post-influenza, nosocomial, ventilator, **pink sputum**		MSSA – amoxicillin-clavulanate MRSA – tetracyclines or TMP/SMX
(Osteomyelitis) Bone pain, fever	Entry through **trauma, lytic lesions on imaging, #1 cause** unless SS is mentioned		Vancomycin, linezolid, daptomycin
Skin or subcutaneous infection	**Mastitis**, new nursing mother		Amoxicillin-clavulanate
	Scalded Skin Syndrome Diffuse **epidermal peeling**	Above plus **exfoliatins** (proteases cleave cadherin desmoglein 1)	Oxacillin, cephalosporin, clindamycin
	(Impetigo) bullous vesicles, children and adolescents		Mupirocin (topical)
	Post-surgical	As above, plus **TSST-1** (superantigen)	See discussion of MSSA, MRSA, VRSA above
Fever, prostration	**Toxic Shock Syndrome** Surgical packing or extended use tampons, **scarlatiniform rash desquamates** and **involves palms and soles,** hypotension, multi-organ failure	**TSST-1**	Vancomycin, linezolid, daptomycin

b. Coagulase-negative Staphylococci (CoNS)

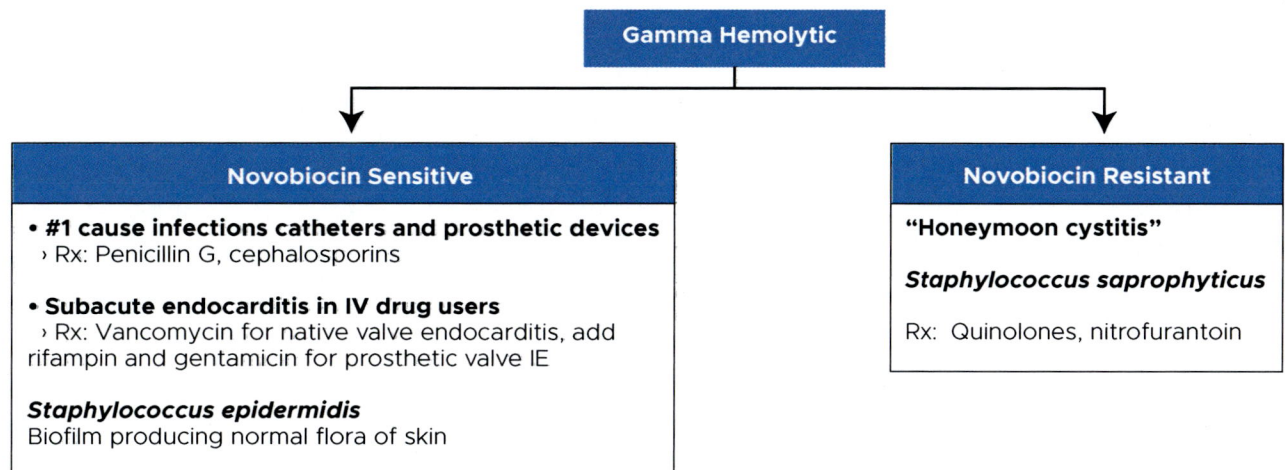

Gamma Hemolytic

Novobiocin Sensitive
- **#1 cause infections catheters and prosthetic devices**
  › Rx: Penicillin G, cephalosporins

- **Subacute endocarditis in IV drug users**
  › Rx: Vancomycin for native valve endocarditis, add rifampin and gentamicin for prosthetic valve IE

Staphylococcus epidermidis
Biofilm producing normal flora of skin

Novobiocin Resistant
"Honeymoon cystitis"

Staphylococcus saprophyticus

Rx: Quinolones, nitrofurantoin

Gram positive, Catalase negative Cocci

Streptococcus (chains or pairs of cocci)

Matrix-Assisted Laser Desorption/Ionization Time of Flight Mass Spectrometry (MALDI-TOF MS) has revolutionized diagnosis in clinical labs and is causing massive reassessments of the taxonomic groupings of these organisms. For now, the genera of **gram positive, catalase negative, cocci in pairs or chains** are analyzed first by their pattern of hemolysis and are referenced by their **Lancefield Group** (an homage to Rebecca Lancefield who received a Nobel Prize for her analysis their cell wall carbohydrates.) Stay tuned for more taxonomic shuffling, but here is what I think is testable now.

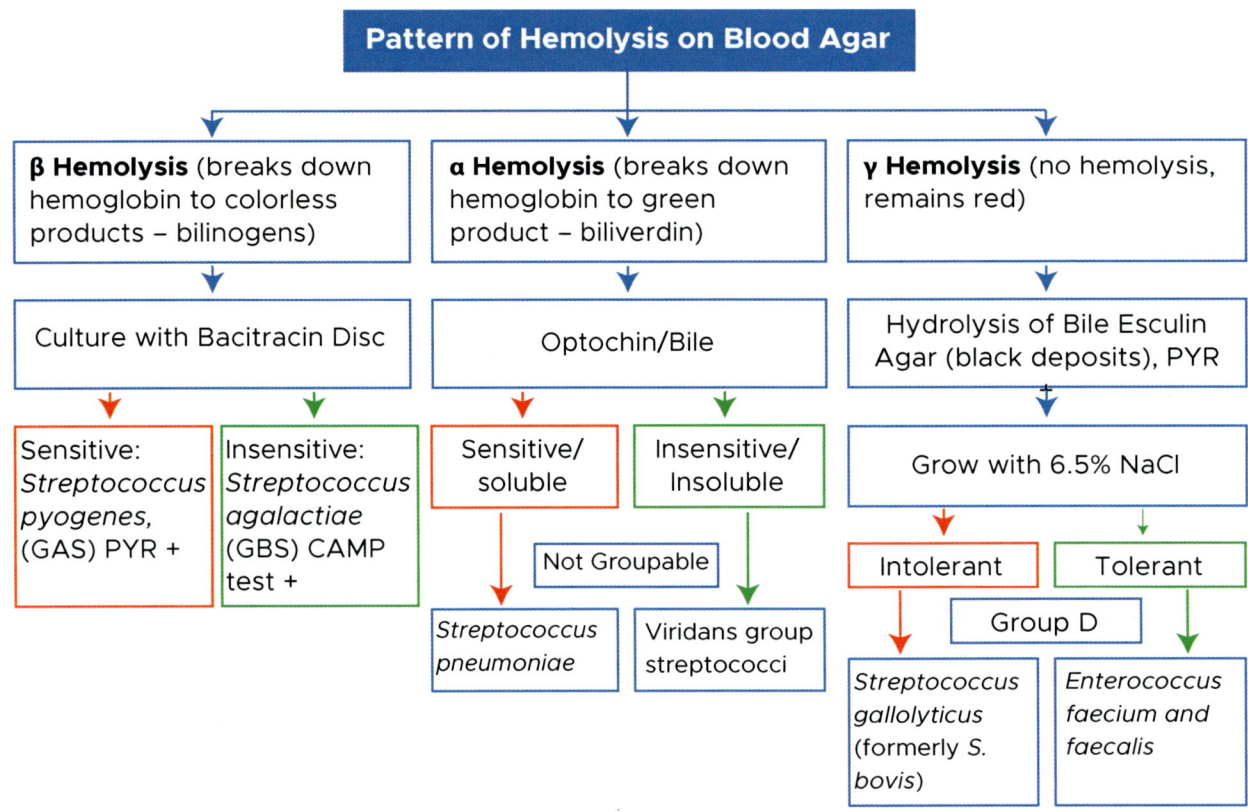

I'm sure this looks like hopeless memorization, but here's a handy memory tool:
In each case, **the diagnostic test is one alphabetical letter off from the Lancefield Group** name.
- Group **A** – **B**acitracin sensitive
- Group **B** – **C**AMP test (A test for an incomplete hemolysin demonstrated by growth next to *Staphylococcus aureus*). The two growing together produce an arrowhead of increased hemolysis over the amount that either would produce independently.
- Group **D** – **E**sculin agar
- Pneumococcus (no group letter) – **O**ptochin sensitive

Beta Hemolytic Streptococci

a. *Streptococcus pyogenes* (GAS)
1) Epidemiology:
- 2-4 per 100,000 population in developed countries
- Children 3 years and older
- Throat and skin, transferred via respiratory droplets, direct contact

2) Patients, Pathogenesis, and Pharmacotherapy
Suppurative Infections:

Chief Complaint	Vignette Clues	Pathogenesis	Rx
Sore throat, fever (Strep throat)	Acute, abscesses on tonsillar pillars, tender cervical lymphadenopathy. Rapid strep test misses ¼, culture all negatives with bacitracin disc on blood agar, PYR+	• Pili, fibronectin binding protein and teichoic acids for adherence • Hyaluronic acid capsule is anti-phagocytic and non-immunogenic • M protein (serotyping) prevents C3b opsonization	Penicillin, amoxicillin
Sore throat, fever, rash (Scarlet fever)	Immigrant child, blanching circumoral sandpaper rash. Strawberry tongue, nausea, vomiting	Above plus: • erythrogenic exotoxins act as superantigens (phage encoded), • streptokinase • hyaluronidase • streptolysins O and S (hemolytic exotoxins)	Penicillins
Skin infection	Keratinized layers, weeping, oozing, **honey-crusted** (impetigo)	Adherence factors, anti-phagocytic factors as above	Topical mupirocin, retapamulin, fusidic acid
	Superficial epidermis (erysipelas)	Exotoxins from superficial infections	Penicillin
Subcutaneous infection, cellulitis, fasciitis	Rapid spread from point of initial wound, flesh eating	Spreading factors: • Hyaluronidase • Streptokinase • Streptodornase	Debridement Penicillin, ampicillin, clindamycin

Non-Suppurative Sequelae:

Chief Complaint	Vignette Clues	Pathogenesis	Rx
Joint pain, rash, fever 3-4 weeks after pharyngitis	Immigrant child, ASO titer > 200, 6-15 year old, erythema marginatum (Rheumatic Fever)	M types 1,3,5,6,18 X-reaction between M protein and collagen. Type II hypersensitivity	Penicillin, anti-inflammatories
Edema, hematuria 10 days post pharyngitis or impetigo	6-8 years old, proteinuria, hypertension (Post-streptococcal glomerulonephritis)	Type III hypersensitivity	Penicillin Symptomatic therapy

b. *Streptococcus agalactiae (GBS)*

1) Epidemiology:
- 15-20% of women are colonized, vaginal flora
- Transmitted intrapartum to neonate, particularly in prolonged, difficult labors
- Inhaled, into blood, survives neutrophil phagocytosis to cross BB barrier
- #1 cause of neonatal meningitis and septicemia

2) Pathogenesis:
- Encapsulated
- β hemolysin and CAMP factor (partial hemolysin)

3) Treatment/Prophylaxis:
- For neonate – ampicillin with aminoglycoside or cephalosporin
- For women who are carriers – ampicillin or penicillin during delivery

Alpha Hemolytic Streptococci

a. *Streptococcus pneumoniae*
1) Epidemiology:
- Reservoir in upper respiratory tract
- Transmission by respiratory droplets
- 93 serotypes of capsule, transformation common because of natural competence
- Number one cause of typical pneumonia, adult meningitis, otitis media and sinusitis

2) Patients, Pathogenesis and Pharmacotherapy:

Chief Complaint	Vignette Clues	Pathogenesis	Rx
Cough, fever (typical pneumonia)	Productive cough, **rusty sputum**, lobar consolidation, acute onset, sputum with **encapsulated diplococci**	• **Previous damage to mucociliary escalator** by antecedent influenza, COPD, congestive heart failure, alcoholism (loss of gag reflex) • **IgA protease** • Teichoic acids for attachment • **Pneumolysin O** anatomical toxin damages epithelium, inhibits respiratory burst and complement fixation	Penicillin, Cefotaxime, Fluoroquinolones
Headache, stiff neck, fever (meningitis)	Acute onset, CSF: ↑PMNs, ↓ glucose, ↑ protein, gram + diplococci. Quellung or **latex particle agglutination positive** for capsular antigens	Asplenia allows encapsulated organisms to survive transit in blood	Ceftriaxone or cefotaxime
Pain in ear or sinuses, fever (Otitis media + sinusitis)	Bulging red tympanic membrane	IgA protease, teichoic acids	Amoxicillin

Prevention:
- PCV13 (pneumococcal conjugate vaccine) pediatric vaccine – 13 capsular serotypes conjugated to diphtheria toxoid.
- PPSV23 (pneumococcal polysaccharide vaccine) for adult, immunocompromised, asplenics – 23 serotypes without protein. (Current recommendation is one dose of PCV followed by boosters of PPSV23).

b. Viridans Group Streptococci (S. anginosus, S. mutans, S. oralis, S. sanguinis, S. sobrinus)

1) Epidemiology:
- Normal flora oropharynx (plaque and dental caries)
- Transmission endogenous
- Most common cause of subacute endocarditis in patients with preexisting damage to heart valves.

2) Patients, Pathogenesis and Pharmacotherapy:

Chief Complaint	Vignette Clues	Pathogenesis	Rx
Fatigue, fever, malaise, weight loss (subacute bacterial endocarditis)	• Indolent onset, post oral surgery • Heart murmur • Splinter hemorrhages and Janeway lesions, (non-tender) from septic emboli, • Osler nodes, Roth spots, (tender; immune complex disease) Rheumatoid factor	• Patient with known or unknown valvular disease but strong immunity to normal flora • Transient bacteremia causes immune complexes • Infectious endotheliosis (endothelial cells secrete IL-1, IL-6, IL-8 and TNF-α) • Biofilm (?) S. sanguinis makes H_2O_2 to damage valves.	Penicillin Ceftriaxone Antibiotics prior to dental work in patients with preexisting damage to valves

Gamma Hemolytic Gram+Cocci; Group D Streptococci

a. Enterococcus faecium and faecalis and Streptococcus gallolyticus

1) Epidemiology:
- Normal flora of colon and urogenital
- Transmission endogenous
- 5-15% of cases of subacute bacterial endocarditis
- One of top 3 causes of hospital-acquired infection

2) Patients, Pathogenesis and Pharmacotherapy:

Chief Complaint	Vignette Clues	Pathogenesis	Rx
Fatigue, fever, malaise, weight loss (subacute endocarditis)	**Elderly male**, prostate issues or bowel damage, preexisting damage to valves. Left sided (aortic valve). **Subacute endocarditis** (splinter hemorrhages, murmur). **PYR+, black deposits on bile-esculin agar.** *Enterococcus* tolerates 6.5% NaCl, *S. gallolyticus* does not.	**Colon cancer lesions** or medical procedures allow access to blood. **Preexisting damage to valves.**	All strains have some drug resistance. VRE have D-Ala-D-Lac pentapeptide bridges that will not bind drug. Penicillin and gentamicin prophylaxis before GI/GU surgery
Fever, right upper quadrant pain (cholescystitis)	Cholecystitis and cholangitis	**Bile and salt tolerance** allow survival in gall bladder and bowel	Ampicillin, vancomycin, sensitivity testing. VRE – daptomycin, linezolid
Fever, dysuria, flank pain (urinary tract infection)	UTI; nosocomial, associated with catheterization or instrumentation	Medical instrumentation	Ampicillin, Nitrofurantoin, Fosfomycin

Gram-Positive Bacilli

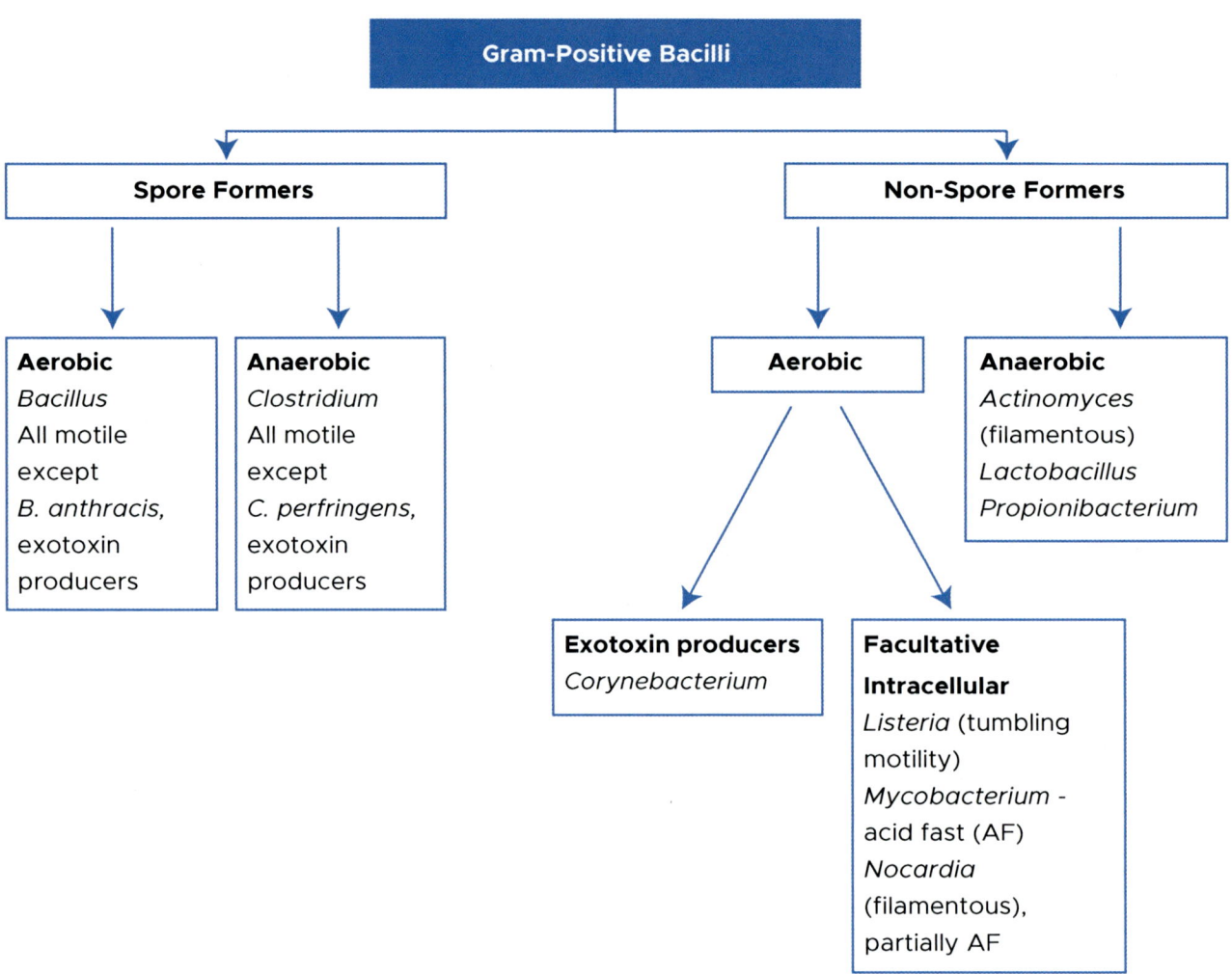

Spore Formers
Aerobic

Bacillus

1) Epidemiology:
- B. anthracis
    - Widespread in nature, animal hides, soil
    - Transmission by inhalation or implantation of spores (form inside bacillus)
    - Concern as potential biowarfare agent
- B. cereus
    - Rice and vegetable dishes
    - Foodborne disease associated with buffet-style restaurants

2) Patients, Pathogenesis and Pharmacotherapy

Chief Complaint	Vignette Clues	Pathogenesis	Rx
Black skin ulcer **Cutaneous anthrax**	Traumatic injury from animal hides, wool. Gram positive bacillus cultured from lesion.	Local production of toxin **Capsule** – **poly-D-glutamate.** Prevents phagocytosis, immunogenic	Ciprofloxacin Doxycycline
Fever, malaise, cough **Pulmonary anthrax**	*B.anthracis* acute onset, rapidly fatal pneumonia, **mediastinal widening, importer of animal hides or wool.** Postal worker exposed to white powder. Gram positive bacillus cultured from blood, sputum.	**Anthrax toxin – 3 component**, heat labile. **Edema factor** – binds calmodulin and acts as adenylate cyclase **Lethal factor** – kills cells **Protective antigen** – binding component	Ciprofloxacin Doxycycline Toxoid vaccine used by military
Vomiting, diarrhea **B. cereus food poisoning.**	1-6 hours after meal. Rice dishes in buffet-style restaurant	**Emetic toxin** preformed **Diarrheal toxin** produced in vivo (18 hours) increases cAMP	Supportive

Spore Formers
Anaerobic

Clostridium and Clostridioides

1) Epidemiology:
- Widespread in soil, persists as spore
- Transmission by traumatic implantation (*C. tetani, C. perfringens, C. botulinum*)
- Transmission food borne – *C. botulinum*
- Normal flora – *Clostridioides difficile*
    - #1 nosocomial, antibiotic-associated diarrhea, #3 nosocomial overall; 400% increase in last decade

2) Patients, Pathogenesis and Pharmacotherapy:

Chief Complaint	Vignette Clues	Pathogenesis	Rx
Muscle spasms *Clostridium tetani*	Unvaccinated, dirty puncture wound (**trismus** – lock jaw, **risus sardonicus** – facial grimace, **opisthotonos** – contraction of back muscles.	**Tetanospasmin** carried intraxonally to CNS, **blocks glycine and GABA, rigid paralysis.**	Hyperimmune globulin plus metronidazole or penicillin Vaccine – toxoid in DTaP, Tdap

Prevention – Wound Management:

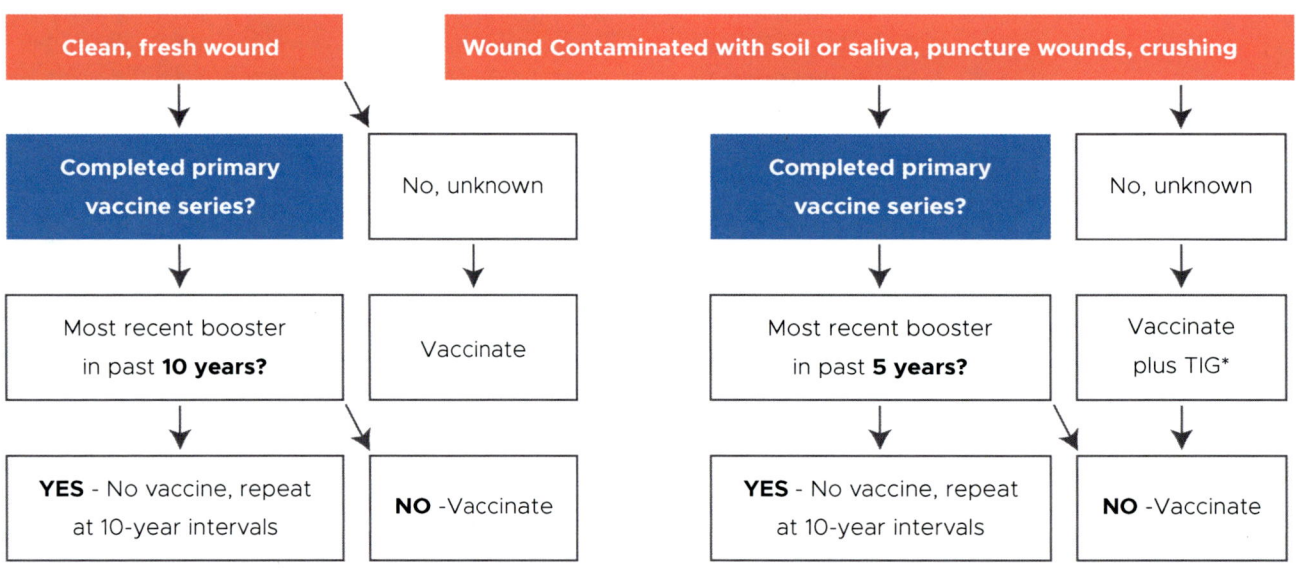

* Tetanus immune globulin

C. botulinum

Chief Complaint	Vignette Clues	Pathogenesis	Rx
Paralysis (**descending, flaccid**)	**Infantile botulism** – infant < 1 yr, fed **honey**, constipation, weak crying.	**Toxi-infection (spores ingested.** pH of infantile gut is alkaline and allows germination of spores.) **Toxin blocks acetylcholine release**, absorbed by gut, carried by blood to peripheral nerve synapses.	Antitoxin, penicillin G
	Food borne – adult, home canned alkaline vegetables, smoked fish	**Toxicosis**, toxin action as above	Antitoxin Prevention - proper heating of food over 60°C
	Wound botulism, traumatic implantation of spores	As above without GI symptoms	Antitoxin Penicillin

C. perfringens

Chief Complaint	Vignette Clues	Pathogenesis	Rx
Wound pain, myonecrosis **(gas gangrene)**	**Gas gangrene** Traumatic injury with loss of blood flow. Foul smelling wound. Fever, diaphoresis, tachycardia. Nagler Rxn – identifies alpha toxin with specific Ab.	Alpha toxin – lecithinase destroys cell membranes, liquifies tissues, hepatic toxicity. Many other toxins	Clindamycin, penicillin, debridement, hyperbaric oxygen
Watery diarrhea (food poisoning)	*C. perfringens* **food poisoning, reheated meat dishes,** noninflammatory	Enterotoxin works like *E. coli* LT	Supportive

Clostridioides difficile

Chief Complaint	Vignette Clues	Pathogenesis	Rx
Diarrhea (pseudomembranous colitis)	Patient on **antibiotics one week or longer**, pseudomembranous	Normal flora. Overgrows when competing flora are killed. **Toxin A** – enterotoxin **Toxin B** - cytotoxin	Fidaxomicin Isolation, autoclave bedpans

Non- Spore Forming, Aerobic Bacilli

a. *Corynebacterium diphtheriae*

1) Epidemiology:
- Diphtheroids (not lysogenized with β-corynephage) are normal flora
- Disease can occur via transmission of phage or lysogenized bacterium.
- **Unvaccinated** individuals
- Transmitted via respiratory droplets

2) Patients, Pathogenesis and Pharmacotherapy:

Chief Complaint	Vignette Clues	Pathogenesis	Rx
Sore throat, fever, cough (diphtheria)	**Unvaccinated**, dense gray **pseudomembrane** in oropharynx, **bleeds profusely** if dislodged. Club shaped rods, gray to black colonies on **tellurite agar, Elek** test or EIA identifies toxin	Toxin (produced by lysogeny) **ADP-ribosylates eEF-2**, binds to **nerve, heart and epithelial cells**. Organism is non-invasive but produces pseudomembrane of dead cells, fibrin, bacterial pigment.	Erythromycin and anti-toxin

For endocarditis, iv penicillin and aminoglycosides

Vaccine – toxoid in DTap, boosters 10 years |

b. *Listeria monocytogenes*

1) Epidemiology:
- Widespread animal GI and GU
- Dairy, deli foods kept in chilled cases (**cold enrichment**)
- Adult food borne, disease in **immunocompromised**
- Pregnant women – can transmit **transplacentally**
- **#1 cause of septicemia** and meningitis in cancer and kidney transplant patients

2) Patients, Pathogenesis and Pharmacotherapy:

Chief Complaint	Vignette Clues	Pathogenesis	Rx
Fever, hypotension, tachycardia (Septicemia)	**Immunocompromised patient**, gram + tumbling rods, cold enrichment	Facultative intracellular, listeriolysin (β **hemolysin**) helps escape from phagosome	Ampicillin plus gentamicin Immunocompromised and pregnant should avoid chilled dairy or deli foods
	Neonate, granulomatous septicemia, high mortality **(granulomatosis infantisepticum)**	Transplacental transmission	
Fever, irritability, bulging fontanelles **neonatal meningitis and septicemia**	3-4 weeks after birth, #3 cause	Acquired in parturition, as above	

Gram positive, Anaerobic, Filamentous Bacilli

a. *Actinomyces israelii*

1) Epidemiology:
- Normal flora in anaerobic niches: gingival crevices, portions of abdomen and female reproductive tract
- Spreads endogenously

2) Patients, Pathogenesis and Pharmacotherapy:

Chief Complaint	Vignette Clues	Pathogenesis	Rx
Subcutaneous swelling with rupture **non-mycotic mycetoma**	Erupts to surface from anaerobic focus (jaw line – lumpy jaw, pelvic from IUDs, abdominal following surgery or trauma), drains yellow granular pus from sinus tracts (**mycetoma**), pus grows gram +, filamentous, anaerobic bacilli (**non-mycotic**)	Invades into areas with diminished oxygen supply	Surgical drainage with penicillin G, ceftriaxone or amoxicillin

Gram-positive, Aerobic, Filamentous Bacilli

a. *Nocardia (N. asteroides and N. brasiliensis)*

1) Epidemiology:
- Soil and dust
- Inhalation or traumatic implantation

2) Patients, Pathogenesis and Pharmacotherapy:

Chief Complaint	Vignette Clues	Pathogenesis	Rx
Cough with sputum, fever **cavitary broncho-pulmonary disease** *N. asteroides*	**Immunocompromised patient**, acute, subacute pneumonia with cavitation, abscess formation, pleural effusion. Spread to CNS via blood. Branching, beaded, filamentous gram + bacilli, **weakly acid-fast.**	Immunosuppression and cancer predispose. T cell immunity is paramount	Sulfonamides or TMS
Subcutaneous swelling with rupture **Non-mycotic mycetoma**	**Southern US, Central or South America.** multiple nodules from puncture wounds *N. brasiliensis*	Traumatic implantation	

Acid-Fast, Anatomically Gram-positive, Aerobic Bacilli

a. *Mycobacterium tuberculosis*

1) Epidemiology:
- Globally, 130 cases per 100,000. US – 2.8 per 100,000 (associated with low socioeconomic status, crowding)
- Most common cause of ID death worldwide
- Respiratory droplets, nuclei 5 μm or less, resistant to drying and disinfectants, but sensitive to UV light

2) Anatomy

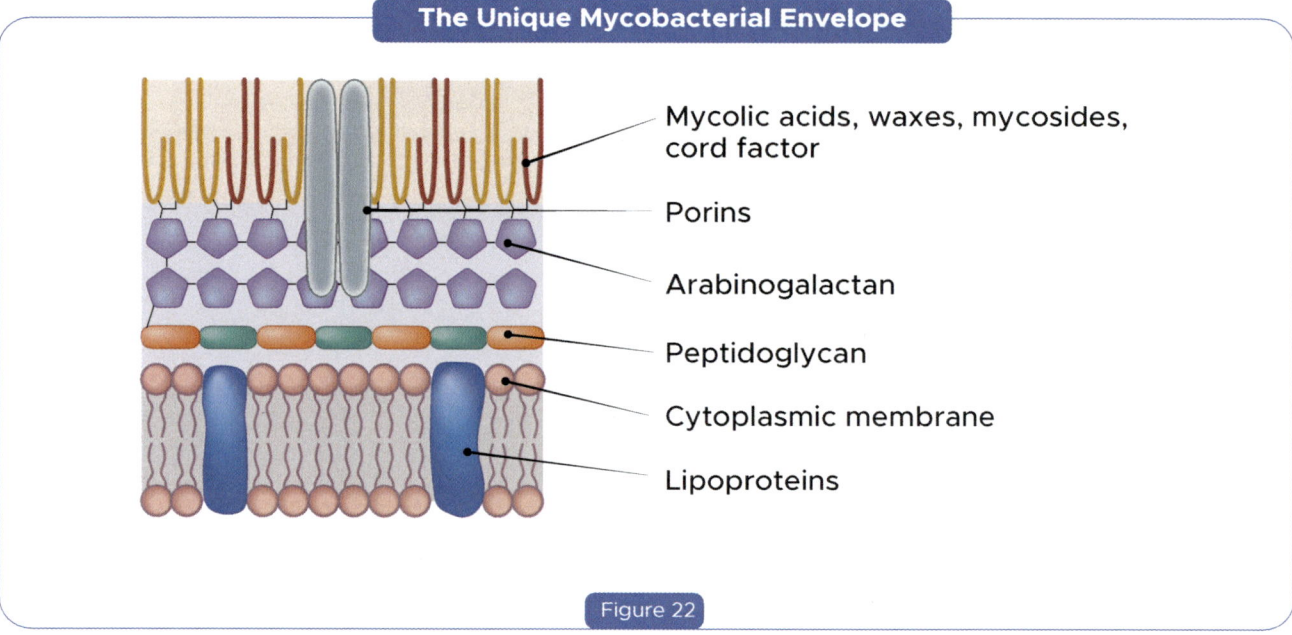

Figure 22

3) Patients, Pathogenesis and Pharmacotherapy:

Chief Complaint	Vignette Clues	Pathogenesis	Rx
Cough, weight loss, fatigue, fever, night sweats (in the endemic area, children acquire infection and are asymptomatic. Adults develop reactivational disease) **(Primary TB)**	**Hx of travel to endemic area** or immigrant child. (2 months after exposure) **Mediastinal lymphadenopathy.** X-ray with lesions in **base of lung. Ghon focus → Ghon complex** with involvement of mediastinal nodes. **Positive tuberculin test.**	Facultative intracellular. **Cord factor (trehalose dimycolate** – surface glycolipid present only in virulent strains. Inhibits diapedesis, disrupts mitochondrial respiration. **Lipoarabinomannan** – inhibits macrophage activation by IFN-γ and induces secretion of TNF-α which causes fever, weight loss and tissue damage. **Sulfatides** – sulfolipids which hydrolyze to create H_2SO_4 – inhibit fusion of phagosome and lysosome. **Mycobactin** - siderophore	2 months isoniazid, rifampin, pyrazinamide, followed by 4 months isoniazid and rifampin or 4 month regimen of rifapentine moxifloxacin, isoniazid, pyrazinamide. Add ethambutol or streptomycin if DR. MDRTB – bedaquiline (a diarylquinoline which ↓ proton pump for ATP synthase). Prophylaxis – Isoniazid for 9 months. BCG vaccine – live attenuated, not used in US (prevents dissemination but not pulmonary disease)
Cough, **hemoptysis**, weight loss, fever, night sweats, chest pain, fatigue **(Post primary TB)**	Hx of prior TB treatment, **homelessness, incarceration.** Reactivational disease, **cavitary lesions in apices** by X-ray. Positive tuberculin test. AFB in sputum, positive **auramine/rhodamine stain, niacin +**, NAAT		
Weakness, fatigue, weight loss, headache **(Miliary TB)**	**Disseminated disease (miliary)** spread to any oxygen-rich location		

With concurrent HIV infection, progression occurs at a rate of 10% each year. Lesions will be in base of lung. In all other cases, progression from latent TB occurs at a rate of 5% within 2 years, and lesions will be in the apices.

4) Diagnosis:

- **Auramine-rhodamine dye** – sensitive but not specific. Use to "rule out"
- Confirm with **Acid-fast stain**
- **Niacin** production
- **Quantiferon test** (interferon-γ release assay; IGRA)
- **Tuberculin test** (Mantoux test, type IV hypersensitivity) – positive reaction indicates exposure but not necessarily active disease. May be false positive after BCG vaccine.
    ◇ >5 mm = **positive in AIDS** or immunosuppressed
    ◇ >10 mm = **positive in health care workers**, IV drug users, immigrants
    ◇ >15 mm = **positive in general population**
- Chest x-ray if positive.

b. *Mycobacterium leprae*

1) Epidemiology:
- Extremely rare, fewer than 100 cases/yr in US
- Endemic in India, Myanmar and Nepal, Brazil, Tanzania
- Obligate intracellular infecting nerves, mucosa, skin
- Transmitted by prolonged contact
- Incubation period months to decades (mean 10 years for lepromatous, 4 years for tuberculoid)

2) Patients, Pathogenesis and Pharmacotherapy:

Chief Complaint	Vignette Clues	Pathogenesis	Rx
Hypoesthetic, hypopigmented macules (Tuberculoid leprosy)	Endemic area or travel. Cooler areas of skin affected. Lepromin test positive (type IV hypersensitivity) Acid-fast bacilli in punch biopsy (paucibacillary) or nasal scrapings	Tuberculoid form: strong M1/Th1 response, IL-12 production by macrophages, nerve damage due to CMI, loss of sensation predisposes to burns and trauma	Dapsone with rifampicin and clofazimine
Multiple hypopigmented skin macules, ulnar neuropathy (Lepromatous leprosy)	Endemic area or travel, Lepromin test negative, acid-fast bacilli (multibacillary) in punch biopsy or nasal scrapings	Lepromatous form: weak CMI, strong Th2 response with IL-4 predominating. Nerve damage from overgrowth of bacilli, loss of sensation predisposes to burns and trauma	

c. Atypical Mycobacteria (Mycobacteria other than Tuberculosis; MOTTs)

1) Epidemiology:
- Sources – soil, water. Not transmissible human to human
- Immunocompromised patients (AIDS)
- Species distinguished on production of yellow/orange (carotenoid) pigments
- Non-chromogens – no pigment produced
- Photo-chromogens – pigment made after exposure to light
- Scoto-chromogens – pigment made in the dark

2) Patients, Pathogenesis and Pharmacotherapy:

Chief Complaint	Vignette Clues	Pathogenesis	Rx
Chronic cough, hemoptysis, fatigue, malaise and weight loss	**AIDS patient**, pulmonary, gastrointestinal, disseminated. Photo-chromogen – *M. kansasii*, non-chromogen – *M. avium intracellulare*.	Facultative intracellular, granuloma formers	Macrolide + ethambutol. Standard prophylaxis at 50 CD4 cells and below
Ulcerating skin lesions on the hands **(fish tank granuloma)**,	Patient has tropical fish ulcerating granuloma on hands. *M. marinum* photochromogen		Rifampicin plus ethambutol or tetracycline, doxycycline, clarithromycin
Cervical lymphadenopathy	Child with water exposure, single lymph node. *M. scrofulaceum* scotochromogen		Surgery is both diagnostic and curative

Gram-Negative Cocci

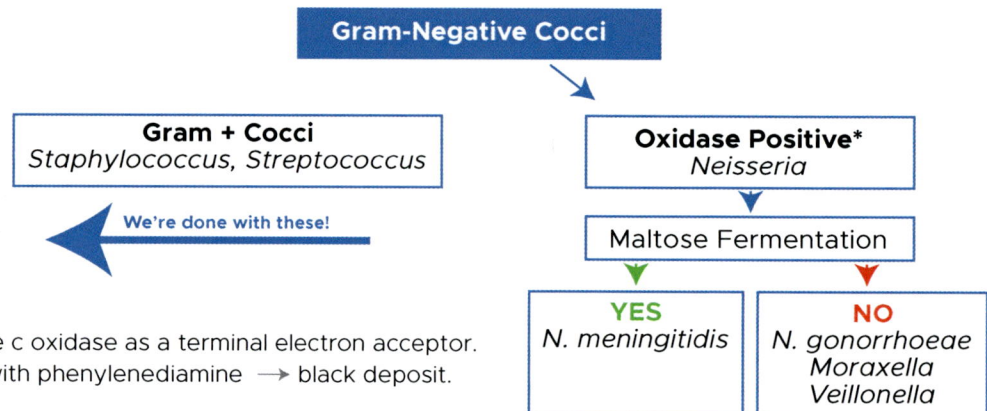

*use cytochrome c oxidase as a terminal electron acceptor. Flood colonies with phenylenediamine → black deposit.

Neisseria

1) Epidemiology:

- *N. meningitidis* – rates of invasive disease peak children younger than 1 year, adolescents and young adults 15-25)
    - Serogroup b – **non-immunogenic sialic acid capsule** – most common in US
    - Incidence worldwide greatly diminished since the advent of the conjugate vaccine.
    - Respiratory droplet transmission, colonization of oropharynx, natural transformation
- *N. gonorrhoeae* – **# 2 STI in US**, 2nd most commonly reported notifiable disease.
    - Sexually transmitted, increasing threat of drug resistance

2) Patients, Pathogenesis and Pharmacotherapy:

Chief Complaint	Vignette Clues	Pathogenesis	Rx
Abrupt onset fever, petechial rash, headache, prostration *Neisseria meningitidis* (meningococcal meningitis/ meningococcemia)	Adolescent – college student, crowded living situation, high transmissibility. High and rapid mortality, CSF with gram-negative kidney bean-shaped diplococci. Culture on chocolate agar, utilize maltose and glucose, oxidase positive	Entry across respiratory mucosa using IgA protease, pili and outer membrane proteins mediate attachment. Overproduction of outer membrane fragments (lipooligosaccharide), endotoxin shock, Waterhouse-Friderichsen syndrome. Non-immunogenic capsule (type b). Capsules for A, C, W-135 and Y impede phagocytosis. Deficiency of C5-9 (MAC) predisposes to bacteremias	Cefotaxime, ceftriaxone with or without vancomycin. Treat empirically before diagnosis confirmed. Rifampin to contacts to cut down transmission in outbreaks

Chief Complaint	Vignette Clues	Pathogenesis	Rx
Painful urethritis in male, vaginal discharge in female **Gonorrhea** (*N. gonorrhoeae*)	Sexually active age group, gram – diplococci on **Thayer-Martin agar** (selective against normal flora). Test for all other STIs	No capsule, pili for attachment, antigenic variation (no immunity to reinfection) IgA protease, oxidizes only glucose.	Ceftriaxone Plasmid encoded β-lactamase gives high level resistance to penicillin
Hot, swollen, painful knee, ankle or wrist joints (Gonococcal arthritis)	More common in female	Septic spread assisted by LOS/endotoxin action on endothelial cells	Ceftriaxone plus azithromycin, contact tracing. Increasing multi-drug resistance.
Painful ophthalmia (Ophthalmia neonatorum)	**Neonate, purulent exudate** bilaterally	**Neutrophilic infiltrate** rapidly leads to blindness	Erythromycin ointment in neonatal eyes

Moraxella catarrhalis

Chief Complaint	Vignette Clues	Pathogenesis	Rx
URTI	Gram negative diplococcus. Butyrate esterase positive	Normal flora of URT	Amoxicillin plus clavulanate

Gram-Negative Bacilli

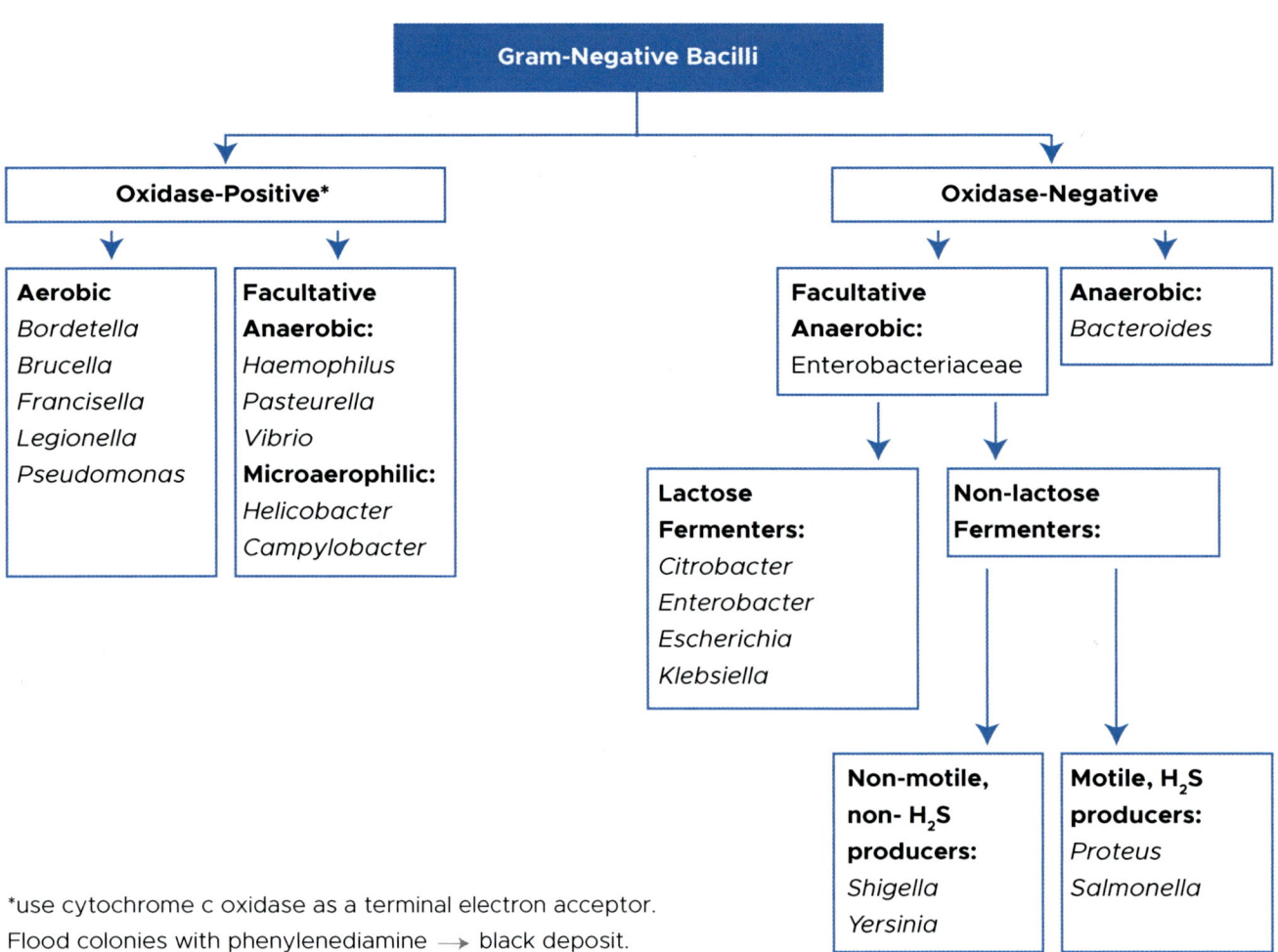

*use cytochrome c oxidase as a terminal electron acceptor.
Flood colonies with phenylenediamine → black deposit.

Oxidase-Positive, Aerobic, Gram-Negative Bacilli

a. *Bordetella pertussis* (not a "sister Ella")

1) Epidemiology:
- Reservoir in adolescents and adults (resembles the common cold). Vaccine not boosted outside of childhood.
- Highly transmissible to unvaccinated children (highest in catarrhal phase)
- Respiratory droplets
- Incidence decreased from advent of vaccine until 2005, now on the rise in unvaccinated populations

2) Patients, Pathogenesis and Pharmacotherapy:

Chief Complaint	Vignette Clues	Pathogenesis	Rx
Cough, fever (Whooping cough)	**Unvaccinated child**, or infant before first series. • **Catarrhal phase** – (1-2 wks) rhinorrhea, malaise, sneezing, anorexia. • **Paroxysmal phase** (2-4 wks) – fits of coughing with inhalational stridor, vomiting, leukocytosis. • **Convalescent** – (4-6 weeks) secondary complications – pneumonia, seizures, subconjunctival or cerebral hemorrhage. Dx immunofluorescence or serology	• Filamentous hemagglutinin for attachment • Encapsulated • **Toxin ADP ribosylates Gi**: promotes edema, lymphocytosis, sensitizes to histamine, enhances insulin secretion (hypoglycemia) • **Tracheal cytotoxin**, dermonecrotic toxin (necrosis of tracheal tissues) • **Adenylate cyclase toxin** – edema, inhibits chemotaxis and PMN function	Macrolides

Vaccine – acellular pertussis. (DTaP) has filamentous hemagglutinin and pertussis toxoid.

b. *Brucella spp.* (our first "sister Ella")

1) Epidemiology:
- Zoonosis – disease of animals transmissible to man
- California and Texas are states with highest number of cases
- Travel to Mexico
- *B. melitensis* – goats
- *B. abortus* – cattle
- *B. suis* - swine

2) Patients, Pathogenesis and Pharmacotherapy:

Chief Complaint	Vignette Clues	Pathogenesis	Rx
Chronic fever (sometimes nocturnal), chills, weight loss, altered mental status (Brucellosis)	Hx of occupational or other **exposure to animals.** Dx serology	**Facultative intracellular** Granulomatous septicemia	Doxycycline with an aminoglycoside. Prevention – vaccination of animals, pasteurization of dairy foods. No human vaccine

c. *Francisella spp.* (our second "sister Ella")

1) Epidemiology:
- Zoonosis: exposure to rabbits, deer, rodents (Arkansas, Missouri, Oklahoma)
- Transmission by aerosol, implantation, ingestion, *Dermacentor* tick
- Extremely transmissible (culture is hazardous)

2) Patients, Pathogenesis and Pharmacotherapy:

Chief Complaint	Vignette Clues	Pathogenesis	Rx
Fever, chills, malaise → • Ulcer of skin or conjunctiva • Abdominal pain • cough (Tularemia)	Hunter of rabbits or deer If inhaled → pneumonia, if ingested resembles → typhoid fever, if traumatically implanted → granulomatous ulcer	Facultative intracellular	Streptomycin or gentamicin Prophylaxis – live, attenuated vaccine for at-risk groups

d. *Legionella spp.* (our third "sister Ella")

1) Epidemiology:
- Most common atypical pneumonia of the elderly
- Aerosols inhaled from water sources (organisms resistant to chlorine and heat. Use copper ionization system)
- No human-to-human transmission

2) Patients, Pathogenesis and Pharmacotherapy:

Chief Complaint	Vignette Clues	Pathogenesis	Rx
Fever, dry **cough**, **confusion, diarrhea** (Legionnaire's Disease)	Elderly smoker, high alcohol consumption, immunosuppressed. **Atypical pneumonia.** Silver stain, urine antigen test, culture on buffered charcoal-yeast agar	**Facultative intracellular.** Pore-forming toxin kills macrophages. Alveoli fill with fibrin, PMNs, macrophages, RBCs. No bacteria in brain or GI so cause of confusion and diarrhea are uncertain – **hyponatremia?**	Fluoroquinolone, azithromycin, erythromycin. Add rifampin for immunocompromised

e. *Pseudomonas aeruginosa*

1) Epidemiology:
- Sources of water worldwide, direct contact (hot tub folliculitis, eye ulcers) trauma (osteomyelitis) or aerosols (pneumonia)
- #1 cause of death in CF patients

2) Patients, Pathogenesis and Pharmacotherapy:

Chief Complaint	Vignette Clues	Pathogenesis	Rx
Cough, fever (**Pseudomonal Pneumonia**)	Patient population: CF, ventilators, neutropenic patients, CGD patients. **Pyocyanin (blue green) and fluorescein (fluorescent) pigments** (give color to pus), **grape-like odor**. Gram stain and culture, non-fermenters on EMB or MacConkey agar	Huge **capsule** impedes phagocytosis. **Exotoxin A** – ADP ribosylates eEF-2, target liver. Endotoxin – shock Elastase – hemorrhagic destruction of blood vessel walls (contributes to appearance of ecthyma gangrenosum)	Anti-pseudomonal penicillin plus aminoglycoside Susceptibility testing: **High levels of drug resistance** Disinfection of any hospital water-bearing equipment
Eye ulcers	Prolonged contact lens wear		
Rash below neck	Hot tub folliculitis		
Dysuria	Catheterized patients, pigmented urine, odor		
Fever, confusion, black necrotic skin lesions (**Septicemia**)	Septicemia in burn patients, neutropenic patients, CGD patients. **Ecthyma gangrenosum** can resemble anthrax eschar.		

Gram-Negative, Oxidase-Positive Facultative Anaerobic Coccobacillus

a. *Pasteurella spp.*
(our fourth and final "sister Ella") and a mixed bag of things you can get from being bitten...

1) Epidemiology:
- Animal mouths
- Bites, scratches

2) Patients, Pathogenesis and Pharmacotherapy:

Chief Complaint	Vignette Clues	Pathogenesis	Rx
Animal bite	• Cat and many others – **Pasteurella** • Cat scratch – *Bartonella henselae* • Dog bite – *Capnocytophaga canimorsus* • Human bite or fist fight – *Eikenella corrodens* • Rat bite – *Streptobacillus moniliformis*	Endotoxin Capsule	Amoxicillin, clavulanate

b. *Haemophilus influenzae*

1) Epidemiology:
- Meningitis and epiglottitis in unvaccinated children 3 months to 3 years
- Human to human
- Respiratory droplets
- Also causes otitis media (non-typeable strains), bronchitis and pneumonia in smokers or patients with COPD.

2) Patients, Pathogenesis and Pharmacotherapy:

Chief Complaint	Vignette Clues	Pathogenesis	Rx
Headache, fever, stiff neck *(Haemophilus meningitis)*	3 month to 3 year old, unvaccinated child. Coccobacillus, require factors X (hemin) and V (NAD) for growth	Type b – 90% of invasive disease, **polyribitol phosphate capsule.** IgA protease	Cefotaxime, ceftriaxone. Rifampin in outbreaks to reduce nasal carriage. **HiB vaccine** – conjugated capsular polysaccharide/protein, 95% effective

c. *Haemophilus ducreyi*

1) Epidemiology:
- Human to human (not in US)
- Sexual transmission

2) Patients, Pathogenesis and Pharmacotherapy:

Chief Complaint	Vignette Clues	Pathogenesis	Rx
Painful genital ulcer (you do cry with ducreyi) Chancroid	Hx of travel to Africa, Asia, India, Latin America Coccobacillus, require factors X (hemin) and V (NAD) for growth	Pili – attachment Toxin – cytolethal distending toxin kills T lymphocytes	Azithromycin, ceftriaxone, ciprofloxacin, erythromycin Safe sex

Gram-Negative, Oxidase-Positive Facultative Anaerobic Curved Bacilli

a. *Vibrio* spp

1) Epidemiology:
- Human-human, fecal/oral, no carriers
- Shellfish and seafood may be contaminated
- Very high infectious dose (10^7 organisms), so associated with poor sanitation

2) Patients, Pathogenesis and Pharmacotherapy:

Chief Complaint	Vignette Clues	Pathogenesis	Rx
Watery diarrhea (Cholera)	*Vibrio cholerae*: Traveler or immigrant from endemic area, "rice water stools", hypovolemic shock, electrolyte imbalance	Cholera toxin ADP ribosylates Gsα, activates adenylate cyclase, increases cAMP, produced by lysogeny	Supportive – fluids and electrolytes. Doxycycline or ciprofloxacin may shorten course. Vaccines for travelers (whole cell, toxin B subunit and live-attenuated). Prevent with sanitation, chlorination, cook shellfish.
	V. parahaemolyticus and *V. vulnificus* – marine undercooked seafood	Thermostable direct hemolysin - enterotoxic and cytotoxic	None required. Properly cook seafood
Skin infection following trauma (cellulitis)	*V. vulnificus*, "shucking oysters", rapidly spreading ulcerative abscess		Tetracycline, 3rd generation cephalosporin

Gram-Negative, Oxidase-Positive, Microaerophilic, Curved Bacilli

a. *Campylobacter jejuni*

1) Epidemiology:
- #1 cause of bacterial gastroenteritis in the US
- Poultry, fecal/oral contamination
- 1 in 4 cases will develop Guillain-Barré Syndrome

2) Patients, Pathogenesis and Pharmacotherapy:

Chief Complaint	Vignette Clues	Pathogenesis	Rx
Bloody diarrhea, fever	Requires **10% CO_2 incubator at 42°C**, **curved rods** with polar flagella **(seagull wings)**	Invades mucosa, inflammatory diarrhea with blood, pus, fever. ID = 500 (resistant to acid), self-limiting 3-5 days	Supportive, fluids and electrolytes Severe cases: Macrolides and fluoroquinolones
Ascending paralysis	**Guillain-Barré Syndrome.** Recent or ongoing *Campylobacter* infection.	Autoimmune, molecular mimicry. **Serotype O19** oligosaccharides cross-react with glycosphingolipids on neural tissue.	Plasmapheresis
Reactive arthritis	HLA B27-linked arthritis, with conjunctivitis and urethritis/cervicitis	Cross-reactivity	Tetracycline and analgesics

b. *Helicobacter pylori*

1) Epidemiology:
- Human reservoir, fecal-oral, oral/oral transmission

2) Patients, Pathogenesis and Pharmacotherapy:

Chief Complaint	Vignette Clues	Pathogenesis	Rx
Dyspepsia, epigastric pain (gastritis + ulcers)	Biopsy and culture spirillar rods, grow at 37°C. **Fecal antigen test, Breath test** (swallow of radiolabeled C-urea yields radiolabeled CO_2 in exhalation due to action of urease.	**Urease** neutralizes gastric acidity, motility assists invasion, **mucinase** dissolves stomach mucus protection, cytotoxin kills cells and promotes inflammation. Gastric cancer near incisura, MALToma, B cell lymphoma result from type IV secretion system encoded in *cag* pathogenicity island.	Proton pump inhibitor plus 2 antibiotics (amoxicillin, clarithromycin, metronidazole, tetracycline).

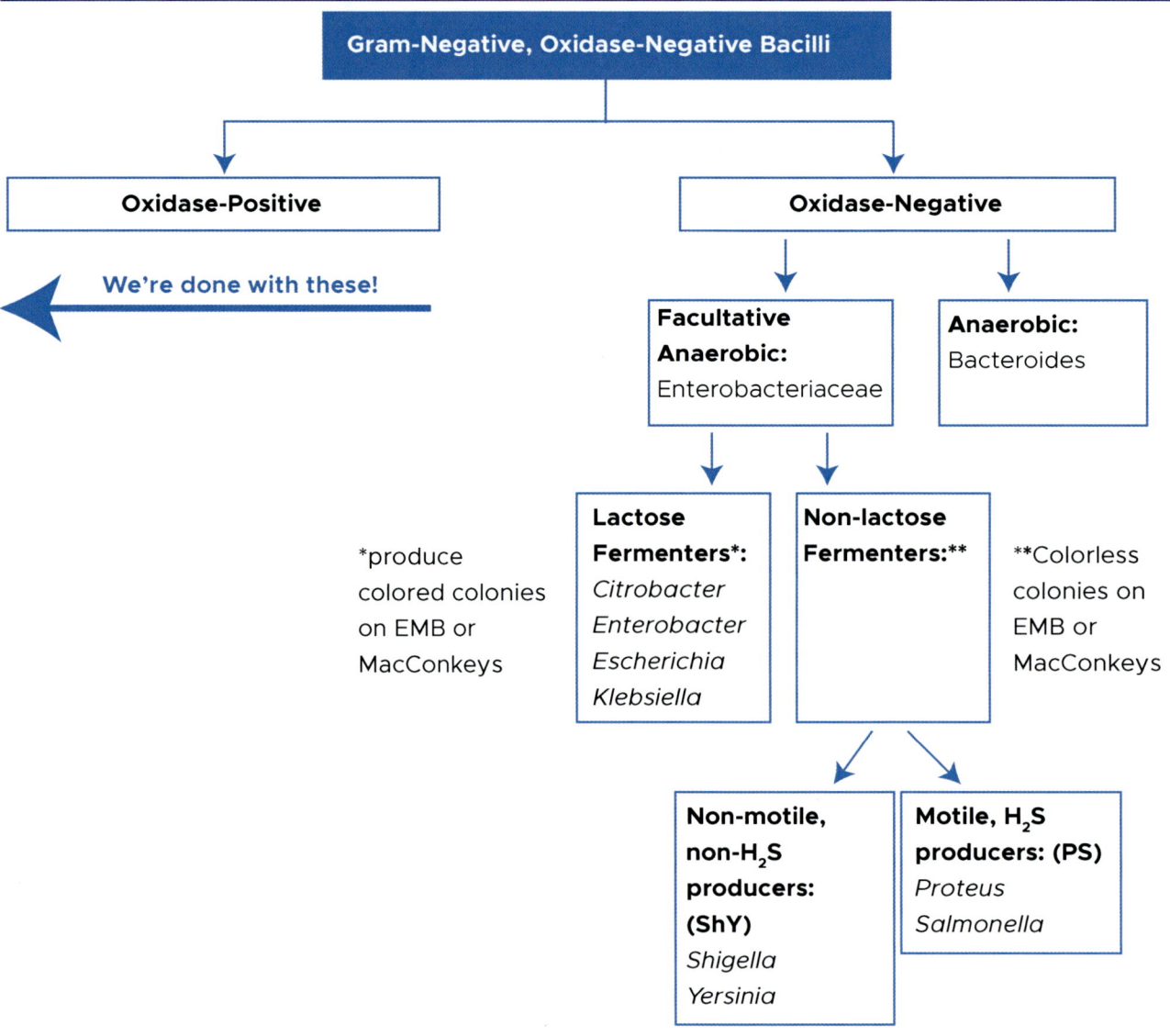

Family Enterobacteriaceae
(Gram-negative, Oxidase-negative)

- Ferment glucose
- Catalase positive
- Use nitrate as their terminal electron acceptor, reducing it to nitrite
- Have endotoxin and some make exotoxins
- Antigens: O – envelope, H – flagellar, K- capsule, Vi – capsule of *Salmonella*

1. Lactose-Fermenters
a. *Escherichia coli*
1) Epidemiology:
- Human and animal colonic flora
- Spread endogenously, during parturition, fecal/oral in food
- Enterohemorrhagic strains (EHEC) from cattle feces
- #1 cause of UTI overall
- #2 cause of neonatal meningitis and septicemia

2) Patients, Pathogenesis and Pharmacotherapy:

Chief Complaint	Vignette Clues	Pathogenesis	Rx
Dysuria (*E.coli* UTI)	10^5 CFU/mL, nitrite positive	• Transmission from normal flora. • **Adherence** with pili, adhesins • **Motility** allows movement against the flow of urine • Many β hemolytic	Fluoroquinolones or sulfonamides
Fever, irritability (*E.coli* neonatal meningitis)	Infant, within 2 weeks of birth. Gram negative rod in CSF or blood culture	• Maternal fecal flora contaminate during delivery • Endotoxin • K1 capsule	Ceftriaxone
Fever, confusion (*E.coli* Septicemia)	Indwelling vascular catheters or cytotoxic drugs allow escape from intestine	**Endotoxin** causes hypotension, peripheral vascular collapse	Carbapenems, piperacillin/ tazobactam

Chief Complaint	Vignette Clues	Pathogenesis	Rx
Vomiting, diarrhea (*E.coli* gastroenteritides)	**EHEC** – Child under 5, **no fever, no pus, bloody diarrhea**. Progression to HUS. **Colorless colonies on sorbitol MacConkeys agar** (non-fermenter of sorbitol)	**Verotoxin (Shiga-like toxin)** interferes with 60S ribosomal subunit	Antibiotics contraindicated, may increase risk of HUS
	EIEC – inflammatory (**blood, pus, fever**), developing country, children under 5.	Invades colonic mucosa	TMS or fluoroquinolones
	ETEC – traveler's diarrhea. Hx of travel outside of US, watery diarrhea. Immunoassay for toxin.	• Colonizing factor adhesins mediate attachment • Capsule • **LT ribosylates Gs** and stimulates adenylate cyclase • **ST stimulates guanylate cyclase**	Supportive, TMS only in severe cases
	EAEC – "stacked brick" biofilm on mucosal cells, watery diarrhea, infants and children in developing countries	**Pili, biofilm** production	Fluoroquinolones, macrolides
	EPEC – infants, developing countries	**Bundle-forming pili** promote attachment and effacing lesions	β lactams, macrolides

EHEC – Enterohemorrhagic *E. coli*; EIEC – Enteroinvasive *E. coli*; ETEC – Enterotoxigenic *E. coli*; EAEC – Enteroaggregative *E. coli*; EPEC – enteropathogenic *E. coli*.

b. *Klebsiella pneumoniae*

1) Epidemiology:
- Reservoir human colon and upper respiratory tract
- Spread endogenous

2) Patients, Pathogenesis and Pharmacotherapy:

Chief Complaint	Vignette Clues	Pathogenesis	Rx
Cough, fever (broncho-pneumonia)	Bronchopneumonia, **thick gelatinous red sputum (currant jelly)**. Alcoholic patient or chronic lung disease. Culture of sputum.	• Capsule interferes with phagocytosis and complement activation. • Pili mediate attachment. • Endotoxin	High levels of drug resistance (sensitivity testing) Fluoroquinolones, 3rd generation cephalosporin with or without aminoglycoside
Dysuria (UTI)	Nosocomial contamination of **catheters**, culture of urine.	Catheter introduction	
Fever, confusion (septicemia)	Immunocompromised patient with invasion of IV lines, cancer chemotherapy patient with escape from gut. Culture of blood.	Endotoxin, capsule	

Non-Lactose Fermenting
Non-motile, Non-H$_2$S Producing

a. *Shigella* spp

1) Epidemiology:
- Human-to-human transmission
- *Shigella dysenteriae* (not in the US), ***S. sonnei*** – most common in US, does not make Shiga toxin
- Fecal/oral contamination, extremely acid resistant, 1-10 organisms = ID
- No carrier state

2) Patients, Pathogenesis and Pharmacotherapy:

Chief Complaint	Vignette Clues	Pathogenesis	Rx
Bloody diarrhea	Infant or adult daycares	Invasive, **shiga toxin is enterotoxic, cytotoxic, neurotoxic acting on 60S ribosomal subunit**	Self-limiting, but TMS, fluoroquinolones, ceftriaxone shorten symptoms. Careful hygiene with adult and infant diapers.

b. *Yersinia* spp

1) Epidemiology:

- *Y. pseudotuberculosis* and *Y. enterocolitica*
    - Zoonotic, northern climates
    - Unpasteurized dairy, pork
- *Y. pestis*
    - Zoonotic, rodents/flea bite
    - Pneumonic form – human-to-human
    - Desert southwest

2) Patients, Pathogenesis and Pharmacotherapy:

Chief Complaint	Vignette Clues	Pathogenesis	Rx
Fever, abdominal pain *Y. pseudotuberculosis* *Y. enterocolitica*	**Pseudoappendicitis** in children. Stool culture at 25°C, **unpasteurized dairy from northern climate.** May cause reactive arthritis.	Invades M cells, **facultative intracellular**	Self-limiting except in immunocompromised. Fluoroquinolones or 3rd generation cephalosporins. Prevent with pasteurization and properly cook pork
Fever, conjunctivitis, confusion (*Y. pestis*)	**Bubonic plague** – rapid ↑ fever, buboes (hemorrhagic lymph nodes near flea bite), conjunctivitis, septicemia, death. Culture is hazardous, serodiagnosis	Coagulase clogs mouthparts of flea, ↑ transmission. **Facultative intracellular**, endotoxin, F1 envelope Ag is anti-phagocytic	Aminoglycosides, fluoroquinolones. **72-hr quarantine** after starting therapy. Military killed vaccine Rodent control
	Pneumonic plague – spread from human or progression from bubonic form. More rapid progression to death		

Non-Lactose Fermenting Motile, H$_2$S Producing

a. *Proteus* spp

1) Epidemiology:
- Reservoir in human colon and environment
- Transmission endogenous or from water, soil

2) Patients, Pathogenesis and Pharmacotherapy:

Chief Complaint	Vignette Clues	Pathogenesis	Rx
Dysuria (UTI)	Elevated urinary pH, Urease +, Nitrite +, culture urine or blood in septicemias, kidney stones, ammoniac odor to urine	Swarming motility (peritrichous flagellae) Urease raises pH → struvite (staghorn) stones Endotoxin in septicemias	Fluoroquinolones, 3rd generation cephalosporin, TMS

b. *Salmonella enterica* serovars

1) Epidemiology:
- 2000 serovars of species distinguished by O, H, and Vi antigens
- Reservoir human colon
- *S. enterica* serovar *typhi* transmission fecal/oral from **carriers** (persons infected with a pathogen with no overt signs of disease.
- High infectious dose (10^5)
- Important clinical distinction is between typhoidal (not US) and non-typhoidal (worldwide) salmonellae
- Non-typhoidal salmonellae are normal flora and transmitted from **poultry products and reptile pets.**
- Non-typhoidal salmonellae are **#1 cause of osteomyelitis in sickle cell patients**

2) Patients, Pathogenesis and Pharmacotherapy:

Chief Complaint	Vignette Clues	Pathogenesis	Rx
Fever, abdominal pain **(typhoid fever)**	Traveler to endemic area. *S. e.* serovar *typhi* – typhoid fever. 1 week positive blood cultures. (Rose spots on abdomen), **Widal** test for O, H, Vi antigens. 3 weeks positive stool cultures	Infection of M cells in ileocecum, carried by macrophages throughout lymphatics. Return to intestine via biliary tree. Vi capsule protects against phagocytosis	Treat carriers. Ceftriaxone, cefixime, ciprofloxacin. Vaccines for travelers: Vi antigen conjugated to protein
Nausea, vomiting, fever, diarrhea	**Non-typhoidal salmonellae**, poultry products, reptile pets. **Widal** test.	Invasion to lamina propria, induces prostaglandin synthesis which then ↑cAMP	Supportive only. Anti-microbics ↑chance of carrier state
Fever, focal bone pain **(osteomyelitis)**	Sickle cell anemia patient **(Non-typhoidal salmonellae)**	Adolescents with sickle cell anemia are functionally asplenic. Normal flora can escape into blood from micro-infarcts, spread to bone.	Ciprofloxacin

Gram-Negative, Oxidase-Negative Anaerobic Bacilli

a. *Bacteroides fragilis*

1) Epidemiology:
- Predominant anaerobe in the colon (aerotolerant, catalase-positive)
- Transmission endogenous following bowel trauma/damage

2) Patients, Pathogenesis and Pharmacotherapy:

Chief Complaint	Vignette Clues	Pathogenesis	Rx
Abdominal pain, nausea, vomiting, fever	**Peritonitis, abscess or septicemia.** Hx of abdominal trauma or surgery. Culture after anaerobic transport protocols.	**Pili** – attachment **Capsule** – anti-phagocytic **Endotoxin missing part of lipid A** (less pathogenic)	Usually treated presumptively. Metronidazole, cefoxitin, clindamycin. Antibiotics before GI surgery.

Atypical (Poorly Gram Staining) Prokaryotes

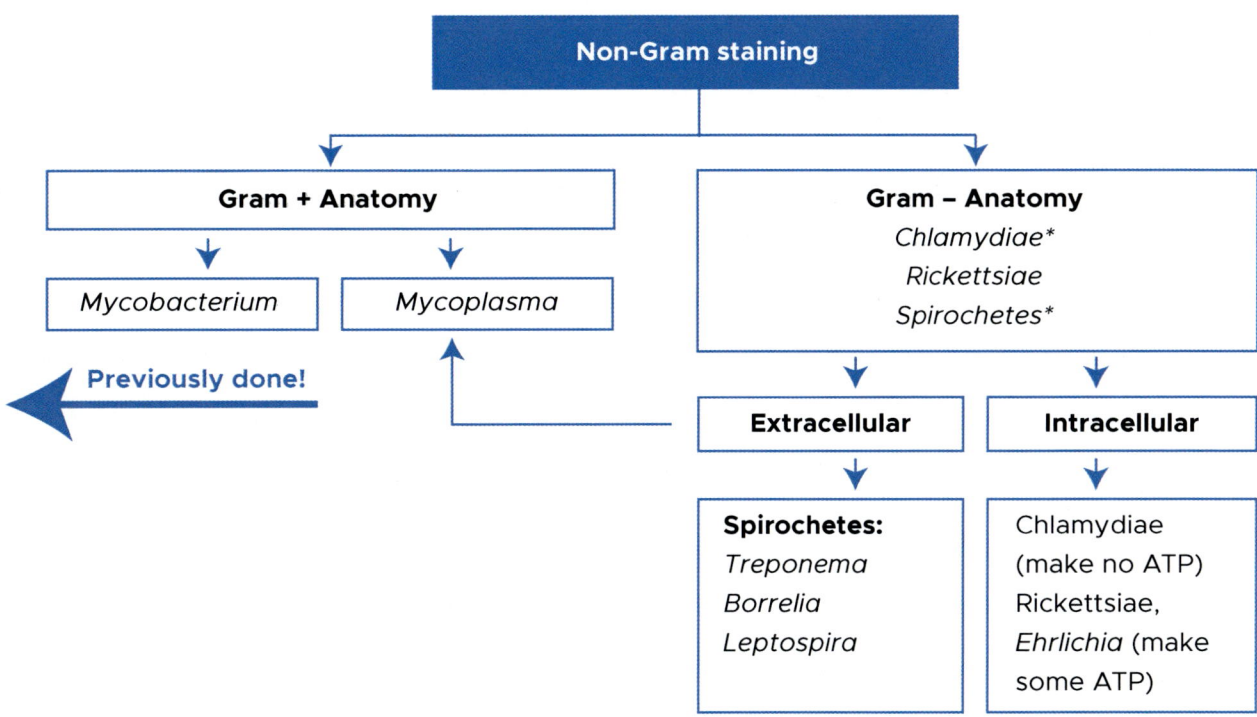

Non-Gram Staining (Anatomically Gram Positive) No Cell Wall, Extracellular

a. *Mycoplasma pneumoniae*
1) Epidemiology:
- Most common atypical pneumonia of adolescents and young adults
- Transmission human-to-human via respiratory droplets

2) Patients, Pathogenesis and Pharmacotherapy:

Chief Complaint	Vignette Clues	Pathogenesis	Rx
Dry cough, sore throat, fever (Walking pneumonia)	Indolent onset and protracted course. Young adult. Atypical pneumonia. Slow growing (10 days), mulberry-shaped colonies on agar containing sterols. **Cold agglutinins** in 65% of patients (isohemagglutinins functional at 4°C)	Microbe lacks signaling for acute inflammation, so the body develops a TH1 response to an extracellular organism. P1 protein – mediates attachment. Ciliary action stopped, leads to desquamation. Infiltration with lymphocytes, plasma cells, macrophages	Erythromycin, doxycycline (no cell wall antibiotics!)

b. *Ureaplasma urealyticum*
1) Epidemiology:
- Human genital tract
- Sexually transmitted, moves up urinary tract

2) Patients, Pathogenesis and Pharmacotherapy:

Chief Complaint	Vignette Clues	Pathogenesis	Rx
Dysuria, colicky flank pain (UTI)	UTI that did not respond to cell wall antibiotics, **alkaline pH** of urine, **nitrite negative**	Urease allows survival in acid pH, **struvite/staghorn** calculia	Doxycycline

Spirochetes

a. *Treponema pallidum*
1) Epidemiology:
- 12.1 cases per 100,00 population, rates rising since 2010
- Human genital tract
- Transmission sexual, transplacental, transfusion

2) Patients, Pathogenesis and Pharmacotherapy:

Chief Complaint	Vignette Clues	Pathogenesis	Rx
Painless genital ulcer (1° syphilis)	10 days to 3 months after unprotected sex. Indurated lesion. **Darkfield microscopy** of biopsy or scraping	Endotoxin. Endarteritis and endothelialitis. Granulomatous cuffs of lymphocytes, plasma cells, monocytes surround blood vessels. **Jarish-Herxheimer rxn** – endotoxin shock response within 24 hours of drug treatment.	Benzathine penicillin, doxycycline. Contact tracing
Bronzing generalized rash (2° syphilis)	1-3 months later, condylomata lata, rash involves palms and soles, alopecia. **VDRL (non-specific) positive, confirm with specific serology (FTA-Abs or MHA-TP)**		
Numbness, dementia (Neurosyphilis)	5-20 years later. Granulomas **(gummas)** throughout CNS and vasculature. Tabes dorsalis. **Specific serology only**, non-specific usually negative.		Penicillin G

b. *Borrelia burgdorferi*

1) Epidemiology:
- Most common tick-borne disease in the US **(Lyme Disease)**
- 30,000 cases per year in US, all 50 states. Incidence highest in northeast, Great Lakes States, Washington State.
- Dogs, mice, deer reservoir, transmitted by **Ixodes** *dammini* tick.

2) Patients, Pathogenesis and Pharmacotherapy:

Chief Complaint	Vignette Clues	Pathogenesis	Rx
Fever, fatigue, myalgia, headache, joint pain (Lyme Disease)	1st month after tick bite. **Target (bull's eye) rash.** Summer months, geography of tick. EIA or IFA followed by Western blot	Inflammation caused by peptidoglycan, lacks classic endotoxin, outer surface proteins inhibit complement fixation. Arthritis may be autoimmune	Doxycycline, amoxicillin, cefuroxime
Facial muscle paralysis	**2-3 months** (Bell's palsy)		
Memory and sleep disorder, decreased concentration, joint pain	More than **3 months** to years later.		

c. *Leptospira interrogans*

1) Epidemiology:
- **Zoonosis**, humid subtropical and tropical climates
- **Hawaii** state of highest incidence
- Rodents, dogs, cattle reservoir, transmitted through water contaminated with urine
- Enters through breaks in skin or mucosa

2) Patients, Pathogenesis and Pharmacotherapy:

Chief Complaint	Vignette Clues	Pathogenesis	Rx
Fever, nausea, vomiting, headache, abdominal and muscle pain (Leptospirosis)	Occupational or recreational exposure to water. Specific serology.	Spirochetes with hooks on the ends. Bind to extracellular matrix, endotoxin action on endothelium, Weil Disease: jaundice, vasculitis, kidney damage, rash.	Penicillin, doxycycline, ceftriaxone

Non-Gram Staining, Obligate Intracellular
Do not make ATP, Cell Wall lacks Muramic Acid

a. *Chlamydiaceae*

1) Epidemiology:

- **Obligate intracellular** inside epithelial cells as reproductive reticulate bodies. Transmission form is the **elementary body** released from cells
- Contact (hand-to-eye) or sexual transmission, intrapartum (neonatal eyes)
- *Chlamydia trachomatis* **D-K is the most common bacterial STI** in the US
- *Chlamydia trachomatis* (A-C) Trachoma is the **#1 cause of infectious preventable blindness** in the world.

2) Patients, Pathogenesis and Pharmacotherapy:

Chief Complaint	Vignette Clues	Pathogenesis	Rx
Dysuria in male (female asymptomatic to dyspareunia) (STI)	*Chlamydia trachomatis*, serotypes D-K. Scraping of affected area yields intracytoplasmic inclusions in epithelia. Tissue culture. Chandelier sign on pelvic exam.	Granulomatous inflammation results in fibrosis and scarring. IL-8 released from infected cells, causes early neutrophilic infiltrate. **Transmitted to neonatal eyes during delivery**	Tetracyclines, macrolides Erythromycin in neonatal eyes.
Eye infection Trachoma	Serotypes A, B, Ba, C.	Entropion leads to scarring	
Soft, painless genital lesion Lymphogranuloma venereum	Serotypes L1-L3	Multilocular suppurative involvement of inguinal lymph nodes.	
Fever, dry cough *Chlamydophila psittaci*	Exposure to birds, **parrots**, turkeys, excreta. Intracytoplasmic inclusions in epithelial cells, tissue culture. Serology	Atypical pneumonia. M1-Th1-CTL response.	Tetracycline or doxycycline
Fever, dry cough, chest pain *Chlamydophila pneumoniae*	Human to human transmission via respiratory droplets	Infects smooth muscle, endothelial cells, Atypical pneumonia	Tetracycline, erythromycin

Non-Gram Staining, Obligate Intracellular
Make limited ATP, Normal Peptidoglycan
Order Rickettsiales

a. *Rickettsia rickettsii, Erhlichia, Anaplasma*

1) Epidemiology:
- Obligate intracellular, vector borne
- Rocky Mountain Spotted Fever (RMSF) is common in the mountain regions of Oklahoma, Tennessee, North and South Carolina
- Mite, louse and flea-borne rickettsiae are associated with poverty and trench warfare.

2) Patients, Pathogenesis and Pharmacotherapy:

Chief Complaint	Vignette Clues	Pathogenesis	Rx
Fever, headache, rash, shock (RMSF)	*Rickettsia rickettsii* Rash is **maculopapular to petechial**. Begins on **ankles and wrists**, spreads **centripetally** to trunk. **Palms and soles** involved. May also have GI symptoms, periorbital swelling, signs of meningitis and arthralgia. Hx tick bite in endemic area. **Weil-Felix** test (heterophile antibody agglutinates *Proteus*). ***Dermacentor*** tick	**Obligate intracellular in endothelial cells.** Cytokine storm and endothelialitis	Doxycycline Begin therapy without confirmation
Fever, headache, shock (no rash)	***Ehrlichia chaffeensis.*** *Amblyomma* ticks. Human monocytic ehrlichiosis. Leukopenia, thrombocytopenia, **morulae inside monocytes**. Ehrlichiosis.	Obligate intracellular	Doxycycline
	Anaplasma phagocytophilum. ***Ixodes*** **tick** transmission. Leukopenia, thrombocytopenia, **morulae inside neutrophils**. Anaplasmosis		

Before you leave, can you...

1. Describe the anatomy and physiology of the major groups of medically important prokaryotes.
2. Explain the mechanism of action of the major anti-bacterial drugs.
3. Diagnose the causal agents of the major bacterial diseases from symptoms, lab results and epidemiologic clues.
4. Explain the mechanism of pathogenesis for the major bacterial pathogens from the symptoms to the molecular basis of disease.

Microbiology
Chapter four

Medically Important Viruses

Medically Important Viruses

Definitions
- **Virus** - **acellular, obligate intracellular**, infectious agents. Contain RNA or DNA, with or without polymerase enzymes to complete their life cycles, and a protective covering which assists their travel from cell to cell, as well as their attachment to specific host cells.
- **Capsid** - the protein shell which surrounds the nucleic acid and the polymerase enzyme (if any). If this is all that comprises the virus, it is referred to as a **naked capsid virus**. The underlying shape of the capsid or nucleocapsid is described as **icosahedral** (having 20 triangular faces) or **helical** (having the underlying shape of the nucleic acid strand).
- **Envelope** - the membrane (captured from the host cell in all cases except poxviruses) which surrounds the **nucleocapsid** (the protein/genome complex) of the virus. Viruses that have a nucleocapsid plus an envelope are said to be enveloped viruses.
All helical **viruses must have an envelope**, but there are both naked and enveloped icosahedral viruses.

Virus Genomes

Viruses may have single- or double-stranded RNA or DNA as their genome.
Remember that in eukaryotic cells like ours, the flow of genetic information is from DNA to RNA to protein:

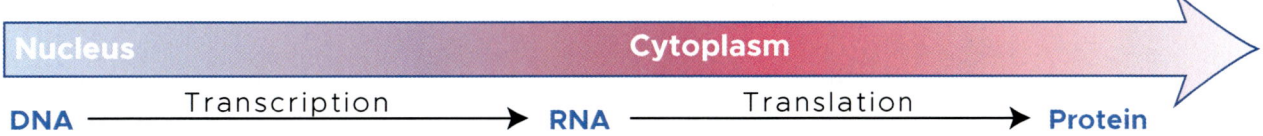

So, in our cells:
- We replicate DNA using **DNA-dependent DNA polymerases**.
- We transcribe DNA into RNA using **DNA-dependent, RNA polymerases** (transcriptases).
- We use RNA as a messenger to carry the genetic code out of the nucleus, so that it can be translated into protein using ribosomes in the cytoplasm.

If viruses are performing these processes, then they simply need to be in the right place to use cellular enzymes, so **DNA viruses (except poxviruses) replicate DNA in the nucleus**. RNA viruses carry out their lifecycles in the cytoplasm.

So how do viruses replicate RNA?

They make a second, complementary strand. So again, let's clear up some terminology:
- **Eukaryotic mRNA is created by complementation of the template strand of DNA.** It thus is a coding strand and **reads from 5' to 3'**. A virus with this genomic structure is said to be a **positive-sense RNA virus**. Viruses that have this type of strand can simply begin the translation process as soon as they find a ribosome.
- Some viruses have RNA which is the complementary strand: its **polarity is 3' to 5'** and is defined as **negative-sense RNA,** because it has the sequence of ribonucleotides which are complementary to the mRNA strand. Notice that this sequence could not be used on the ribosomes because of its polarity, so such viruses must carry **RNA-dependent, RNA polymerases** into the cell with them or their lifecycle cannot be completed. In other words, they must replicate RNA as a first step in order to create the mRNA that they need to produce their proteins.

The Virus Life Cycle

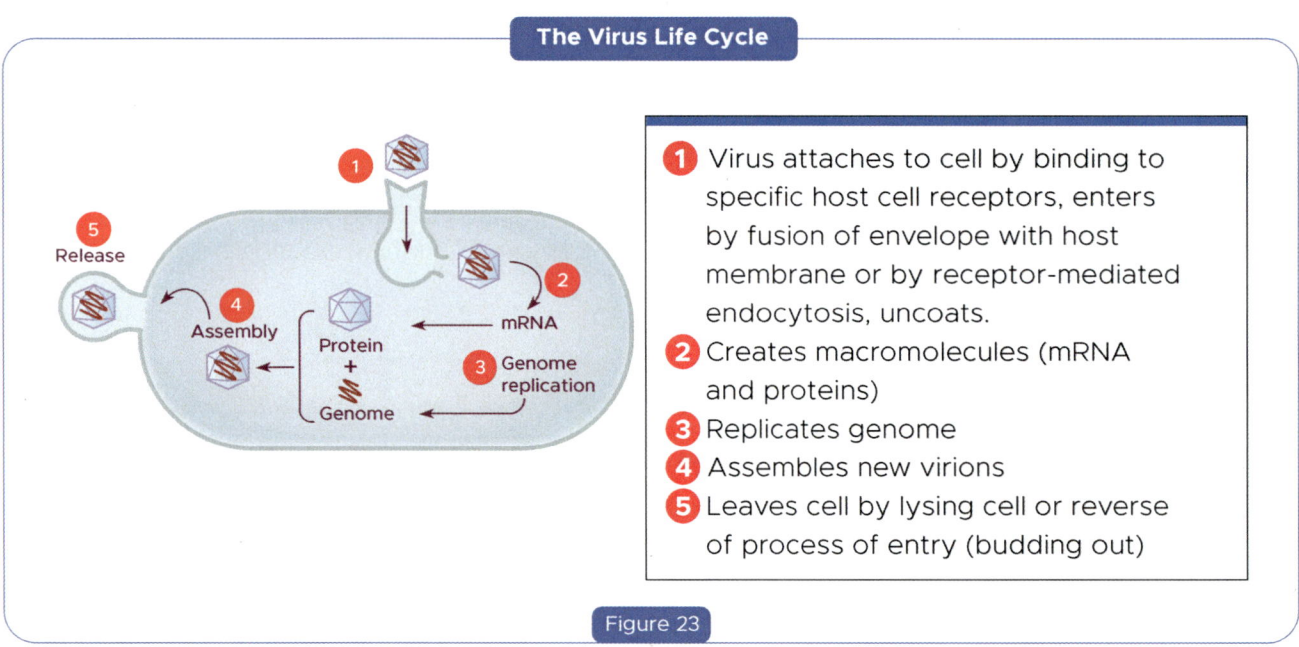

1. Virus attaches to cell by binding to specific host cell receptors, enters by fusion of envelope with host membrane or by receptor-mediated endocytosis, uncoats.
2. Creates macromolecules (mRNA and proteins)
3. Replicates genome
4. Assembles new virions
5. Leaves cell by lysing cell or reverse of process of entry (budding out)

Figure 23

How are viruses spread?
As with all microbes:
- Direct contact, airborne, fecal/oral, sexual/parenteral.
- Viruses spread using arthropods as vectors are identified by the acronym **AR**thropod **BO**rne viruses (Arboviruses).

Step 1: binding, entry, uncoating

Virus receptors that are testable:
- HIV – CD4 plus CXCR4 (TH cells) or CCR5 (macrophages)
- Epstein-Barr virus – CD21
- Rabies – acetylcholine receptor
- Rhinovirus – ICAM-1
- Parvovirus – Erythrocyte P antigen
- Cytomegalovirus and Herpes simplex – heparan sulfate

Mechanisms of entry:

Receptor-mediated endocytosis or fusion. Viruses that enter cells by fusion **(paramyxoviridae, herpesviridae, retroviridae)** leave viral proteins on the surface of the cells they infect. These proteins cause the first infected cell to adhere to uninfected cells around it, and this allows the virus to move from one cell to the next through fused cell membranes. This **protects from the action of antibodies** which could otherwise coat the virus and prevent its ability to bind to a new cell and infect it. These **multinucleated giant cells (syncytia)** are sometimes diagnostic clues in tissue specimens or cultures.

Step 2: How do viruses make their macromolecules?

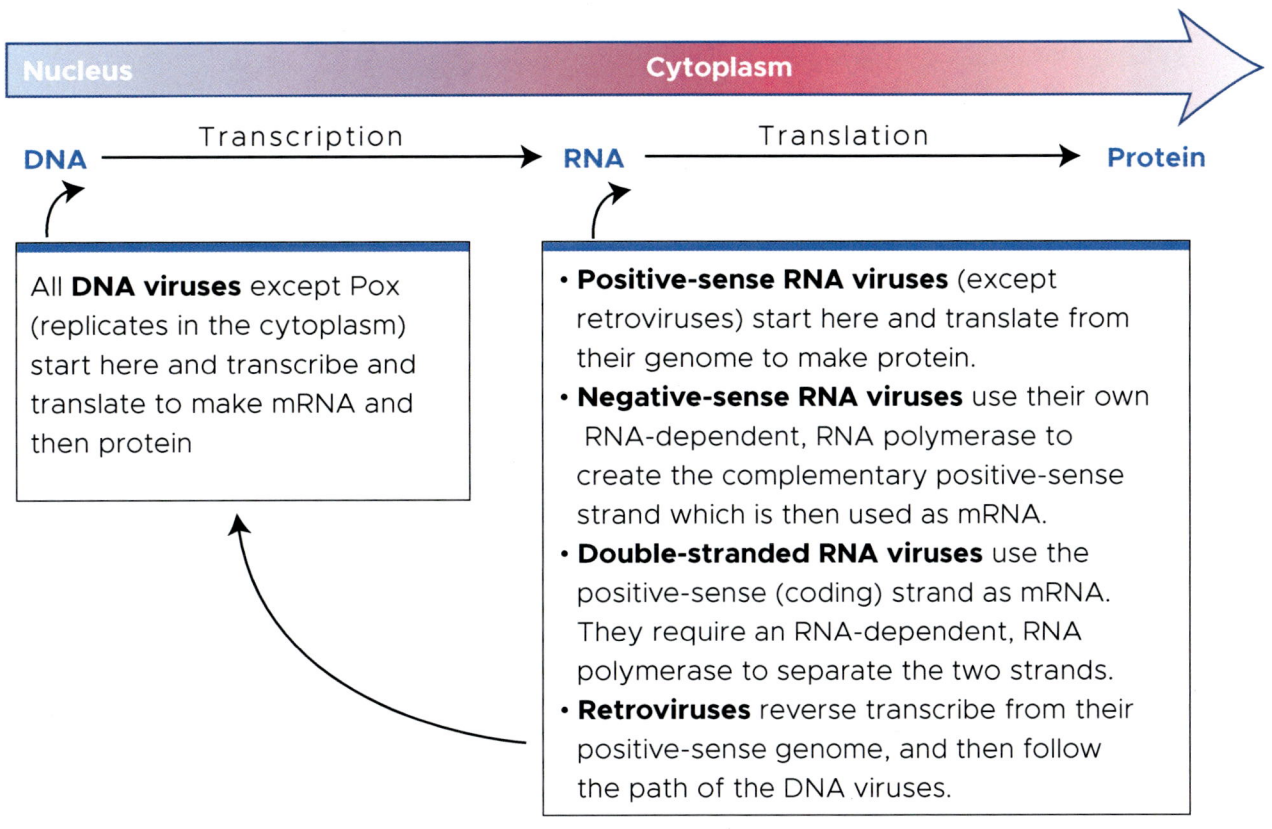

All **DNA viruses** except Pox (replicates in the cytoplasm) start here and transcribe and translate to make mRNA and then protein

- **Positive-sense RNA viruses** (except retroviruses) start here and translate from their genome to make protein.
- **Negative-sense RNA viruses** use their own RNA-dependent, RNA polymerase to create the complementary positive-sense strand which is then used as mRNA.
- **Double-stranded RNA viruses** use the positive-sense (coding) strand as mRNA. They require an RNA-dependent, RNA polymerase to separate the two strands.
- **Retroviruses** reverse transcribe from their positive-sense genome, and then follow the path of the DNA viruses.

Step 3: How do viruses replicate their genomes?

- **DNA Viruses:**

  Most use cellular polymerases to semi-conservatively replicate their DNA genomes.
  - ◇ **Hepadnaviruses** – infect hepatocytes, which are stable cells and do not dependably have the polymerases for DNA replication available. The virus therefore allows the hepatocyte to make mRNA from its genomic DNA, and then uses its own reverse transcriptase enzyme to create more DNA copies of its genome.

- **Positive-sense RNA Viruses:**

  Most use an RNA-dependent, RNA polymerase which is encoded in their genome and create a complementary template strand which is then used to create multiple genomic (positive-sense) copies.
  - ◇ **Retroviruses** – Use their reverse transcriptase to create a double-stranded DNA version of their positive-sense RNA genome. This **"provirus"** is transported into the nucleus and integrated into the chromosomes. From there, genomic replication is the process of transcription; positive-sense, single stranded RNA molecules that are unspliced are simply packaged into the next generation of viral capsids.

- **Negative-sense RNA viruses:**

  Use the positive-sense strand that they must create to make proteins as the template off of which to make more negative-sense strands.

Step 4 and 5: Assembly and release

- **Most naked capsid viruses** leave the cell by lysing it. The viral progeny simply assemble and accumulate inside the cell until it cannot swell any further, and bursts.
- **Most enveloped viruses** capture their envelope from the cell membrane and must keep the cell alive to continuously produce their covering. They therefore bud off the surface of the cell as they are assembled, by a process which is almost the reverse of the way in which they entered.

The Effects of Virus Infections

At the cellular level:
- **Abortive Infections** – no viral progeny produced, cell is not affected.
- **Cytolytic infections** – viral progeny produced, cell is killed
- **Persistent infections** – may be **productive** (progeny produced) or latent (no progeny) or **transforming** (cell becomes malignant).

At the patient level:
- **Acute, self-limited.** Most virus infections, e.g. influenza, coronavirus). Patient is contagious before symptoms, during acute presentation and for a diminishing time afterwards, but the virus is eventually eliminated and the patient has adaptive immune memory to that strain.
- **Persistent with continuous or intermittent shedding** (e.g. Epstein-Barr virus)
- **Persistent latent with reactivation** (e.g. herpes simplex or varicella zoster). The patient is non-infectious in the periods between outbreaks, but transmission can occur with each new acute episode.
- **Acute infection followed by persistent slow viral growth** (e.g. subacute sclerosing panencephalitis (SSPE), progressive multifocal leukoencephalopathy (PML), HTLV leukemia)
- **Persistent slow accumulation without acute presentation,** e.g. prion disease. (Creutzfeldt-Jakob disease)

Viral Infections as a Function of Patient Age Group

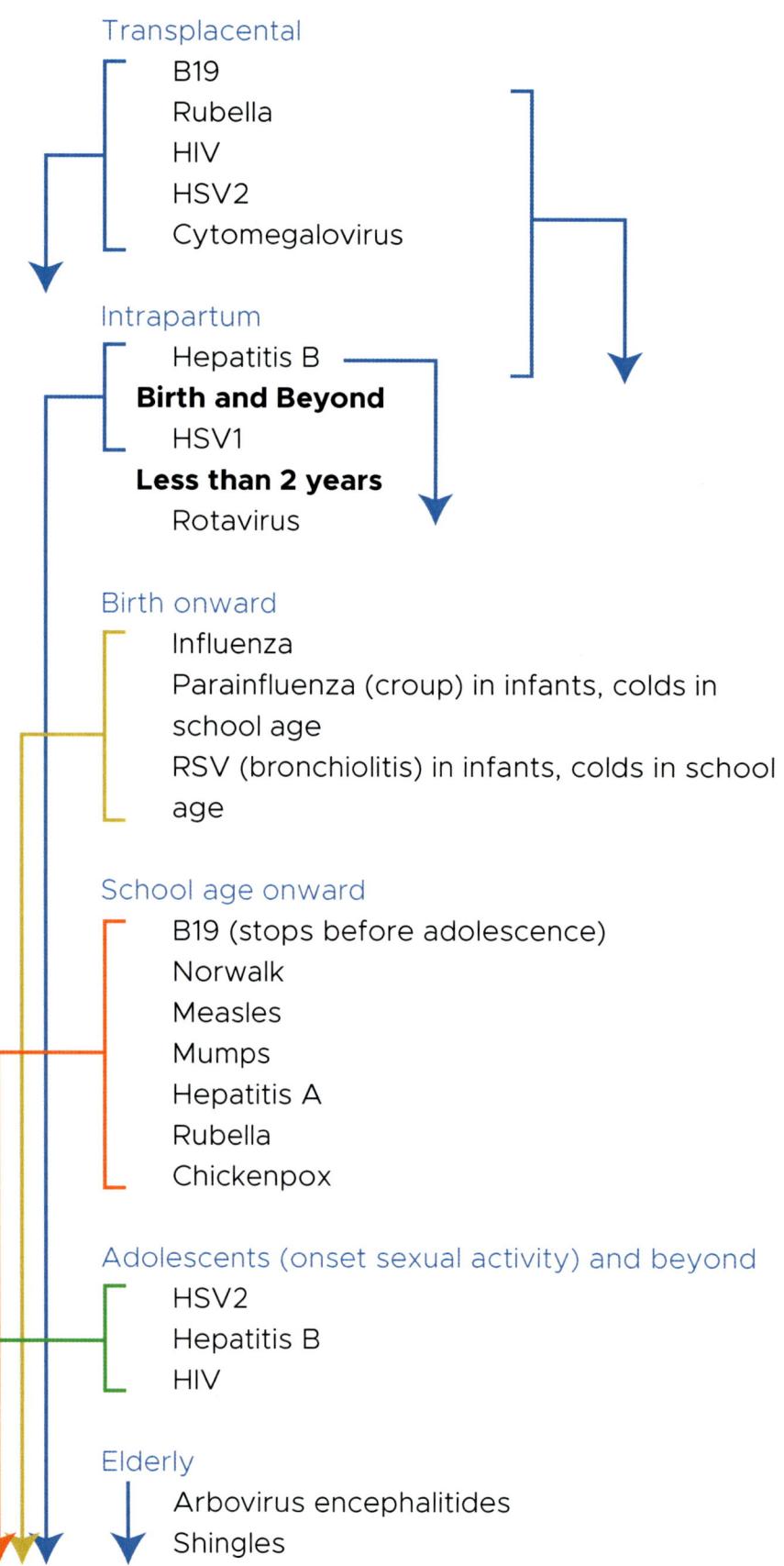

Transplacental
- B19
- Rubella
- HIV
- HSV2
- Cytomegalovirus

Intrapartum
- Hepatitis B
- **Birth and Beyond**
- HSV1
- **Less than 2 years**
- Rotavirus

Birth onward
- Influenza
- Parainfluenza (croup) in infants, colds in school age
- RSV (bronchiolitis) in infants, colds in school age

School age onward
- B19 (stops before adolescence)
- Norwalk
- Measles
- Mumps
- Hepatitis A
- Rubella
- Chickenpox

Adolescents (onset sexual activity) and beyond
- HSV2
- Hepatitis B
- HIV

Elderly
- Arbovirus encephalitides
- Shingles

Immunity to Virus Infections

- Viruses are obligate intracellular parasites, so the adaptive immune response that eradicates infected cells is the classical APC stimulating the TH1 and activating the effectors of CMI.
- Anti-viral interferons are a component of the innate immune response to viruses. These are **type 1 interferons, IFN-α and IFN-β**, and they act by slowing the viral life cycle until the adaptive response can take over. They are secreted by infected cells, and act on uninfected cells in the vicinity to slow the virus life cycle and enhance immunity by:
    - Activation of an RNA endonuclease
    - Activation a protein kinase that inactivates eIF2
    - Increasing expression of MHC1 and MHC2
    - Activation of NK cells and phagocytosis
    - Induction of chemokines to attract WBC

IFN-α is in clinical use in the treatment of hepatitis B and C, Kaposi sarcoma, hairy B cell leukemia and chronic myelogenous leukemia.

IFN-β increases the length of remissions in multiple sclerosis.

IFN-γ (a type 2 interferon) is used to treat chronic granulomatous disease.

Viral Genetics

Viruses are simple agents that use the strategy of producing volumes of progeny as quickly as possible, with little attention to the accuracy of their replication. Changes in phenotype can indeed be beneficial for avoidance of adaptive immunity, so there is little care placed in stringent proofreading for mutational errors. When viruses use the polymerase enzymes of the host cell, the proofreading capacity of the native polymerase is retained, but the polymerases that viruses bring for their own purposes are notoriously sloppy. The mutational changes that occur as a result are referred to as **genetic drift**, and they can be responsible for epidemics of disease.

Complementation

While it is certainly true that genetic shift can generate virions that are defective and unable to complete their life cycle in some way, remember that when two defective viruses get into a single cell, they can complement each other's genetic defects as long as the defects are different. An example of this is the co-infection of cells with **hepatitis B virus and the delta agent (hepatitis D)**. The delta agent is a defective virus but can complete its life cycle inside cells infected with hepatitis B because it can use the gene products that it needs by complementation. On its own, the delta agent creates abortive infections.

Genetic Shift

For viruses that have a segmented genome (their nucleic acid strands in separate pieces), it is possible to have a more dramatic change in phenotype due to the process of **reassortment**. This is referred to as **genetic shift** and is responsible for the development of pandemics of these viral infections (**R**eovirus, **O**rthomyxovirus, **B**unyavirus and **A**renavirus: **ROBA**, sounds like robot, and robots have segmented appendages). This is what happens in influenza virus infections at about 10 year intervals: when animal and human influenza viruses infect a single cell, they can accidentally reassort the segments of their genome and the product is a generation of new progeny with attributes that are different from those of either parental virus. This requires a novel immune response, and large populations of humans become ill.

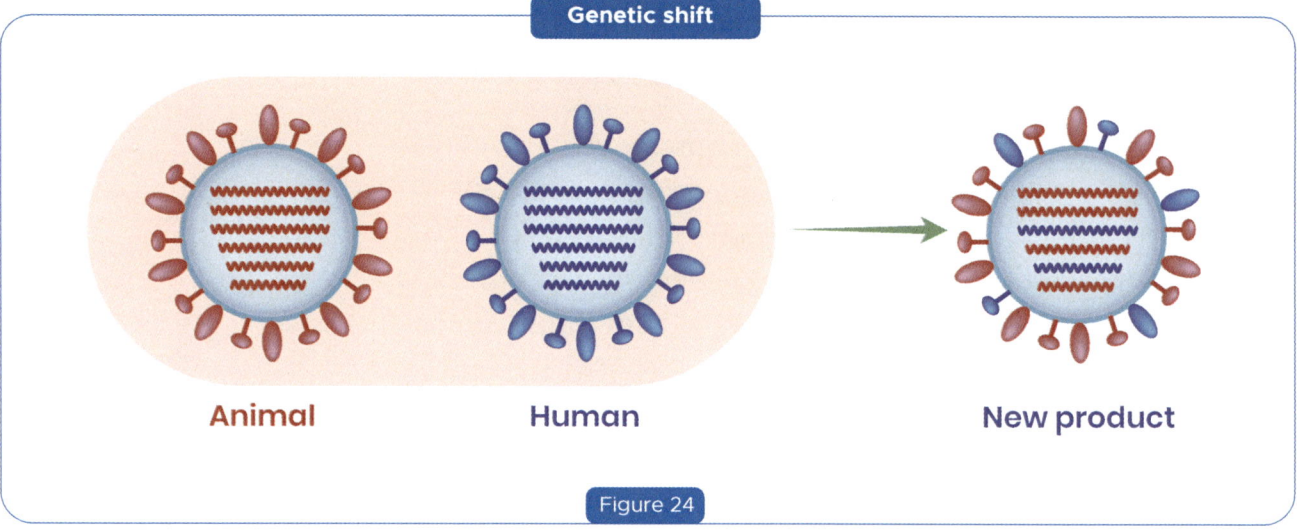

Figure 24

Microbial Oncogenesis

Microbial Oncogensis

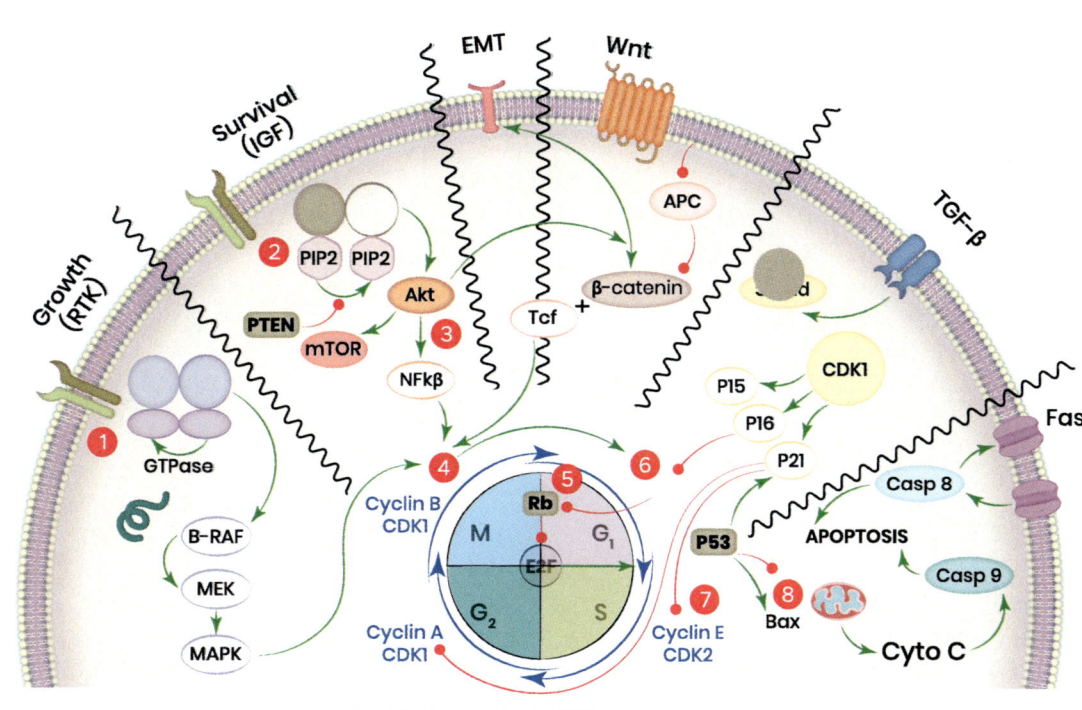

Molecular Basis of Neoplasms

1. Growth factor pathways – *Helicobacter pylori CagA* products

2. P13K – HTLV-1 *tax* gene activates

3. NFKB activation – latent membrane protein-1 (LMP-1) of EBV, HBV, HCV, HTLV-1

4. Transcription factors: EBV – polyclonal mitogenesis of B cells promotes translocation t(8:14) and ↑ expression of *myc*. EBV (Hodgkin) LMP-1 activates Jak/STAT. HBV (HBx protein) and HBcAg ↑ signal transduction

5. pRB inactivation - Polyomavirus large T antigen, HBV E7 protein and adenovirus E1A proteins

6. Activation cyclin D – EBNA-2 antigen, HHV-8 produces viral homolog of cyclin D

7. Inhibition p53 – HPV E6 protein, adenovirus E1B protein, HBV x protein, HHV-8

8. Activation Bcl (prevents apoptosis) – EBV

Figure 25

Anti-Viral Pharmacotherapy

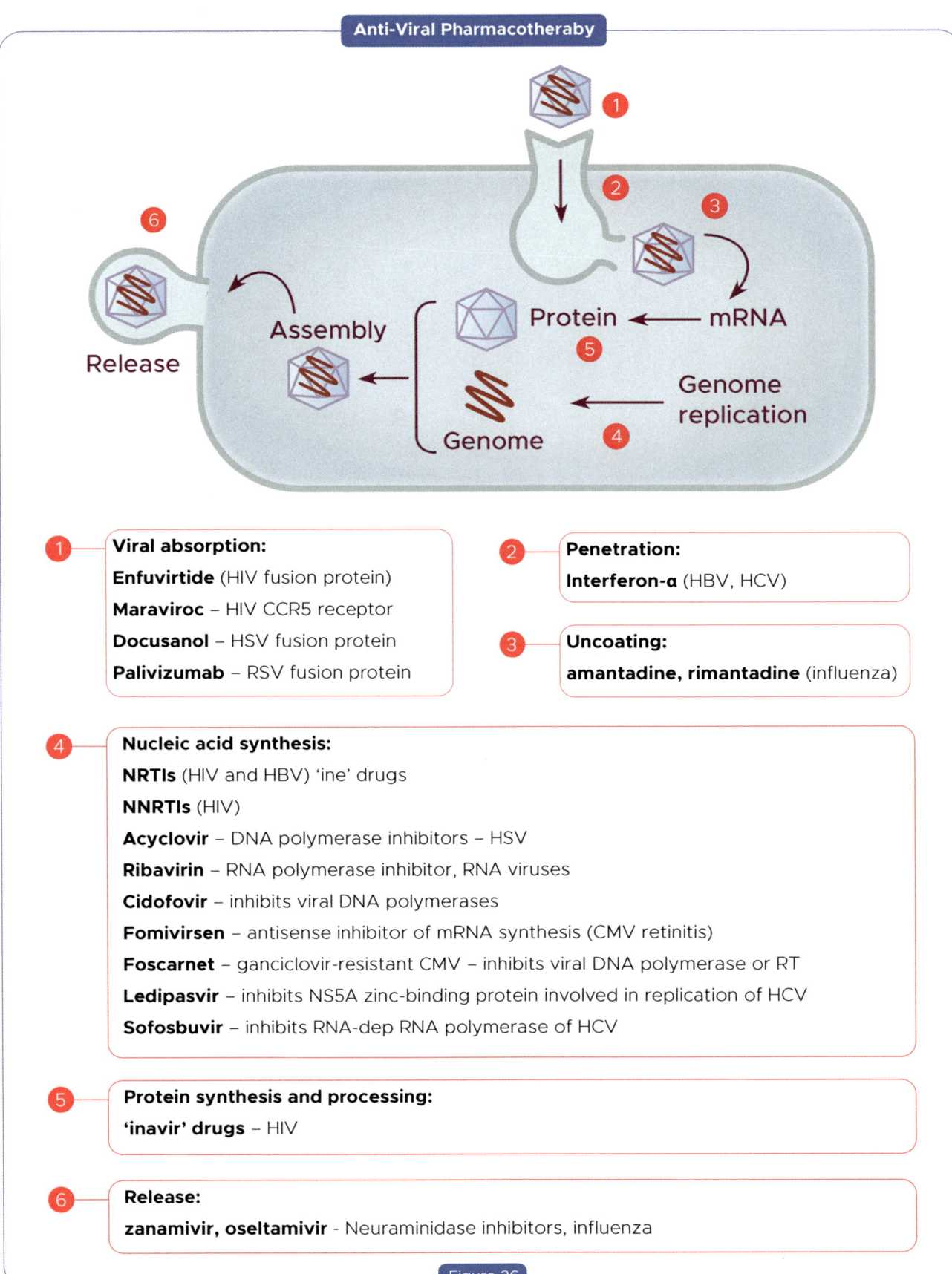

1 Viral absorption:
Enfuvirtide (HIV fusion protein)
Maraviroc – HIV CCR5 receptor
Docusanol – HSV fusion protein
Palivizumab – RSV fusion protein

2 Penetration:
Interferon-α (HBV, HCV)

3 Uncoating:
amantadine, rimantadine (influenza)

4 Nucleic acid synthesis:
NRTIs (HIV and HBV) 'ine' drugs
NNRTIs (HIV)
Acyclovir – DNA polymerase inhibitors – HSV
Ribavirin – RNA polymerase inhibitor, RNA viruses
Cidofovir – inhibits viral DNA polymerases
Fomivirsen – antisense inhibitor of mRNA synthesis (CMV retinitis)
Foscarnet – ganciclovir-resistant CMV – inhibits viral DNA polymerase or RT
Ledipasvir – inhibits NS5A zinc-binding protein involved in replication of HCV
Sofosbuvir – inhibits RNA-dep RNA polymerase of HCV

5 Protein synthesis and processing:
'inavir' drugs – HIV

6 Release:
zanamivir, oseltamivir - Neuraminidase inhibitors, influenza

Figure 26

Hepatitis (Hepatotropic) Viruses

Epidemiology
- **A, B, C, and D are worldwide** in distribution. **E occurs only in Africa and Asia**
- **A and E (the vowels) are transmitted by the bowels** (fecal/oral), all others are sexual/parenteral.
- **A and E cause only acute** infections
- **B and D cause acute and chronic** infections
- **C causes only chronic (85%)**

Symptoms of hepatitis:
- fever
- malaise
- headache
- anorexia
- vomiting
- dark urine
- clay-colored stools
- jaundice

The changes in color of skin, sclera, urine, serum and stool can be understood as alterations of the liver's ability to metabolize hemoglobin.

Heme	
Biliverdin	Spleen
Bilirubin	
Bilirubin-albumin	Blood
Bilirubin	
Bilirubin diglucuronide	Liver
Urobilinogen	Intestine
Stercobilin	Feces

Because of inflammation and fibrosis in the bile canaliculi, conjugated bilirubin is prevented from entering the intestine and passed back into the blood. From there it is eventually cleared out via the kidney. The stool is pale because the stercobilin is not being produced there, and the urine is dark because the kidney is handling the urobilinogen.

Medical Microbiology Essentials

The Differential Diagnosis of Jaundice:

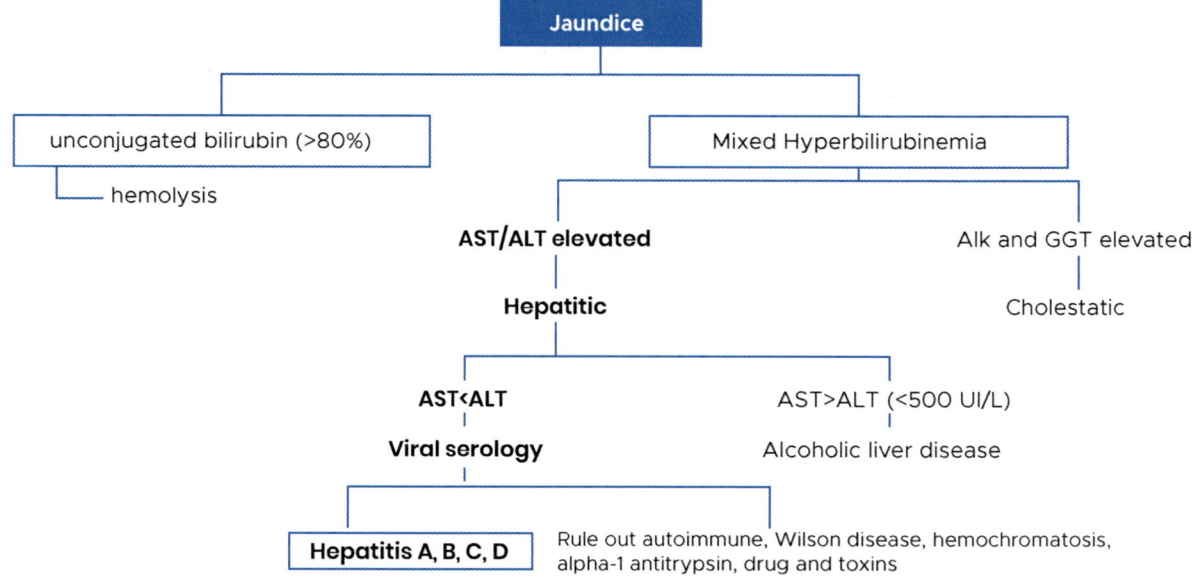

	Hepatitis A	**Hepatitis B**	**Hepatitis C**	**Hepatitis D**	**Hepatitis E**
Virus	Picorna, +ssRNA, naked	Hepadna, dsDNA, enveloped	Flavi, +ssRNA, enveloped	Defective, ss+RNA with HBV envelope	Hepe, +ssRNA, naked
Transmission	Fecal/oral	Sexual/parenteral	Sexual/parenteral	Sexual/parenteral	Fecal/oral
Dx	IgM anti HAV	IgM anti-HBcAg and HBsAg	EIA for anti-HCV	Anti-HDV plus HBsAg	serology
Rx	Pooled Igs	Acute – supportive Chronic – IFN-α plus lamivudine, entecavir, tenofovir, telbivudine	Direct-acting antivirals, ledipasvir, daclatasvir, sofosbuvir, elbasvir, glecaprevir etc.	IFN-α, hepcludex (entry inhibitor), lonafarnib (prenylation inhibitor) plus ritonavir	Ribavirin Supportive
Prevention	Killed vaccine	Recombinant DNA vaccine with HBsAg	Vaccine unlikely because of genomic mutations	HBV vaccine	None
Natural Hx		10% chronicity in adults 90% infants	Hepatocellular carcinoma. 1-5% progression/yr after cirrhosis develops	Coinfection – same as monoinfection. Superinfection – 70-90% → severe disease, → cirrhosis 10 years before monoinfected pts	20% mortality in pregnant women

Hepatitis B Structure

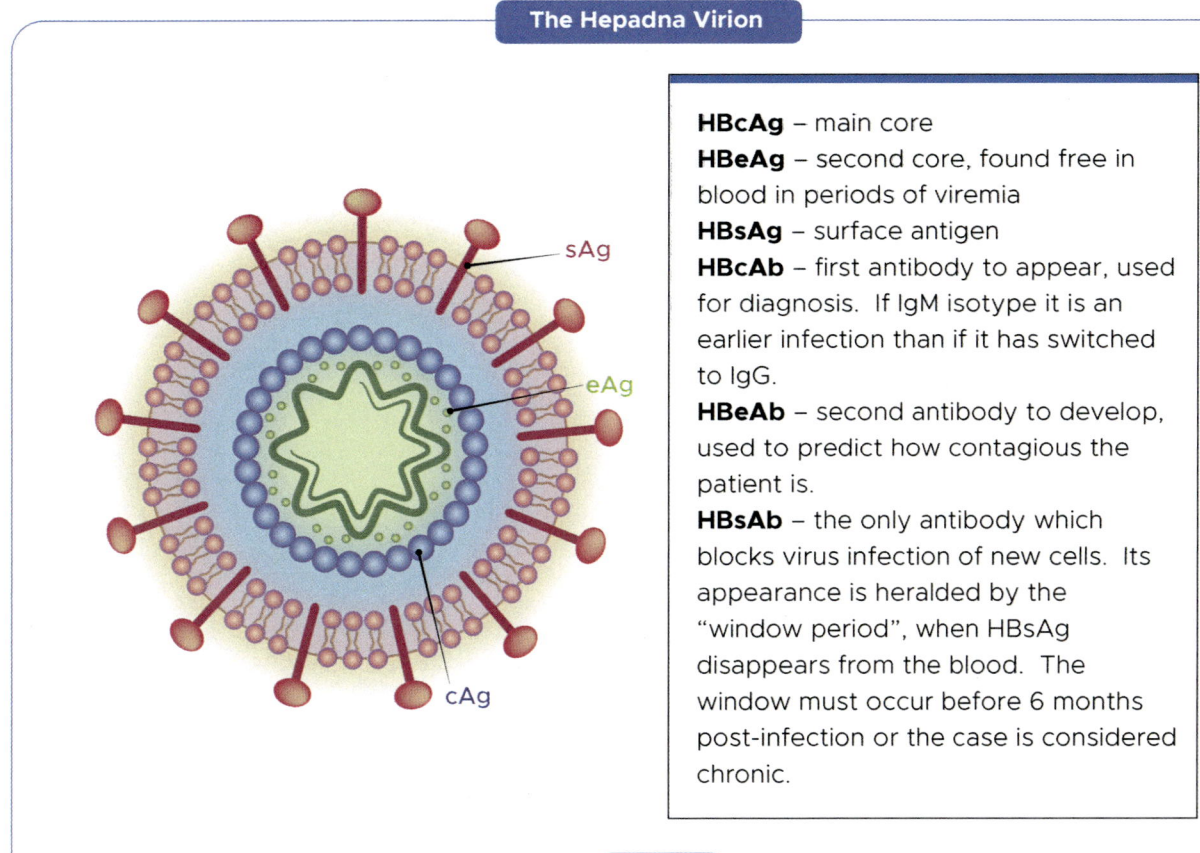

HBcAg – main core
HBeAg – second core, found free in blood in periods of viremia
HBsAg – surface antigen
HBcAb – first antibody to appear, used for diagnosis. If IgM isotype it is an earlier infection than if it has switched to IgG.
HBeAb – second antibody to develop, used to predict how contagious the patient is.
HBsAb – the only antibody which blocks virus infection of new cells. Its appearance is heralded by the "window period", when HBsAg disappears from the blood. The window must occur before 6 months post-infection or the case is considered chronic.

Figure 27

Hepatitis B Serology

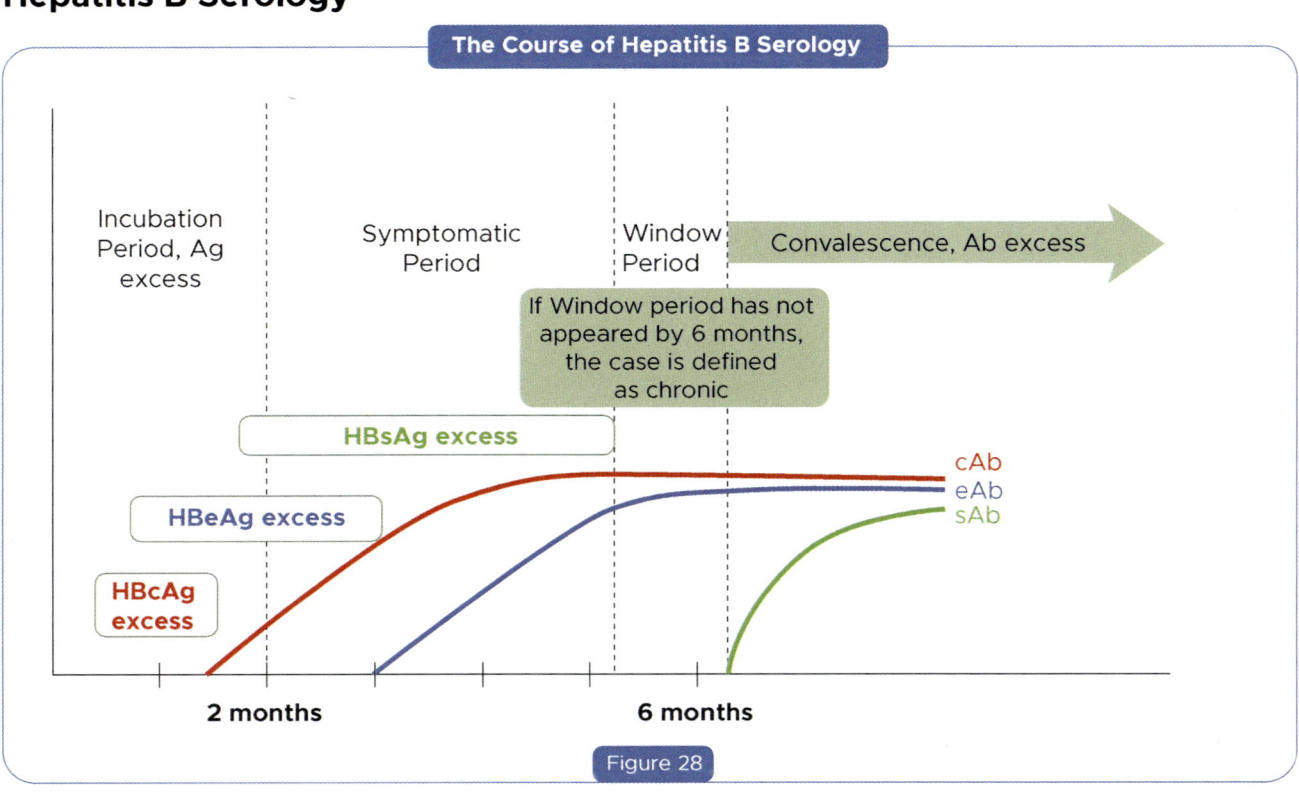

Figure 28

Summary of Serologic Markers during Acute and Chronic HBV infection

Marker	Acute <3 mo	Acute 3-6 mo	Window	Acute convalescent	Chronic	Vaccinated
HBcAg	-	-	-	-	-	-
HBeAg	+	-	-	-	-	-
HBsAg	+	+	-	-	+	-
HBcAb	IgM	IgG	+	+	+	-
HBeAb	-	+	+	+	+/-	-
HBsAb	-	-	-	+	-	+

DNA Viruses

The Life Cycle of DNA Viruses

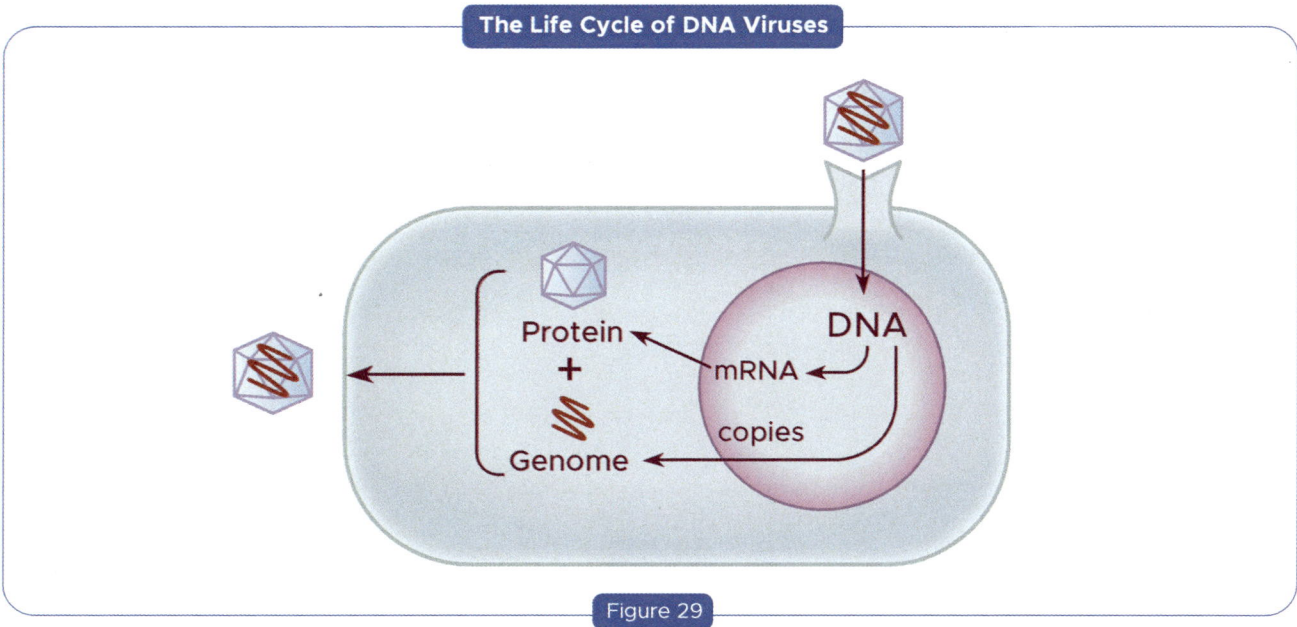

Figure 29

DNA viruses replicate in the nucleus (they produce intra-nuclear inclusion bodies). Most use the cell's polymerases.
- **Hepadna** virus replicates DNA through the mRNA intermediate using its own reverse transcriptase.
- **Poxviruses** replicate in the cytoplasm so they have to carry their own DNA-dependent, RNA polymerase and make their DNA replicases in the cytoplasm.
- DNA viruses use cellular polymerases for transcription and create proteins in the cytoplasm.

Assembly occurs in the cytoplasm, and they leave the cell by either lysing it (naked capsid viruses) or capturing membrane for their envelope.
- **Herpesviruses assemble new virions in the nucleus**, bud their envelope from the **nuclear membrane** and leave the cell through the Golgi complex.
- Poxviruses create their own envelope from lipid leaflets in the cytoplasm.

Medical Microbiology Essentials

Algorithm for Families of DNA Viruses

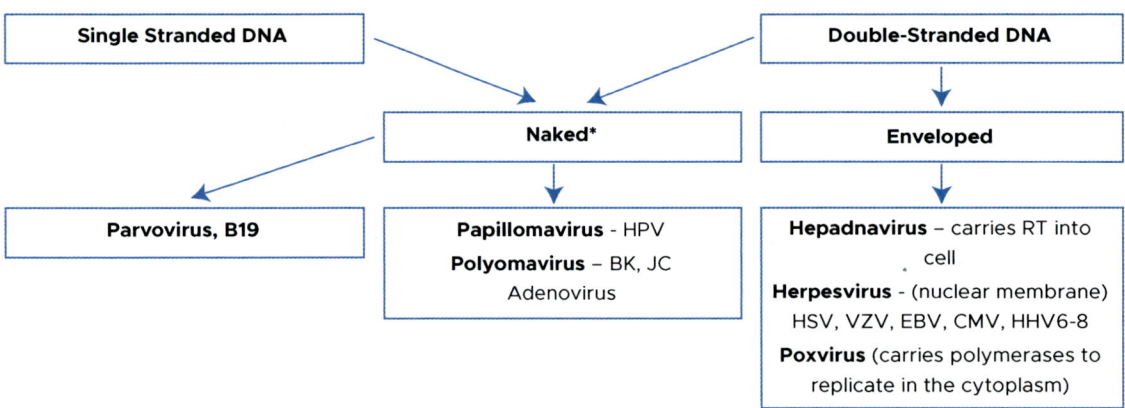

*The naked DNA viruses are **PAPP** – you have to be naked for a Pap smear.
Mnemonic: **P**ardon **P**a**P**a **A**s **H**e **H**as **P**ox (**P**arvo, **P**apilloma, **P**olyoma, **A**deno, **H**epadna, **H**erpes, **P**ox)

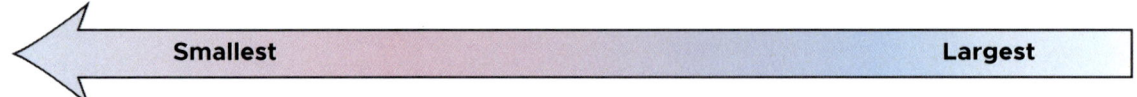

Single-Stranded DNA, Naked Parvovirus (B19) Fifth Disease (Erythema infectiosum)

Epidemiology:
- Common worldwide
- Children 2-5 years 5-10% seropositive
- 50% positive by 15 years
- 60% by 30 years
- 90% in over 60-year-old group
- Annual seroconversion rate in pregnant women 1.5%
- Transmission – respiratory route

Patients, Pathogenesis and Pharmacotherapy:

Chief Complaint	Vignette Clues	Pathogenesis	Rx
Fever, rash (Slapped cheek fever)	Young child, raised erythematous facial rash. Circumoral pallor. Serology, PCR	Tropism for erythroid progenitors, binds to P blood antigen receptor (globoside). Virus is cytotoxic, suppresses erythrogenesis. Aplastic crises in sickle cell patients. Arthropathy due to immune complexes	Supportive
Rash and joint pain			
Hydrops fetalis	Transmission across the placenta before 20 weeks gestation		

Double-Stranded DNA, Naked
Papillomaviridae (Human Papillomavirus)

Epidemiology:
- Common worldwide, most common STI in US.
    ◇ **99.7% of all cervical cancers** (serotypes 16, 18, 31, 35)
- Transmission skin-to-skin, sexual contact, fomites
- **Vaccine introduced in 2006, infections down 83%** in some age groups

Patients, Pathogenesis and Pharmacotherapy:

Chief Complaint	Vignette Clues	Pathogenesis	Rx
Warts	Plantar – serotype 1 Common – serotypes 2,4 Anogenital – serotypes 6, 11 (benign). Clinical description.	Infects basal layer of skin and mucous membranes, hyperkeratosis leads to warts	Salicylic acid, podophyllin (arrests mitosis in metaphase), imiquimod, podophyllotoxin, 5-fluorouracil (cytotoxic) Liquid nitrogen or laser
Abnormal vaginal discharge or bleeding, growth or sore on penis (HPV neoplasia)	**Koilocytosis** on pap smear: perinuclear vacuolization and nuclear enlargement), DNA probes and PCR.	Viral E6 and E7 proteins inactivate p53 and p105Rb (tumor suppressor genes), respectively.	Electrocautery, radiation therapy or surgery. Vaccine-recombinant DNA capsid proteins from serotypes 6, 11, 16, 18.

Double-Stranded DNA, Naked Polyomaviridae (BK Virus, JC Virus)

Epidemiology:
- Common (70-80% seropositive) but asymptomatic in immunocompetent individuals.
- Transmission respiratory or oral/oral from early childhood.

Patients, Pathogenesis and Pharmacotherapy:

Chief Complaint	Vignette Clues	Pathogenesis	Rx
Dysuria, flank pain	**Immunocompromised** patient, urine cytology with decoy cells (virus-infected urothelial cells with intranuclear inclusions). Virus culture, PCR, kidney biopsy.	BK virus – hemorrhagic cystitis and tubulointerstitial nephritis	Cidofovir, leflunomide (immunomodulatory, reduces denovo synthesis of DNA and RNA), reduce immunosuppression
Mental impairment, vision loss, speech disturbance	**Immunocompromised** patient (AIDS) with hemiparesis, hemianopsia, cognitive deterioration. PCR of brain or CSF	JC virus – progressive multifocal leukoencephalopathy. Targets oligodendroglial cells. Foci of demyelination, giant astrocytes with intranuclear inclusions.	Initiation of anti-retroviral therapy

Double-Stranded DNA, Naked
Adenovirus

Epidemiology:
- Common worldwide, responsible for between 2-5% of all respiratory infections.
- High incidence in crowded military training situations caused development of **live non-attenuated** vaccine for serotypes 4 and 7
- Tropism for epithelial cells
- Site of entry determines site of infection:
- Respiratory – droplet inhalation
- GI – fecal/oral

Patients, Pathogenesis and Pharmacotherapy:

Chief Complaint	Vignette Clues	Pathogenesis	Rx
Fever, dry cough	Children – serotypes 3, 7 Adults – serotypes 3, 7, 14 All diagnosed by serology	Lytic infection in epithelial cells. Penton fibers act as hemagglutinins and are cytotoxic. E3 protein decreases MHC 1 expression.	Supportive, cidofovir, ribavirin, sanitary precautions, live **non-attenuated vaccine** in the military
Pink eye	Serotypes 3, 19, conjunctivitis or keratoconjunctivitis		
Dysuria	Serotype 11, hemorrhagic cystitis		
Diarrhea	Serotypes 40, 41, watery diarrhea		

Double-Stranded DNA, Enveloped
Hepadnavirus (discussed previously)

Double-Stranded DNA, Enveloped
(Nuclear Membrane)
Herpesviruses

Epidemiology:
- Common worldwide, life-long latencies
- HSV-1 is #1 cause of viral encephalitis in the US. Bimodal distribution...primary infection in early adulthood, reactivational disease in 50+ year age group
- Transmission –
    - close personal contact – all
    - sexual – HSV-2, HHV-8, CMV
    - saliva – EBV, CMV, HHV-8
    - respiratory – VZV (also contact with ruptured vesicles)

1. Herpes simplex-1
Patients, Pathogenesis and Pharmacotherapy:

Chief Complaint	Vignette Clues	Pathogenesis	Rx
Painful mucosal blisters	Mostly above the waist. **Tzanck smear** detects multinucleated giant cells. **Eczema herpeticum** in children with eczema or atopic dermatitis.	Replicate in mucoepithelial cells, produce lytic, productive infection. **Syncytial virus**, protects against HI. latency in sensory ganglia: **trigeminal ganglia** if inoculated above the waist. Stress causes reactivation.	Acyclovir, valacyclovir, famciclovir. Acyclovir is a nucleoside analog, administered in prodrug form, requires the viral thymidine kinase to phosphorylate. Once activated by cellular kinases, it inhibits the viral DNA polymerase.
Painful eye ulcers, tearing, photophobia	**Dendritic ulcers**, may lead to blindness		Acyclovir ophthalmic plus steroid eyedrops
Fever, lethargy, confusion, delirium (encephalitis)	Age group within **bimodal distribution**. Focal temporal lesions, RBCs in CSF, high opening pressure	70% mortality if untreated.	**Medical emergency, treat presumptively**

2. Herpes simplex-2
Patients, Pathogenesis and Pharmacotherapy:

Chief Complaint	Vignette Clues	Pathogenesis	Rx
Painful genital blisters	Most common below the waist. **Tzanck test,** viral culture, PCR	As above, with latency in **sacral ganglia** if inoculated below the waist.	Acyclovir, valacyclovir, famciclovir
Seizures, mucocutaneous blisters	Infant, first two weeks of life, CSF pleocytosis, fever	As above.	Intravenous ganciclovir, valganciclovir

3. Varicella zoster virus
Epidemiology:
- Transmitted by respiratory droplet and contact with ruptured vesicles.
- Prior to vaccine 4 million infected, 10-13,000 hospitalized and 100-150 died yearly. Varicella vaccine (live attenuated) introduced in 1995. Incidence declined 78%, deaths down 87%.
- Zoster live attenuated vaccine (Zostavac) introduced 2006, recombinant DNA vaccine (Shingrix) 2017.
- Herpes zoster - 1 in 3 persons in US during their life-time will develop.
- Immunocompromise results in increased risk.

Patients, Pathogenesis and Pharmacotherapy:

Chief Complaint	Vignette Clues	Pathogenesis	Rx
Fever, pruritic vesicular rash (**chickenpox**)	Unvaccinated child, **asynchronous** rash, clinical diagnosis, PCR, Tzanck smear	Infection begins in URT, viremia, spread to reticuloendothelial system and skin (rash). **Latency in dorsal root ganglia**	Acyclovir, valaciclovir, famciclovir in immunocompromised. Immunoglobulins available for post-exposure prophylaxis of immunocompromised. Avoid aspirin (Reye syndrome). LA vaccine
Painful, burning rash **Shingles**	**50 years and above, single dermatome** (does not cross midline)	Reactivation due to waning immunity and stress.	Acyclovir, valaciclovir, famciclovir. LA and recombinant vaccines

4. Epstein-Barr virus

Epidemiology:
- Worldwide, 80-90% infected, mostly in childhood.
- Transmitted in bodily fluids, especially saliva, but also sexual contact, blood transfusions, organ transplantation.

Patients, Pathogenesis and Pharmacotherapy:

Chief Complaint	Vignette Clues	Pathogenesis	Rx
Fever, fatigue, sore throat, swollen cervical lymph nodes (mononucleosis)	Teenager/college student, **heterophile (monospot) positive, lymphocytosis (70%) due to CTLs (Downey cells). Complication splenic rupture.** Specific serologic tests – **high titer of IgM against VCA and no titer to EBNA = acute infection.**	Virus infects B lymphocytes and nasopharyngeal epithelial cells by **binding to CD21.** Causes polyclonal activation to produce antibodies. Splenomegaly and lymphadenopathy from B cell proliferation	Supportive maribavir (investigational oral benzimidazole L-riboside)
Fever, swollen lymph nodes, persistent	**Lymphoproliferative disease,** patient with primary or secondary immunodeficiency.		Immunotherapy
White patches on sides of tongue	**Hairy oral leukoplakia.** Immunocompromised patient. White plaques cannot be dislodged.	Proliferation of lingual epithelia in AIDS	Return immune response to normal, acyclovir
Painless lymph node swelling, fatigue weight loss	**Hodgkin Lymphoma.** Nodes above diaphragm in 80% of cases. Pain in nodes precipitated by drinking alcohol, Reed-Sternberg cells by fine needle biopsy express CD30 and CD15.	**Latent membrane protein-1 (LMP-1) activates NF-KB and Jak/STAT.** Burkitt (Africa and Asia) **t(8:14) translocation** increases expression of *myc*.	Chemotherapy, radiotherapy

5. Cytomegalovirus

Epidemiology:
- Common worldwide, over ½ of adults infected by age 40.
- One out of every 200 babies born with congenital CMV, 1/5 of these will have long-term health effects.
- Transmitted by intimate contact; saliva, breast milk, urine, tears, sexual transmission, transplacental, organ transplant, blood products
- #1 in utero infection in the US

Patients, Pathogenesis and Pharmacotherapy:

Chief Complaint	Vignette Clues	Pathogenesis	Rx
Fever, sore throat, fatigue, swollen lymph nodes	**Heterophile negative mononucleosis, Owl's eye inclusion bodies in biopsy and urine**, PCR, culture, serology	Infects endothelial cells, lymphocytes and monocytes. Latency in monocytes. Severity relates to immunologic damage.	Ganciclovir, foscarnet, cidofovir (maribavir, investigational)
Fever, diarrhea, dyspnea	**Transplant patient** on immunosuppressive therapy, weeks to months after surgery, retinitis.		
Newborn with low Apgar score, rash (**cytomegalic inclusion disease**)	**Blueberry muffin rash**, microcephaly, periventricular brain calcification, sensorineural deafness, thrombocytopenic purpura, hepatomegaly. Inclusions in urine, PCR		

6. HHV-6 and HHV-7

Epidemiology:
- Common worldwide, 90% of children are seropositive by 3 years of age.
- Transmission from respiratory secretions, usually ends when fever breaks.

Patients, Pathogenesis and Pharmacotherapy:

Chief Complaint	Vignette Clues	Pathogenesis	Rx
Fever, rash	HHV-6, Exanthem subitum, roseola infantum, sixth disease. Abrupt onset of high fever. Rash begins on face and trunk **after** fever breaks. Child **6 mo to 3 years**	T cell lymphotropic	Supportive, anti-pyretics
	HHV-7, Child outside of infancy, otherwise same as above		

7. HHV-8 (Kaposi sarcoma-associated herpesvirus)

Epidemiology:
- AIDS indicator disease
- Sexual and nonsexual transmission

Patients, Pathogenesis and Pharmacotherapy:

Chief Complaint	Vignette Clues	Pathogenesis	Rx
Purple, red or brown spots on the skin, in the mouth or throat (Kaposi Sarcoma)	AIDS patient, greatest risk with low CD4 count, Serology, PCR	B cell lymphotropic virus, turns on VEGF	IFN-α or IL-12 Surgery, radiation, chemotherapy liposomal doxorubicin, paclitaxel, vinorelbine

Double-Stranded DNA, Complex (Brick-shaped) Replicates in the Cytoplasm, Carries DNA-dependent RNA polymerase into cell Makes its own Envelope
Poxviruses

Epidemiology:
- Smallpox – last natural case Somalia 1977, respiratory droplets. Now a concern as a potential bioweapon. Vaccine – live, attenuated, in use only in military.
- Molluscum contagiosum – direct contact, sexual, fomites, swimming pools Children 0-14 years, 12 to 14 episodes per 1000 children per year.
- Monkeypox - current worldwide outbreak, 10,000 cases, primarily men who have sex with men.

Patients, Pathogenesis and Pharmacotherapy:

Chief Complaint	Vignette Clues	Pathogenesis	Rx
Fever, rash (Smallpox)	Biowarfare. Synchronous rash, begins in mouth, spreads over entire body. **Guarnieri bodies** (cytoplasmic inclusions) found in infected cells	Viremia causes infection of dermis and internal organs, hemorrhage into the dermis causes pocks.	Cidofovir LA vaccine eradicated
Warts (Molluscum contagiosum)	School age child, **umbilicated warts**, athlete in contact sports (wrestling). **Eosinophilic cytoplasmic inclusions** in epithelial cells.	Virus enters through breaks in skin, causes hyperplasia and acanthosis of epidermis	Curettage, cryotherapy Self-limiting in immunocompetent. Ritonavir, cidofovir for immunocompromised.
Fever, rash (Monkeypox)	MSM, travel outside of US or contact.	as with smallpox?	tecovirimat, vaccination

RNA Viruses

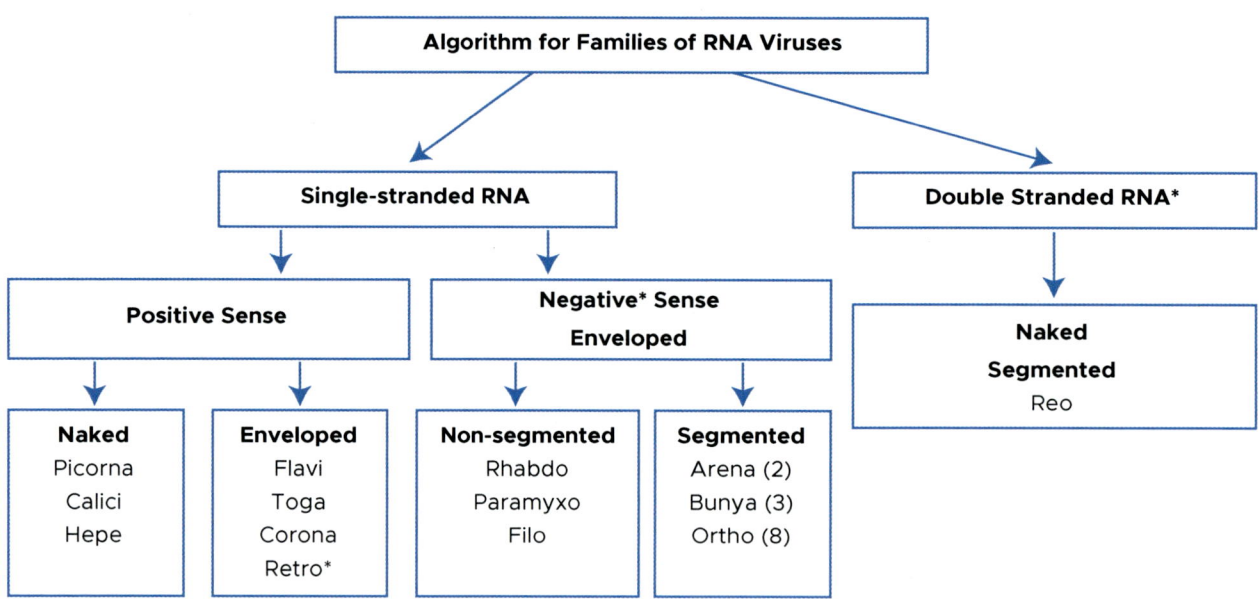

*Viruses which must carry a polymerase with them into the cell.
The naked RNA viruses: **H**elp **R**emove **C**lothes **P**lease! (**H**epe, **R**eo, **C**alici, **P**icorna).
The segmented viruses: **ROBA** (**R**eo, **O**rthomyxo, **B**unya, **A**rena)
Mnemonic for positive sense RNA viruses: **P**ico **C**alls **H**enry and **F**lo **T**o **C**ome **R**ightaway (**P**icorna, **C**alici, **H**epe, **F**lavi, **T**oga, **C**orona, **R**etro)
Mnemonic for negative sense RNA viruses: **B**ring **A** **P**olymerase **O**r **F**ail **R**eplication (**B**unya, **A**rena, **P**aramyxo, **O**rthomyxo, **F**ilo, **R**habdo)

RNA virus Life Cycle

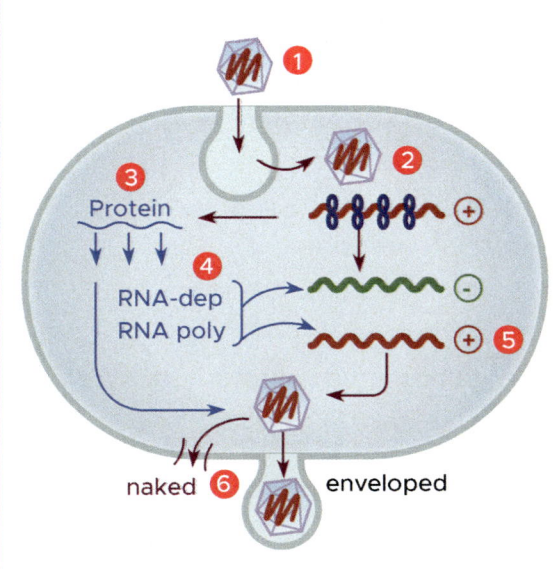

1. Attachment and penetration
2. Uncoating in the cytoplasm
3. Positive sense RNA is used on ribosomes to create protein.
4. One of the encoded proteins is an RNA-dependent RNA polymerase which replicates the viral RNA by making a negative-sense strand.
5. The negative-sense strand is again complemented to make more copies of the positive sense genome. (These can also be used to speed up translation)
6. Proteins and genome copies are assembled and leave the cell either by lysis (naked capsid) or by budding (enveloped capsid viruses).

Figure 30

Medical Microbiology Essentials

Positive-Sense, Single-Stranded RNA Viruses, Naked
Picorna
(PEECoRnA: Polio, Echo, Entero, Coxsackie, Rhino, hep A)

Epidemiology:
- Summer/Fall peak incidence, **fecal/oral transmission** (stable in acid), grow best at body temperature.
- Very large number of members of family, so divided into genera
    - **Enterovirus** genus – leading cause of aseptic meningitis and viral myocarditis
    - **Heparnavirus** genus – Hepatitis A, already discussed
    - **Rhinovirus** genus – **most common cause of common cold (peak summer/fall)**
        - Exception to genus rule: not fecal/oral in transmission, not stable in acid, grows best at 33°C

1. Enterovirus Genus:
Patients, Pathogenesis and Pharmacotherapy:

Chief Complaint	Vignette Clues	Pathogenesis	Rx
Fever, headache, altered mental status, stiff neck, photophobia	Enterovirus #1 cause **aseptic meningitis**, serology or virus culture, echovirus also.	Infection begins in oropharynx, moves into intestinal mucosa and lymphoid tissue. Viremia causes spread throughout body.	Supportive
Oral pain, rash	Coxsackie A16 – **hand-foot-and-mouth**, rash on buttocks hands and feet	Also causes herpangina, aseptic meningitis, pharyngitis, common cold	Supportive
Dyspnea, orthopnea, leg swelling	Coxsackie B (#1 cause of viral **myocarditis** necessitating cardiac transplant)	Also causes pleurodynia, aseptic meningitis, systemic disease of newborns	Interferons, pleconaril, acyclovir
Flaccid paralysis	**Polio** endemic area, unvaccinated, descending paralysis, no sensory loss	Damage to **anterior horn motor** neurons. Post-polio syndrome with muscle atrophy	Supportive Salk – **killed** vaccine (US) Sabin – live attenuated (rest of world)

2. Rhinovirus Genus
Patients, Pathogenesis and Pharmacotherapy:

Chief Complaint	Vignette Clues	Pathogenesis	Rx
Cough, sore throat, fever, congestion, rhinorrhea (**Common cold**)	Summer and fall months, 100 serotypes.	Virus binds to ICAM-1	Zinc lozenges (Zicam) can prevent viral adherence and shorten symptoms. Otherwise supportive.

Calicivirus (Norovirus, Norwalk)

Epidemiology:
- Most common cause of noninflammatory gastroenteritis in US (1/2 of all foodborne disease outbreaks)
- Fecal-oral transmission

Patients, Pathogenesis and Pharmacotherapy:

Chief Complaint	Vignette Clues	Pathogenesis	Rx
Vomiting, diarrhea, stomach pain	**Cruise ship** or confined dining areas. 12-48 hours incubation (Norovirus gastroenteritis)	Virus replicates in small intestine, self-limiting in 24-72 hours	Supportive

Hepevirus
Hepatitis E – discussed previously

Positive-Sense, Single-Stranded RNA Viruses, Enveloped
Flavivirus
(Dengue, Hepatitis C, St. Louis encephalitis, West Nile virus, Yellow Fever virus, Zika)

Epidemiology:
- Arthropod-borne except hepatitis C.
- Geographically distinguished, mostly tropical, not US (except WNV; St. Louis encephalitis)
- Zika – mosquito, transplacental, sex

Patients, Pathogenesis and Pharmacotherapy:

Chief Complaint	Vignette Clues	Pathogenesis	Rx
Fever, headache, muscle pain	Break-bone fever, **dengue**, *Aedes* mosquito, serology	Hemorrhagic fever	Acetaminophen (avoid aspirin)
	Yellow Fever: Tropical, hemorrhage and degeneration of liver, kidney, heart, *Aedes* mosquito		Live attenuated vaccine for travelers
Fever, headache, confusion	**St. Louis encephalitis**, Lower 48 states, *Culex* mosquito, #1 flaviviral encephalitis, serology, PCR	Uncertain, interferes with IFN-α function	Supportive
	WNV: Summer months, North America, kills wild birds.		
Fever, rash, headache, joint pain	**Zika:** traveler to an affected area. Newborn with microcephaly, serology or urine antigen test	Paraibo strain causes most brain cell death	Supportive

Togavirus
(rubella, EEE, VEE, WEE, chikungunya)

Epidemiology:
- Rubella – respiratory droplets, fewer than 10 cases per year in US.
- Encephalitides – mosquito borne, bird reservoir, 1 case/200,000 population per year.
- Chikungunya – Africa, Asia, Europe. Since 2013 - Caribbean

Patients, Pathogenesis and Pharmacotherapy:

Chief Complaint	Vignette Clues	Pathogenesis	Rx
Rash, fever	**Rubella.** Unvaccinated, in adult 3-day fever. Rash starts on face, spreads to trunk. **In utero** – CRS: deafness, **congenital heart defects (PDA, VSD)**, mental retardation, microcephaly, cataracts, thrombocytopenic purpura. Serology, culture, PCR	Infects upper respiratory tract, spreads via blood	Supportive Live attenuated vaccine (part of MMR)
Fever, headache, confusion	**Equine encephalitis viruses.** Sudden onset fever, general myalgia, headache, seizures, coma, Summer months, mosquito borne, bird reservoir. Serology or PCR	Infects monocytes and endothelial cells during viremia, enters CNS	Supportive
Fever, joint pain	**Chikungunya.** Geography, season. Serology, PCR	Immune pathology in joints	Supportive

Coronavirus
(coronavirus, SARS-CoV, MERS, COVID19)

Epidemiology:
- Corona – 2nd most common cause of the common cold
- Winter-spring peak incidence, respiratory droplet, airborne
- SARS, MERS, COVID19 – epidemic respiratory syndromes, animal reservoirs
- COVID-19 is now the most common cause of death in the US

Patients, Pathogenesis and Pharmacotherapy:

Chief Complaint	Vignette Clues	Pathogenesis	Rx
Fever, rhinorrhea, sore throat	Corona - Seasonal, US, self-limiting	Lytic infection in respiratory tissues	Supportive
Fever, sore throat, dyspnea	SARS, MERS, COVID19. Season, travel to endemic area, serology or PCR	Combination of animal and human strains creates newly emerging variants. Sars-COV-2 uses ACE-2 receptor with TMPRSS and HRH coreceptors. Causes respiratory distress, cytokine + bradykinin storms	Supportive. For COVID: remdesivir, paxlovid, dexamethasone, monoclonal antibodies. Vaccines – mRNA, adenoviral vector, recombinant DNA

Retrovirus
Lentivirus Group - HIV (previously discussed)

Oncovirus Group - HTLV

Epidemiology:
- Most common Japan, Caribbean and Central Africa
- Transmission sexual, parenteral

Patients, Pathogenesis and Pharmacotherapy:

Chief Complaint	Vignette Clues	Pathogenesis	Rx
Fatigue, enlarged lymph nodes	**ATLL:** Malignant T cells with flower shaped nucleus, RT-PCR for viral RNA, serology	Virus infects CD4 T lymphocytes. Tax protein increases production of IL-2 and CD25 (high affinity IL-2 receptor). Product of *hbz* gene causes clonal expansion of lymphocytes.	Zidovudine plus IFN-α, chemotherapy

Negative-Sense, Single-Stranded RNA Viruses
All Enveloped and Helical

The -ss RNA Virus Life Cycle

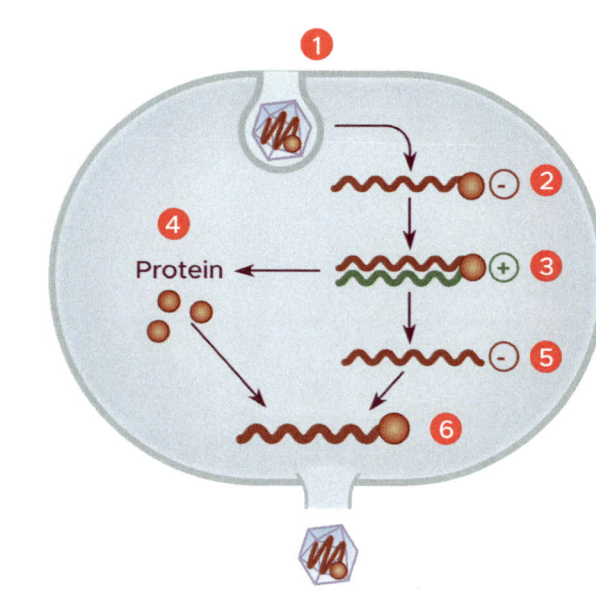

1. Attachment and penetration. Hemagglutinin binds to sialic acid.
2. Uncoating in the cytoplasm
3. Use of viral RNA-dependent RNA polymerase to create a mRNA (positive sense strand)
4. Creation of proteins using cellular ribosomes.
5. Use of viral RNA-dependent RNA polymerase to make more negative sense genomic copies.
6. Assembly of proteins and genomic copies and budding from cell membrane. Neuraminidase cuts off sialic acids and aids release.

Figure 31

Non-Segmented

1. Rhabdovirus (Rabies, Vesicular Stomatitis Virus)

Epidemiology:
- Human disease extremely rare in US. (1-3 cases per year)
- Unvaccinated cats and dogs become infected from rabid wildlife (bats, raccoons, skunks)

Patients, Pathogenesis and Pharmacotherapy:

Chief Complaint	Vignette Clues	Pathogenesis	Rx
Bite wound with itching, fever, headache, hallucinations, coma	Animal bite, or exposure to wildlife (bats). DFA of corneal epithelia, PCR. Animal with Negri bodies (eosinophilic intracytoplasmic inclusions) in purkinje/hippocampal neurons. Fatal if symptoms evident.	Virus binds to nicotinic acetylcholine receptors of nerve or muscle at bite site, moves by retrograde axoplasmic transport to dorsal root ganglia, spinal cord.	Postexposure prophylaxis: anti-rabies Abs into wound, 4 doses of **killed** vaccine (days 1,3,7,14).

2. Paramyxovirus (Measles, Mumps, Parainfluenza, Respiratory Syncytial virus)

Epidemiology:

- Measles declared eliminated from the US in 2011. Since then increasing incidence of cases brought in from outside US, in unvaccinated individuals.
- Resurgence of mumps may be due to waning vaccine protection
- All transmitted by aerosol or respiratory droplets.
- RSV – 177,000 hospitalizations and 14,000 deaths per year

Patients, Pathogenesis and Pharmacotherapy:

Chief Complaint	Vignette Clues	Pathogenesis	Rx
Cough, coryza, conjunctivitis	**Measles:** Unvaccinated child. **Koplik spots**, maculopapular rash begins on face, spreads downward. **Giant cell pneumonia – Warthin-Finkeldey cells.** Fatal neurologic sequela – **SSPE** (build-up of defective virus particles in brain), virus culture or PCR	HA and F protein, no NA. Replicates in respiratory tract, infects T and B cells, monocytes and PMNs impairing their function. **Syncytial** viruses evade humoral immunity	Supportive Live attenuated vaccine - MMR
Fever, swollen neck, cheeks	**Mumps:** unvaccinated child. Parotitis, pancreatitis, orchitis in adult males. **Elevated serum amylase.** Virus isolation from saliva, CSF, urine, serology	Combined HA, NA, separate F protein. Replicates in respiratory tract, lymphoid tissue spreads via blood to salivary glands. Causes necrosis and inflammation of epithelial lining of glands.	Supportive Live attenuated vaccine: MMR
Fever, honking cough	**Parainfluenza (croup).** 6 months to 3-year age group. **Laryngotracheobronchitis**, bronchiolitis, pneumonia. PCR or serology.	Single HA/NA and F proteins. Subglottic airway obstruction causes inspiratory stridor, hoarseness.	Supportive Ribavirin
Fever, wheezing, dyspnea	RSV **bronchiolitis**. Infant 6 weeks to 6 months. Hypoxemia and cyanosis. IFA, PCR, syncytia in cell culture. **Preemies at risk.**	Fusion protein, no HA or NA. Infection confined to respiratory epithelium. Necrosis of cells, interstitial mononuclear infiltrates	Supportive Palivizumab (monoclonal Ab vs. fusion protein) Prophylaxis to preemies ribavirin? Bronchodilators?

Non-segmented, Filamentous Filovirus
(Marburg, Ebola)

Epidemiology:
- Reservoir in Old World simians and rodents
- Transmitted by direct contact with blood, secretions

Patients, Pathogenesis and Pharmacotherapy:

Chief Complaint	Vignette Clues	Pathogenesis	Rx
Fever, fatigue, muscle pain (Marburg, Ebola)	Geography – Africa. Vomiting, diarrhea, internal bleeding, impaired kidney and liver function, Serology, PCR	Virus replicates in endothelium and causes necrosis	Supportive, quarantine Inmazeb (3 monoclonals, application for FDA approval 2020)

Segmented Negative-Sense RNA Viruses

1. Arenavirus (2 segments) "sand" in virions is ribosomes
(Lymphocytic choriomeningitis virus, Lassa fever virus)
Epidemiology:
- LCMV: Worldwide, 1-5% of population of US seropositive
- Transmitted from mice
- Lassa fever – West Africa
- Transmission person to person, contact with rodents

Patients, Pathogenesis and Pharmacotherapy:

Chief Complaint	Vignette Clues	Pathogenesis	Rx
Fever, headache, muscle pain	**LCMV:** Exposure to hamster/rodent breeding colonies, pet center.	Virus is not cytotoxic, immune response causes symptoms. Viremia seeds the meninges.	Supportive, ribavirin
Fever, fatigue, muscle pain	**Lassa fever:** West Africa, December to March, exposure to rats, hemorrhagic fever	Lack of CMI increases severity	Supportive, ribavirin

2. Bunyavirus (3 Segments)
(California encephalitis, LaCrosse encephalitis, Hantavirus)
Epidemiology:
- Hantavirus: worldwide, exposure to excreta of rodents
- US – Four Corners region (Utah, New Mexico, Colorado, Arizona)
- Encephalitis viruses – 80-100 cases per year, mosquito borne.

Patients, Pathogenesis and Pharmacotherapy:

Chief Complaint	Vignette Clues	Pathogenesis	Rx
Fever, dyspnea	**Hantavirus:** 4 Corners region, spring months, rodent exposure	Inhalation from excreta of rodents, infection of respiratory epithelium causes edema, effusion, 35% mortality	Respiratory support, ribavirin - experimental
Fever, headache, confusion	Geography, encephalitis with seizures, 5-18 year age group. **California or LaCrosse encephalitis viruses**	Invades CNS through cerebral capillary endothelial cells or choroid plexus	Supportive Ribavirin?

3. Orthomyxovirus (8 segments)
(Influenza)
Epidemiology:
- Common worldwide, fall and winter in US
- All ages susceptible, hospitalizations greater in over 65 year age group
- Transmission aerosol, respiratory droplet
- **Genetic shift** (Influenza A because strains in humans, swine, birds) due to reassortment causes pandemics
- **Genetic drift** due to mutation causes epidemics and mild disease after vaccination
- Vaccine is yearly epidemiological "best guess" about the serotypes which will prevail.

Patients, Pathogenesis and Pharmacotherapy:

Chief Complaint	Vignette Clues	Pathogenesis	Rx
Dry cough, fever, headache, myalgia (Influenza)	Abrupt onset, season, antigen detection in nasal swab or NAAT. Complications Reye syndrome, GBS	Virus uses HA to bind to sialic acid, multiplies in ciliated respiratory epithelial cells → cell death and desquamation → loss mucociliary escalator predisposes to secondary bacterial infection.	Supportive. Amantadine/rimantadine – prevent uncoating (recent isolates resistant). Zanamivir/oseltamivir – NA inhibitors work on Influenza A and B. Peramivir (i.v.) or baloxavir (oral). Vaccine: killed injectable, prepared in eggs. LA intranasal – ages 2-49

Double-Stranded, Naked RNA Viruses
Reovirus (10-11 segments, double shelled)
(Colorado tick fever virus, reovirus, rotavirus)

Epidemiology:
- Rota – most common watery diarrhea in pre-school age children, fecal-oral transmission
- Reo – fecal oral or respiratory transmission
- CTFV – *Dermacentor tick*

Patients, Pathogenesis and Pharmacotherapy:

Chief Complaint	Vignette Clues	Pathogenesis	Rx
Headache, myalgia, fever (Colorado Tick Fever)	CTFV. Geography, season (tick bite), encephalitis, **rash rare.** Serology	Endothelial cells serve as sites of amplification for spread via blood.	Supportive
Diarrhea or common cold	EIA (Reovirus)		Self-limiting
Diarrhea (Rotavirus)	**Infant**, daycare setting, **non-inflammatory diarrhea,** unvaccinated age group or individual		Self-limiting, supportive. LA oral vaccine

Prions

General Definition:
- Not viruses
- Small infectious particles of protein
- No nucleic acid
- Protein is encoded by a normal cellular gene (PrPc), but converted into a β-pleated sheet, disease-causing form (PrPsc)
- We do not know how to inactivate prions! (not heat, radiation, boiling, disinfectants, autoclave)
- Elicit no inflammatory response.
- Invariably fatal, subacute spongiform encephalopathies (amyloidopathies of the brain)
- Name recognition of diseases: Creutzfeldt-Jakob disease and variant (Mad Cow Disease), Fatal familial insomnia, Gerstmann-Straussler-Scheinker syndrome, Kuru

Before you leave, can you...

1. Explain the anatomy, life cycle and pathogenesis of the major medical virus pathogens.
2. Use serology to interpret the stages of infection in viral hepatitis.
3. Explain the mechanism of action and application of the major categories of anti-viral drugs.
4. Understand the roles of genetic shift and drift in the epidemiology of viral infections and explain the groups of agents which would be likely to possess each.
5. Use epidemiologic, symptomatic and diagnostic clues to diagnose the most important viral diseases (hepatitis, herpes family).

Microbiology
Chapter five

Medically Important Fungi

Medically Important Fungi

1. Anatomy and site of action of major anti-fungals:

The fungi are our first eukaryotes, so they have all the normal internal organelles that our cells do. This produces some complications in the pharmacotherapy of the fungi since our cells can be injured if we target molecules or organelles that are in common. Attributes that are unique to the fungi include:

- Rigid cell wall made of **mannan, glucan and chitin**
- Ergosterol as the major **membrane sterol**

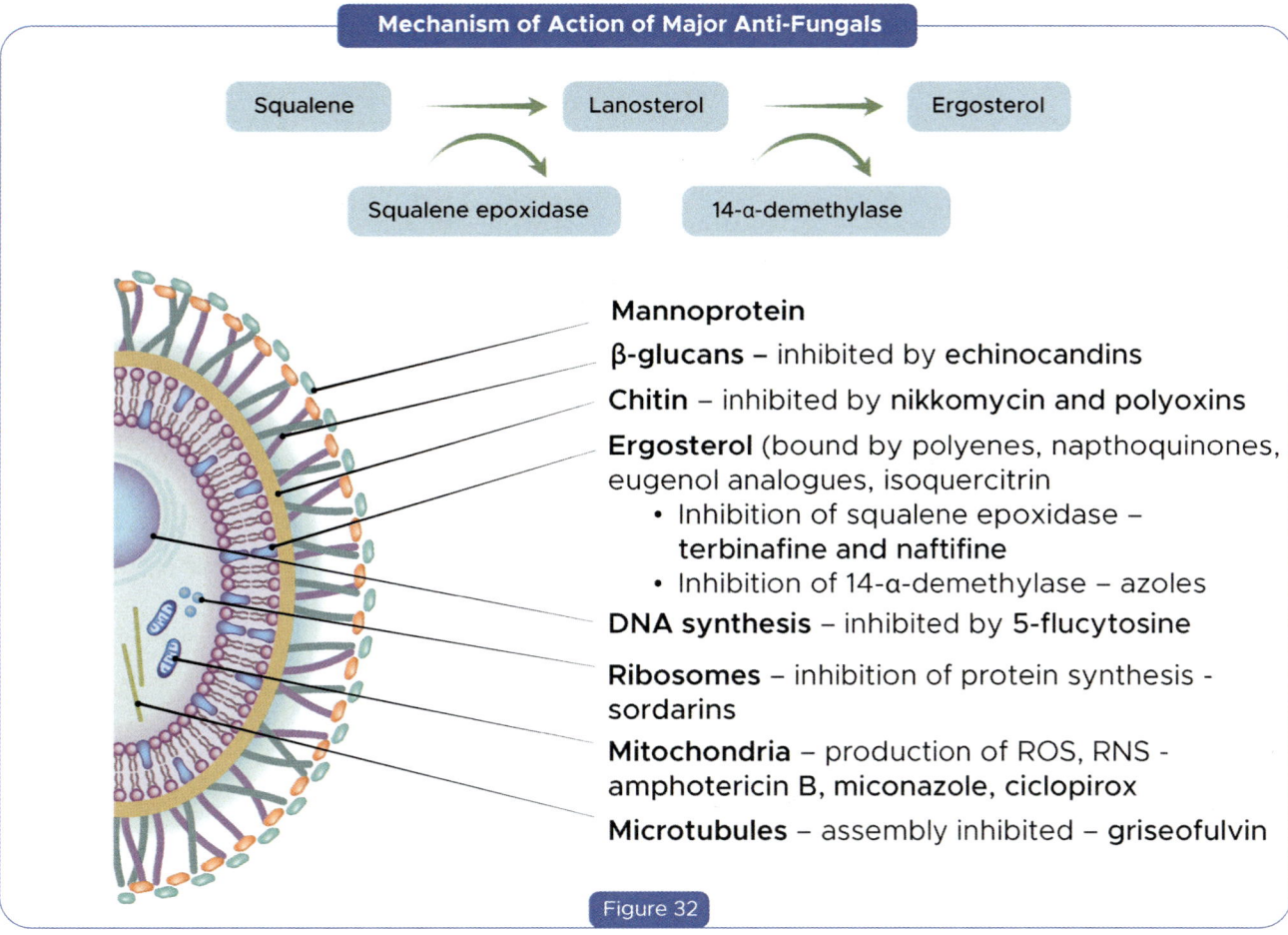

Figure 32

2. Life Cycle:
Fungi reproduce by sexual or asexual means:
- Asexual elements – **conidia** (further described by shape as macro-, micro- or arthro-)
- Sexual elements – **spores** (further described as asco-, basidio-, or zygo-depending on family of fungi). Notice that unlike bacterial spores, fungal spores function in BOTH reproduction and protection from the environment.
- **Yeasts** – single celled fungi that grow by budding, to make **blastoconidia**
- **Molds** – the filamentous forms of fungi. The filament is called a **hypha**, and when the hyphae make intertwined masses, it is referred to as a **mycelium**. Hyphae may grow with cross-walls between cells (**septate**) or without (**aseptate**).
- **Pseudohyphae** form as buds from a yeast cell but fail to detach.
- Dimorphic fungi grow in yeast or hyphal forms depending on the temperature. (Yeast in the beast, mold in the cold). Body Heat Changes Shape: *Blastomyces, Histoplasma, Coccidioides* and *Sporothrix*)

3. Diagnosis:
Fungi are diagnosed by direct examination of scrapings or biopsies. Special stains are used to highlight the unique cell wall:
- **Calcofluor white** – cellulose and chitin fluoresce
- **Silver stains** – blacken polysaccharide components of cell wall
- **India ink** – old, insensitive test to negatively stain the capsule of *Cryptococcus*. Has been supplanted by latex particle agglutination test.
- **Mucicarmine** – stains polysaccharide capsule (also insensitive for *Cryptococcus*)
- **Gram stain** – remember all cells with dense cell walls will retain the primary stain for this technique. Thus, yeast cells like *Candida* are Gram-positive.

Mycoses by Tissue Layers

1. Keratinized tissues:
Malassezia furfur

Epidemiology:

- Geographic areas with high temperatures and relative humidities
- 2-8% of the US population

Patients, Pathogenesis and Pharmacotherapy:

Chief Complaint	Vignette Clues	Pathogenesis	Rx
Blotchy hypo- or hyper-pigmentation of skin	**Pityriasis versicolor.** Woods lamp with fluorescence. KOH skin scraping – short curved septate hyphae and round yeast clusters.	Lipophilic yeast, normal skin flora. Can cause fungemia in premature infants on lipid supplements	Selenium sulfide or ketoconazole topically

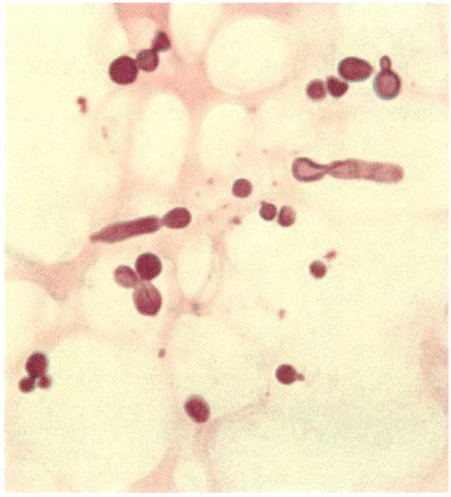

Image courtesy of CDC Public Health Image Library

2. Cutaneous tissues (Dermatophytoses)

Epidemiology:
- Incidence uncertain, but generally an infection of pre-adolescents and young adults
- Direct contact with humans or animals
- Three genera involved
  ◦ *Microsporum* – infects skin and hair shaft
  ◦ *Trichophyton* – infects skin, hair shaft and nail bed
  ◦ *Epidermophyton* – infects skin and nail bed
- Defined by region of skin involved
  ◦ **Tinea capitis** – ringworm of the scalp
  ◦ **Tinea barbae** – ringworm of the bearded area
  ◦ **Tinea cruris** – jock itch
  ◦ **Tinea pedis** – athlete's foot
  ◦ **Tinea corporis** – ringworm of the trunk
  ◦ **Tinea unguium** (or onychomycosis) – infection of the nail bed

Patients, Pathogenesis and Pharmacotherapy:

Chief Complaint	Vignette Clues	Pathogenesis	Rx
Circular, itchy areas on the skin (Ringworm)	Defined by area of skin, diagnose by KOH scraping, filamentous monomorphic septic hyphae. **Woods lamp** may show fluorescence.	Hyphae grow outwards from point of inoculation. Scaling, itching skin in the center reflects healing.	Topical azoles. Griseofulvin, itraconazole, terbinafine necessary systemically if nail bed or hair shaft involved.

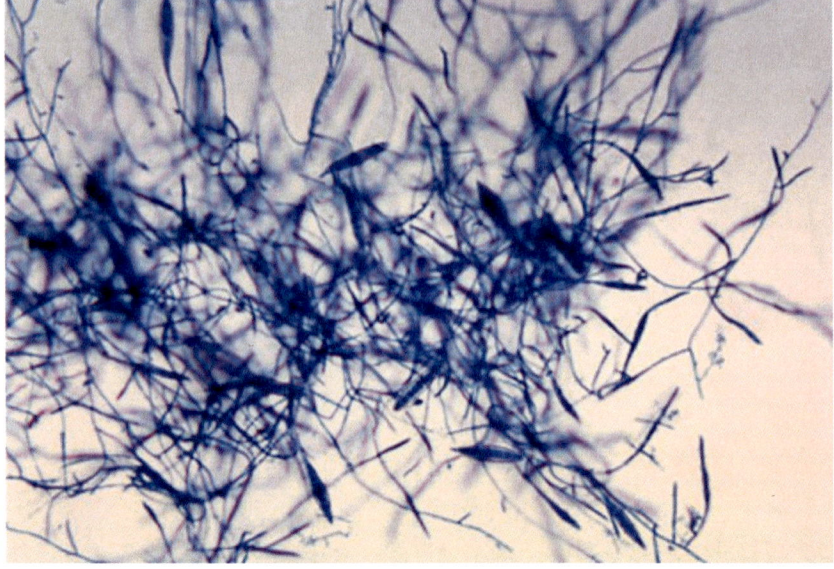

Image courtesy of CDC Public Health Image Library

3. Subcutaneous Tissues: *Sporothrix schenckii*

Epidemiology:
- 1-2 cases per million population
- Worldwide
- Adults with traumatic implantation of hyphae with sleeves and rosettes of conidia (image) from rotting vegetation while gardening (rose gardener's disease)

Patients, Pathogenesis and Pharmacotherapy:

Chief Complaint	Vignette Clues	Pathogenesis	Rx
Infected skin and subcutaneous lesion (Rose Gardener's Disease)	Gardener or employee at a florist. **Eumycotic mycetoma** – abscess draining through multiple sinus tracts, pus with yellow granules in pus. KOH mount of pus – cigar shaped yeasts.	Suppurating granuloma with histiocytes and giant cells, PMNs, lymphocytes and plasma cells. Spread along lymphatic channels.	Itraconazole and amphotericin B

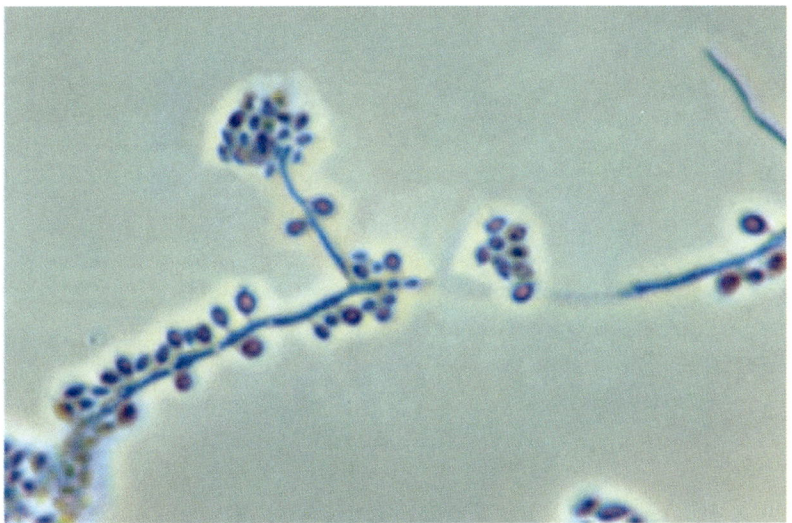

Image courtesy of CDC Public Health Image Library

Systemic Mycoses

- Geographically-associated problems in AIDS patients
- All are dimorphs. Tissue form is a yeast, transmission form a hypha.
- All cause acute or chronic pulmonary or disseminated infections
- Distinguished by examination of sputum or lesions
- Atlantic seaboard to Mississippi river valley – blastomycosis (pink)
- Overlapping with blastomycosis and extending west – histoplasmosis (green)
- Sonoran desert – coccidioidomycosis - yellow

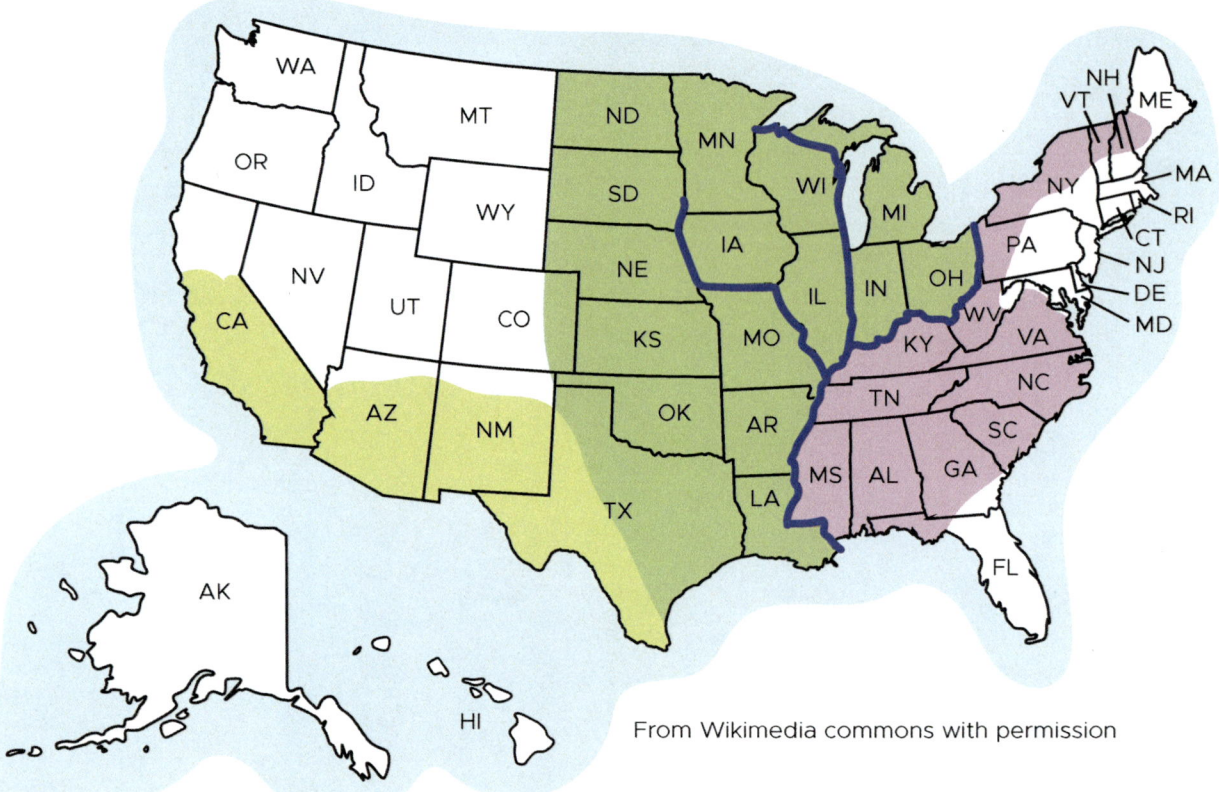

From Wikimedia commons with permission

1. *Blastomyces dermatitidis*

Epidemiology:
- Atlantic seaboard states overlapping with *Histoplasma* in the Mississippi and Missouri River beds
- Exact incidence uncertain
- Inhalation of spores, large construction projects release spores from the soil

Patients, Pathogenesis and Pharmacotherapy:

Chief Complaint	Vignette Clues	Pathogenesis	Rx
Cough, fever (Blasto-mycosis)	Unresponsive to antibiotics. **North Carolina, Wisconsin** highest number of cases. Immunocompromised patients may have dissemination to skin with necrosis and fibrosis. **Broad-based budding** yeast in sputum. (image)	Inhaled spores phagocytized by bronchopulmonary mononuclear cells, disseminates through blood and lymphatics. Pyogranulomatous inflammatory response.	Itraconazole in mild to moderate pulmonary disease. More severe – amphotericin B

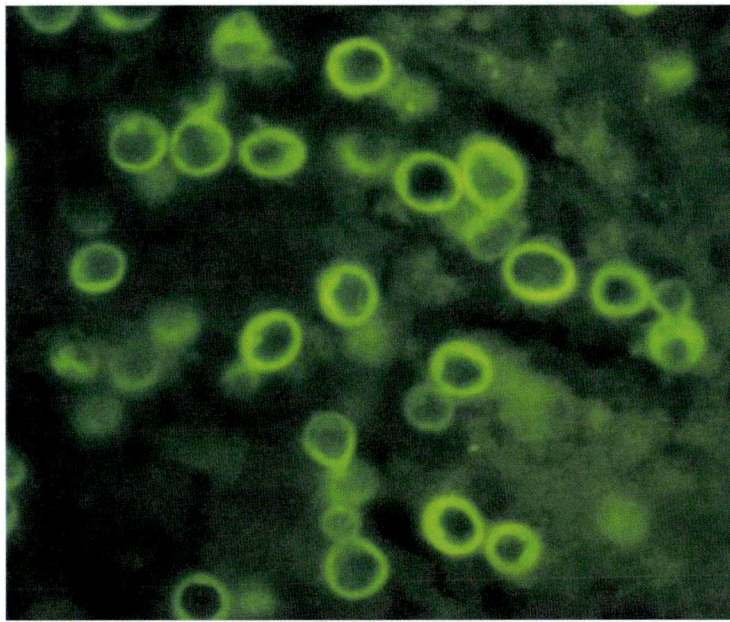

Image courtesy of CDC Public Health Image Library

2. *Histoplasma capsulatum* (not encapsulated)
Epidemiology:
- Endemic in Ohio, Mississippi and Missouri River valleys.
- Soil enriched with bird or bat guano

Patients, Pathogenesis and Pharmacotherapy:

Chief Complaint	Vignette Clues	Pathogenesis	Rx
Fever, dyspnea (Histoplasmosis)	Travel or residence in an endemic area. Activities involving exposure to birds or bats **(chicken coops, caves)**. Painless ulcers on mucous membranes in disseminated form. Mediastinal lymphadenopathy, hepatosplenomegaly and **calcifying lesions** on radiograph. Biopsy with small intracellular yeasts.	**Facultative intracellular.** Infectious form – septate hyphae with microconidia and tuberculate macroconidia. Intracellular form – yeast with halo shrinkage artifact.	Healthy patients resolve with supportive care. Itraconazole, amphotericin B. **AIDS prophylaxis at 100 CD4 cells** in endemic area.

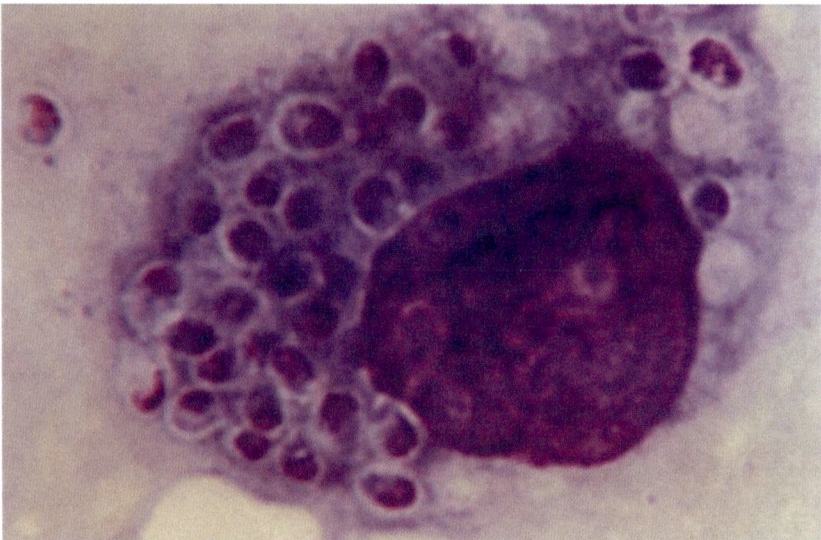

Image courtesy of CDC Public Health Image Library

3. *Coccidioides immitis*

Epidemiology:
- San Joaquin Valley of California, Sonoran desert of southwestern US
- Summer or late fall, outdoor activities
- Inhalation of airborne arthroconidia

Patients, Pathogenesis and Pharmacotherapy:

Chief Complaint	Vignette Clues	Pathogenesis	Rx
Fever, cough, dyspnea Coccidioido-mycosis	Travel to endemic area, Desert biking, after wind storms. **Large, double-walled, round spherule containing multiple endospores.** (image) **Erythema nodosum (desert bumps)** common in endemic area – good prognostic indicator of strong immune response.	Arthroconidia enlarge in bronchioles to form spherules. Endospores engulfed by macrophages, start TH1 – macrophage granuloma formation.	AIDS and immunocompromised – amphotericin B and an azole Self-limiting in patients with normal immunity. **No treatment for desert bumps.**

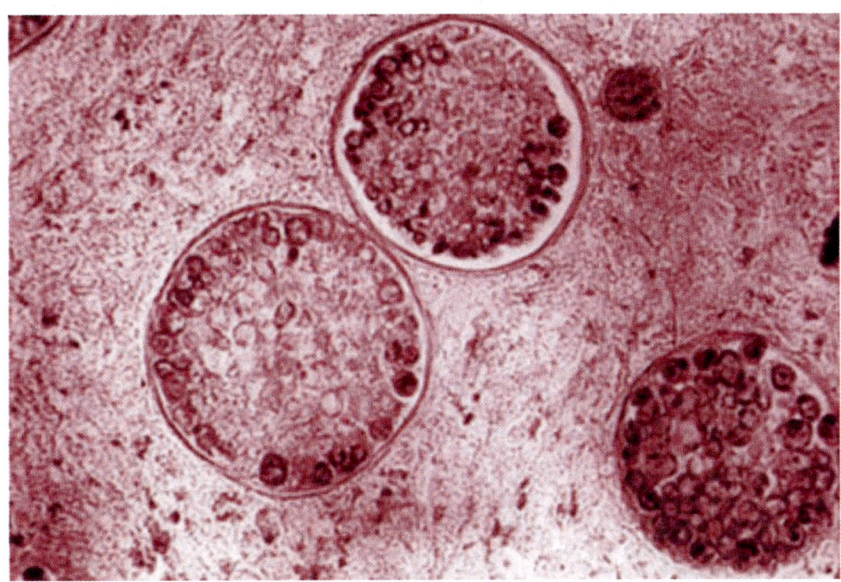

Courtesy of CDC Public Health Image Library

4. *Paracoccidioides brasiliensis* (South American blastomycosis)

Epidemiology:
- Tropical and subtropical Central and South America (Brazil)
- Coffee or tobacco growing areas

Patients, Pathogenesis and Pharmacotherapy:

Chief Complaint	Vignette Clues	Pathogenesis	Rx
Fever, cough (South American blastomycosis)	Tissue phase is a yeast with multiple blastoconidia – "captain's wheel", (image) oral lesions	M1 -TH1 granulomatous response	Itraconazole, amphotericin B

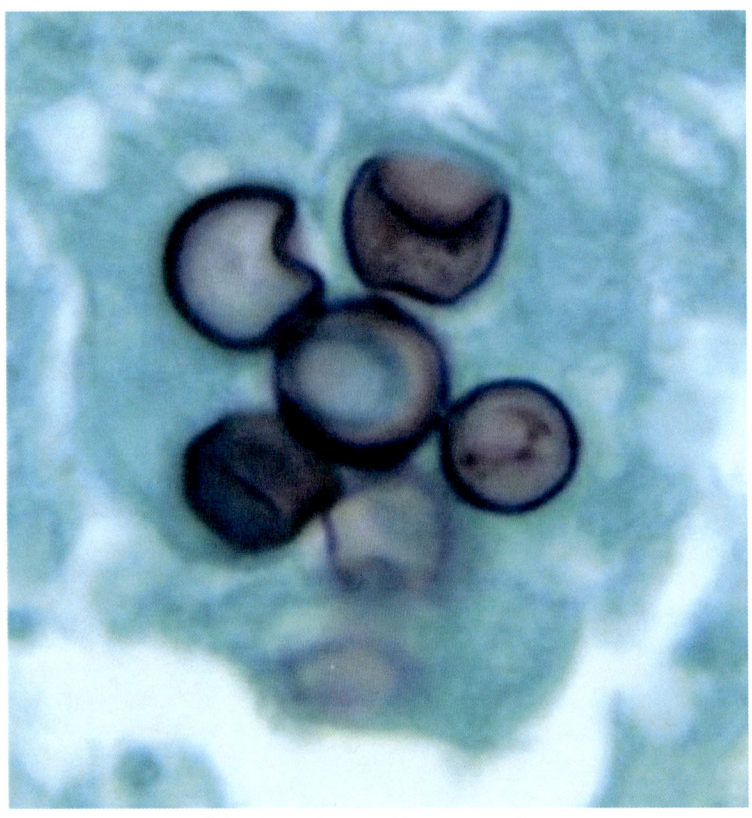

Image courtesy of CDC Public Health Image Library

Opportunistic Fungal Infections

1. *Cryptococcus neoformans*
Epidemiology:
- 2-7 cases/1000 HIV-infected patients
- Inhalation from soil enriched with **bird droppings (pigeons, turkeys, chickens)**
- Monomorphic encapsulated yeast

Patients, Pathogenesis and Pharmacotherapy:

Chief Complaint	Vignette Clues	Pathogenesis	Rx
Headache, fever, mental changes (Cryptococcal Meningitis)	Insidious onset, AIDS Patient with **100 CD4 cells/µL** or fewer. LPA for capsular polysaccharide in CSF. **Capsular halo** visible with **India Ink** or **mucicarmine**.(image)	Spreads hematogenously from lung	Amphotericin B plus flucytosine, with extended course of fluconazole Prophylaxis in AIDS at <50 CD4$^+$ cells/µL

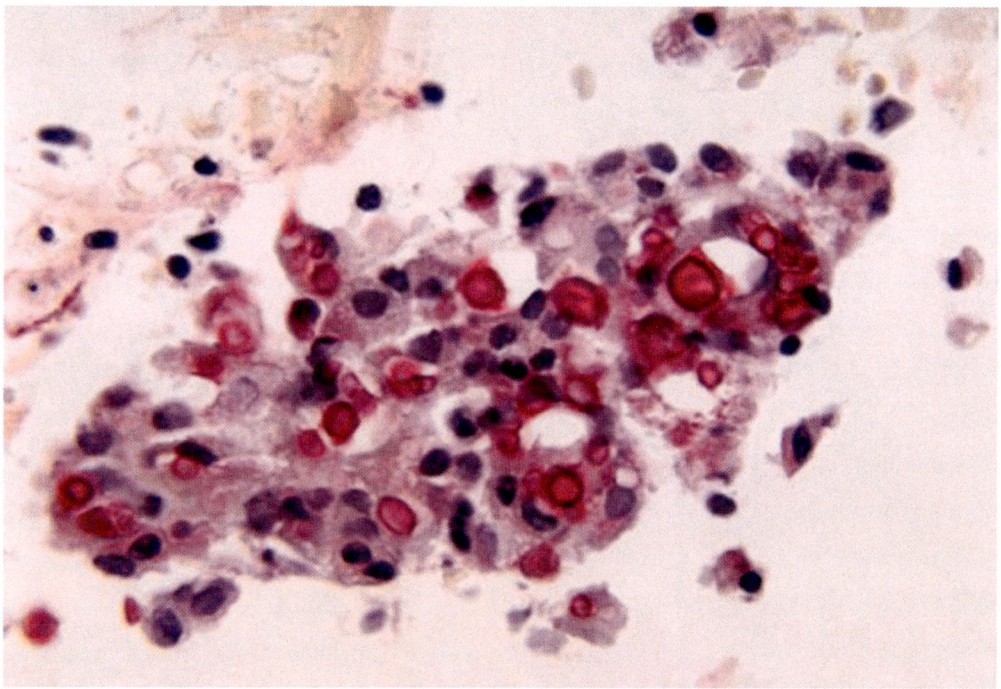

Image courtesy of CDC Public Health Image Library

2. *Aspergillus fumigatus*

Epidemiology:
- Common worldwide, conidia inhaled.
- Monomorphic, filamentous fungus with septate hyphae found in tissues, branch at acute angles. (Image)

Patients, Pathogenesis and Pharmacotherapy:

Chief Complaint	Vignette Clues	Pathogenesis	Rx
Dyspnea, fever, cough (Farmer's Lung)	Asthma and CF patients – allergic aspergillosis.	Grows in mucus plugs (not invasive)	Voriconazole, itraconazole, caspofungin, amphotericin B
	Invasive in severely immunocompromised	Acute pneumonia or sinus infection spreading to CNS	
	Fungus ball, aspergilloma	Growth into pre-existing cavitary lesions	Surgical resection of fungus balls

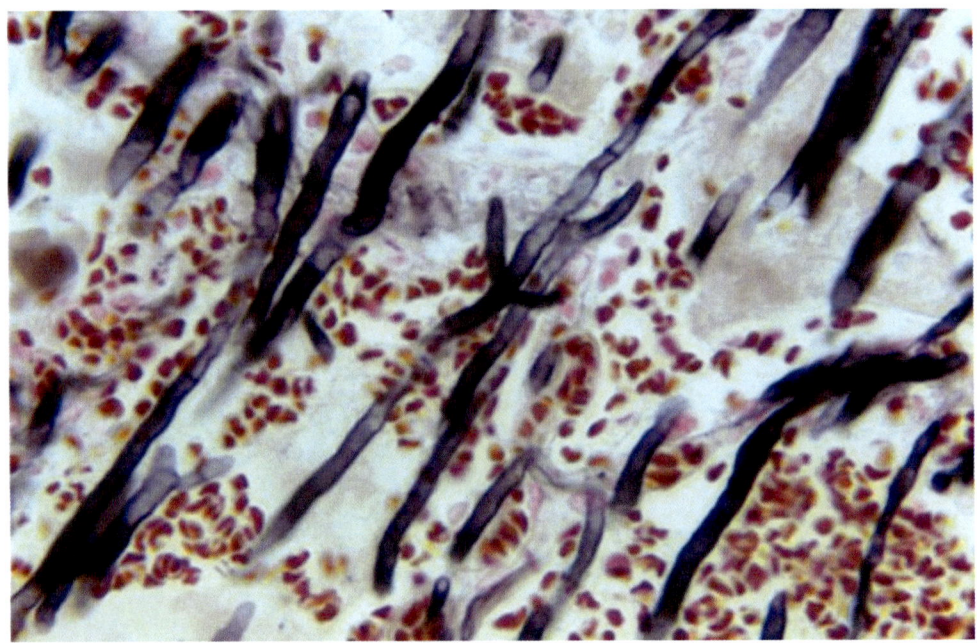

Image courtesy of CDC Public Health Image Library

3. *Candida albicans*
Epidemiology:
- Normal flora of the mucous membranes
- Overgrow in diabetics and immunocompromised

Patients, Pathogenesis and Pharmacotherapy:

Chief Complaint	Vignette Clues	Pathogenesis	Rx
Pain and exudate in mouth	**Thrush**. Premature infant, immunocompromised, antibiotic use. **Germ tube test** detects **pseudohyphae** (image)	Pseudohyphae and hyphae made by invasive strains. Hyphal wall protein mediates binding, proteinases and phospholipases increase invasion.	Nystatin, azoles
Vaginal itching and discharge	Diabetic female. (Vulvo-vaginal Candidiasis)		
Fever, fatigue	**Septicemia, endocarditis**, IV patients, immunocompromised		Fluconazole, amphotericin B, caspofungin
Dysphagia, odynophagia	AIDS, spread from mouth to esophagus or stomach.		
Erythematous skin rash	Infants, obese patients, dental hygienists	Moist skin folds predispose to growth	Nystatin, azoles, keep skin dry

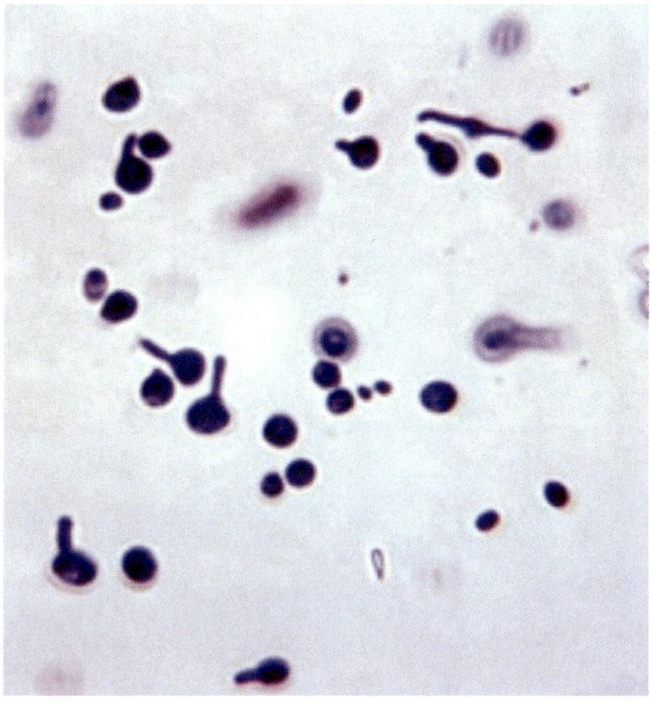

Image courtesy of CDC Public Health Image Library

4. Zygomycosis (Mucormycosis, Rhizomycosis, Absidiomycosis)

Epidemiology:
- Common worldwide in soil, grows on bread and foods
- Infection by inhalation of conidia
- Ketoacidotic diabetics, immunosuppressed

Patients, Pathogenesis and Pharmacotherapy:

Chief Complaint	Vignette Clues	Pathogenesis	Rx
Headache, nasal discharge (Zygomycosis)	Ketoacidotic diabetic or immunosuppressed patient. Rapid progression to coma, death. Biopsy with **irregularly wide, ribbon-like hyphae that branch at 90° angles**. (image)	Invades from sinuses through cavernous sinus into brain. **Rhinocerebral infection** (Black fungus in COVID patients)	Control of underlying condition, amphotericin B

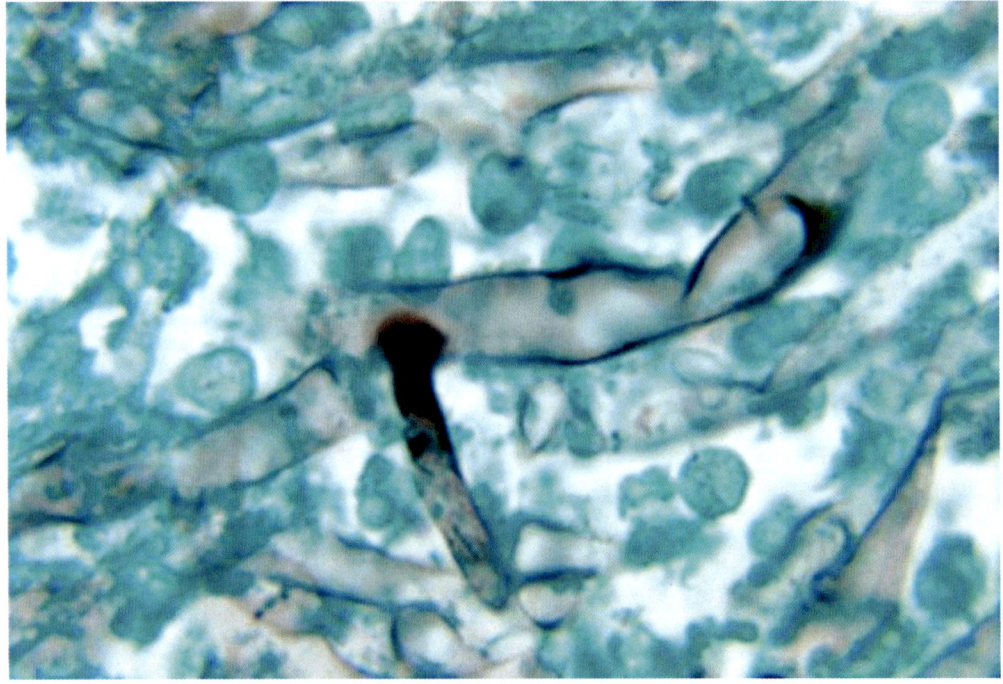

Image courtesy of CDC Public Health Image Library

5. *Pneumocystis jirovecii*

Epidemiology:
- AIDS-defining atypical pneumonia
- Premature infants
- **Atypical fungus:** major membrane sterol is cholesterol, cell wall thin, but contains chitin and glucan. Cannot be cultured.

Patients, Pathogenesis and Pharmacotherapy:

Chief Complaint	Vignette Clues	Pathogenesis	Rx
Fever, shortness of breath, fatigue	**Atypical pneumonia in AIDS.** Biopsy or lavage shows silver staining cysts in honeycomb exudate	Attaches to and **kills type I pneumocytes**, causes excess replication of type II pneumocytes. Alveoli fill with dense exudate, death by asphyxiation.	Trimethoprim-sulfamethoxazole, pentamidine. Start standard **prophylaxis** at CD4 count of 200/µL

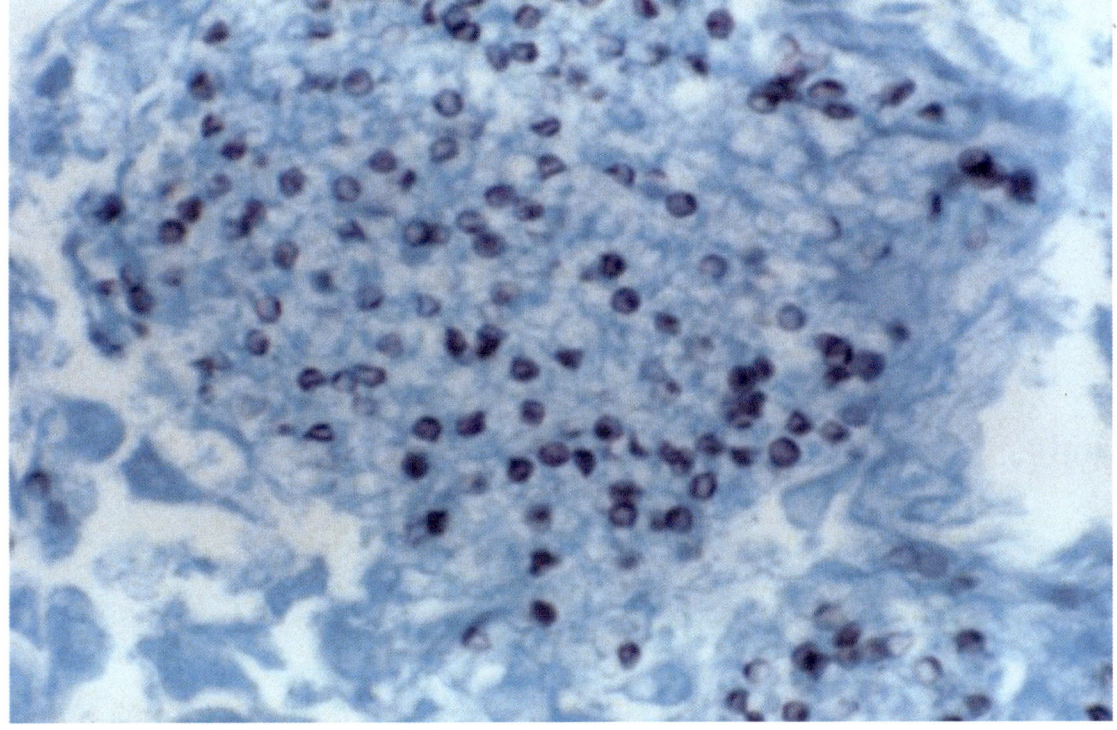

Image courtesy of CDC Public Health Image Library

Before you leave, can you...

1. Identify microscopic images of fungi from diagnostic samples.
2. Identify the geographic areas in which the important fungal pathogens will be endemic.
3. Identify the anatomical/biochemical points of action of the major anti-fungal therapeutics.
4. Diagnose and treat the most important fungal diseases in the United States from symptoms and signs.

Microbiology
Chapter six

Medically Important Parasites

Medically Important Parasites

1. Vocabulary

The parasites are the largest and most diverse group of eukaryotes that cause human disease. As usual, we need some new terminology before we can dive in, but remember these diseases tend to be superficially tested on the USMLE, simply because they are not common in the US.

a. Protozoa
- Single celled protists classified by their motility:
    - **Amebae** – move by pseudopodia
    - **Ciliates** – move by many, short, hair-like processes
    - **Flagellates** – move by few, longer, hair-like processes
    - **Sporozoa/apicomplexa** – **obligate intracellular** protozoa which reproduce sexually and asexually and use an "**apical complex**" to penetrate host cells.
- **Trophozoite** - feeding form
- **Cyst** - transmission form that is resistant to the environment
- **Amastigote** - a flagellate that has only the vestige of a flagellum internally
- **Trypomastigote** - the form of hemoflagellate found in human blood or the insect vector that has external flagella and an undulating membrane going down one side, so movement is both directional and rotational.

b. Helminths (Metazoa) – worms
- **Nematodes** (roundworms) – round in cross-section
    - Most phylogenetically advanced
    - Complete digestive tract (mouth, intestine, anus)
    - Separate sexes
    - Simple life cycles with egg, larva, adult in one or few hosts
- **Flatworms** (flukes and tapeworms) – dorsoventrally flattened
    - **Flukes (trematodes)**
        - Incomplete digestive tract – mouth, intestine, no anus
        - Hermaphroditic (except schistosomes which have separate sexes)
        - Complex life cycles with egg, larvae, adults in multiple hosts
    - **Tapeworms (cestodes)**
        - Most highly adapted to parasitic lifestyle
        - No digestive tract (absorb nutrients through cuticle)
        - Hermaphroditic
        - Complex live cycles with egg, larvae, adults in multiple hosts

c. Hosts

- **Definitive** - harbors the most adult or sexually reproductive stages of the parasite
- **Intermediate** - harbors the immature or asexually reproductive stages of the parasite.
- **Be aware that this does not always follow your anthropomorphic values!** Man is NOT the definitive host for everything we are interested in. For example, in malaria, the mosquito is the definitive host. In toxoplasmosis, the cat is the definitive host. In each of these cases, the human plays the role of the intermediate host.

2. Anti-Parasitic Drugs:

Use	Mechanism of Action	Drug
Protozoa		
Malaria, acute attack	4-aminoquinolone, Inhibits formation of hemazoin	**Chloroquine**
Malaria, prevent relapse (*P. vivax* and *P. ovale*)	8-aminoquinolone. May create ROS or interfere with electron transport	**Primaquine**
Malaria, prophylaxis	Quinoline, mechanism uncertain	**Mefloquine, doxycycline**
Giardiasis, amebiasis	Disrupts DNA synthesis of anaerobic organisms	**Metronidazole**
Amebiasis, luminal phases	Protein synthesis inhibitor	**Paromomycin**
Cryptosporidiosis	Thiazolide. Interferes with pyruvate:ferredoxin oxidoreductase enzyme-dependent ET reaction	**Nitazoxanide**
African trypanosomes	Inhibits glycerol-3-phosphate oxidase and dehydrogenase	**Suramin**
Chagas Disease	Nitroimidazole. Inhibits synthesis of DNA, RNA, proteins	**Benznidazole**
Leishmaniasis	Pentavalent antimonial, reduces available ATP and GTP, inhibits topoisomerase I	**Stibogluconate**
Helminths		
Nematodes	Inhibits polymerization of microtubules	**Mebendazole**
Trematodes and cestodes	Unknown, increases permeability of membranes for calcium ions, causes paralysis in contracted state	**Praziquantel**
Filariasis	Inhibitor of microfilarial arachidonic acid metabolism, makes them susceptible to phagocytosis	**Diethylcarbamazine**
Filariasis, strongyloidiasis	Binds to glutamate-gated chloride channels, paralyzes microfilariae, larvae	**Ivermectin**

Protozoa of the Gastrointestinal and Urogenital Systems

Chief complaint: Diarrhea, transmission fecal/oral, cyst or oocyst

Organism	Geography	Pathogenesis	Diagnosis	Treatment
Entamoeba histolytica	Mexico, tropics	**Inflammatory diarrhea.** Invades wall of colon, inverted **flask-shaped lesions,** hematogenous spread to create **liver abscess**	Cysts or trophozoites in stool. Rapid stool antigen test, serology for hepatic liver abscess	Metronidazole followed by paromomycin to cure luminal infection
Giardia lamblia	US, Russia **Camping or hiking,** drinking water from streams	**Non-inflammatory diarrhea.** Trophozoites attach to mucosa of small intestine, fat malabsorption, **steatorrhea.**	Trophozoites with **falling leaf motility** or non-motile cysts in stool.	Metronidazole, tinidazole, nitazoxanide
Cryptosporidium parvum	US AIDS patients	Obligate intracellular, unrelenting diarrhea in AIDS	**Acid-fast oocysts** in stool	Nitazoxanide. Anti-retroviral therapy. Begin prophylaxis at **50 CD4 cells/µL**
Isospora belli	US AIDS patients			Self-limiting in normal patients

Chief complaint: Vaginitis, transmission sexual, trophozoite

Organism	Geography	Pathogenesis	Diagnosis	Treatment
Trichomonas vaginalis	Worldwide	**Thin, yellow, frothy discharge** after the menses. Males often asymptomatic	**Flagellated trophozoites** in vaginal or urethral smear. **Corkscrew motility**	Metronidazole, contact tracing and treatment

Images courtesy of CDC Public Health Image Library

Protozoa of the Blood and Tissues
Malaria: Plasmodium spp.

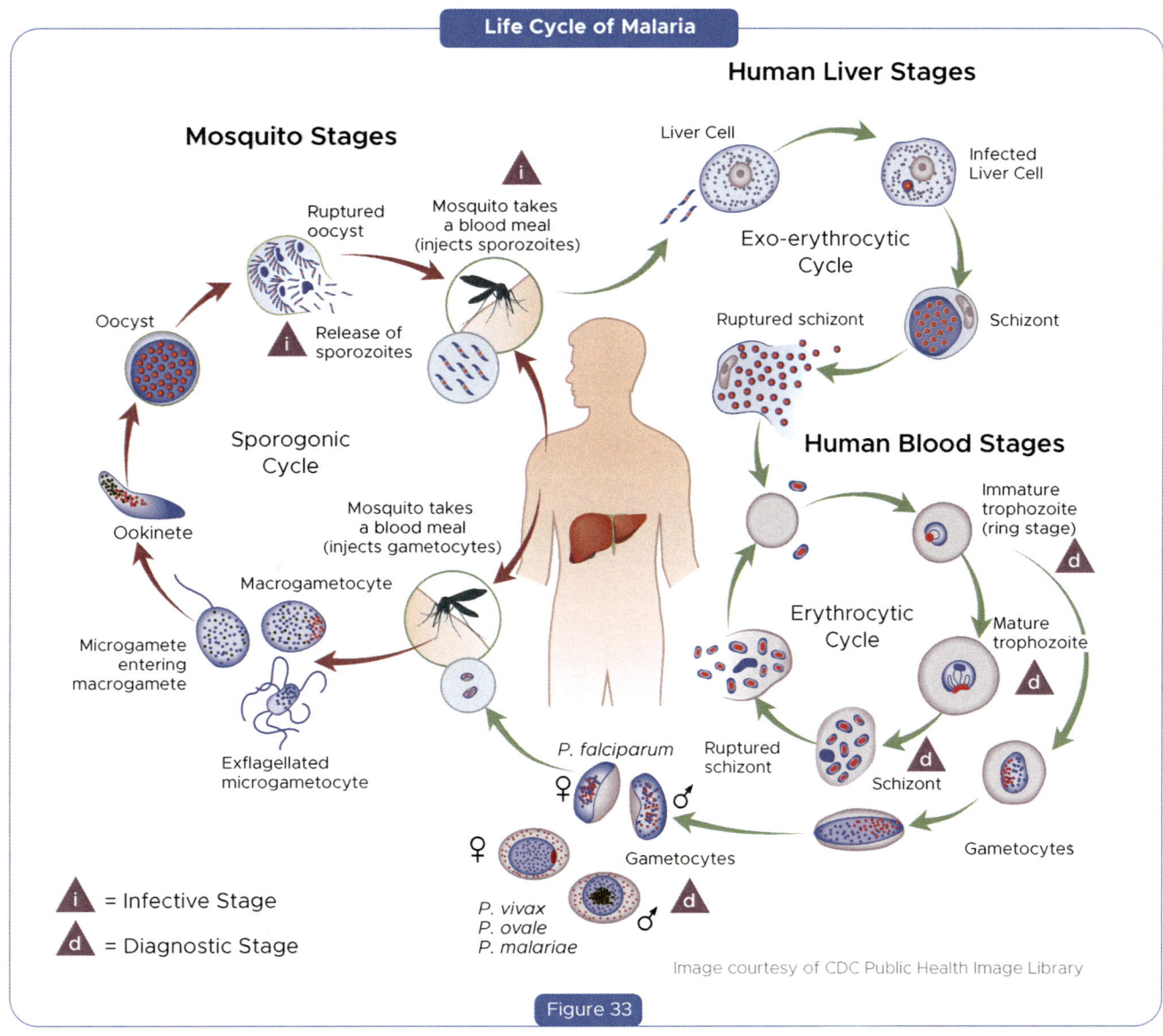

Figure 33

Medical Microbiology Essentials

		Chief complaint: Paroxysms of fever, diaphoresis		
Organism	**Geography**	**Pathogenesis**	**Diagnosis**	**Treatment**
Plasmodium vivax (**benign tertian**)	Central and south America, India and SE Asia, **85% of all infections**, tropics, transmission by female *Anopheles* mosquito. Uses **Duffy blood group** antigen for attachment (reason why it is less common in sub-Saharan Africa)	Intraerythrocytic stages: **48-hour fever spikes** (length of time required for erythrocytic schizogony). Lysis of RBCs dumps hemozoin (partially digested hemoglobin) into blood causing spikes of fever, reticuloendothelial congestion, hemolytic anemia, kidney failure	Blood film with **ameboid** intraerythrocytic trophozoite inside **enlarged** (immature) RBCs	Chloroquine followed by primaquine or tafenoquine (radical cure) to destroy **hypnozoites** and prevent relapse. Drug resistant or severe - artemether + lumefantrine.
Plasmodium ovale, (**benign tertian**)	Sub-Saharan Africa		Infected RBCs are **fimbriated or oval**.	
Plasmodium falciparum, (**malignant tertian**)	**95% of all malarial deaths.** Tropical and subtropical areas of Central and South America, Africa and SE Asia	**Irregular fever pattern**, although erythrocytic schizogony takes the same amount of time as with *vivax* and *ovale*. Parasites fail to synchronize so fever rises and stays high. Infected RBCs stick to endothelium and block blood vessels (**cerebral malaria**). HbS heterozygote is protected.	Mature RBCs (small diameter), are **multiply infected**	Chloroquine, radical cure is not necessary (no hypnozoites left in liver). Return of symptoms (recrudescence) may occur due to rise in global drug resistance. For severe or drug resistant – artemether + lumefantrine.
Plasmodium malariae, (**quartan malaria**)	Same geography as *falciparum*	**72-hour fever spikes.**	Infects normocytes, may have **band forms**	

Images courtesy of CDC Public Health Image Library

Chief complaint: Fatigue, fever. Transmission by *Ixodes* tick				
Organism	Geography	Pathogenesis	Diagnosis	Treatment
Babesia microti (Babesiosis)	US. Northeast, Great Lakes states, California (limited by vector, **same as Lyme disease**)	**Intraerythrocytic trophozoites** destroy RBCs and cause anemia. More severe in splenectomized patients.	**Multiple intraerythrocytic ring forms**, tetrads may be mentioned	Atovaquone plus azithromycin or clindamycin plus quinine

Chief complaint: Fever, fatigue, myalgia. Transmission; cysts in pork, lamb. Cat has sexual stages in intestine (definitive host)				
Organism	Geography	Pathogenesis	Diagnosis	Treatment
Toxoplasma gondii (Toxoplasmosis)	Worldwide	Flu or mono-like in adult. **Transplacental transmission** possible in **tachyzoite** form (retinochoroiditis, hydrocephalus, still birth). **Bradyzoites** may persist for life and cause reactivational disease (encephalitis in AIDS). **#1 diagnosis at autopsy**	Serology	Sulfadiazine, pyrimethamine AIDS patients put on **prophylaxis at 100 CD4 cells/μL** remaining.

Chief complaint: Headache, change in sense of smell, fever, stiff neck, photophobia, confusion				
Organism	Geography	Pathogenesis	Diagnosis	Treatment
Naegleria fowleri (Amebic encephalitis)	Worldwide, warm fresh water lakes	**Free-living amebae** forced through cribriform plate by changes in pressure when **diving in recreational lakes.** Hemorrhagic, purulent inflammation extends from olfactory bulbs to rest of brain.	Flagellated trophozoites in CSF	Amphotericin B, miltefosine, rarely successful
Acanthamoeba spp. (Amebic encephalitis)	Worldwide soil and water	**Acute granulomatous encephalitis** (AGE) in AIDS and immunocompromised **Keratitis** in contact lens wearers	Star shaped cysts on biopsy	Polyhexamethylene biguanide or chlorhexidine digluconate plus propamidine isethionate or hexamidine. Miltefosine.

Images courtesy of CDC Public Health Image Library

Hemoflagellates

\multicolumn{5}{l}{Chief complaint: Fever, headache, altered mentation. Transmission by Tsetse}
Organism	Geography	Pathogenesis	Diagnosis	Treatment
Trypanosoma brucei rhodesiense (east Africa) or T. b. gambiense (West Africa)	Africa	Lymphadenopathy at fly bite (Winterbottom sign) followed by parasitemia. Invades CNS, antigenic variation.	Sleeping sickness. Trypomastigotes in blood or CSF	Pentamidine. Suramin early, melarsoprol late.

Chief complaint: Fatigue, fever. Transmission - feces of Reduviid bug

Organism	Geography	Pathogenesis	Diagnosis	Treatment
Trypanosoma cruzi (**Chagas Disease**, American trypanosomiasis)	South America	Parasite invades bite wound when bug feeds around eye at night (**Romaña's sign**). Parasitemia with trypomastigotes leads to **amastigotes intracellular in cardiac and smooth muscle**. Megaesophagus, megacolon, achalasia, dilated cardiomyopathy.	Trypomastigotes in blood film	Nifurtimox or benznidazole

Images courtesy of CDC Public Health Image Library

Hemoflagellates (continued)

Chief complaint: Fever, weight loss, skin hyperpigmentation. Transmission by phlebotomine sandflies

Organism	Geography	Pathogenesis	Diagnosis	Treatment
Leishmania donovani (**visceral leishmaniasis**, kala azar)	Indian subcontinent, Brazil	**Amastigotes are obligate intracellular** in macrophages in reticuloendothelial organs	Bone marrow, spleen, liver biopsy with amastigotes inside macrophages	Stibogluconate sodium

Chief complaint: Disfiguring skin lesions

Organism	Geography	Pathogenesis	Diagnosis	Treatment
Leishmania tropica, L. major, L. mexicana (**cutaneous leishmaniasis**)	Central and South America (*L. mexicana*), Middle East (*L. tropica* and *L. major*)	Erosive skin lesions on skin exposed to sandfly bite. Intracellular in **macrophages of skin.**	**Leishmanin skin test positive,** amastigotes in skin biopsy	Stibogluconate sodium

Chief complaint: Disfiguring mucocutaneous lesions

Organism	Geography	Pathogenesis	Diagnosis	Treatment
Leishmania braziliensis (**mucocutaneous leishmaniasis,** espundia)	South America	Intracellular in mucocutaneous macrophages	As above	Stibogluconate sodium

Images courtesy of CDC Public Health Image Library

Helminths
Nematodes (roundworms)

1. Transmitted by fecal-oral ingestion of ova

Chief complaint: Abdominal pain, distension.

Organism	Geography	Pathogenesis	Diagnosis	Treatment
Ascaris lumbricoides (large roundworm)	Worldwide. Southern US	Lifecycle involves migration through **lung** (**Loeffler syndrome**). Largest roundworm. Adults may **block intestine**	Large, rough shelled eggs in feces. Larvae in sputum, eosinophilia	Mebendazole

Chief complaint: Abdominal tenderness, blood in stool.

Organism	Geography	Pathogenesis	Diagnosis	Treatment
Trichuris trichiura (**Whipworm**)	Worldwide, Southern US	Larvae invade wall of cecum and colon, mature to adulthood. **Damage muscularis layer.** Diarrhea, rare **rectal prolapse**	Eggs with bipolar plugs in feces	Mebendazole

Chief complaint: Perianal itching.

Organism	Geography	Pathogenesis	Diagnosis	Treatment
Enterobius vermicularis (**Pinworm**)	Worldwide, US	Female migrates out of anus at night, explodes, leaving eggs attached to perianal skin.	**Sticky tape** to perianal skin, flattened on one side, fully formed larvae inside	Mebendazole (treat all contacts)

Chief complaint: Cough, wheezing.

Organism	Geography	Pathogenesis	Diagnosis	Treatment
Toxocara canis (**Visceral larva migrans**)	Worldwide, US Child/family with new puppy	Dog roundworms cannot mature in humans. Wander aimlessly until walled off and killed by the immune response	Serology, eosinophilia	Corticosteroids, mebendazole, keep pets wormed

Images courtesy of CDC Public Health Image Library

Nematodes

2. Transmitted by Skin Penetration or Ingestion of Larvae

Chief complaint: fatigue, weight loss

Organism	Geography	Pathogenesis	Diagnosis	Treatment
Necator americanus (**New World** Hookworm)	New World	**Larvae penetrate skin,** migrate through lung, coughed up and swallowed, mature in small intestine, ingest blood. **Microcytic hypochromic anemia** in heavy infections.	Oval, clear-shelled light brown eggs in feces, eosinophilia	Mebendazole
Ancylostoma duodenale (**Old World** Hookworm)	Old World			

Chief complaint: blood-tinged productive cough, dyspnea

Organism	Geography	Pathogenesis	Diagnosis	Treatment
Strongyloides stercoralis (**Threadworm**)	Worldwide, US. High rates in mental institutions	Larvae penetrate skin, migration like hookworms, **autoinfection** and **hyperinfection syndrome** possible.	Live larvae in stool	Ivermectin, benzimidazoles

Chief complaint: Diarrhea (1st week), myalgia (weeks to months)

Organism	Geography	Pathogenesis	Diagnosis	Treatment
Trichinella spiralis (**Trichinosis**)	Worldwide, cosmopolitan	Ingestion of **larvae in poorly cooked game meat.** Larvae mature to adulthood and mate, producing live larvae which migrate via the blood to encyst in active striated muscle.	Muscle biopsy showing larvae encysted in striated muscle	Early - mebendazole Late - Corticosteroids, antipyretics, analgesics

Chief complaint: pruritic cutaneous eruptions

Organism	Geography	Pathogenesis	Diagnosis	Treatment
Ancylostoma braziliense (**Cutaneous larva migrans**)	SW US, Caribbean, Central and South America, SE Asia, Africa	Dog or cat hookworms penetrate human skin and migrate in the skin until killed by the immune response.	Clinical, eosinophilia	Topical corticosteroids, topical or oral ivermectin

Images courtesy of CDC Public Health Image Library

Filarial Nematodes

1. Transmitted by Arthropods

Chief complaint: Pruritic SQ nodules. Transmission by blackflies (*Simulium*)				
Organism	**Geography**	**Pathogenesis**	**Diagnosis**	**Treatment**
Onchocerca volvulus (River blindness)	Central and South America, West Africa	Larvae mature to adulthood in SQ nodules, produce microfilariae which cause chronic inflammation.	Skin biopsy with microfilariae	Surgical excision of adults from nodules, ivermectin to kill larvae

Chief complaint: Eye irritation, SQ nodules. Transmission by *Chrysops* deerfly				
Organism	**Geography**	**Pathogenesis**	**Diagnosis**	**Treatment**
Loa loa (African eye worm)	Africa	Adults form Calabar swellings in SQ tissue. Adults migrate across conjunctiva	Eosinophilia, blood examination for microfilariae	Diethylcarbamazine

Chief complaint: Fever, inguinal or axillary lymphadenopathy. Transmission by *Anopheles, Culex or Mansonia* mosquitoes				
Organism	**Geography**	**Pathogenesis**	**Diagnosis**	**Treatment**
Wuchereria bancrofti	Africa, Latin America, South Pacific	Repeated episodes of inflammation and lymphedema cause lymphatic damage, chronic swelling and elephantiasis	Microfilariae in peripheral blood, circulating filarial antigens	Diethylcarbamazine
Brugia malayi (Filariasis, elephantiasis)	Asia and South Pacific			

Images courtesy of CDC Public Health Image Library

Filarial Nematodes

2. Transmitted from Ingestion of Larvae in Water

\multicolumn{5}{l}{Chief complaint: Skin papule with pruritus. Ingestion of water containing the intermediate host, *Cyclops*}
Organism	Geography	Pathogenesis	Diagnosis	Treatment
Dracunculus medinensis (Guinea worm)	South Sudan, Mali, Ethiopia	Female migrates from GI tract to SQ tissues, causing intense pain before emerging to create ulcer on lower leg and discharge larvae into water.	Imaging for calcified worms, Increased IgE	Extraction by wrapping the worm around a stick, metronidazole to prevent infection with anaerobic bacteria

Trematodes

1. Transmitted by Skin Penetration by Cercariae

Chief complaint: Pruritic skin rash, hematemesis					
Organism	**Geography**	**Pathogenesis**	**Diagnosis**	**Treatment**
Schistosoma mansoni (Schistosomiasis)	Africa	Adults in mesenteries of intestine, eggs passed into blood and liver, liver fibrosis results in cirrhosis, varices, hematemesis	Eggs in stool; *S. mansoni* – **lateral spine**;	Praziquantel
S. japonicum	Asia		*S. japonicum* – **small lateral hook**	

Chief complaint: Pruritic skin rash, bloody urine					
Organism	**Geography**	**Pathogenesis**	**Diagnosis**	**Treatment**
Schistosoma haematobium	Egypt, Iraq	Adults in vasculature of **urinary bladder**, hematuria, squamous cell cancer of the bladder	Eggs with **terminal spine** in urine	Praziquantel

Images courtesy of CDC Public Health Image Library

Trematodes

2. Transmitted by Ingestion

Chief complaint: Cough, dyspnea. Ingestion of larvae in raw crabs or crayfish				
Organism	**Geography**	**Pathogenesis**	**Diagnosis**	**Treatment**
Paragonimus westermani (oriental lung fluke)	Asia or South America	Invasion of flukes causes abdominal pain, diarrhea and urticaria, followed by fever, pleuritic chest pain, cough and dyspnea. Brown tinged sputum	Sputum examination for operculated eggs	Praziquantel

Chief complaint: Abdominal pain, fever. Ingestion of metacercariae on water plants				
Organism	**Geography**	**Pathogenesis**	**Diagnosis**	**Treatment**
Fasciola hepatica (sheep liver fluke)	Bolivia or Peru	Damage to bile ducts causes inflammation and blockage	Fecal exam for operculated eggs	Praziquantel

Chief complaint: Epigastric pain, nausea, diarrhea. Ingestion of metacercariae on water chestnuts				
Organism	**Geography**	**Pathogenesis**	**Diagnosis**	**Treatment**
Fasciolopsis buski (Giant intestinal fluke)	India, China, SE Asia	Inflammation, ulceration at site of attachment in duodenum and jejunal mucosa.	Operculated eggs in stool	Praziquantel

Chief complaint: Fatigue, fever. Ingestion of cysts in raw fish				
Organism	**Geography**	**Pathogenesis**	**Diagnosis**	**Treatment**
Clonorchis sinensis (Chinese liver fluke)	Asia	Inflammation and deformation of bile duct. Risk of cholangiocarcinoma	Operculated eggs in stool	Praziquantel

Images courtesy of CDC Public Health Image Library

Cestodes

1. Transmitted by Ingestion

Chief complaint: Vague abdominal pain. Transmission by ingestion of cysticerci in beef				
Organism	**Geography**	**Pathogenesis**	**Diagnosis**	**Treatment**
Taenia saginata (Beef tapeworm)	Worldwide	Compete with host for calories	Proglottids or eggs in stool	Praziquantel

Chief complaint: Vague abdominal pain. Ingestion of cysticerci in poorly cooked pork				
Organism	**Geography**	**Pathogenesis**	**Diagnosis**	**Treatment**
Taenia solium (Pork tapeworm)	Worldwide	Compete with host for calories	Proglottids or eggs in stool	Praziquantel

Chief complaint: Adult onset epilepsy. Ingestion of eggs from fecal contamination or autoinfection				
Organism	**Geography**	**Pathogenesis**	**Diagnosis**	**Treatment**
Taenia solium (cysticercosis)	South and Central America, Africa, Asia	Ingestion of eggs by inappropriate host (human) causes development of cysticerci which encyst in tissues. Symptoms depend on locations of encystment. **Neurocysticercosis** – eye and neurologic signs. Adult onset epilepsy	Imaging, calcifying lesions	Praziquantel, surgery

Chief complaint: Abdominal pain. Ingestion of spargana (larvae) from poorly cooked fish				
Organism	**Geography**	**Pathogenesis**	**Diagnosis**	**Treatment**
Diphyllobothrium latum (Fish tapeworm)	Great Lakes, Northern Europe, Scandanavia	Competes with host for vitamin B12, causes megaloblastic anemia	Operculated eggs in stool	Praziquantel

Images courtesy of CDC Public Health Image Library

Cestodes (continued)

Chief complaint: Space occupying mass. Fecal/oral contamination from eggs in canine feces, human is aberrant intermediate host.				
Organism	Geography	Pathogenesis	Diagnosis	Treatment
Echinococcus granulosus (Hydatid disease)	Worldwide, rare in North America	Unilocular cysts cause symptoms depending on location	Imaging, serology	Surgery

Chief complaint: Space occupying mass. Fecal-oral contamination from eggs in feces of wild canids.				
Organism	Geography	Pathogenesis	Diagnosis	Treatment
Echinococcus multilocularis (Multilocular hydatid)	Northern latitudes of Europe, Asia and North America	Multilocular cysts, produce symptoms depending on location	Imaging, serology	Surgery

Before you leave, can you...

1. Identify the diagnostic stages of parasites from images
2. Identify the geographic areas in which the important parasites will be endemic.
3. Name the major anti-parasitic therapeutics and anticipate their use.
4. Diagnose the most important parasitic diseases in the United States from symptoms and signs.

Made in the USA
Coppell, TX
16 August 2023